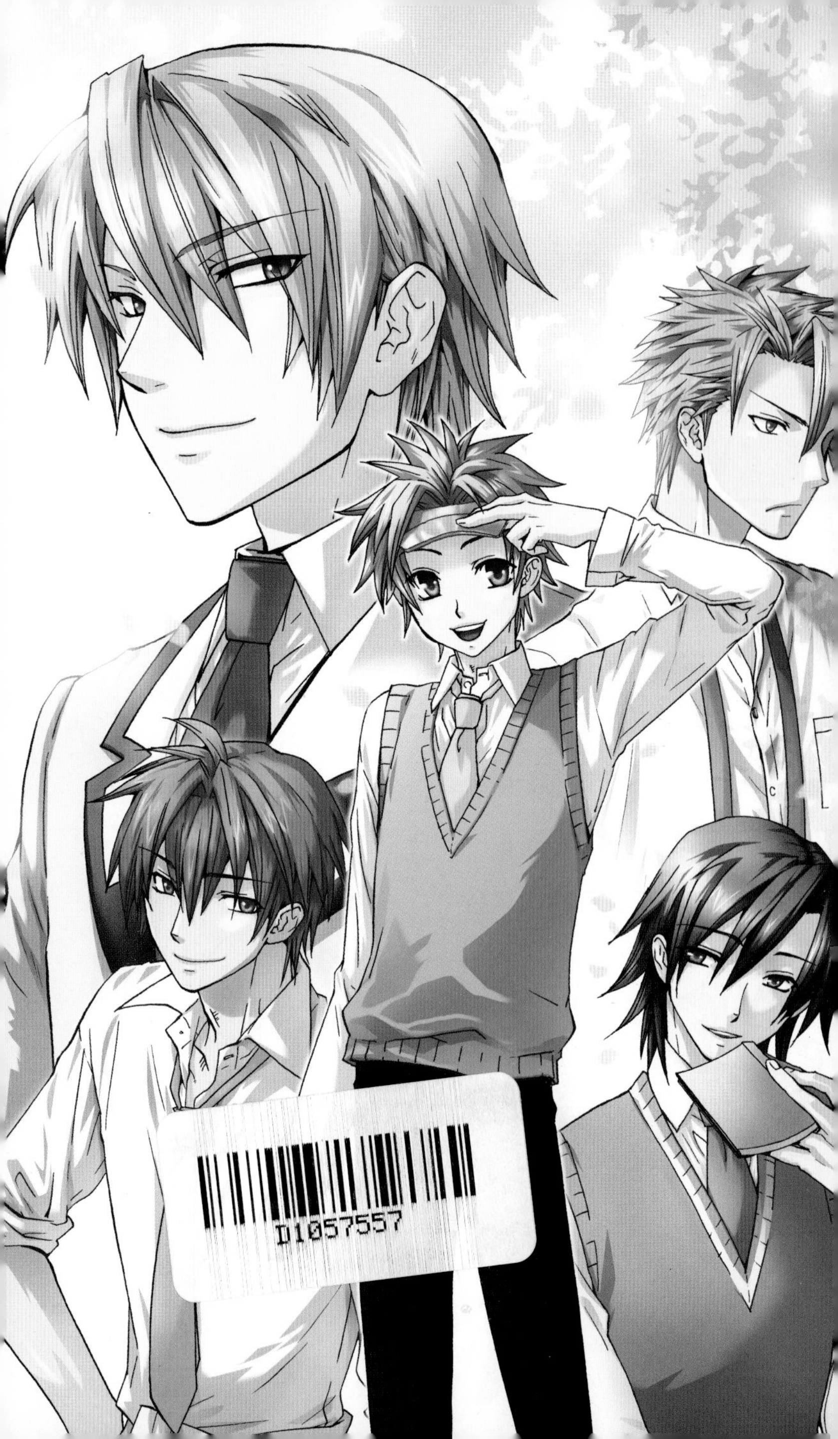

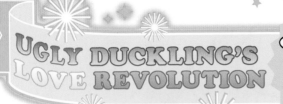

UGLY DUCKLING'S LOVE REVOLUTION

1

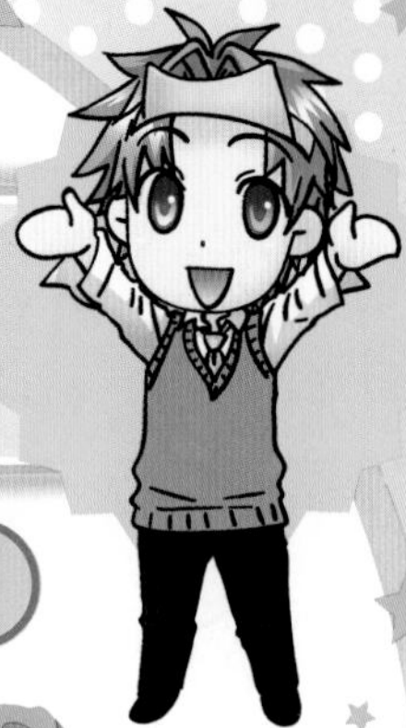

CONTENTS

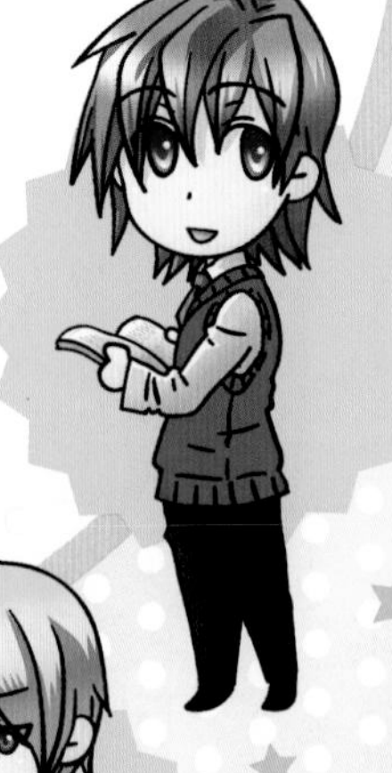

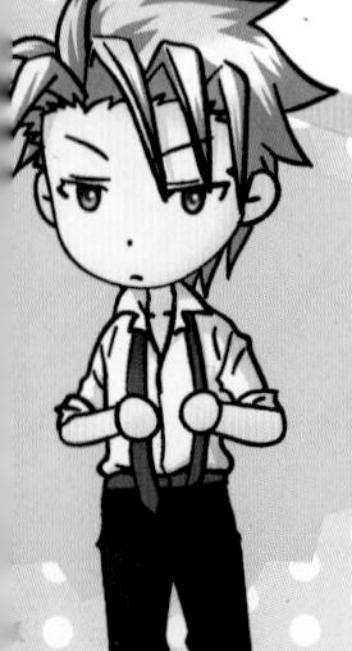

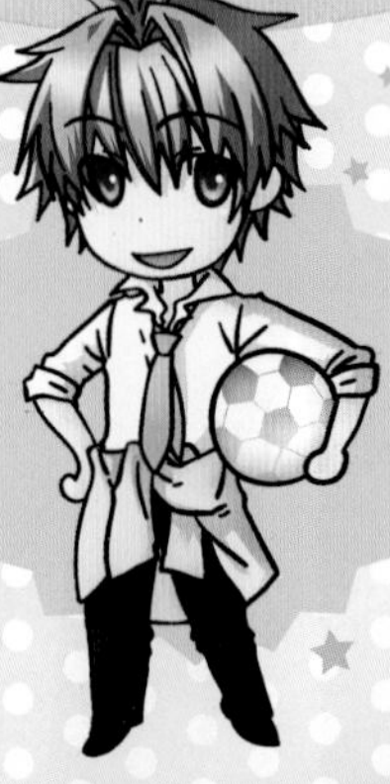

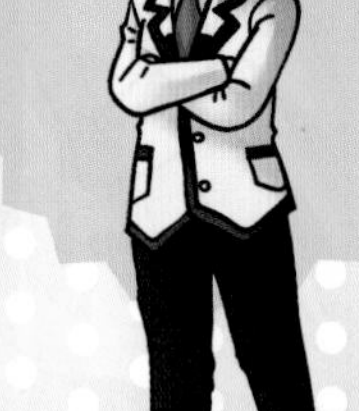

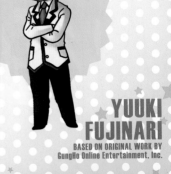

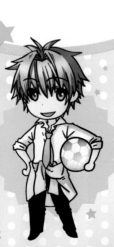

YUUKI FUJINARI

BASED ON ORIGINAL WORK BY GungHo Online Entertainment, Inc.

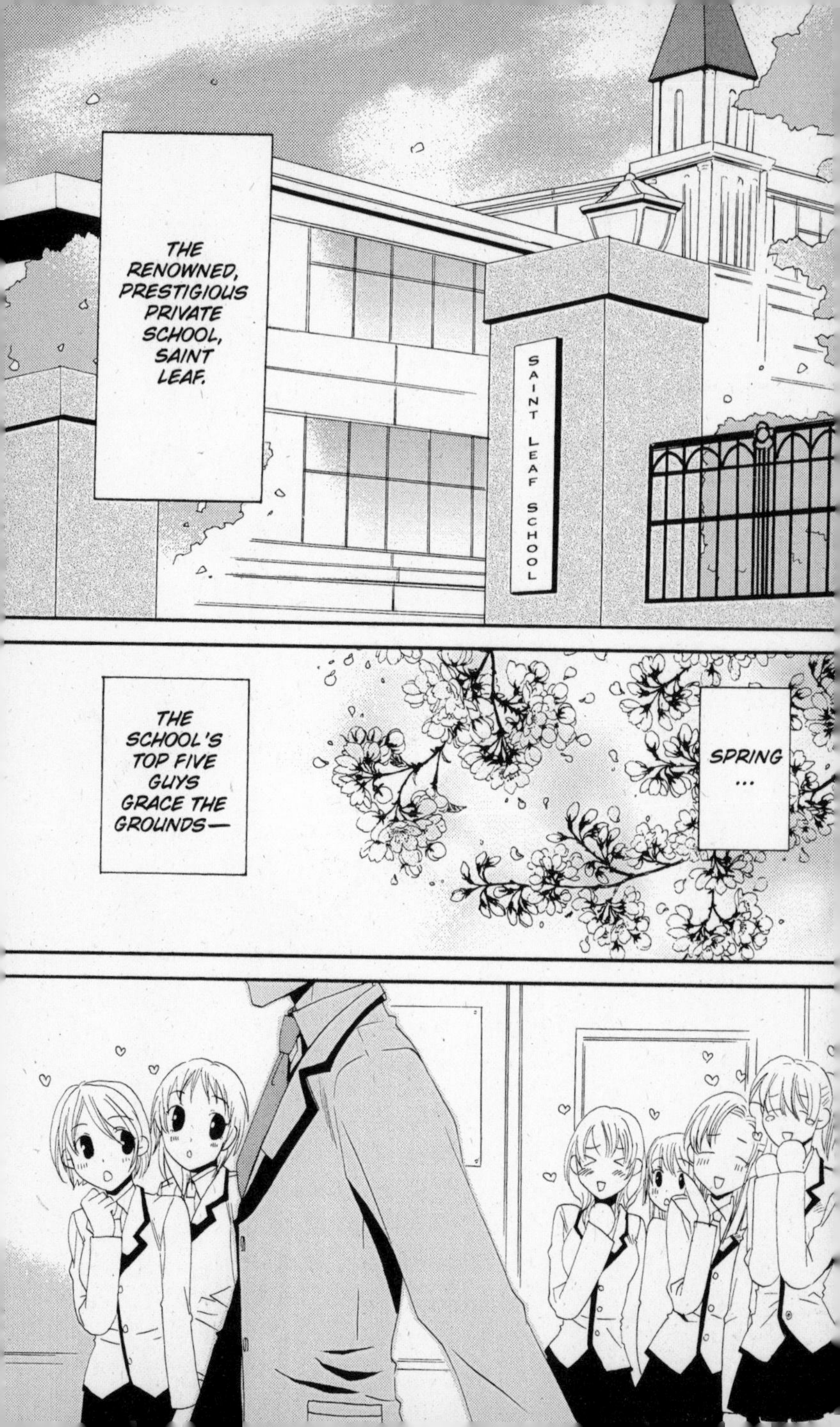
THE RENOWNED, PRESTIGIOUS PRIVATE SCHOOL, SAINT LEAF.
SAINT LEAF SCHOOL
SPRING...
THE SCHOOL'S TOP FIVE GUYS GRACE THE GROUNDS—

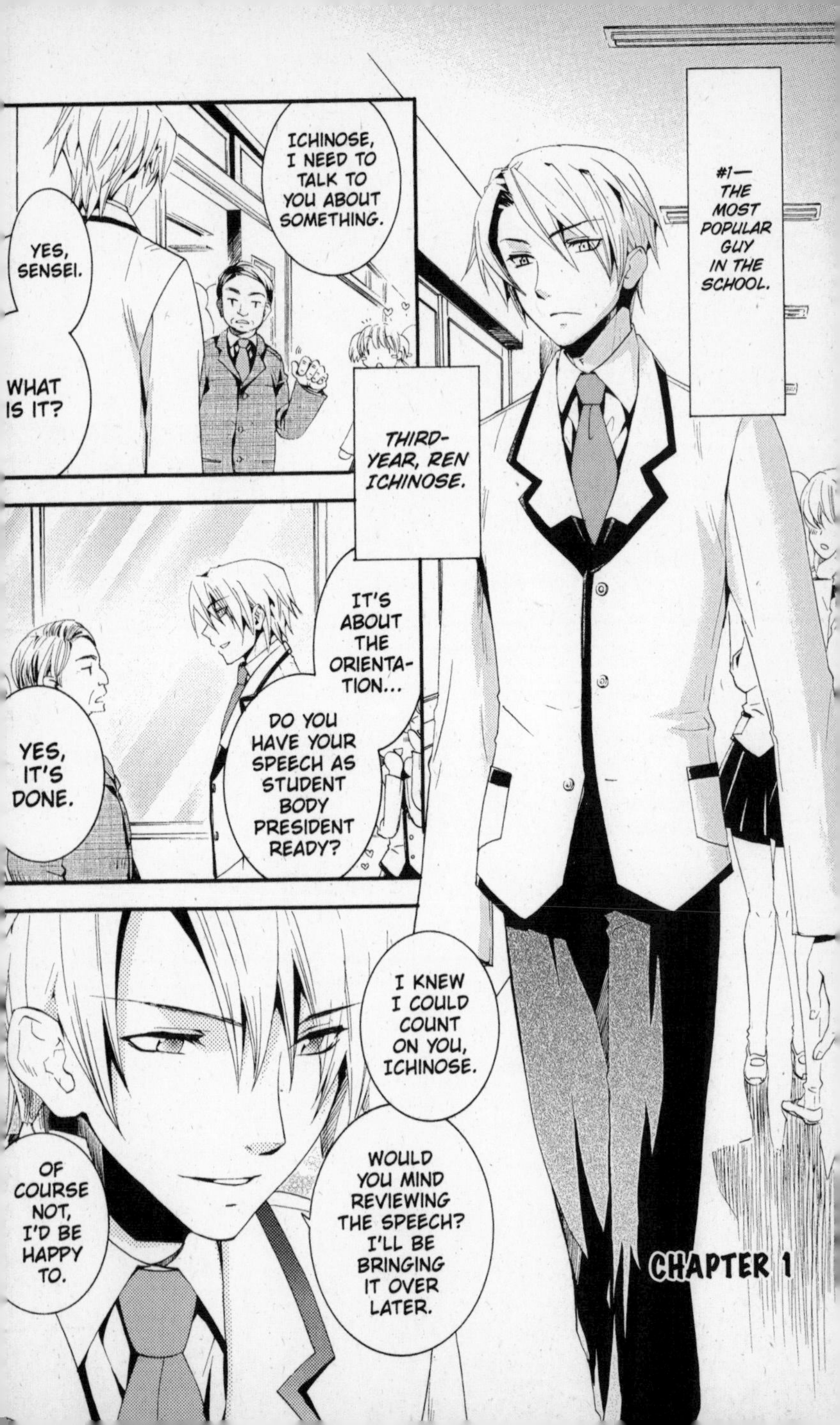
#1—THE MOST POPULAR GUY IN THE SCHOOL.
THIRD-YEAR, REN ICHINOSE.
CHAPTER 1
ICHINOSE, I NEED TO TALK TO YOU ABOUT SOMETHING.
YES, SENSEI.
WHAT IS IT?
IT'S ABOUT THE ORIENTATION-TION...
DO YOU HAVE YOUR SPEECH AS STUDENT BODY PRESIDENT READY?
YES, IT'S DONE.
I KNEW I COULD COUNT ON YOU, ICHINOSE.
WOULD YOU MIND REVIEWING THE SPEECH? I'LL BE BRINGING IT OVER LATER.
OF COURSE NOT, I'D BE HAPPY TO.

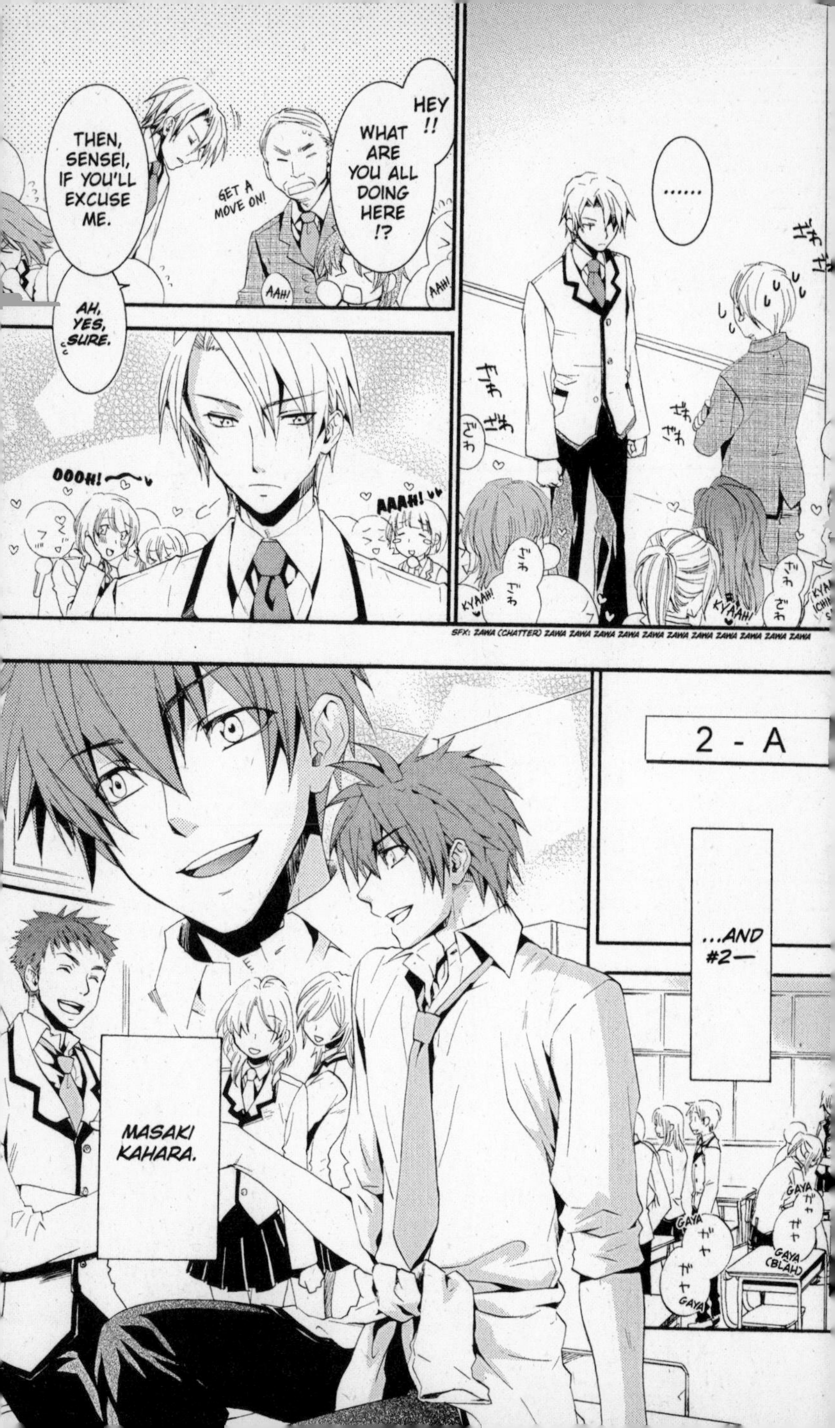
......
ざわ ざわ
ざわ ざわ
ざわ ざわ
ざわ ざわ
ざわ ざわ
KYAAH!
KYAAH!
HEY!!
WHAT ARE YOU ALL DOING HERE!?
GET A MOVE ON!
AAH!
AAH!
THEN, SENSEI, IF YOU'LL EXCUSE ME.
AH, YES, SURE.
OOOH!
AAAH!
SFX: ZAWA (CHATTER) ZAWA ZAWA ZAWA ZAWA ZAWA ZAWA ZAWA ZAWA ZAWA ZAWA ZAWA
2 - A
...AND #2—
GAYA ガヤ
ガヤ GAYA (BLAH)
GAYA ガヤ
ガヤ GAYA
MASAKI KAHARA.

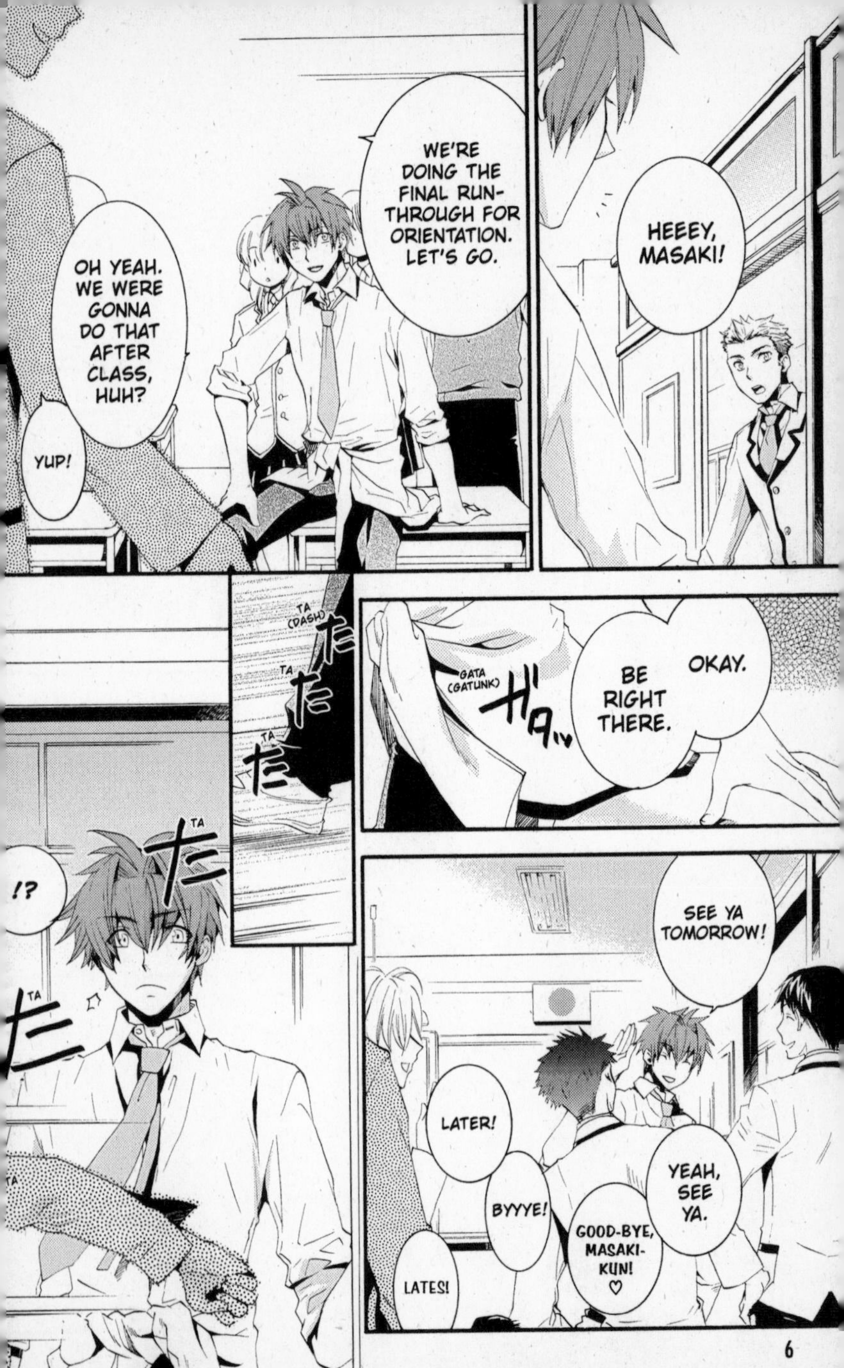
HEEEY, MASAKI!
WE'RE DOING THE FINAL RUN-THROUGH FOR ORIENTATION. LET'S GO.
OH YEAH. WE WERE GONNA DO THAT AFTER CLASS, HUH?
YUP!
OKAY.
BE RIGHT THERE.
GATA (GATUNK)
ガタッ
TA (DASH)
た
TA
た
TA
た
SEE YA TOMORROW!
YEAH, SEE YA.
GOOD-BYE, MASAKI-KUN! ♡
LATER!
BYYYE!
LATES!
TA
た
!?
TA
た
TA

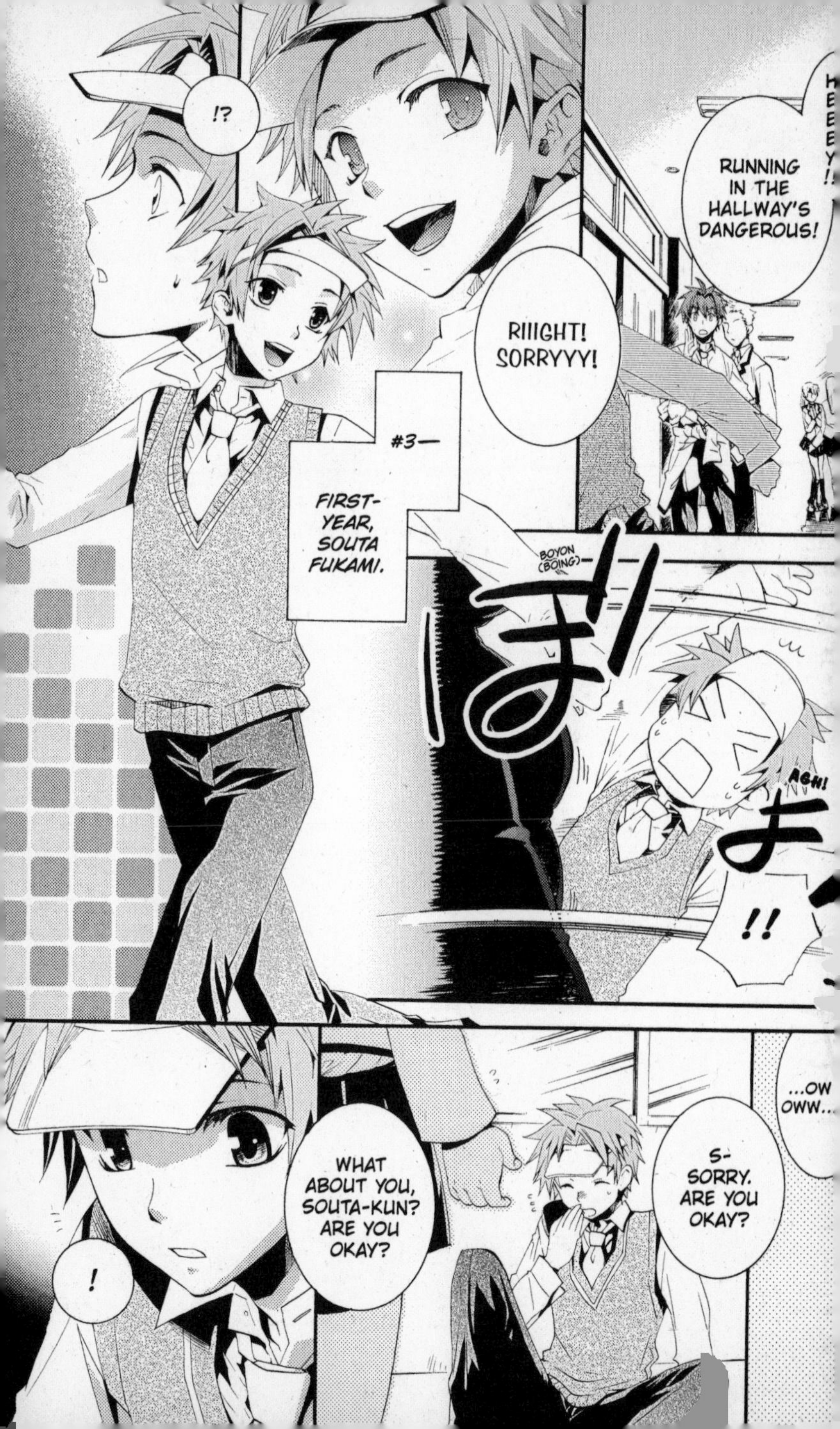

HEEEY!!
RUNNING IN THE HALLWAY'S DANGEROUS!
RIIIGHT! SORRYYY!
BOYON (BOING)
AGH!
!!
!?
#3—
FIRST-YEAR, SOUTA FUKAMI.
...OW OWW...
S- SORRY. ARE YOU OKAY?
WHAT ABOUT YOU, SOUTA-KUN? ARE YOU OKAY?
!

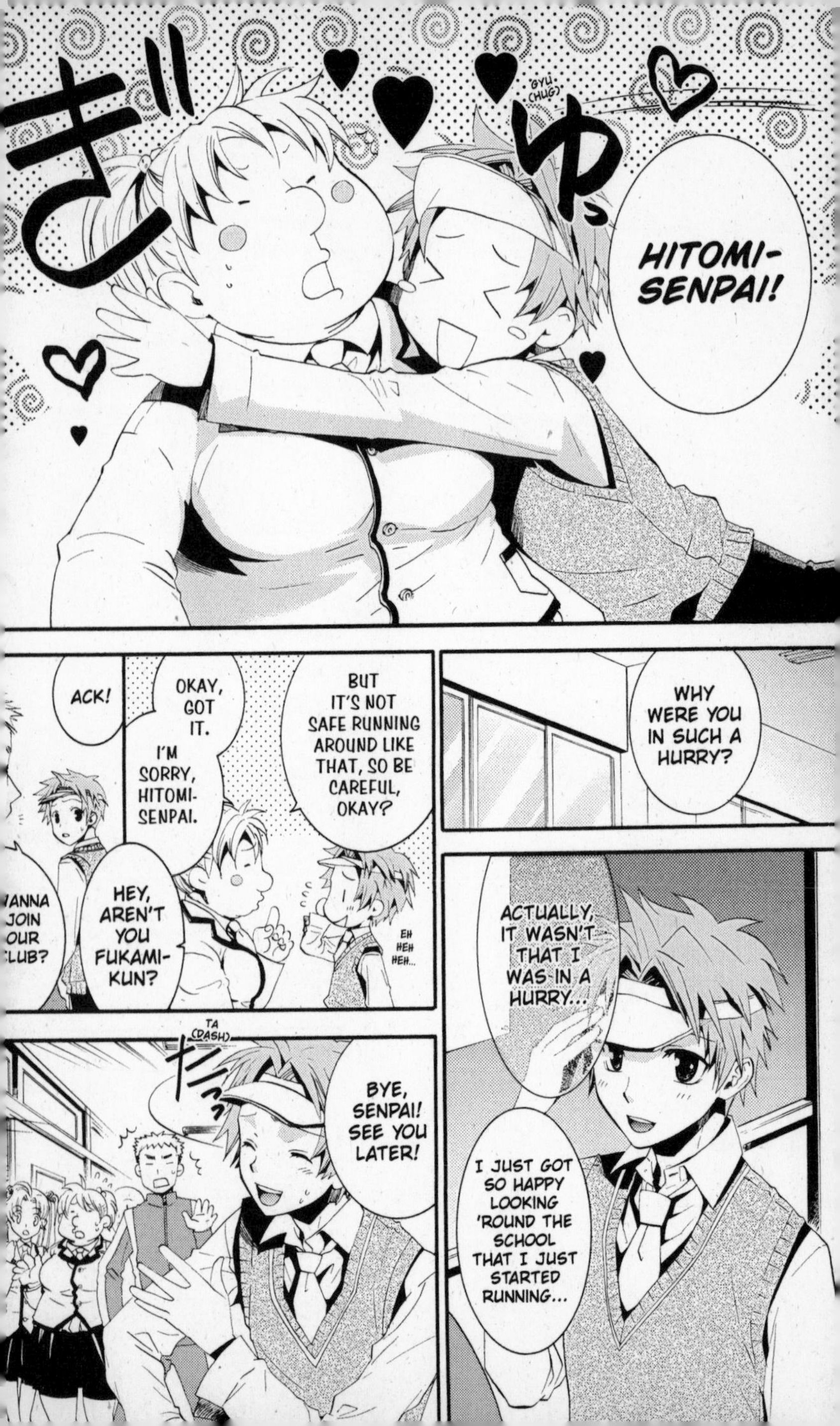
きゅ
GYU (HUG)
HITOMI-SENPAI!
WHY WERE YOU IN SUCH A HURRY?
ACTUALLY, IT WASN'T THAT I WAS IN A HURRY...
I JUST GOT SO HAPPY LOOKING 'ROUND THE SCHOOL THAT I JUST STARTED RUNNING...
BUT IT'S NOT SAFE RUNNING AROUND LIKE THAT, SO BE CAREFUL, OKAY?
OKAY, GOT IT.
I'M SORRY, HITOMI-SENPAI.
EH HEH HEH...
ACK!
HEY, AREN'T YOU FUKAMI-KUN?
ANNA JOIN OUR LUB?
TA (DASH)
BYE, SENPAI! SEE YOU LATER!

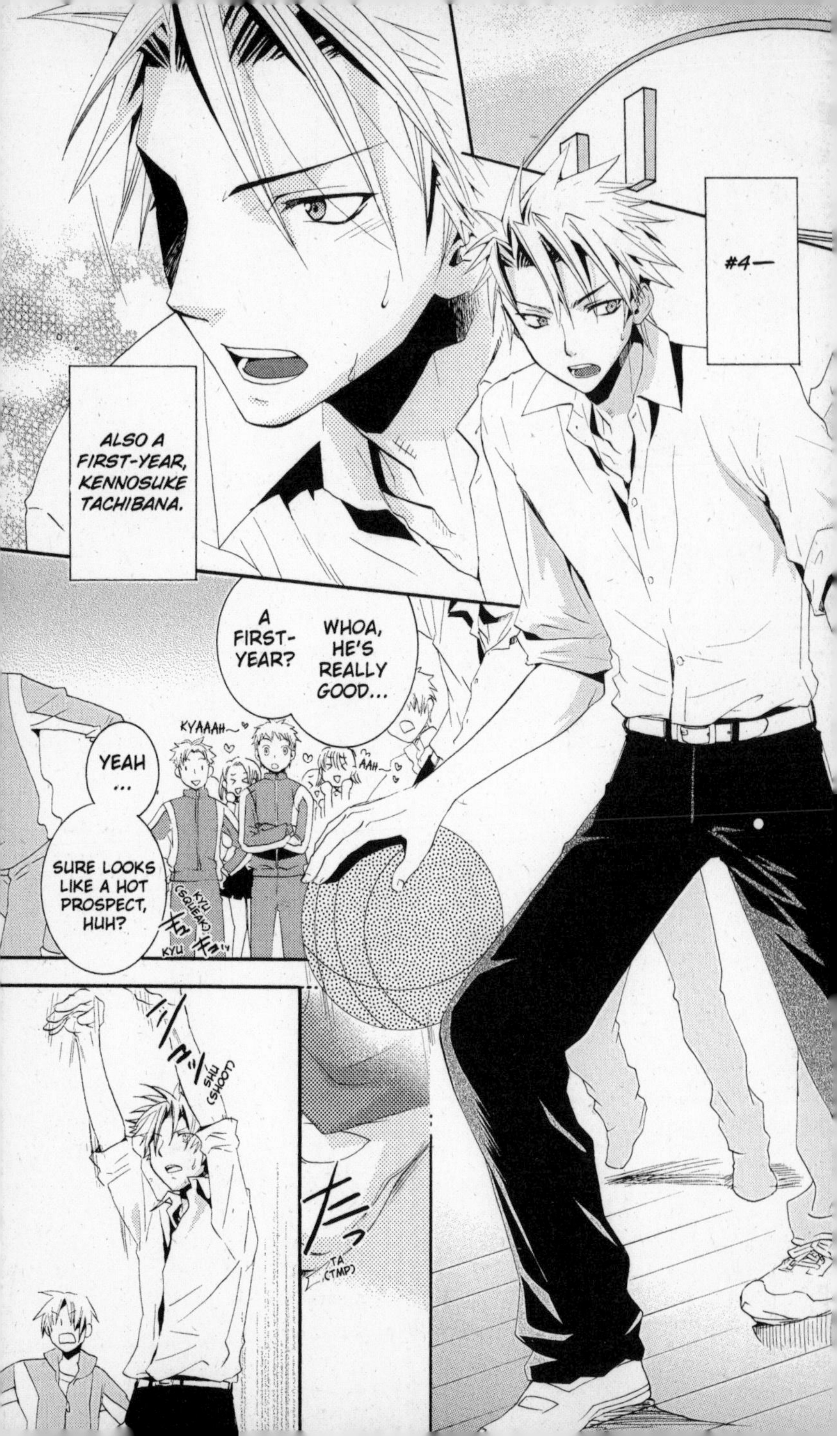
#4—
ALSO A FIRST-YEAR, KENNOSUKE TACHIBANA.
WHOA, HE'S REALLY GOOD...
A FIRST-YEAR?
KYAAAH~
AAH~
YEAH...
SURE LOOKS LIKE A HOT PROSPECT, HUH?
KYU (SQUEAK) KYU
TA (TMP)
SHU (SHOOT)

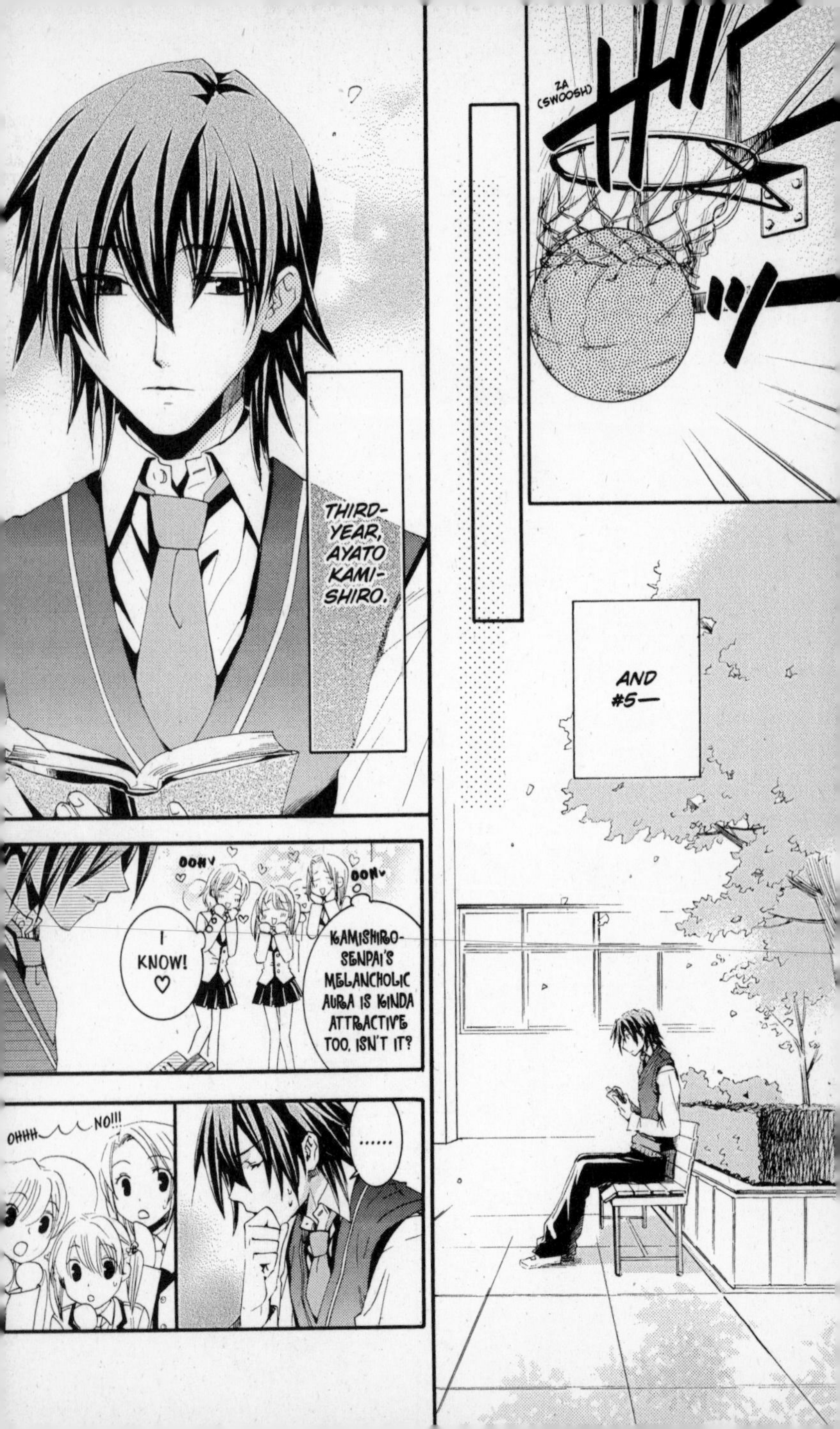
ZA (SWOOSH)
AND #5—
THIRD-YEAR, AYATO KAMISHIRO.
OOH♥
KAMISHIRO-SENPAI'S MELANCHOLIC AURA IS KINDA ATTRACTIVE TOO, ISN'T IT?
OOH♥
I KNOW! ♡
......
OHHH~~NO!!!

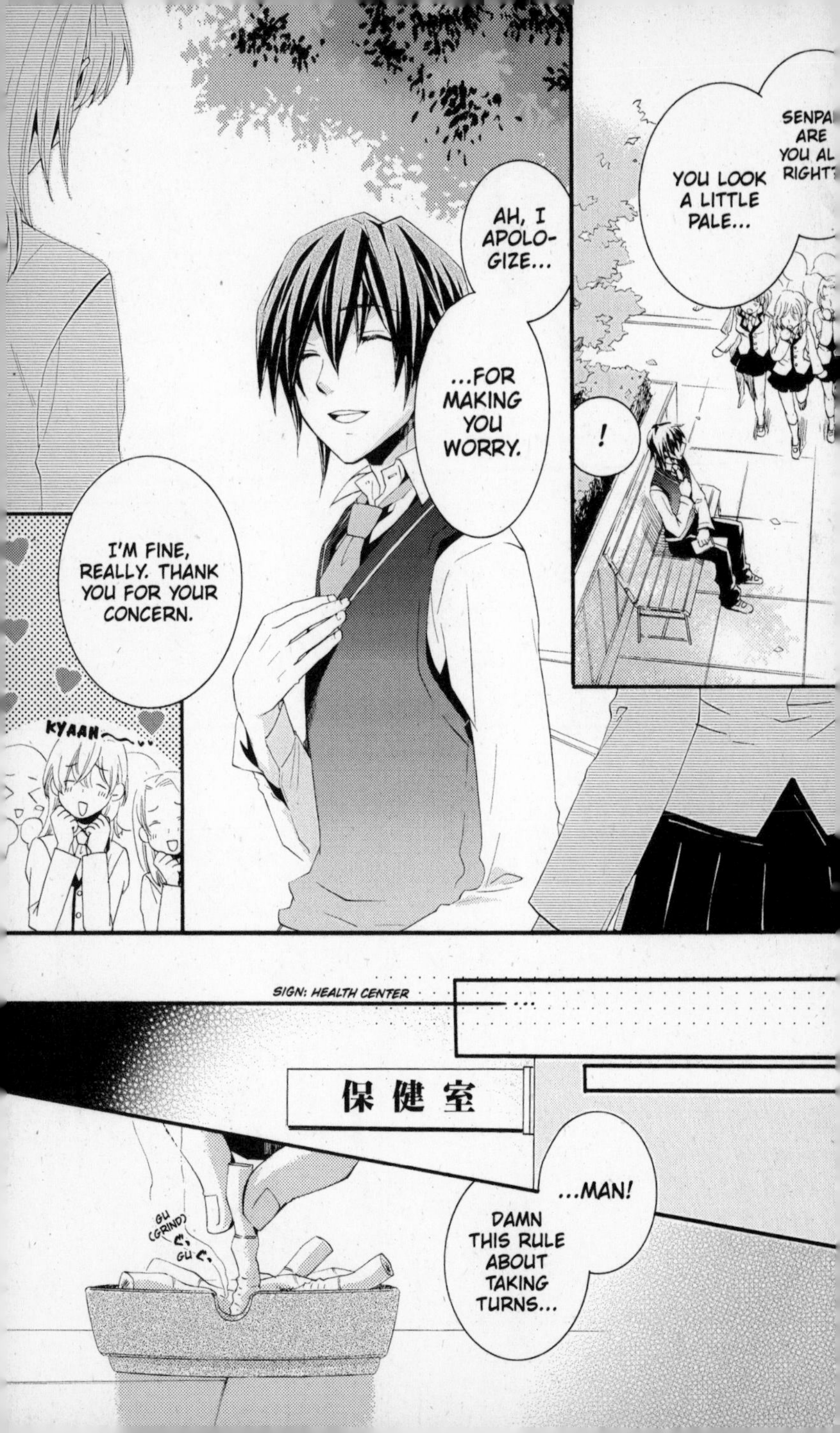
SENPA ARE YOU AL RIGHT?
YOU LOOK A LITTLE PALE...
!
AH, I APOLO-GIZE...
...FOR MAKING YOU WORRY.
I'M FINE, REALLY. THANK YOU FOR YOUR CONCERN.
KYAAH~~
SIGN: HEALTH CENTER
......
保健室
...MAN!
DAMN THIS RULE ABOUT TAKING TURNS...
GU (GRIND) ぐ、GU ぐ、

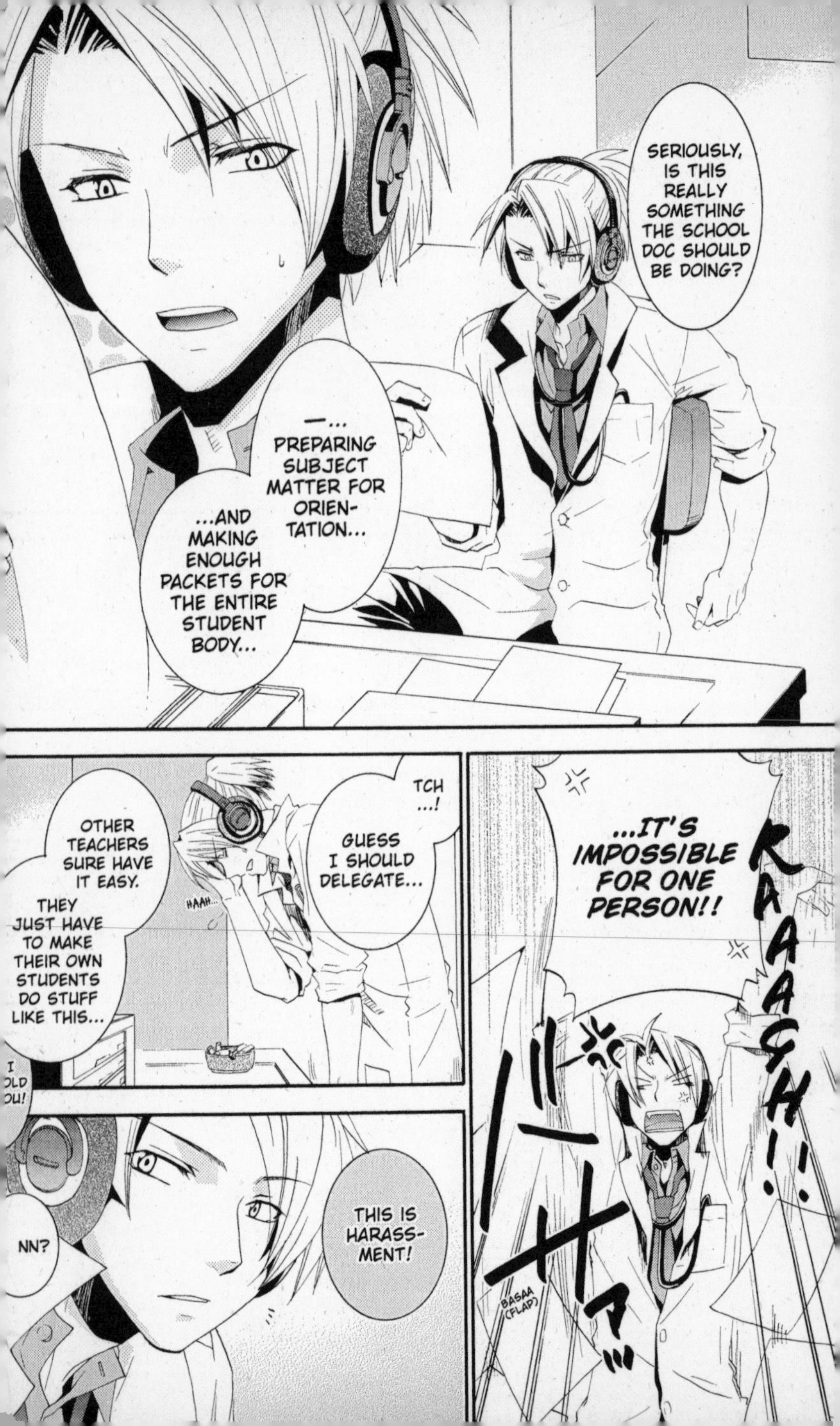
SERIOUSLY, IS THIS REALLY SOMETHING THE SCHOOL DOC SHOULD BE DOING?
—... PREPARING SUBJECT MATTER FOR ORIEN-TATION...
...AND MAKING ENOUGH PACKETS FOR THE ENTIRE STUDENT BODY...
...IT'S IMPOSSIBLE FOR ONE PERSON!!
RAAAGH!!
BASAA (FLAP)
TCH ...!
GUESS I SHOULD DELEGATE...
HAAH...
OTHER TEACHERS SURE HAVE IT EASY.
THEY JUST HAVE TO MAKE THEIR OWN STUDENTS DO STUFF LIKE THIS...
THIS IS HARASS-MENT!
NN?

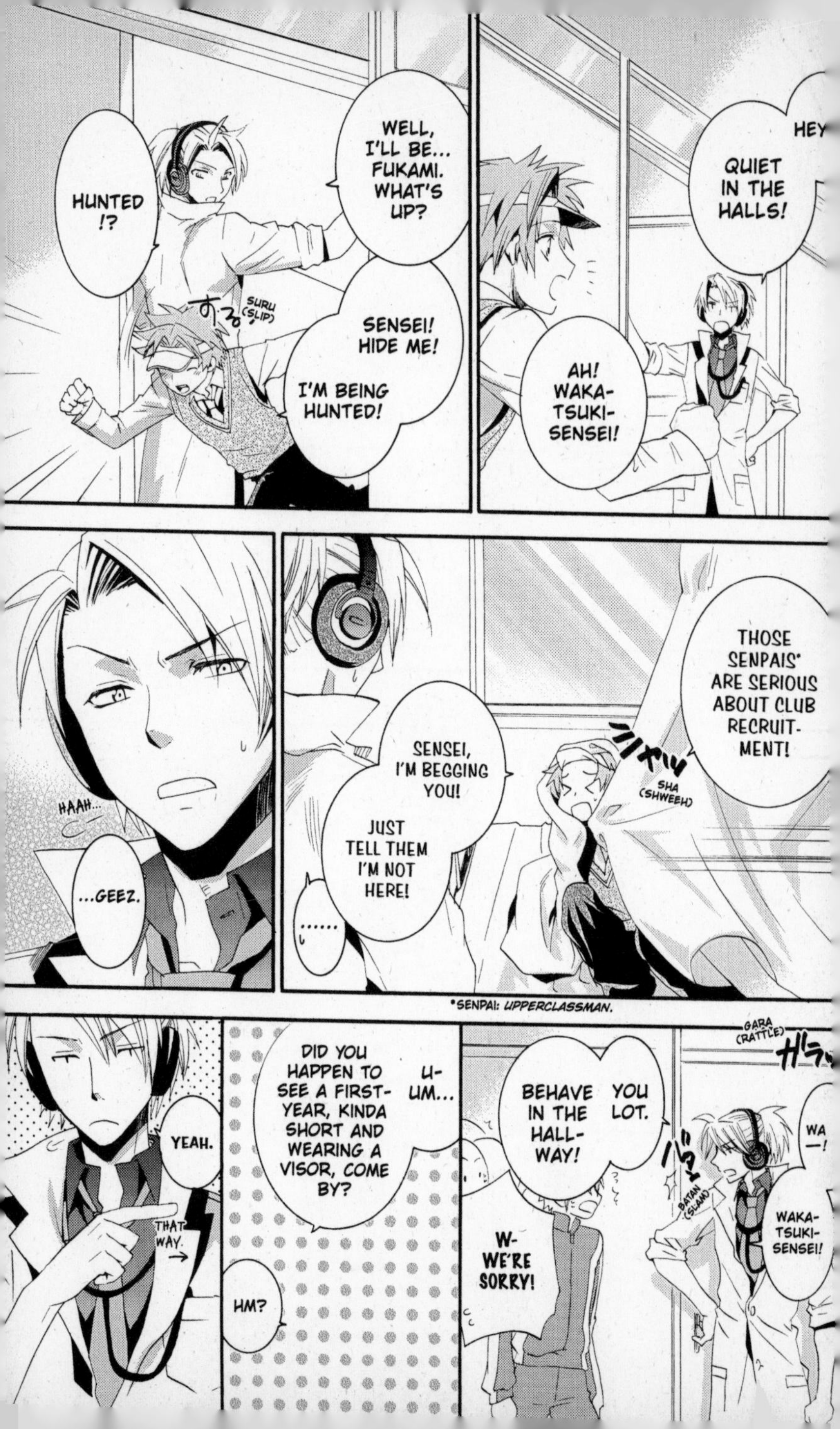
HEY
QUIET IN THE HALLS!
AH! WAKATSUKI-SENSEI!
WELL, I'LL BE... FUKAMI. WHAT'S UP?
SENSEI! HIDE ME!
I'M BEING HUNTED!
SURU (SLIP)
HUNTED!?
THOSE SENPAIS* ARE SERIOUS ABOUT CLUB RECRUITMENT!
SHA (SHWEEH)
SENSEI, I'M BEGGING YOU!
JUST TELL THEM I'M NOT HERE!
......
HAAH...
...GEEZ.
GARA (RATTLE)
WA—!
WAKATSUKI-SENSEI!
BATAN (SLAM)
YOU LOT.
BEHAVE IN THE HALLWAY!
W-WE'RE SORRY!
U-UM...
DID YOU HAPPEN TO SEE A FIRST-YEAR, KINDA SHORT AND WEARING A VISOR, COME BY?
HM?
YEAH.
THAT WAY.

*SENPAI: *UPPERCLASSMAN.*

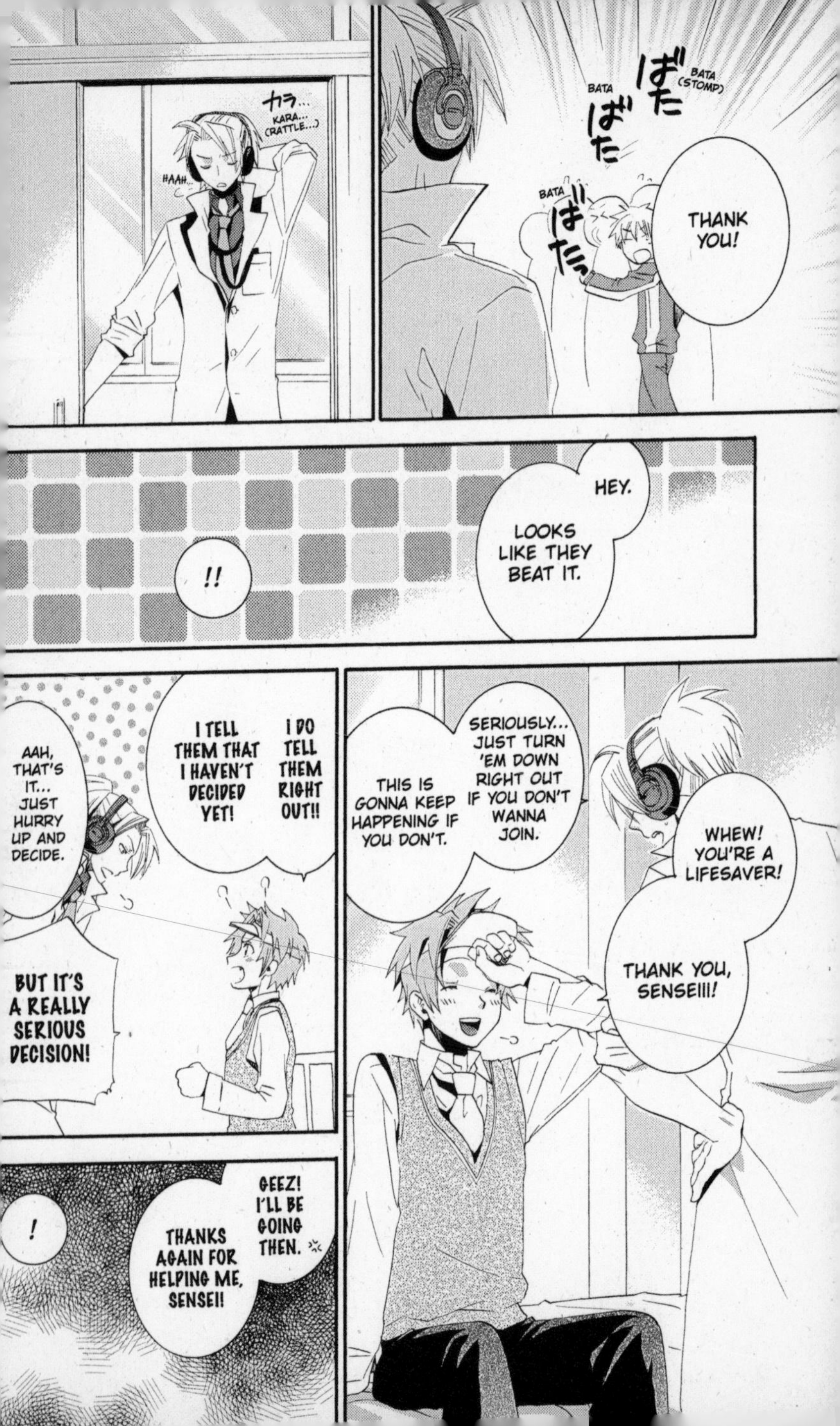
ばた
BATA (STOMP)
ばた
BATA
ばたっ
BATA
THANK YOU!
カラ...
KARA... (RATTLE...)
HAAH...
HEY.
LOOKS LIKE THEY BEAT IT.
!!
WHEW! YOU'RE A LIFESAVER!
THANK YOU, SENSEI!!!
SERIOUSLY... JUST TURN 'EM DOWN RIGHT OUT IF YOU DON'T WANNA JOIN.
THIS IS GONNA KEEP HAPPENING IF YOU DON'T.
I DO TELL THEM RIGHT OUT!!
I TELL THEM THAT I HAVEN'T DECIDED YET!
AAH, THAT'S IT... JUST HURRY UP AND DECIDE.
BUT IT'S A REALLY SERIOUS DECISION!
GEEZ! I'LL BE GOING THEN.
THANKS AGAIN FOR HELPING ME, SENSEI!
!

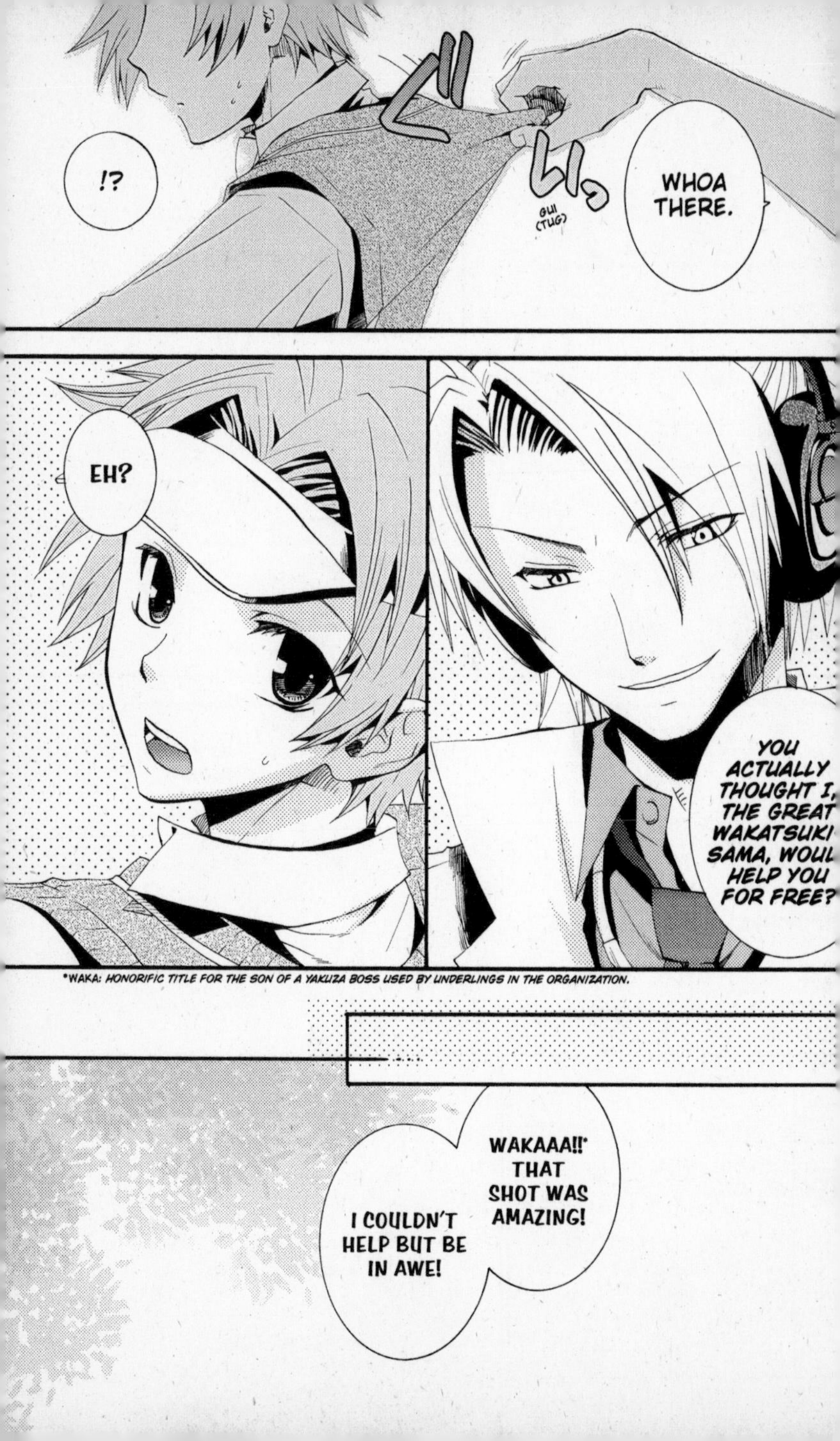
WHOA THERE.
GUI (TUG)
!?
YOU ACTUALLY THOUGHT I, THE GREAT WAKATSUKI SAMA, WOUL HELP YOU FOR FREE?
EH?
......
WAKAAA!!* THAT SHOT WAS AMAZING!
I COULDN'T HELP BUT BE IN AWE!

*WAKA: HONORIFIC TITLE FOR THE SON OF A YAKUZA BOSS USED BY UNDERLINGS IN THE ORGANIZATION.

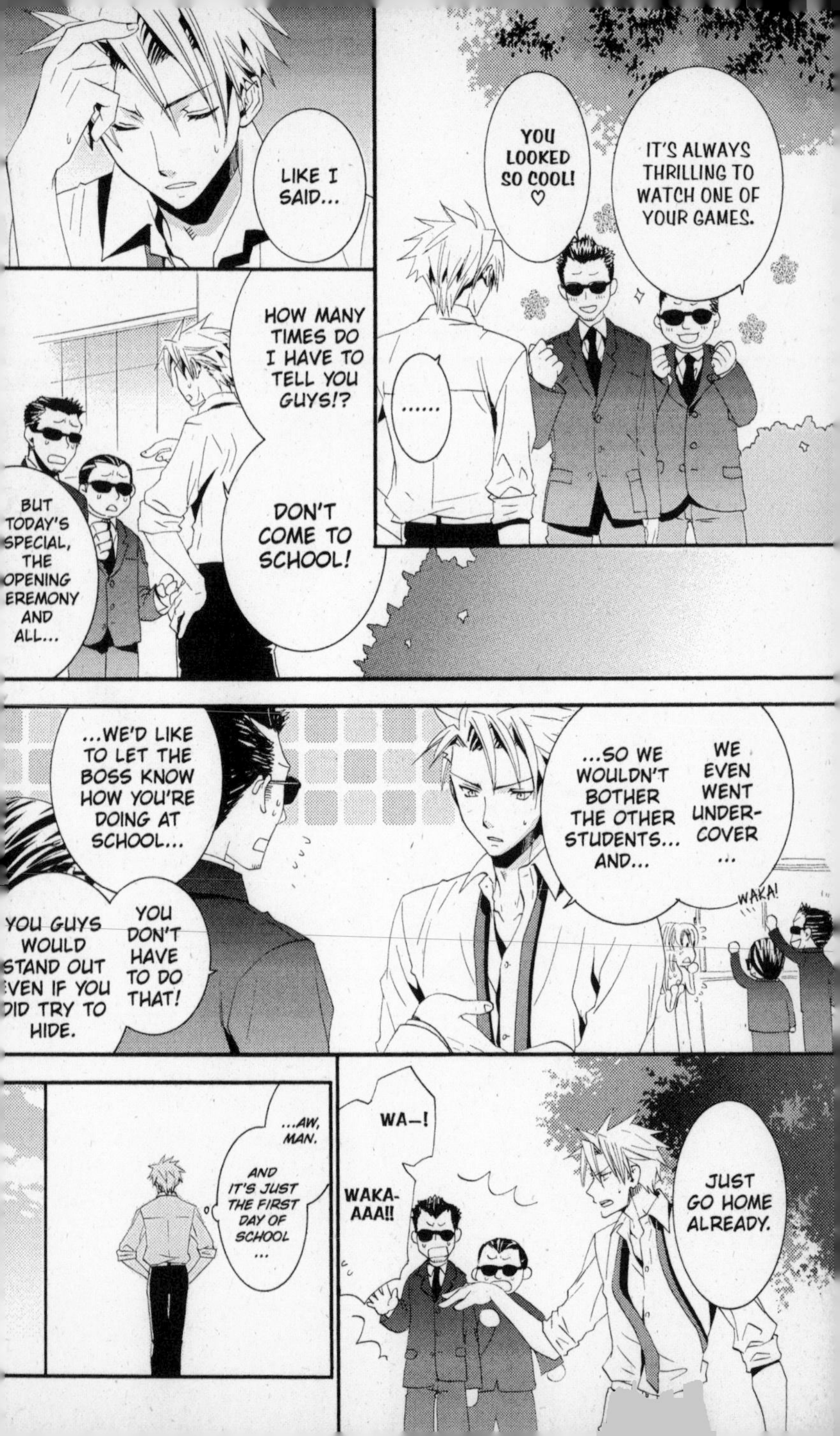
IT'S ALWAYS THRILLING TO WATCH ONE OF YOUR GAMES.
YOU LOOKED SO COOL! ♡
......
LIKE I SAID...
HOW MANY TIMES DO I HAVE TO TELL YOU GUYS!?
DON'T COME TO SCHOOL!
BUT TODAY'S SPECIAL, THE OPENING EREMONY AND ALL...
WE EVEN WENT UNDER-COVER ...
...SO WE WOULDN'T BOTHER THE OTHER STUDENTS... AND...
WAKA!
...WE'D LIKE TO LET THE BOSS KNOW HOW YOU'RE DOING AT SCHOOL...
YOU DON'T HAVE TO DO THAT!
YOU GUYS WOULD STAND OUT VEN IF YOU ID TRY TO HIDE.
JUST GO HOME ALREADY.
WA—!
WAKA-AAA!!
...AW, MAN.
AND IT'S JUST THE FIRST DAY OF SCHOOL ...

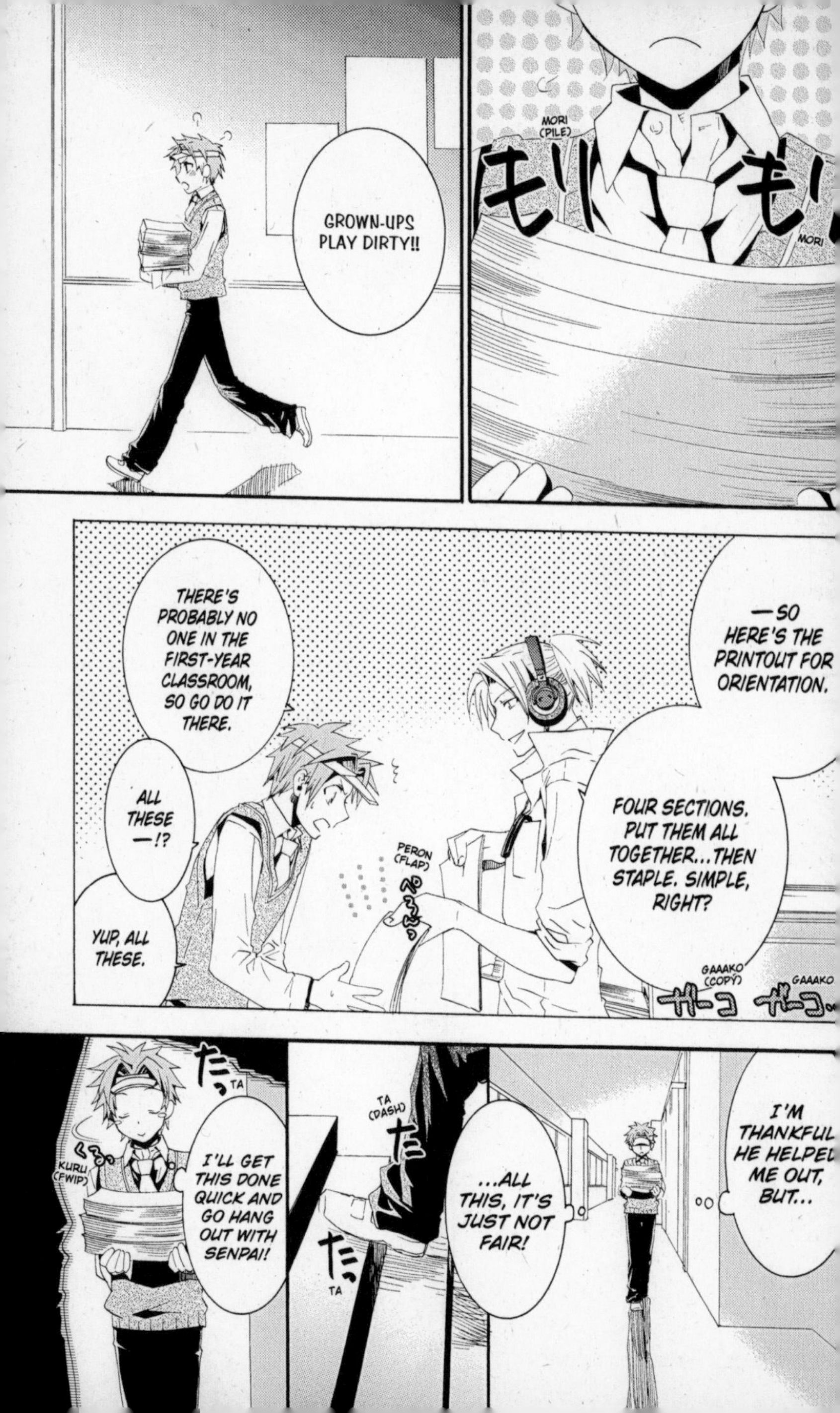
MORI (PILE)
MORI
GROWN-UPS PLAY DIRTY!!
—SO HERE'S THE PRINTOUT FOR ORIENTATION.
FOUR SECTIONS. PUT THEM ALL TOGETHER...THEN STAPLE. SIMPLE, RIGHT?
GAAAKO (COPY)
GAAAKO
PERON (FLAP)
THERE'S PROBABLY NO ONE IN THE FIRST-YEAR CLASSROOM, SO GO DO IT THERE.
ALL THESE—!?
YUP, ALL THESE.
I'M THANKFUL HE HELPED ME OUT, BUT...
...ALL THIS, IT'S JUST NOT FAIR!
TA (DASH)
TA
TA
KURU (FWIP)
I'LL GET THIS DONE QUICK AND GO HANG OUT WITH SENPAI!

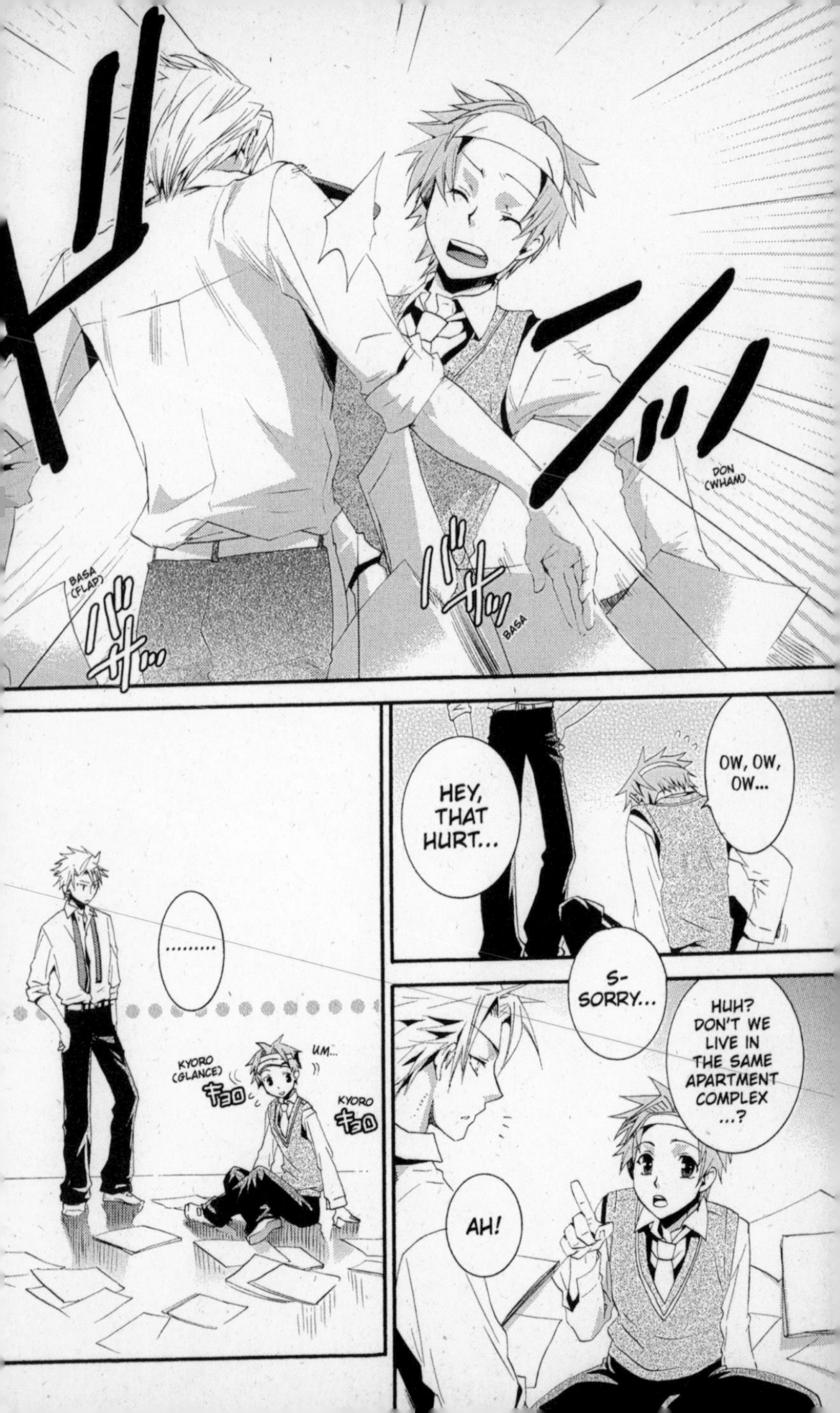
DON (WHAM)
BASA
BASA (FLAP)
OW, OW, OW...
HEY, THAT HURT...
S-SORRY...
HUH? DON'T WE LIVE IN THE SAME APARTMENT COMPLEX ...?
AH!
....
UM...
KYORO
KYORO (GLANCE)

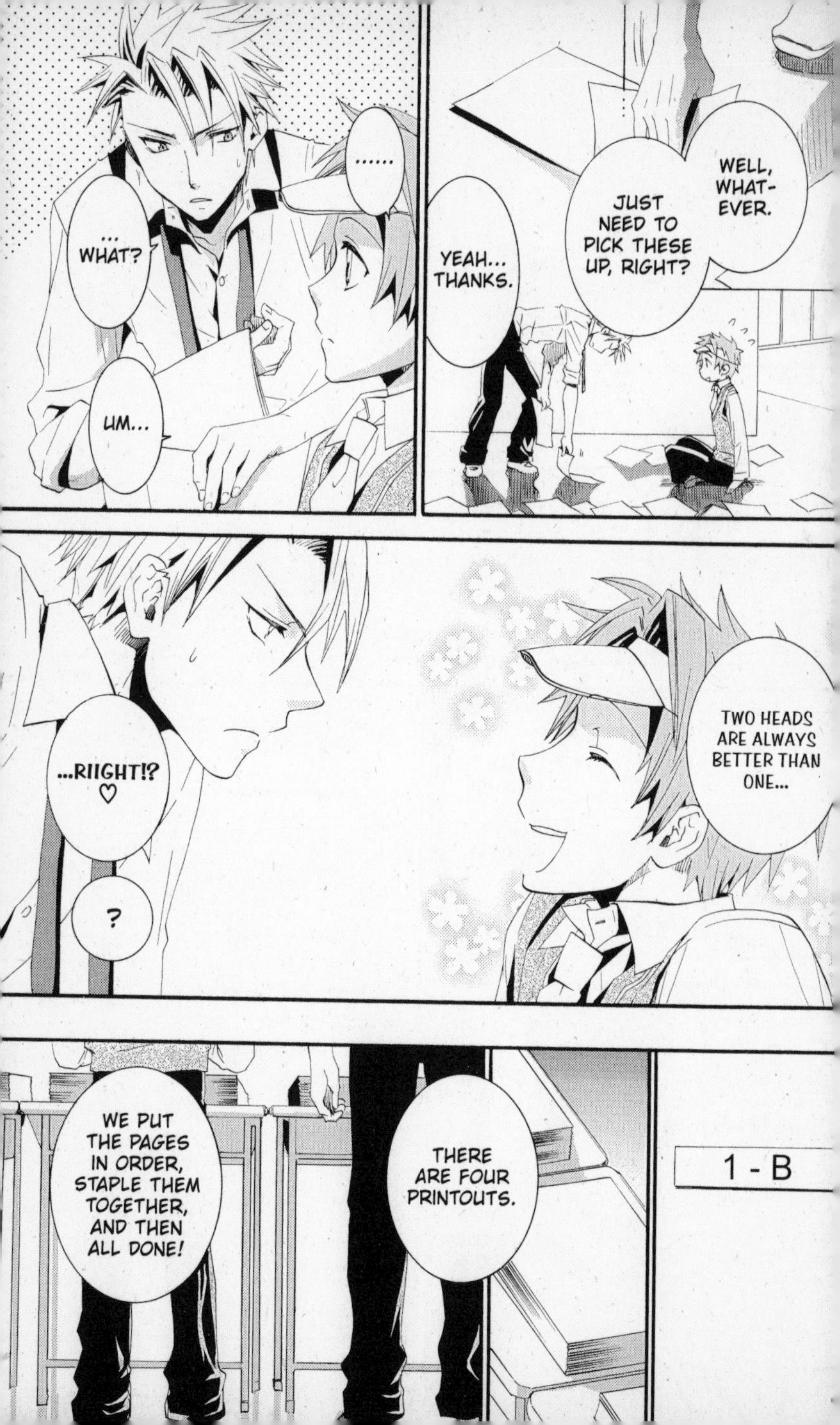
WELL, WHAT-EVER.
JUST NEED TO PICK THESE UP, RIGHT?
YEAH... THANKS.
......
... WHAT?
UM...
TWO HEADS ARE ALWAYS BETTER THAN ONE...
...RIIGHT!? ♡
?
1 - B
THERE ARE FOUR PRINTOUTS.
WE PUT THE PAGES IN ORDER, STAPLE THEM TOGETHER, AND THEN ALL DONE!

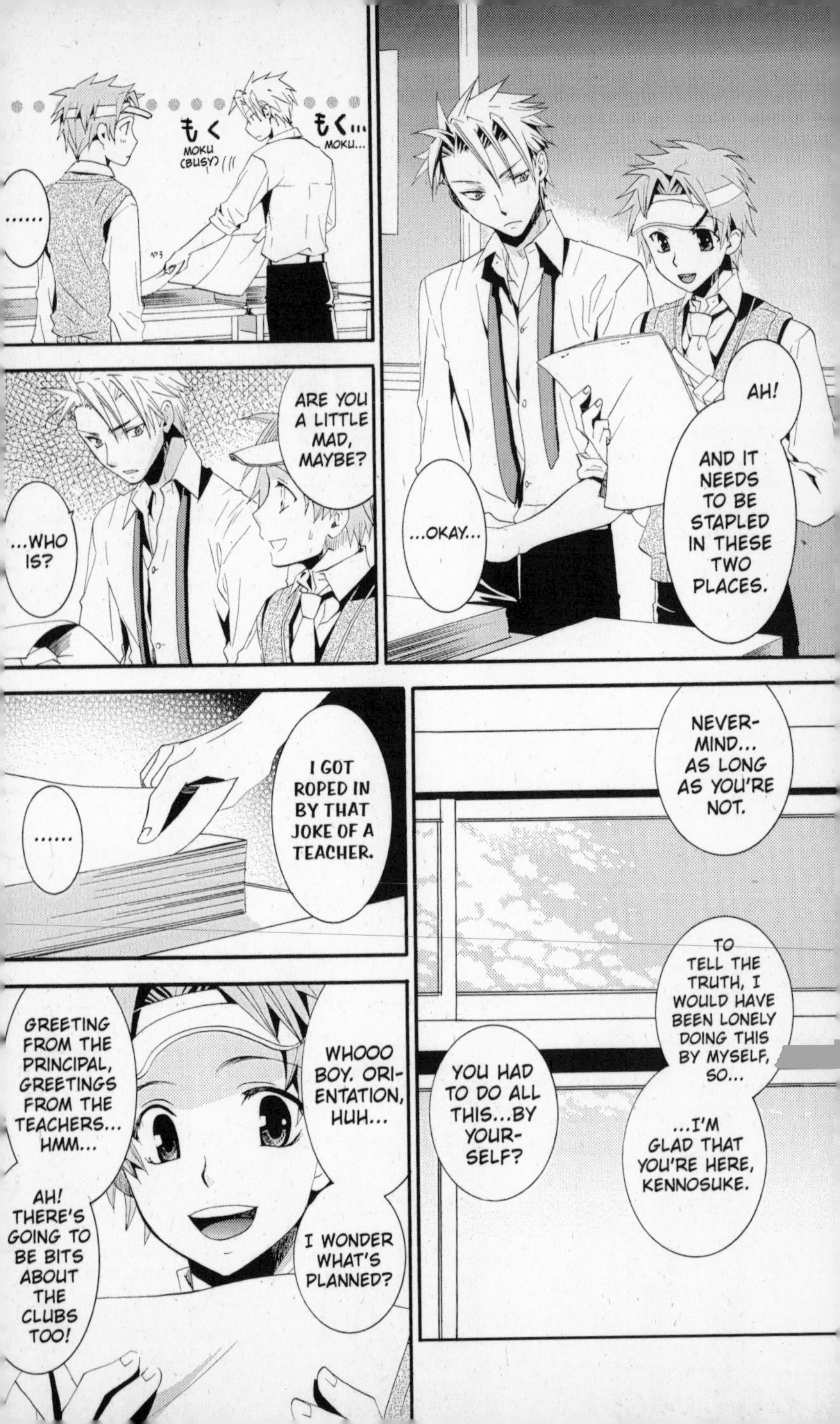
AH!
AND IT NEEDS TO BE STAPLED IN THESE TWO PLACES.
...OKAY...
もく... MOKU...
もく MOKU (BUSY)
......
ARE YOU A LITTLE MAD, MAYBE?
...WHO IS?
NEVER-MIND... AS LONG AS YOU'RE NOT.
TO TELL THE TRUTH, I WOULD HAVE BEEN LONELY DOING THIS BY MYSELF, SO...
...I'M GLAD THAT YOU'RE HERE, KENNOSUKE.
YOU HAD TO DO ALL THIS...BY YOURSELF?
I GOT ROPED IN BY THAT JOKE OF A TEACHER.
......
WHOOO BOY. ORI-ENTATION, HUH...
I WONDER WHAT'S PLANNED?
GREETING FROM THE PRINCIPAL, GREETINGS FROM THE TEACHERS... HMM...
AH! THERE'S GOING TO BE BITS ABOUT THE CLUBS TOO!

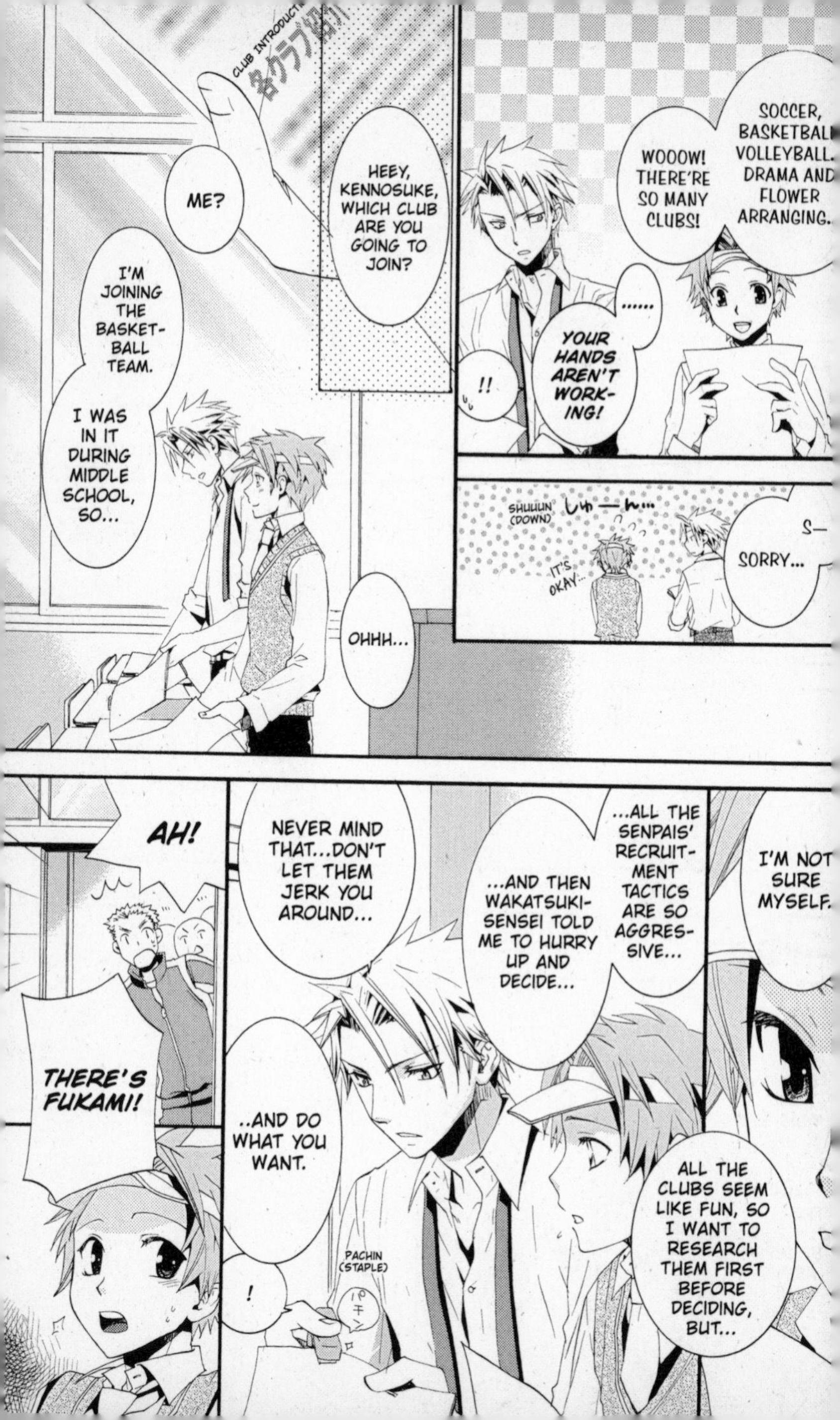

SOCCER, BASKETBALL VOLLEYBALL. DRAMA AND FLOWER ARRANGING.
WOOOW! THERE'RE SO MANY CLUBS!
......
YOUR HANDS AREN'T WORKING!
!!
S— SORRY...
SHUUUN (DOWN)
しゅーん…
IT'S OKAY...
CLUB INTRODUCT
HEEY, KENNOSUKE, WHICH CLUB ARE YOU GOING TO JOIN?
ME?
I'M JOINING THE BASKET-BALL TEAM.
I WAS IN IT DURING MIDDLE SCHOOL, SO...
OHHH...
I'M NOT SURE MYSELF.
ALL THE CLUBS SEEM LIKE FUN, SO I WANT TO RESEARCH THEM FIRST BEFORE DECIDING, BUT...
...ALL THE SENPAIS' RECRUIT-MENT TACTICS ARE SO AGGRES-SIVE...
...AND THEN WAKATSUKI-SENSEI TOLD ME TO HURRY UP AND DECIDE...
NEVER MIND THAT...DON'T LET THEM JERK YOU AROUND...
..AND DO WHAT YOU WANT.
PACHIN (STAPLE)
パチン
!
AH!
THERE'S FUKAMI!

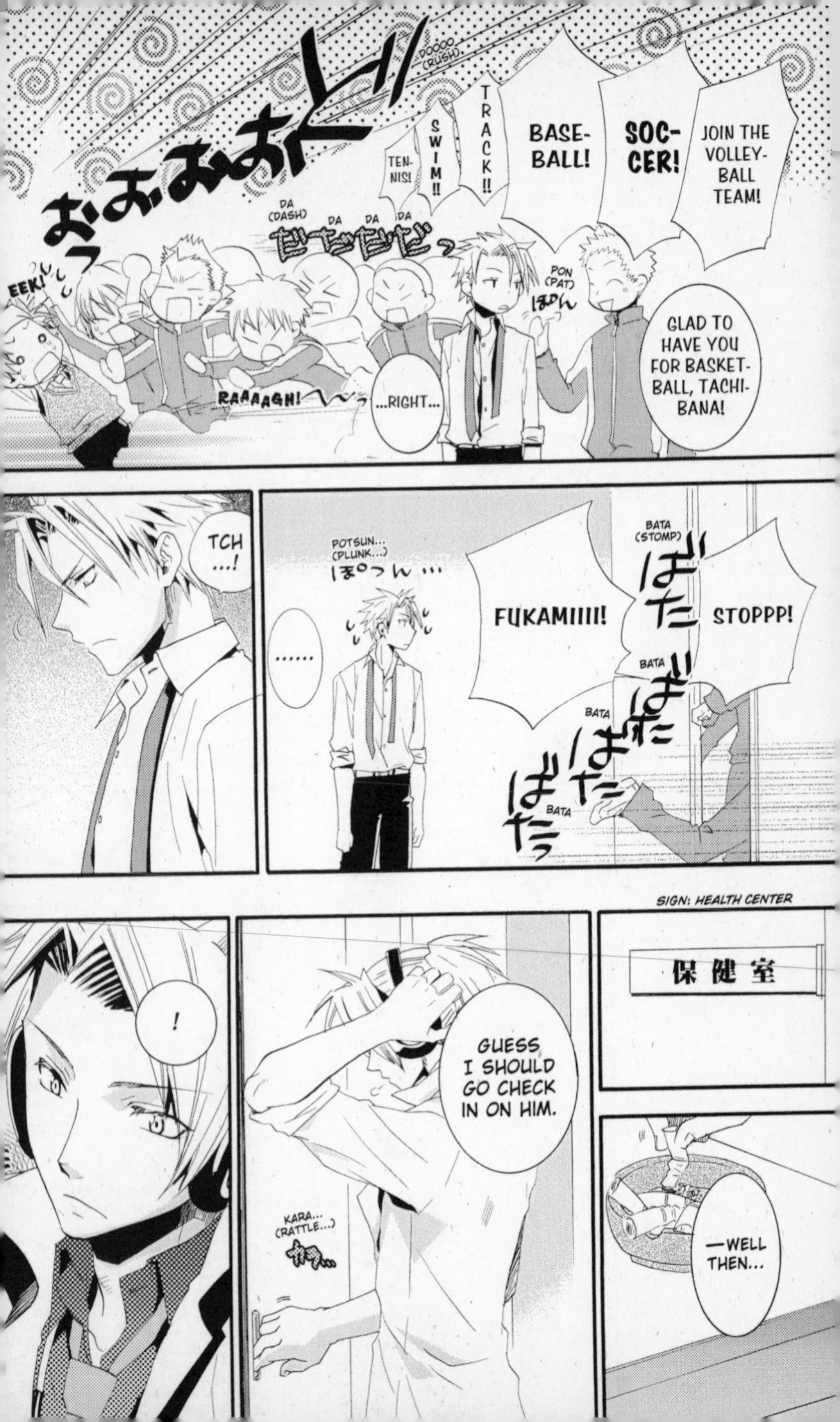
JOIN THE VOLLEY-BALL TEAM!
SOC-CER!
BASE-BALL!
TRACK!!
DOOOO (RUSH)
SWIM!!
TEN-NIS!
DA (DASH) DA DA DA
PON (PAT)
GLAD TO HAVE YOU FOR BASKET-BALL, TACHI-BANA!
EEK!
RAAAAGH!
...RIGHT...
STOPPP!
BATA (STOMP)
FUKAMIIIII!
BATA
BATA
BATA
POTSUN... (PLUNK...)
......
TCH ...!
SIGN: HEALTH CENTER
保健室
—WELL THEN...
GUESS I SHOULD GO CHECK IN ON HIM.
KARA... (RATTLE...)
!

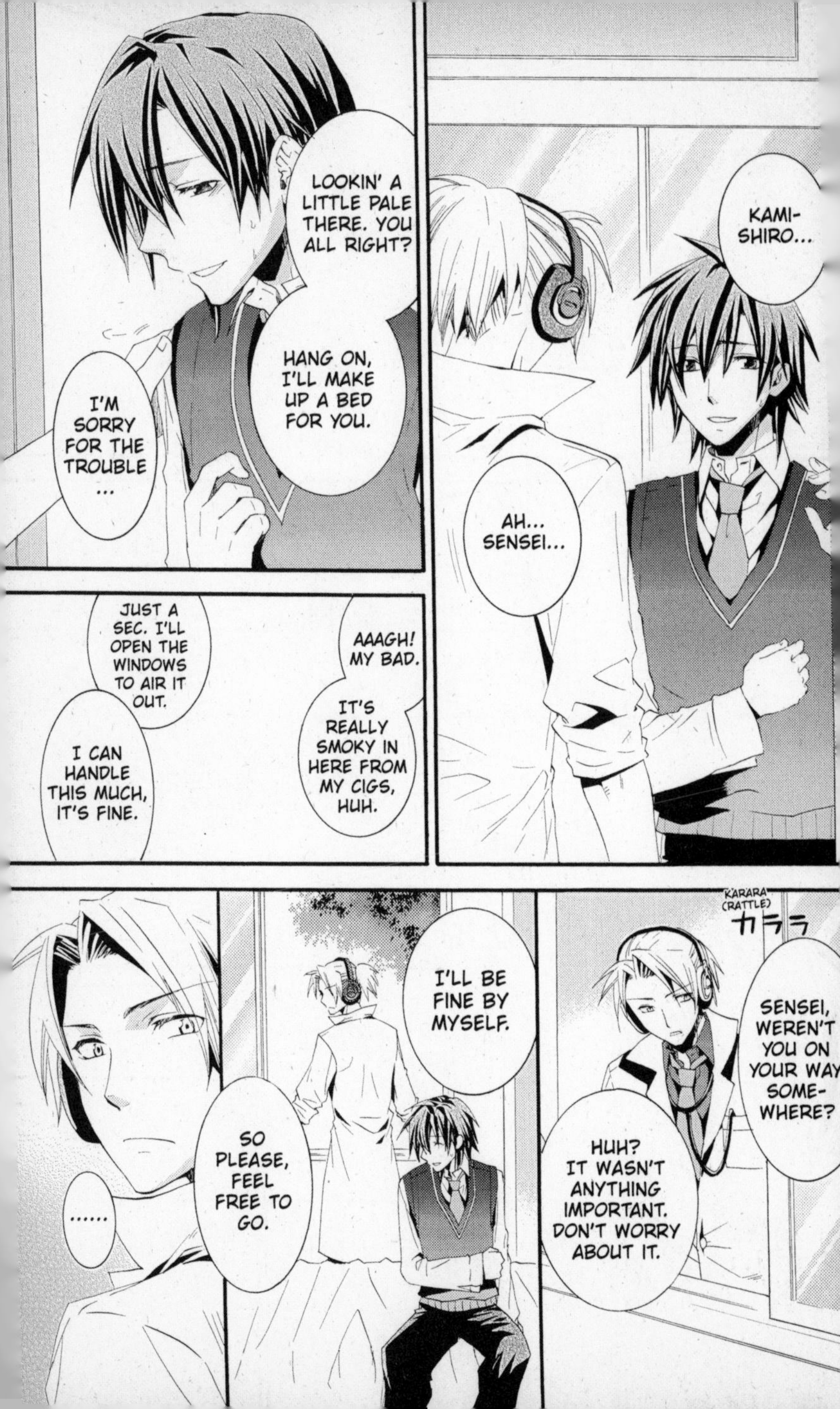
KAMI-SHIRO...
AH... SENSEI...
LOOKIN' A LITTLE PALE THERE. YOU ALL RIGHT?
HANG ON, I'LL MAKE UP A BED FOR YOU.
I'M SORRY FOR THE TROUBLE ...
AAAGH! MY BAD.
IT'S REALLY SMOKY IN HERE FROM MY CIGS, HUH.
JUST A SEC. I'LL OPEN THE WINDOWS TO AIR IT OUT.
I CAN HANDLE THIS MUCH, IT'S FINE.
KARARA (RATTLE)
カララ
SENSEI, WEREN'T YOU ON YOUR WAY SOME-WHERE?
HUH? IT WASN'T ANYTHING IMPORTANT. DON'T WORRY ABOUT IT.
I'LL BE FINE BY MYSELF.
SO PLEASE, FEEL FREE TO GO.
......

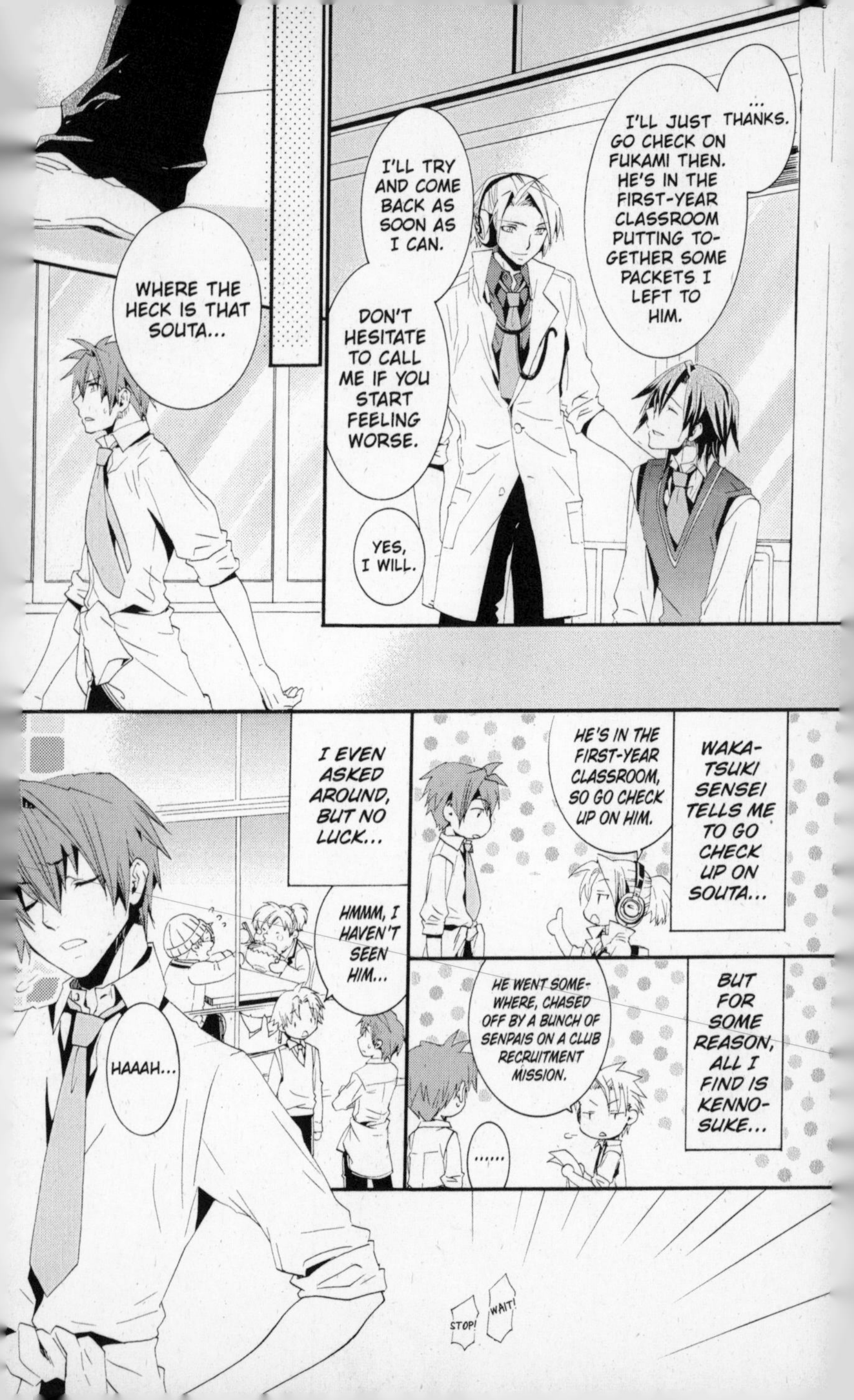

... THANKS.
I'LL JUST GO CHECK ON FUKAMI THEN. HE'S IN THE FIRST-YEAR CLASSROOM PUTTING TO-GETHER SOME PACKETS I LEFT TO HIM.
I'LL TRY AND COME BACK AS SOON AS I CAN.
DON'T HESITATE TO CALL ME IF YOU START FEELING WORSE.
YES, I WILL.
WHERE THE HECK IS THAT SOUTA...
WAKA-TSUKI SENSEI TELLS ME TO GO CHECK UP ON SOUTA...
HE'S IN THE FIRST-YEAR CLASSROOM, SO GO CHECK UP ON HIM.
BUT FOR SOME REASON, ALL I FIND IS KENNO-SUKE...
HE WENT SOME-WHERE, CHASED OFF BY A BUNCH OF SENPAIS ON A CLUB RECRUITMENT MISSION.
......
I EVEN ASKED AROUND, BUT NO LUCK...
HMMM, I HAVEN'T SEEN HIM...
HAAAH...
WAIT!
STOP!

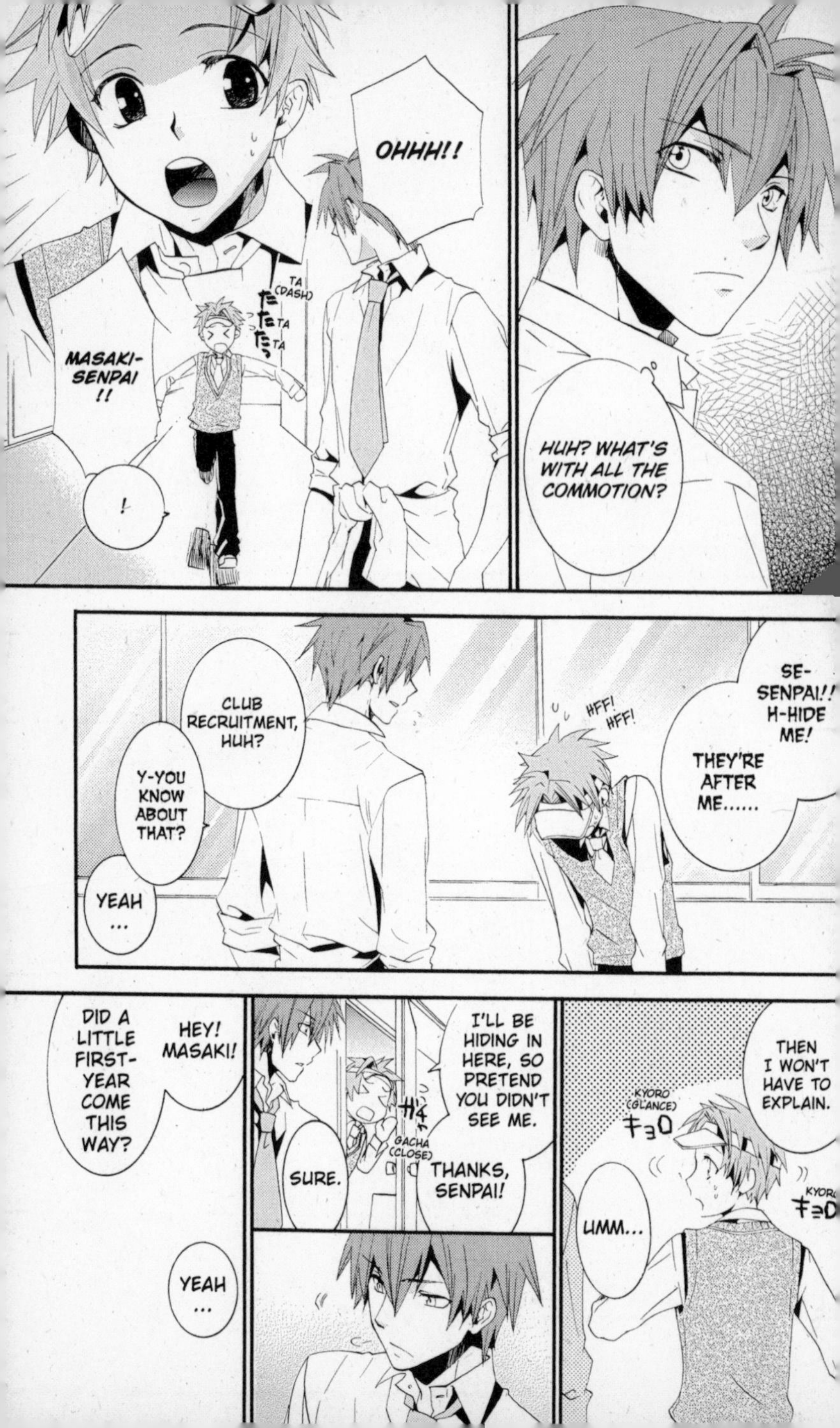
HUH? WHAT'S WITH ALL THE COMMOTION?
OHHH!!
TA (DASH)
TA
TA
MASAKI-SENPAI!!
!
SE-SENPAI!! H-HIDE ME!
THEY'RE AFTER ME......
HFF! HFF!
CLUB RECRUITMENT, HUH?
Y-YOU KNOW ABOUT THAT?
YEAH...
THEN I WON'T HAVE TO EXPLAIN.
KYORO (GLANCE)
KYORO
UMM...
I'LL BE HIDING IN HERE, SO PRETEND YOU DIDN'T SEE ME.
GACHA (CLOSE)
THANKS, SENPAI!
SURE.
HEY! MASAKI!
DID A LITTLE FIRST-YEAR COME THIS WAY?
YEAH...

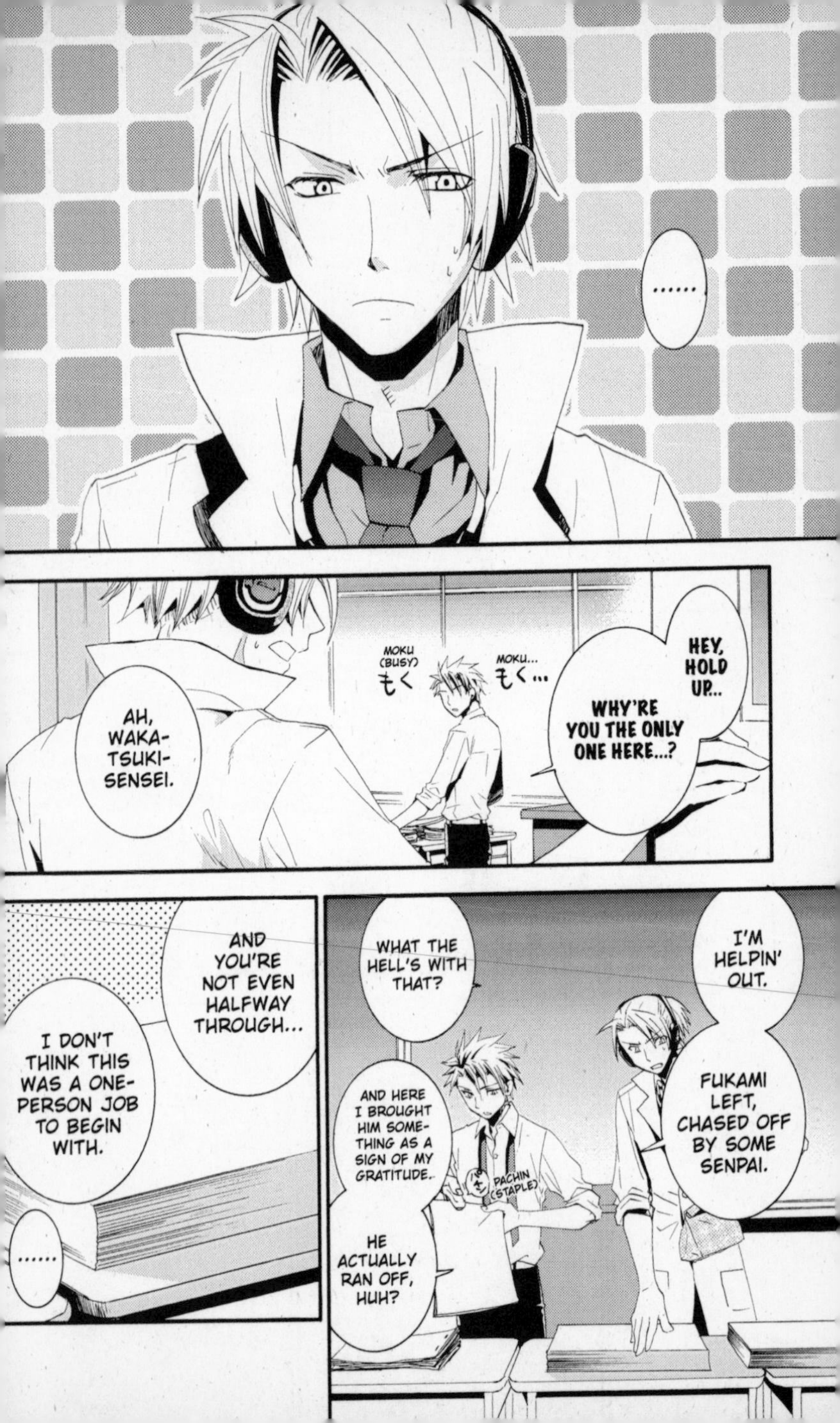
......
HEY, HOLD UP...
WHY'RE YOU THE ONLY ONE HERE...?
MOKU... もく...
MOKU (BUSY) もく
AH, WAKA-TSUKI-SENSEI.
I'M HELPIN' OUT.
FUKAMI LEFT, CHASED OFF BY SOME SENPAI.
WHAT THE HELL'S WITH THAT?
AND HERE I BROUGHT HIM SOME-THING AS A SIGN OF MY GRATITUDE.
PACHIN (STAPLE)
HE ACTUALLY RAN OFF, HUH?
AND YOU'RE NOT EVEN HALFWAY THROUGH...
I DON'T THINK THIS WAS A ONE-PERSON JOB TO BEGIN WITH.
......

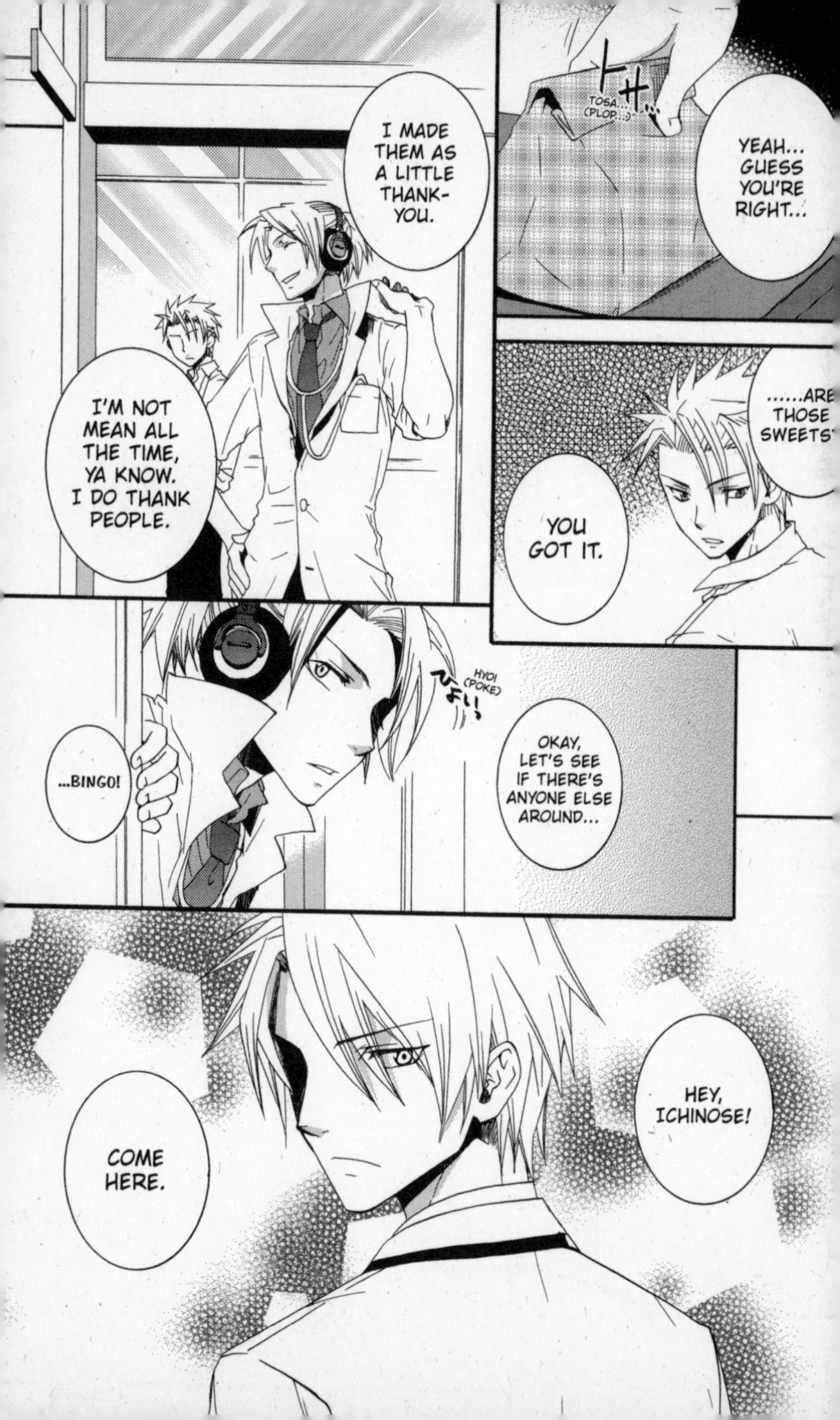
TOSA... (PLOP...)
YEAH... GUESS YOU'RE RIGHT...
......ARE THOSE SWEETS
YOU GOT IT.
I MADE THEM AS A LITTLE THANK-YOU.
I'M NOT MEAN ALL THE TIME, YA KNOW. I DO THANK PEOPLE.
HYOI (POKE)
OKAY, LET'S SEE IF THERE'S ANYONE ELSE AROUND...
...BINGO!
HEY, ICHINOSE!
COME HERE.

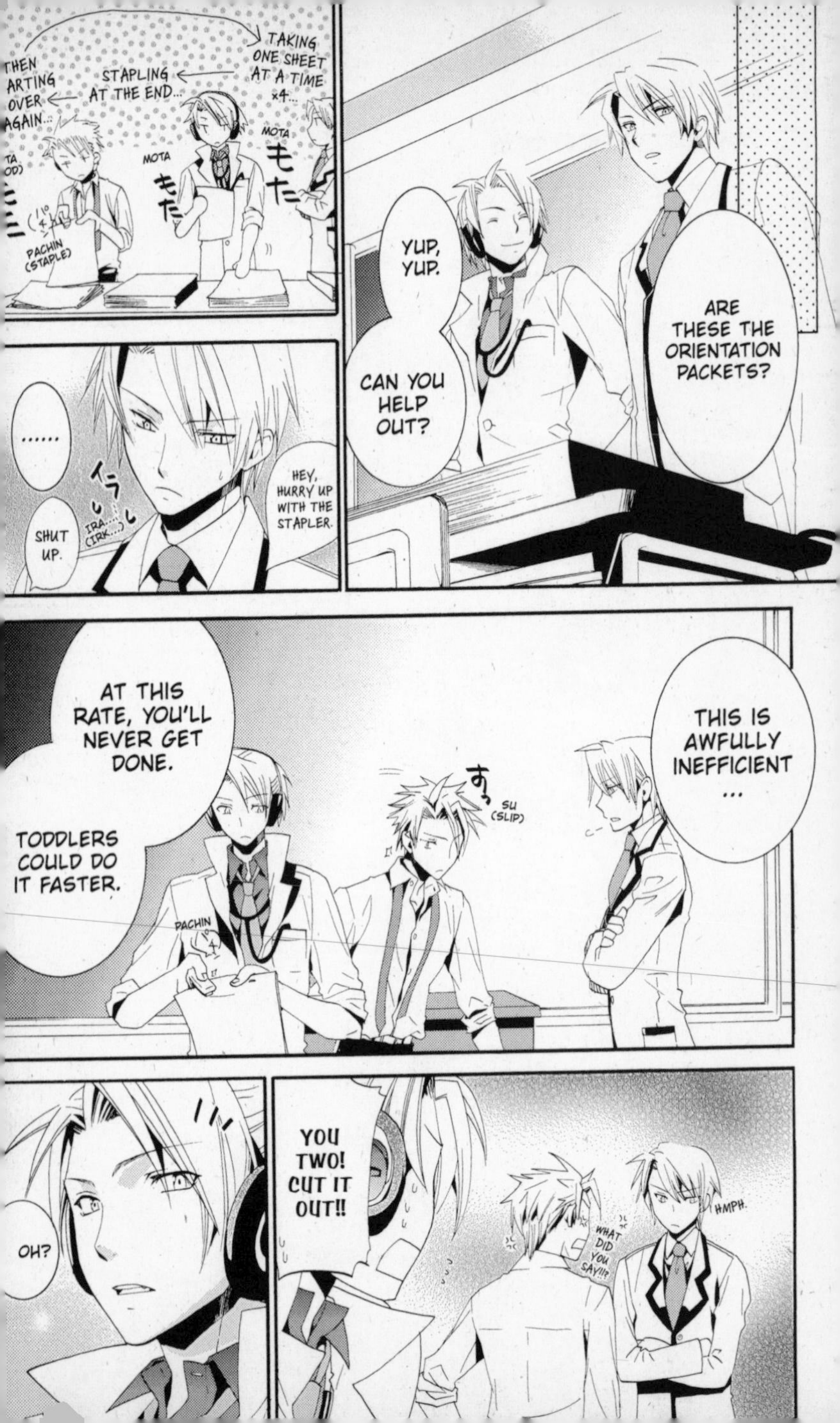
ARE THESE THE ORIENTATION PACKETS?
YUP, YUP.
CAN YOU HELP OUT?
TAKING ONE SHEET AT A TIME x4...
MOTA
もた
STAPLING AT THE END...
MOTA
もた
THEN ARTING OVER AGAIN...
PACHIN (STAPLE)
HEY, HURRY UP WITH THE STAPLER.
イラ
IRA... (IRK...)
......
SHUT UP.
THIS IS AWFULLY INEFFICIENT ...
す
SU (SLIP)
AT THIS RATE, YOU'LL NEVER GET DONE.
TODDLERS COULD DO IT FASTER.
PACHIN
HMPH.
WHAT DID YOU SAY!!?
YOU TWO! CUT IT OUT!!
OH?

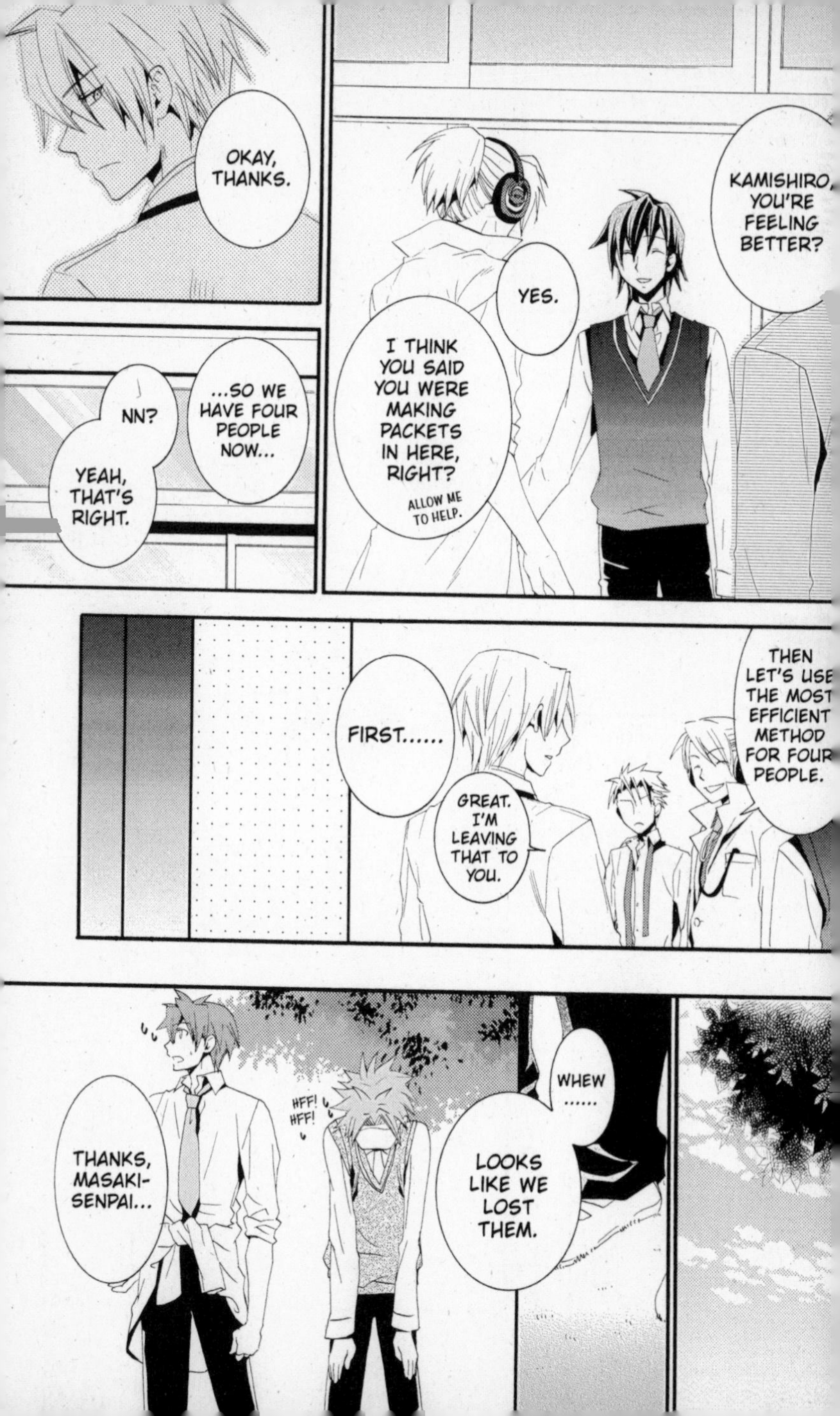
KAMISHIRO, YOU'RE FEELING BETTER?
YES.
I THINK YOU SAID YOU WERE MAKING PACKETS IN HERE, RIGHT?
ALLOW ME TO HELP.
OKAY, THANKS.
...SO WE HAVE FOUR PEOPLE NOW...
NN?
YEAH, THAT'S RIGHT.
THEN LET'S USE THE MOST EFFICIENT METHOD FOR FOUR PEOPLE.
FIRST......
GREAT. I'M LEAVING THAT TO YOU.
WHEW ......
LOOKS LIKE WE LOST THEM.
HFF! HFF!
THANKS, MASAKI-SENPAI...

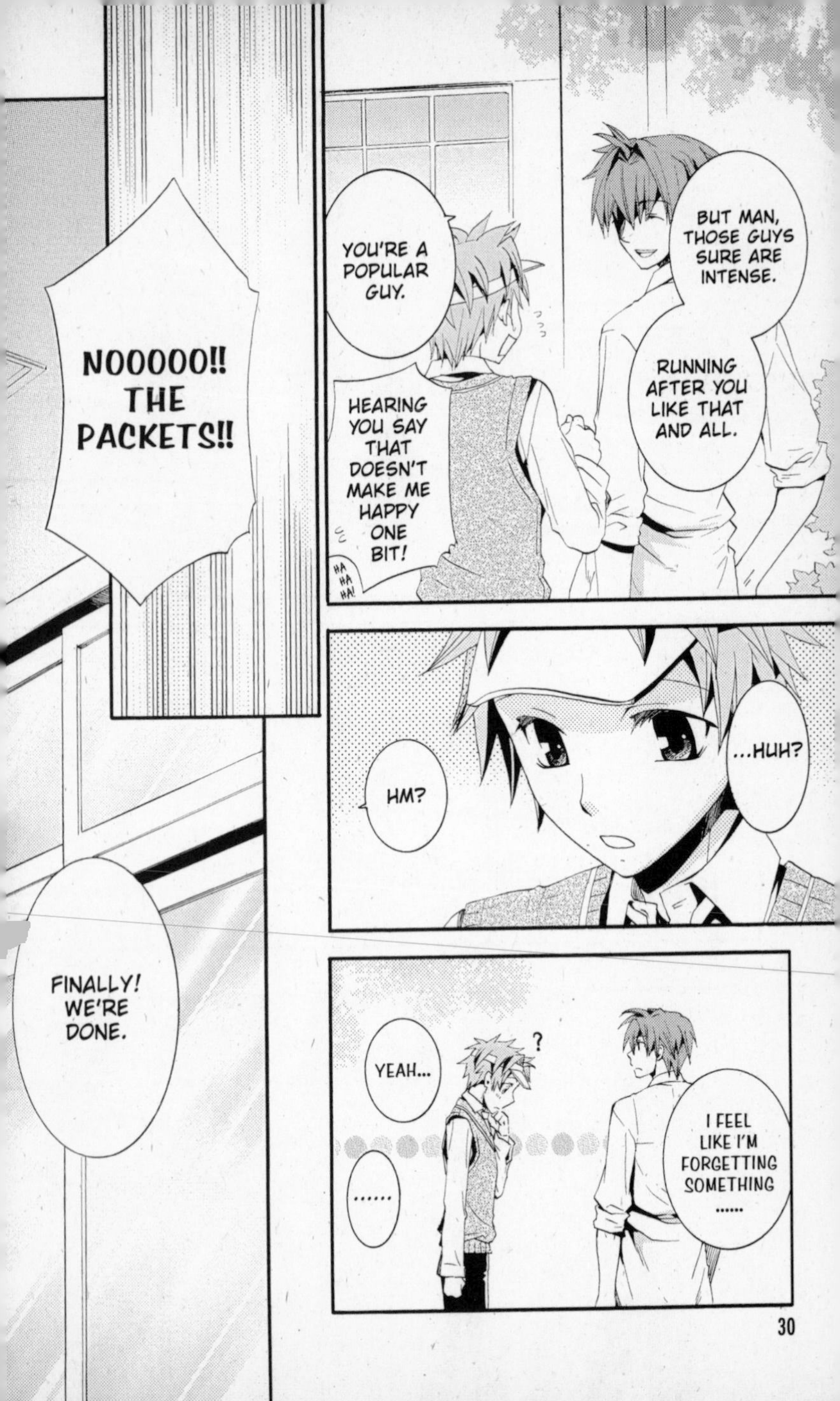
BUT MAN, THOSE GUYS SURE ARE INTENSE.
RUNNING AFTER YOU LIKE THAT AND ALL.
YOU'RE A POPULAR GUY.
HEARING YOU SAY THAT DOESN'T MAKE ME HAPPY ONE BIT!
HA HA HA!
...HUH?
HM?
I FEEL LIKE I'M FORGETTING SOMETHING ......
YEAH...
......
NOOOOO!! THE PACKETS!!
FINALLY! WE'RE DONE.

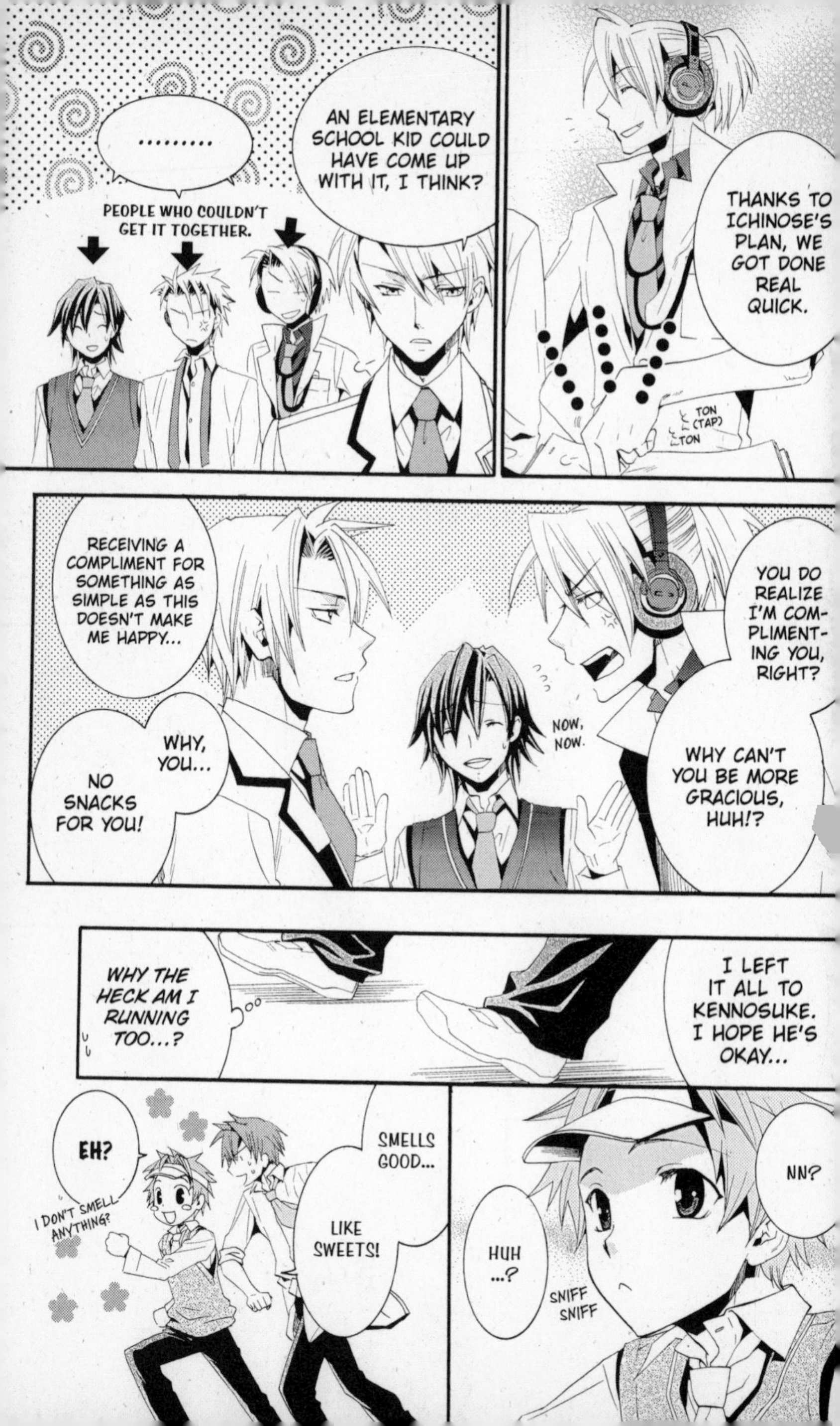
THANKS TO ICHINOSE'S PLAN, WE GOT DONE REAL QUICK.
TON (TAP) TON
AN ELEMENTARY SCHOOL KID COULD HAVE COME UP WITH IT, I THINK?
....
PEOPLE WHO COULDN'T GET IT TOGETHER.
YOU DO REALIZE I'M COMPLIMENTING YOU, RIGHT?
RECEIVING A COMPLIMENT FOR SOMETHING AS SIMPLE AS THIS DOESN'T MAKE ME HAPPY...
WHY CAN'T YOU BE MORE GRACIOUS, HUH!?
NOW, NOW.
WHY, YOU...
NO SNACKS FOR YOU!
I LEFT IT ALL TO KENNOSUKE. I HOPE HE'S OKAY...
WHY THE HECK AM I RUNNING TOO...?
NN?
HUH ...?
SNIFF SNIFF
SMELLS GOOD...
LIKE SWEETS!
EH?
I DON'T SMELL ANYTHING?

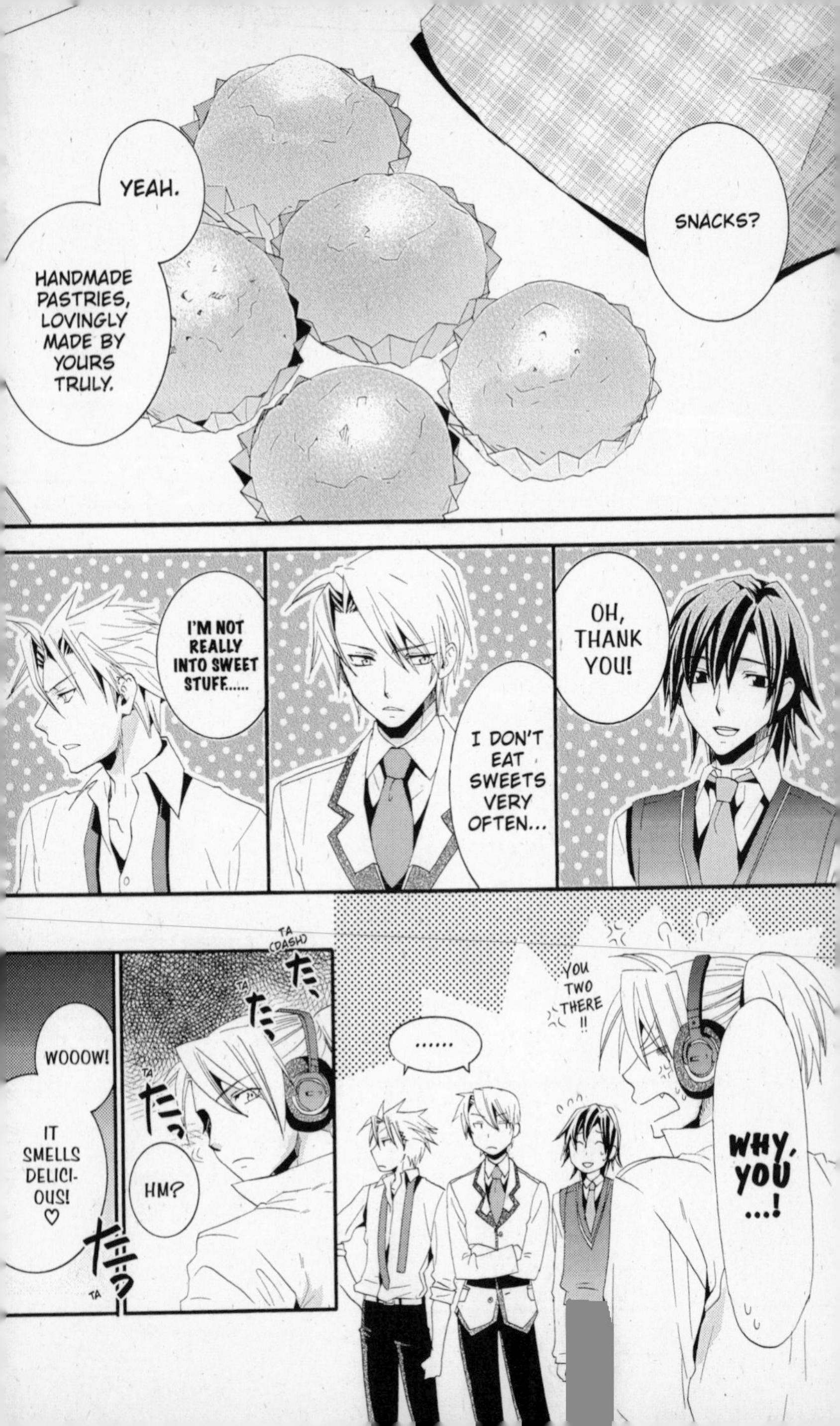
SNACKS?
YEAH.
HANDMADE PASTRIES, LOVINGLY MADE BY YOURS TRULY.
OH, THANK YOU!
I DON'T EAT SWEETS VERY OFTEN...
I'M NOT REALLY INTO SWEET STUFF......
YOU TWO THERE!!
WHY, YOU...!
......
TA (DASH)
TA
TA
HM?
WOOOW!
IT SMELLS DELICIOUS! ♡
TA

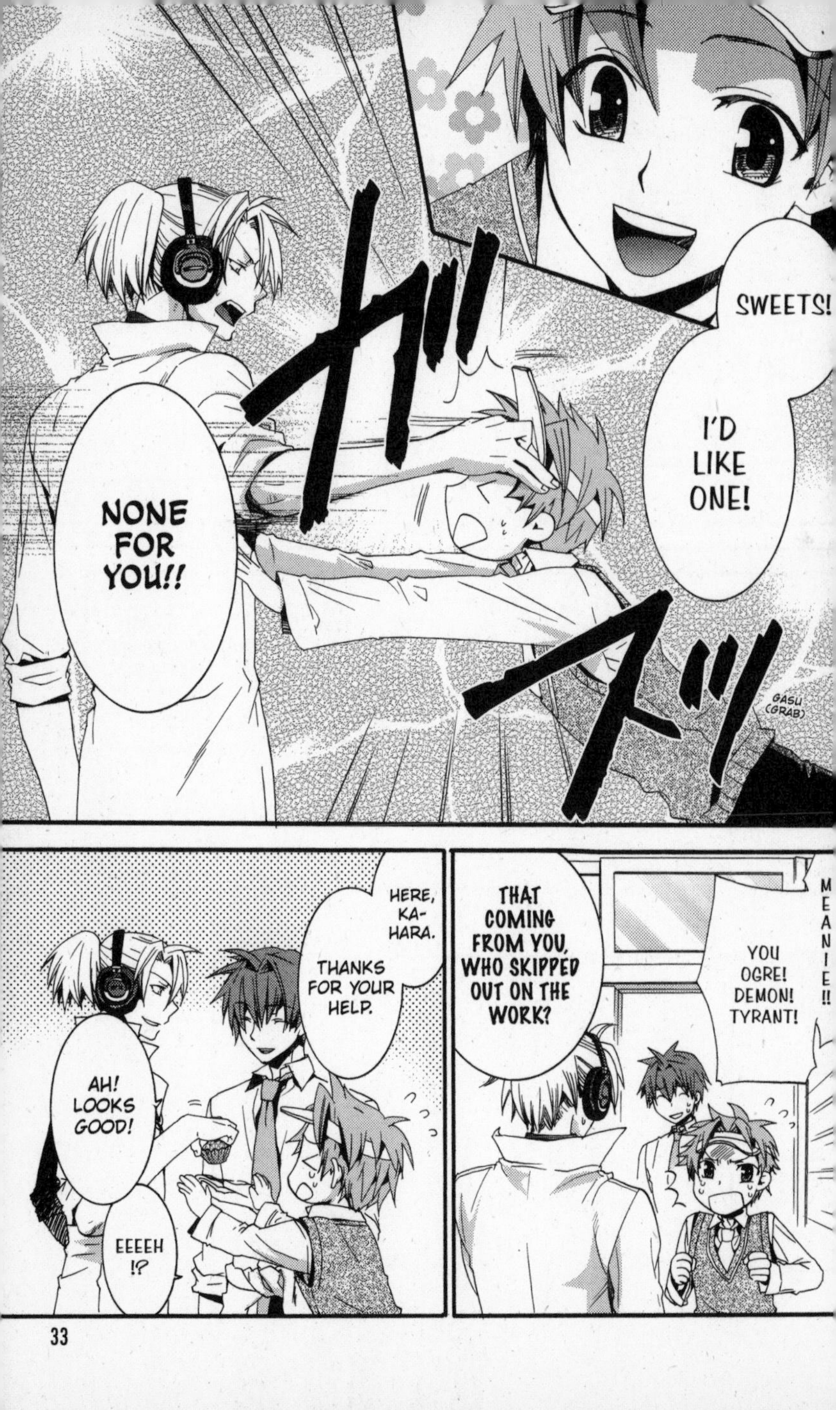
SWEETS!
I'D LIKE ONE!
GASU (GRAB)
NONE FOR YOU!!
MEANIE!!
YOU OGRE! DEMON! TYRANT!
THAT COMING FROM YOU, WHO SKIPPED OUT ON THE WORK?
HERE, KA-HARA.
THANKS FOR YOUR HELP.
AH! LOOKS GOOD!
EEEEH !?

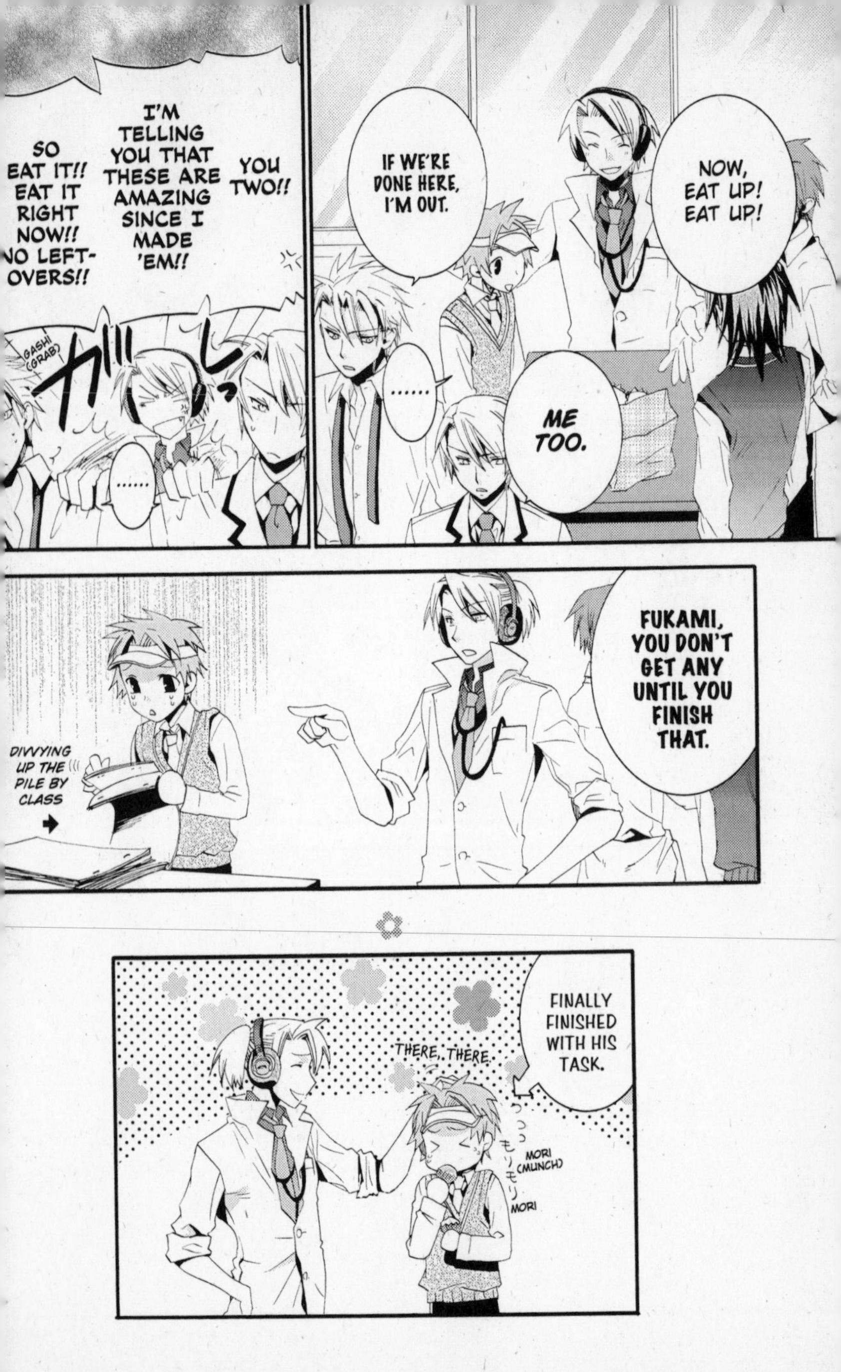
NOW, EAT UP! EAT UP!
IF WE'RE DONE HERE, I'M OUT.
ME TOO.
......
YOU TWO!!
I'M TELLING YOU THAT THESE ARE AMAZING SINCE I MADE 'EM!!
SO EAT IT!! EAT IT RIGHT NOW!! NO LEFT-OVERS!!
GASHI (GRAB)
......
FUKAMI, YOU DON'T GET ANY UNTIL YOU FINISH THAT.
DIVVYING UP THE PILE BY CLASS
FINALLY FINISHED WITH HIS TASK.
MORI (MUNCH) MORI
THERE, THERE.

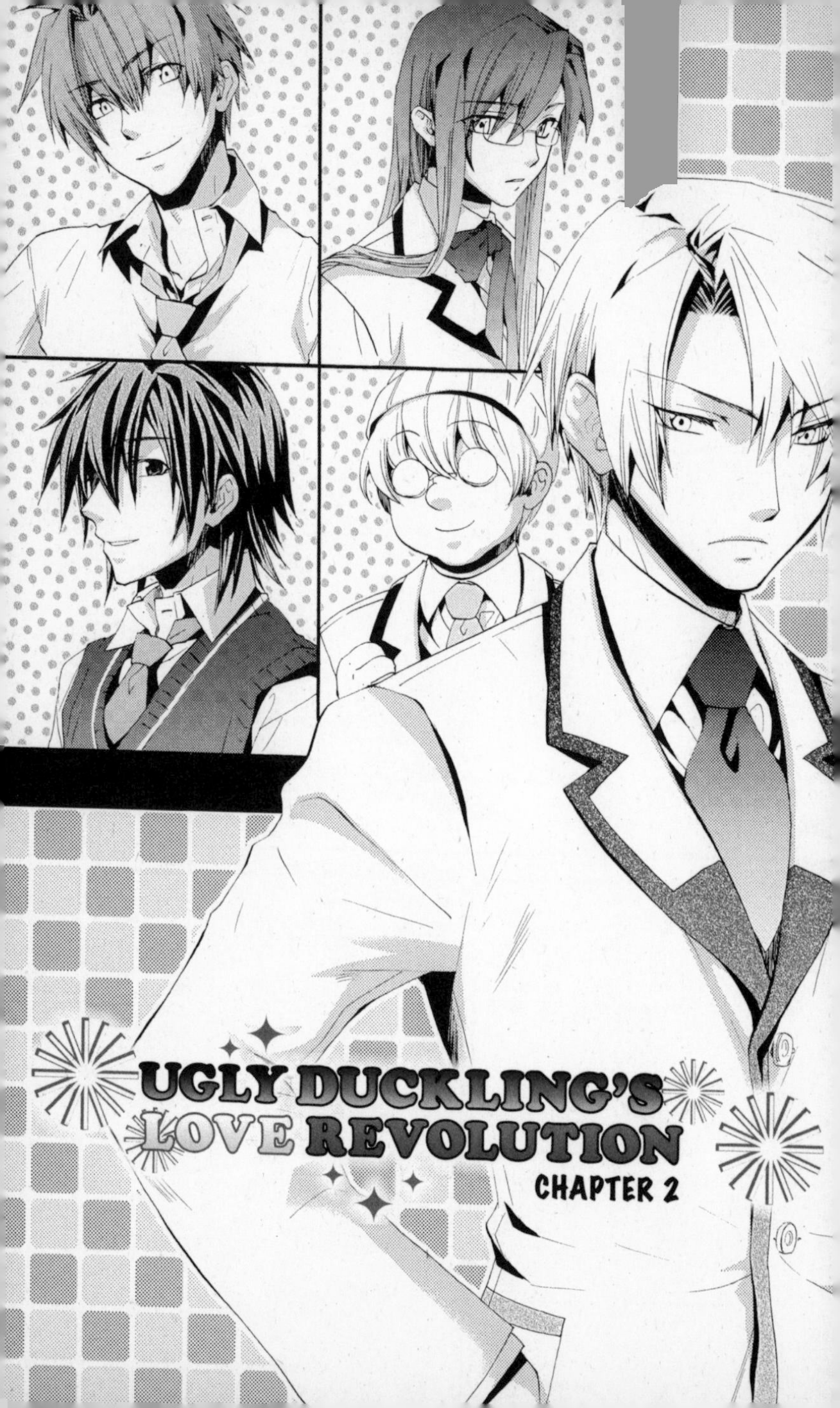
UGLY DUCKLING'S LOVE REVOLUTION
CHAPTER 2

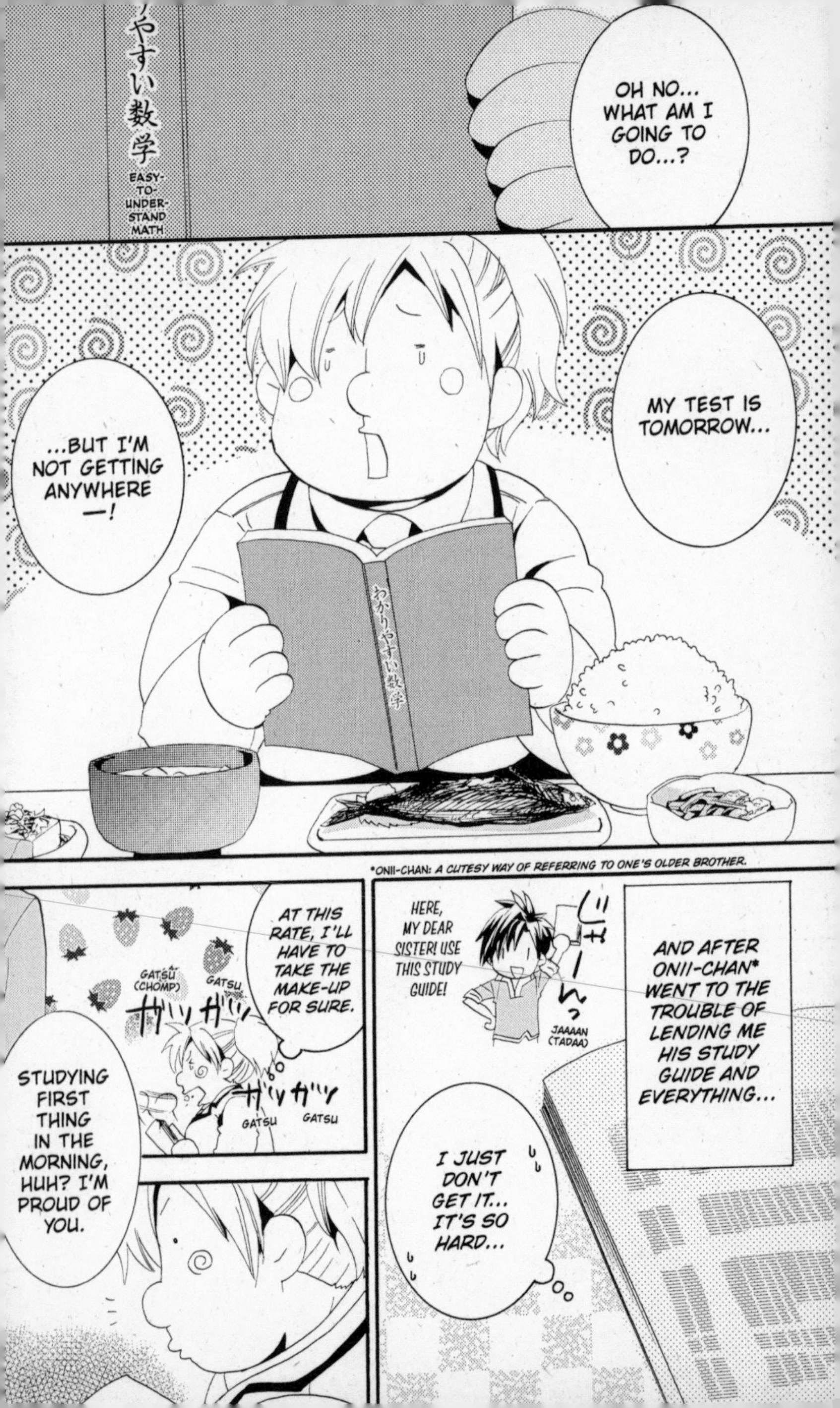
OH NO... WHAT AM I GOING TO DO...?
やすい数学
EASY-TO-UNDER-STAND MATH
MY TEST IS TOMORROW...
...BUT I'M NOT GETTING ANYWHERE—!
わかりやすい数学
AND AFTER ONII-CHAN* WENT TO THE TROUBLE OF LENDING ME HIS STUDY GUIDE AND EVERYTHING...
じゃーんっ
JAAAAN (TADAA)
HERE, MY DEAR SISTER! USE THIS STUDY GUIDE!
I JUST DON'T GET IT... IT'S SO HARD...
AT THIS RATE, I'LL HAVE TO TAKE THE MAKE-UP FOR SURE.
ガツガツ
GATSU (CHOMP) GATSU
ガツガツ
GATSU GATSU
STUDYING FIRST THING IN THE MORNING, HUH? I'M PROUD OF YOU.

*ONII-CHAN: A CUTESY WAY OF REFERRING TO ONE'S OLDER BROTHER.

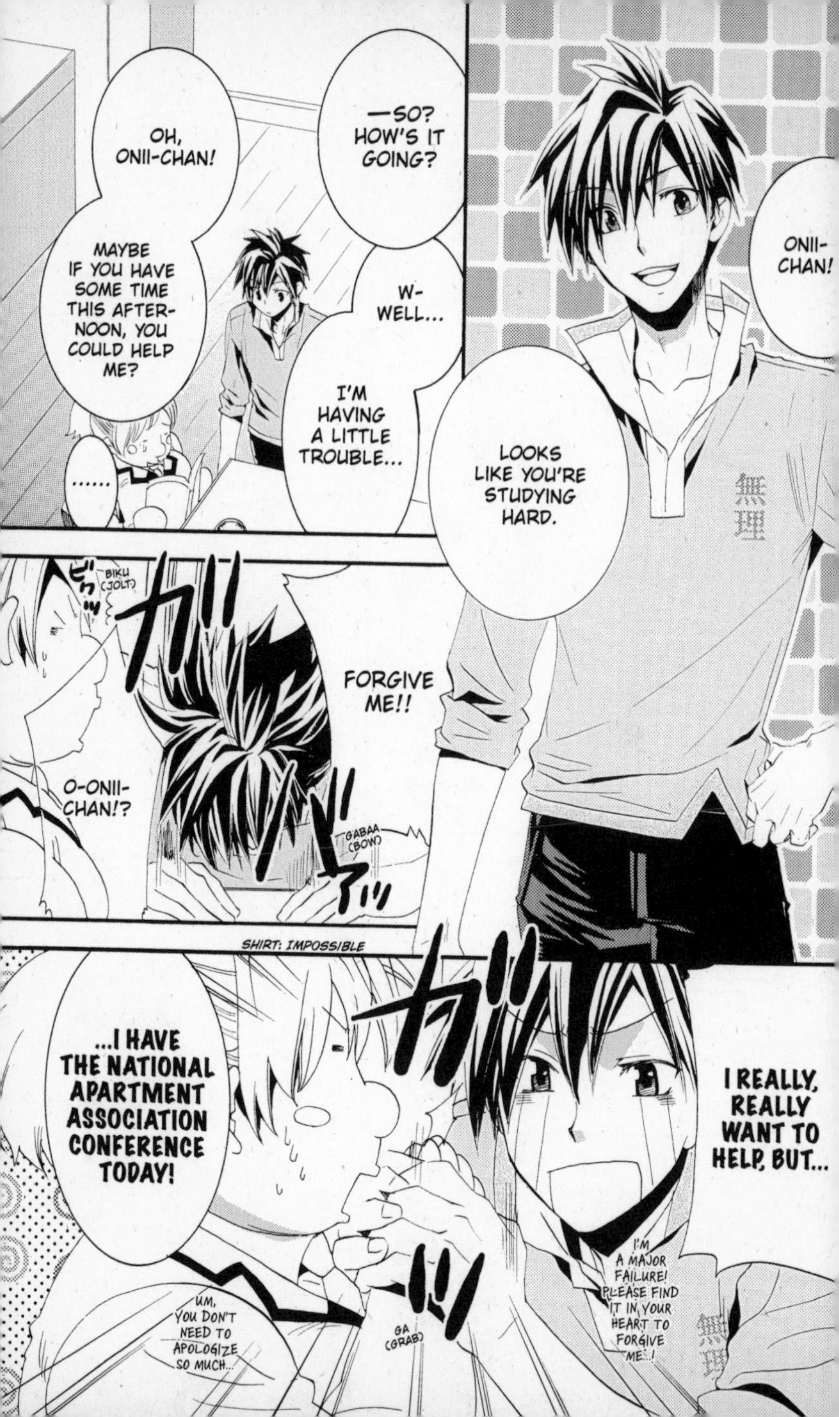
ONII-CHAN!
LOOKS LIKE YOU'RE STUDYING HARD.
SHIRT: IMPOSSIBLE
—SO? HOW'S IT GOING?
W-WELL...
I'M HAVING A LITTLE TROUBLE...
OH, ONII-CHAN!
MAYBE IF YOU HAVE SOME TIME THIS AFTER-NOON, YOU COULD HELP ME?
......
BIKU (JOLT)
FORGIVE ME!!
O-ONII-CHAN!?
GABAA (BOW)
I REALLY, REALLY WANT TO HELP, BUT...
...I HAVE THE NATIONAL APARTMENT ASSOCIATION CONFERENCE TODAY!
I'M A MAJOR FAILURE! PLEASE FIND IT IN YOUR HEART TO FORGIVE ME...!
GA (GRAB)
UM, YOU DON'T NEED TO APOLOGIZE SO MUCH...

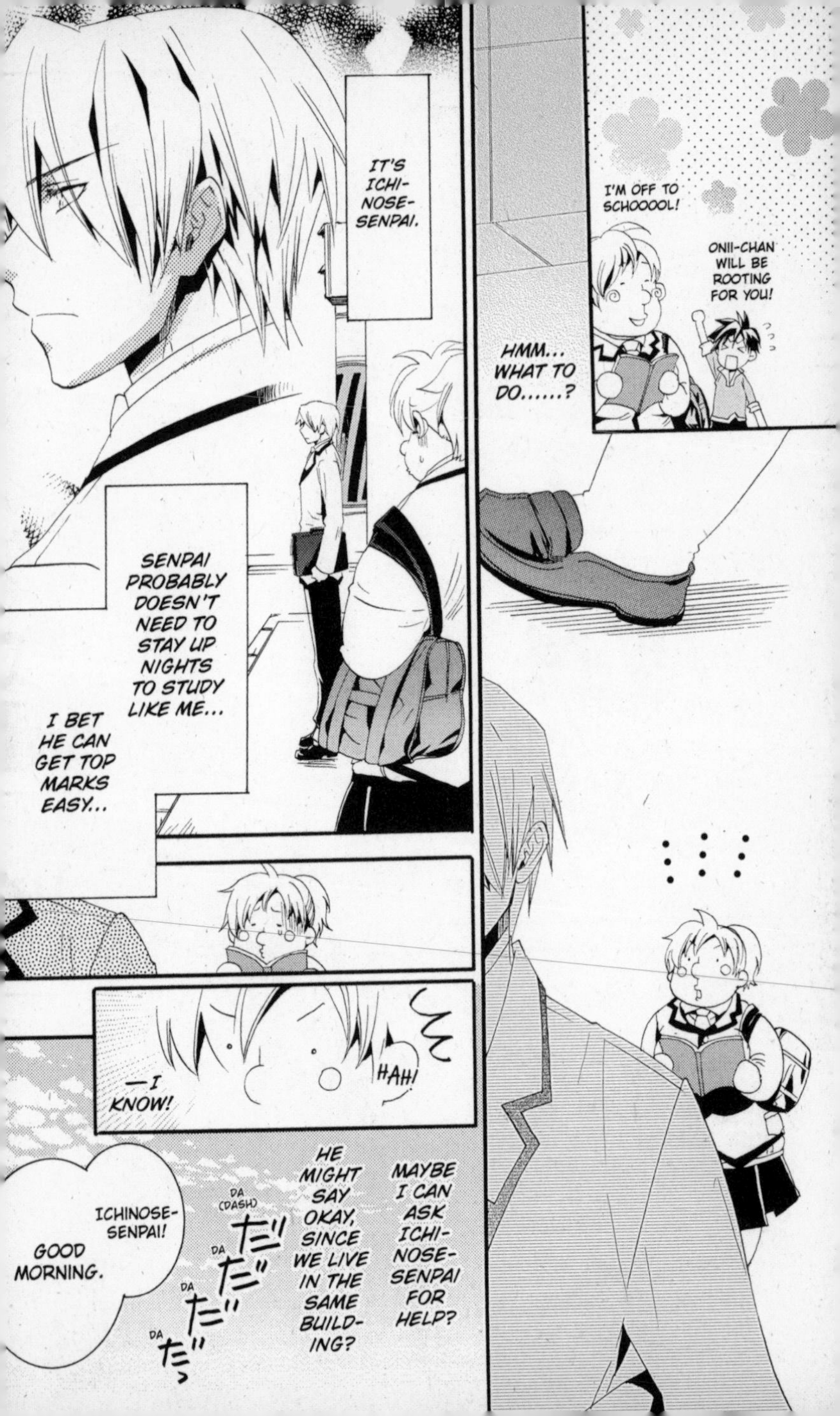
I'M OFF TO SCHOOOOL!
ONII-CHAN WILL BE ROOTING FOR YOU!
HMM... WHAT TO DO......?
......
IT'S ICHINOSE-SENPAI.
SENPAI PROBABLY DOESN'T NEED TO STAY UP NIGHTS TO STUDY LIKE ME...
I BET HE CAN GET TOP MARKS EASY...
HAH!
—I KNOW!
MAYBE I CAN ASK ICHINOSE-SENPAI FOR HELP?
HE MIGHT SAY OKAY, SINCE WE LIVE IN THE SAME BUILD-ING?
DA (DASH) だ
DA だ
DA だ
DA だ
ICHINOSE-SENPAI!
GOOD MORNING.

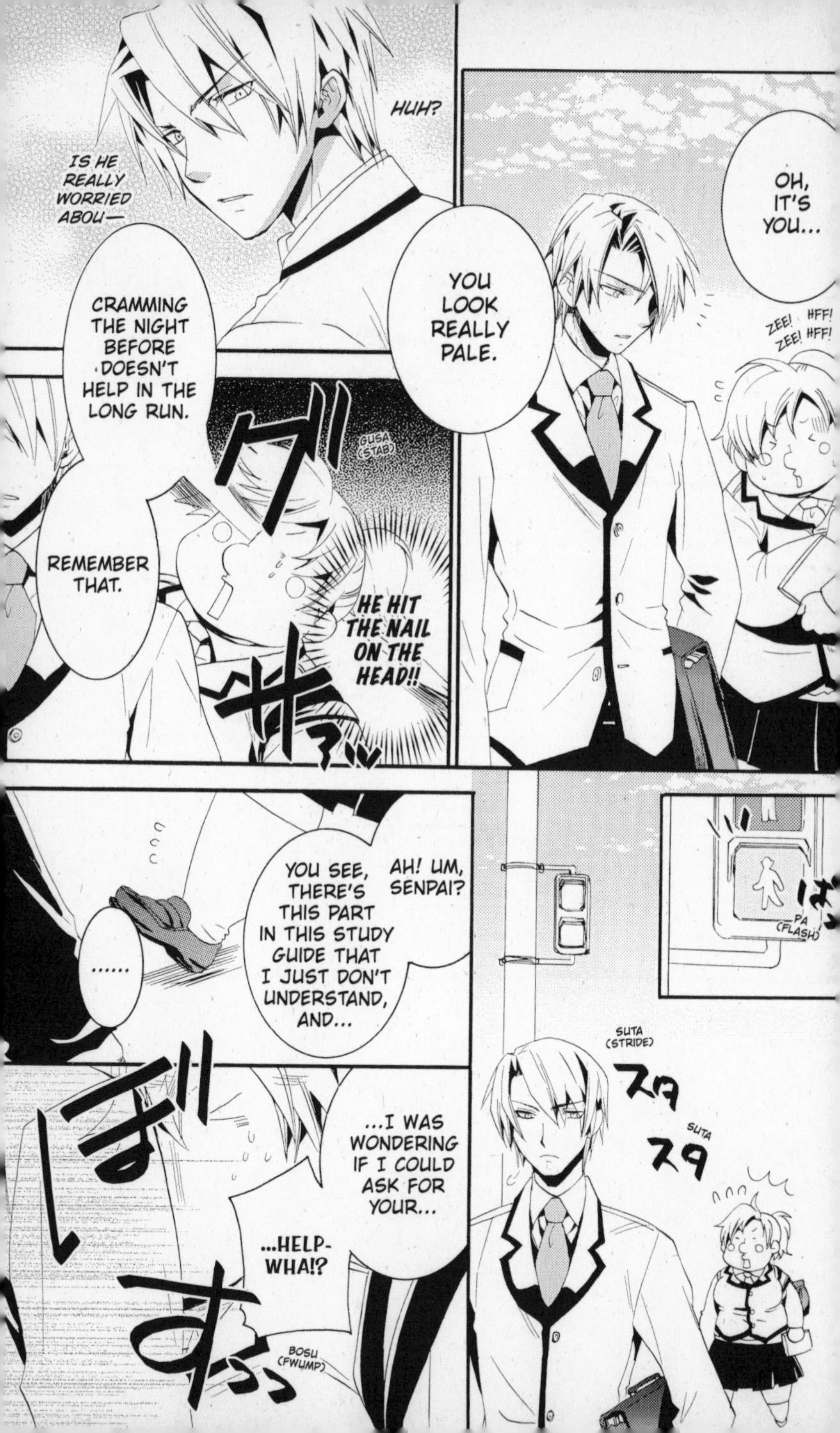
OH, IT'S YOU...
ZEE! HFF! ZEE! HFF!
YOU LOOK REALLY PALE.
HUH?
IS HE REALLY WORRIED ABOU—
CRAMMING THE NIGHT BEFORE DOESN'T HELP IN THE LONG RUN.
GUSA (STAB)
HE HIT THE NAIL ON THE HEAD!!
REMEMBER THAT.
PA (FLASH)
SUTA (STRIDE)
SUTA
AH! UM, SENPAI?
YOU SEE, THERE'S THIS PART IN THIS STUDY GUIDE THAT I JUST DON'T UNDERSTAND, AND...
......
...I WAS WONDERING IF I COULD ASK FOR YOUR...
...HELP-WHA!?
BOSU (FWUMP)

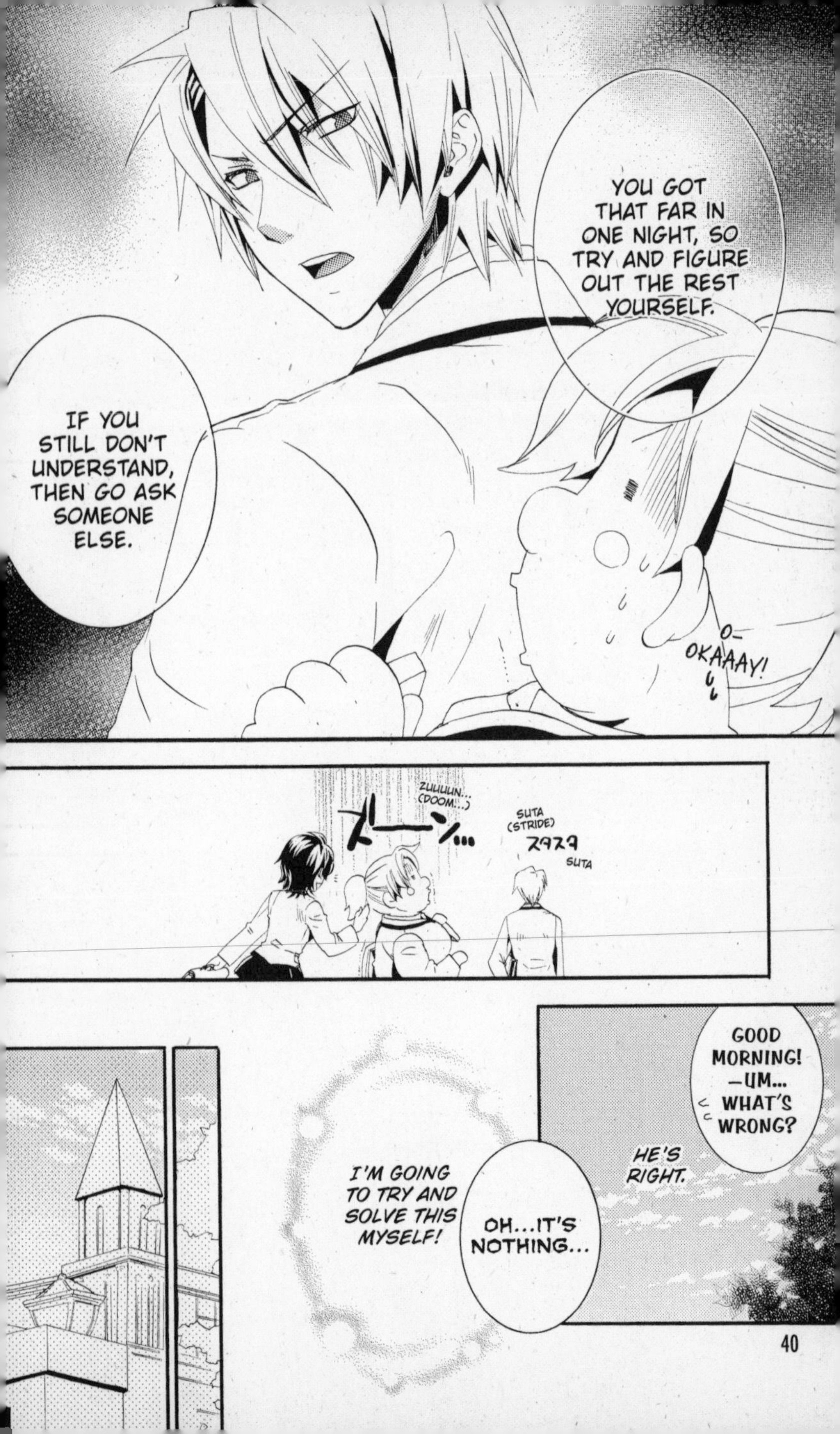
YOU GOT THAT FAR IN ONE NIGHT, SO TRY AND FIGURE OUT THE REST YOURSELF.
IF YOU STILL DON'T UNDERSTAND, THEN GO ASK SOMEONE ELSE.
O-OKAAAY!
SUTA (STRIDE)
スタスタ
SUTA
ZUUUUN... (DOOM...)
ズーン...
GOOD MORNING! —UM... WHAT'S WRONG?
HE'S RIGHT.
OH...IT'S NOTHING...
I'M GOING TO TRY AND SOLVE THIS MYSELF!

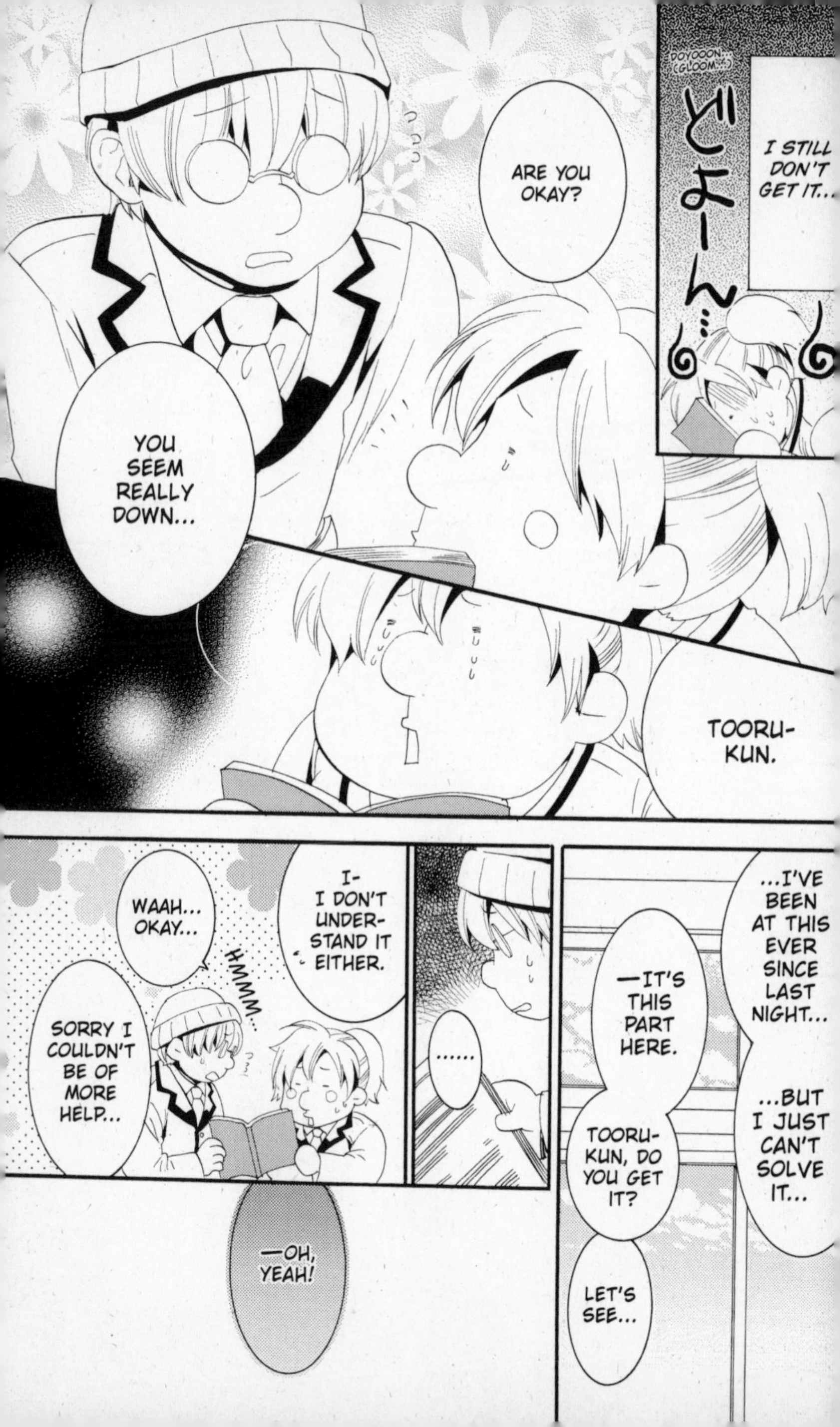
DOYOOON... (GLOOM)
どよーん…
I STILL DON'T GET IT...
ARE YOU OKAY?
YOU SEEM REALLY DOWN...
TOORU-KUN.
...I'VE BEEN AT THIS EVER SINCE LAST NIGHT...
—IT'S THIS PART HERE.
...BUT I JUST CAN'T SOLVE IT...
TOORU-KUN, DO YOU GET IT?
LET'S SEE...
......
I- I DON'T UNDERSTAND IT EITHER.
WAAH... OKAY...
HMMM...
SORRY I COULDN'T BE OF MORE HELP...
—OH, YEAH!

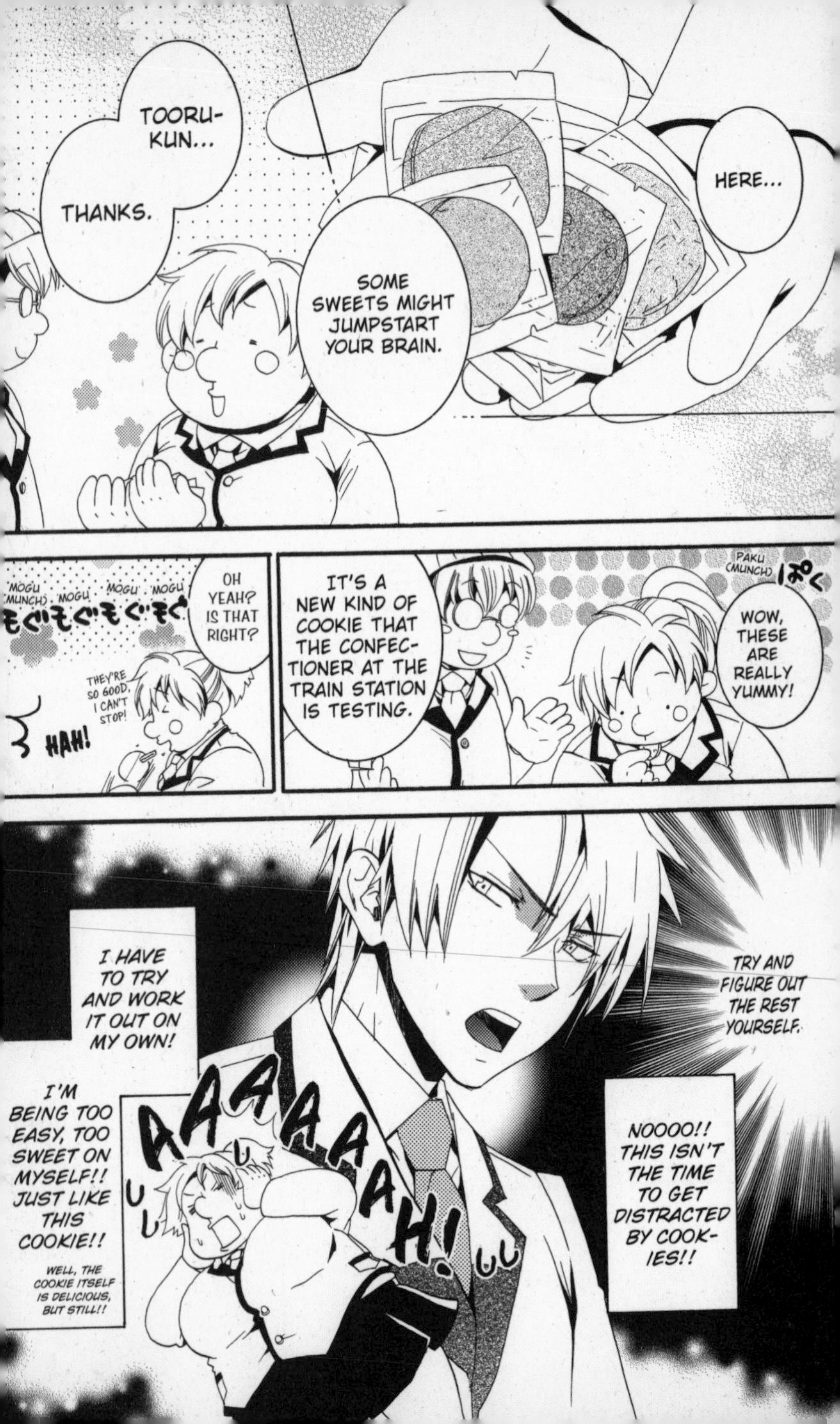
HERE...
SOME SWEETS MIGHT JUMPSTART YOUR BRAIN.
TOORU-KUN...
THANKS.
PAKU (MUNCH) ぱく
WOW, THESE ARE REALLY YUMMY!
IT'S A NEW KIND OF COOKIE THAT THE CONFEC-TIONER AT THE TRAIN STATION IS TESTING.
OH YEAH? IS THAT RIGHT?
MOGU (MUNCH) MOGU MOGU MOGU もぐもぐもぐもぐ
THEY'RE SO GOOD, I CAN'T STOP!
HAH!
TRY AND FIGURE OUT THE REST YOURSELF.
I HAVE TO TRY AND WORK IT OUT ON MY OWN!
NOOOO!! THIS ISN'T THE TIME TO GET DISTRACTED BY COOK-IES!!
AAAAAAAH!
I'M BEING TOO EASY, TOO SWEET ON MYSELF!! JUST LIKE THIS COOKIE!!
WELL, THE COOKIE ITSELF IS DELICIOUS, BUT STILL!!

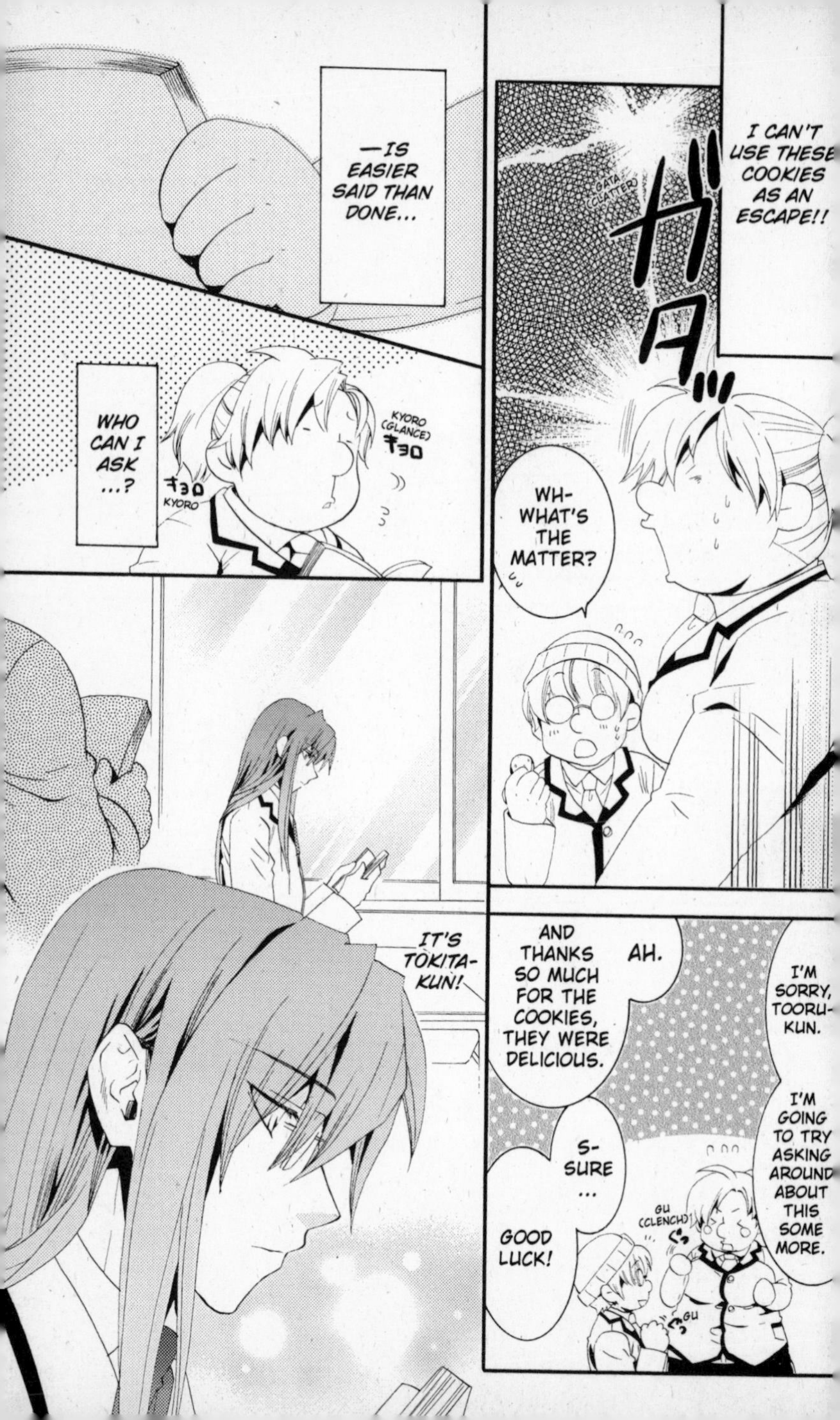
I CAN'T USE THESE COOKIES AS AN ESCAPE!!
GATA (CLATTER)
WH-WHAT'S THE MATTER?
I'M SORRY, TOORU-KUN.
I'M GOING TO TRY ASKING AROUND ABOUT THIS SOME MORE.
AH.
AND THANKS SO MUCH FOR THE COOKIES, THEY WERE DELICIOUS.
S-SURE...
GOOD LUCK!
GU (CLENCH)
GU
—IS EASIER SAID THAN DONE...
WHO CAN I ASK...?
KYORO (GLANCE)
KYORO
IT'S TOKITA-KUN!

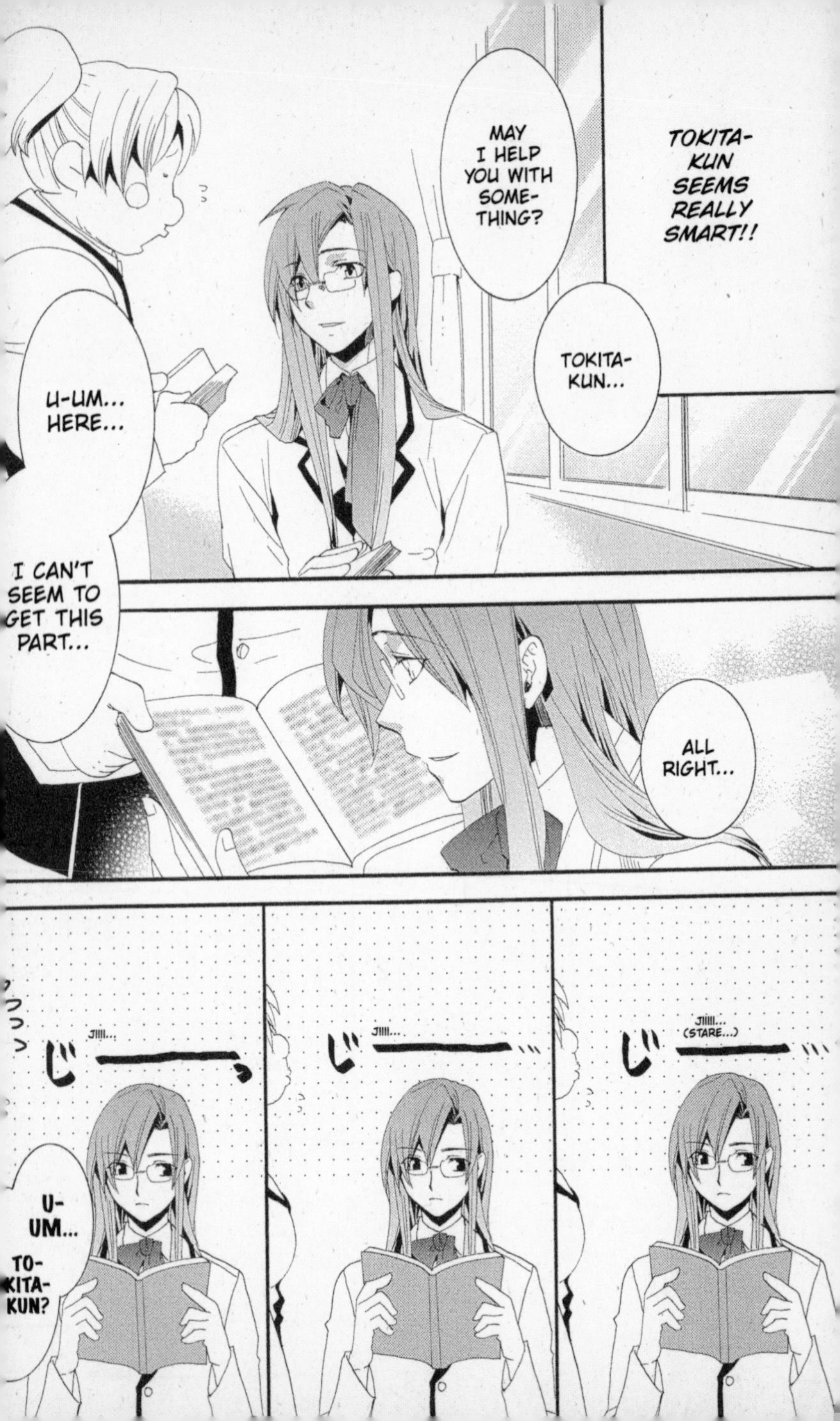
TOKITA-KUN SEEMS REALLY SMART!!
MAY I HELP YOU WITH SOME-THING?
TOKITA-KUN...
U-UM... HERE...
I CAN'T SEEM TO GET THIS PART...
ALL RIGHT...
じーー
JIIIII... (STARE...)
じーー
JIIII...
じーー
JIIII...
U-UM... TO-KITA-KUN?

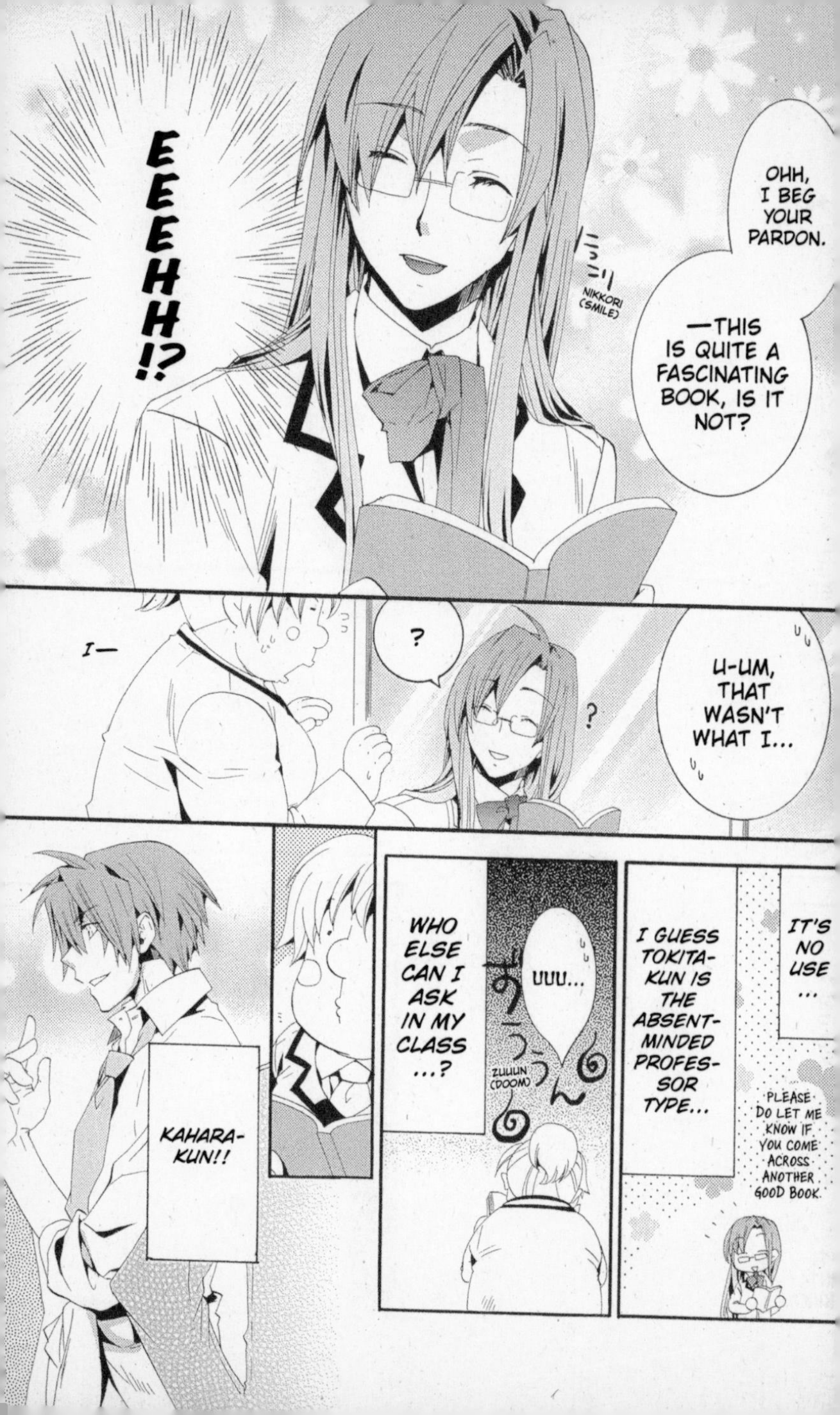
OHH, I BEG YOUR PARDON.
—THIS IS QUITE A FASCINATING BOOK, IS IT NOT?
NIKKORI (SMILE)
EEEEHH!?
U-UM, THAT WASN'T WHAT I...
?
?
I—
IT'S NO USE ...
I GUESS TOKITA-KUN IS THE ABSENT-MINDED PROFESSOR TYPE...
PLEASE DO LET ME KNOW IF YOU COME ACROSS ANOTHER GOOD BOOK.
UUU...
ZUUUN (DOOM)
WHO ELSE CAN I ASK IN MY CLASS ...?
KAHARA-KUN!!

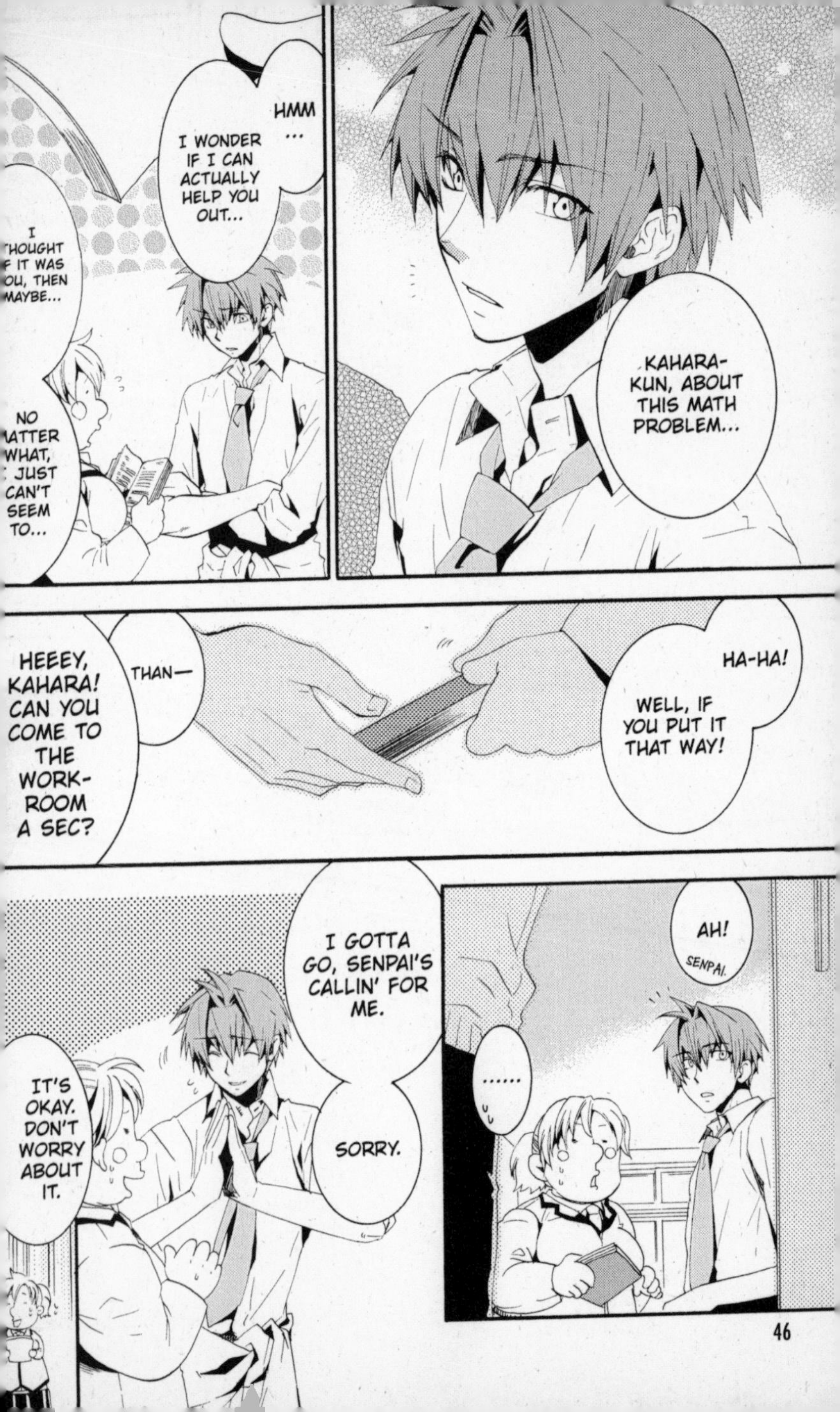
KAHARA-KUN, ABOUT THIS MATH PROBLEM...
HMM...
I WONDER IF I CAN ACTUALLY HELP YOU OUT...
I HOUGHT F IT WAS OU, THEN MAYBE...
NO ATTER WHAT, JUST CAN'T SEEM TO...
HA-HA!
WELL, IF YOU PUT IT THAT WAY!
THAN—
HEEEY, KAHARA! CAN YOU COME TO THE WORK-ROOM A SEC?
AH!
SENPAI.
......
I GOTTA GO, SENPAI'S CALLIN' FOR ME.
SORRY.
IT'S OKAY. DON'T WORRY ABOUT IT.

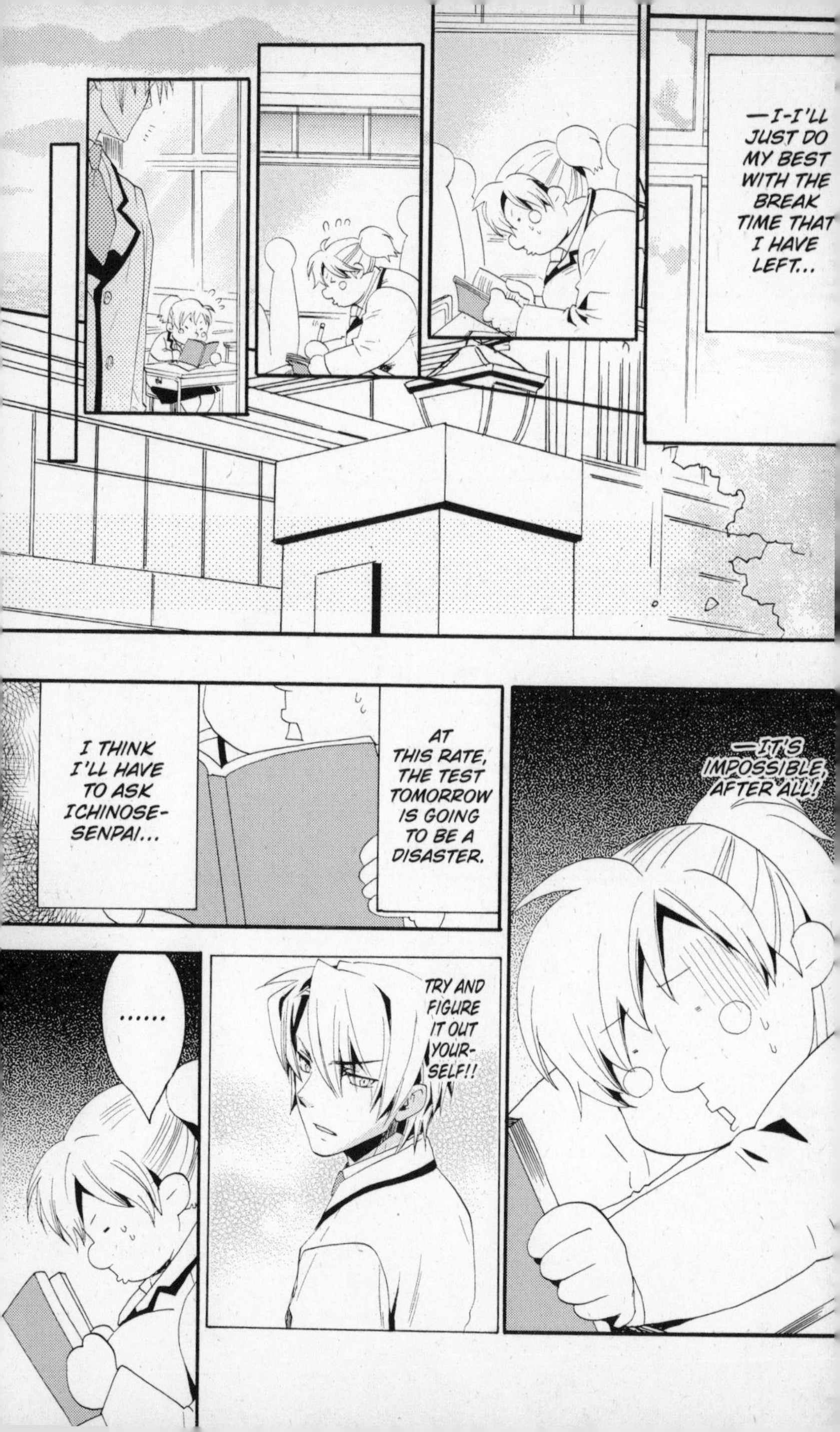
—I-I'LL JUST DO MY BEST WITH THE BREAK TIME THAT I HAVE LEFT...
—IT'S IMPOSSIBLE, AFTER ALL!
AT THIS RATE, THE TEST TOMORROW IS GOING TO BE A DISASTER.
I THINK I'LL HAVE TO ASK ICHINOSE-SENPAI...
TRY AND FIGURE IT OUT YOUR-SELF!!
......

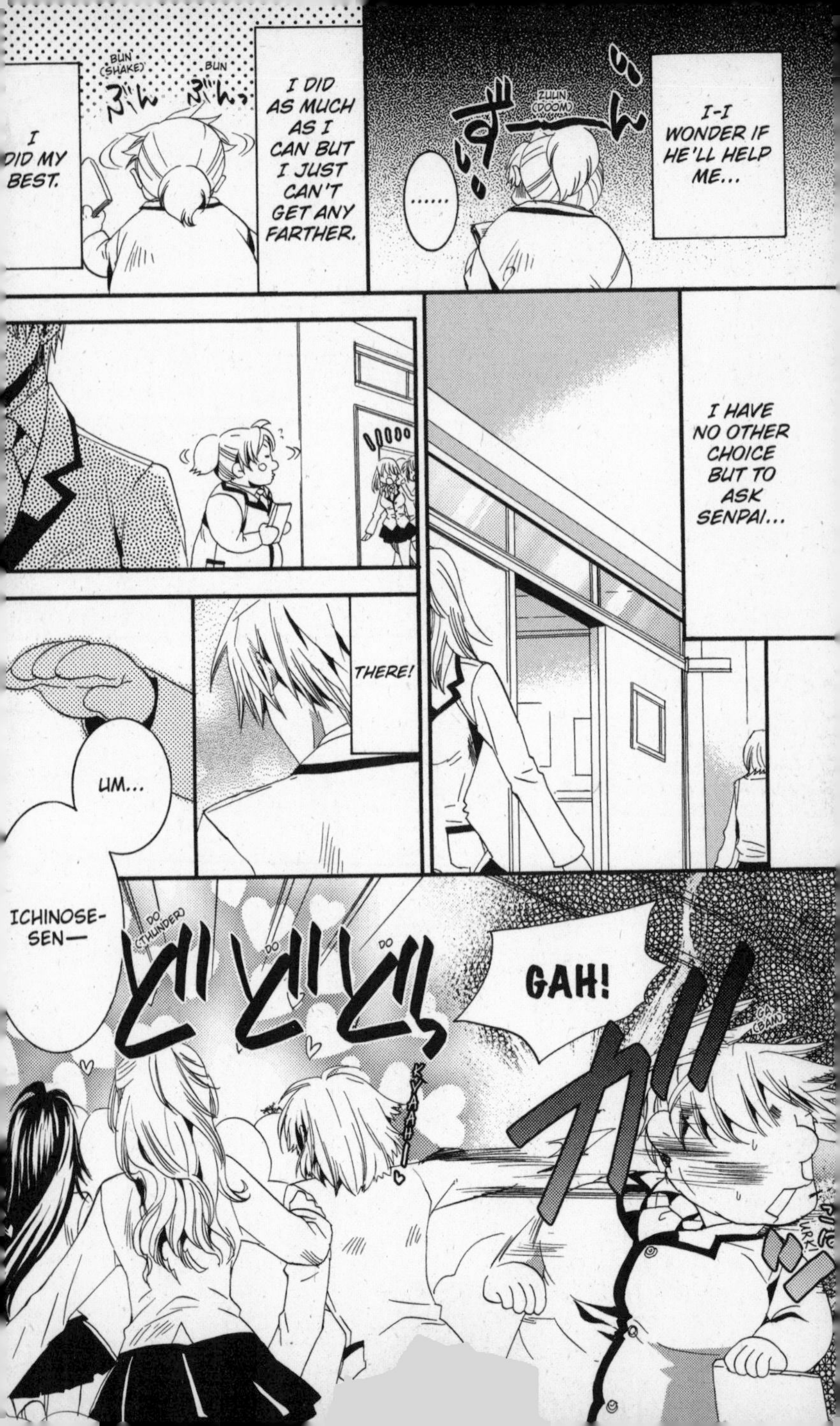

I-I WONDER IF HE'LL HELP ME...
ZUUN (DOOM)
......
I DID AS MUCH AS I CAN BUT I JUST CAN'T GET ANY FARTHER.
BUN (SHAKE) BUN
I DID MY BEST.
I HAVE NO OTHER CHOICE BUT TO ASK SENPAI...
THERE!
UM...
ICHINOSE-SEN—
GAH!
GA (BAN)
URK!
KYAAAH!
DO (THUNDER) DO DO

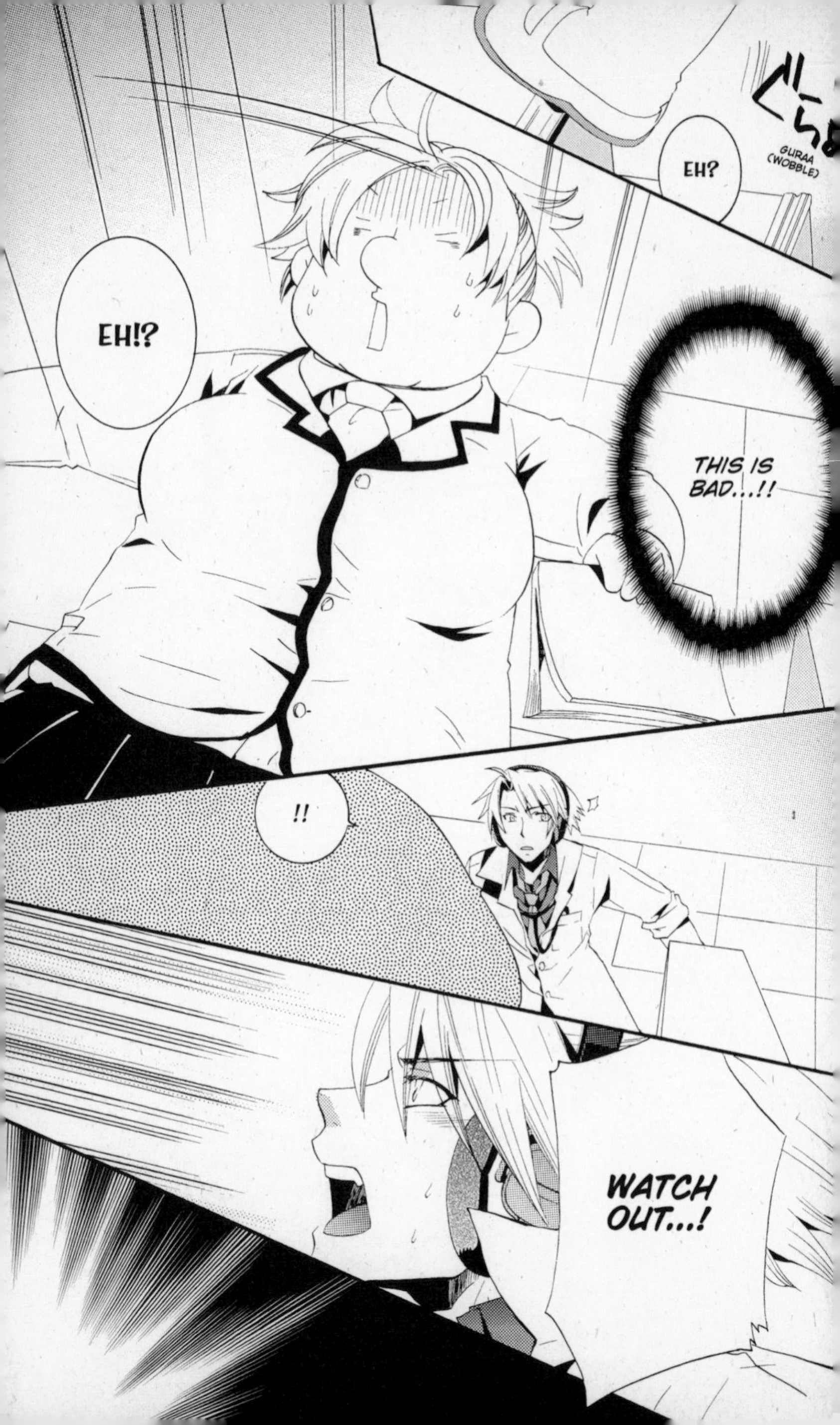
ぐら〜
GURAA (WOBBLE)
EH?
EH!?
THIS IS BAD...!!
!!
WATCH OUT...!

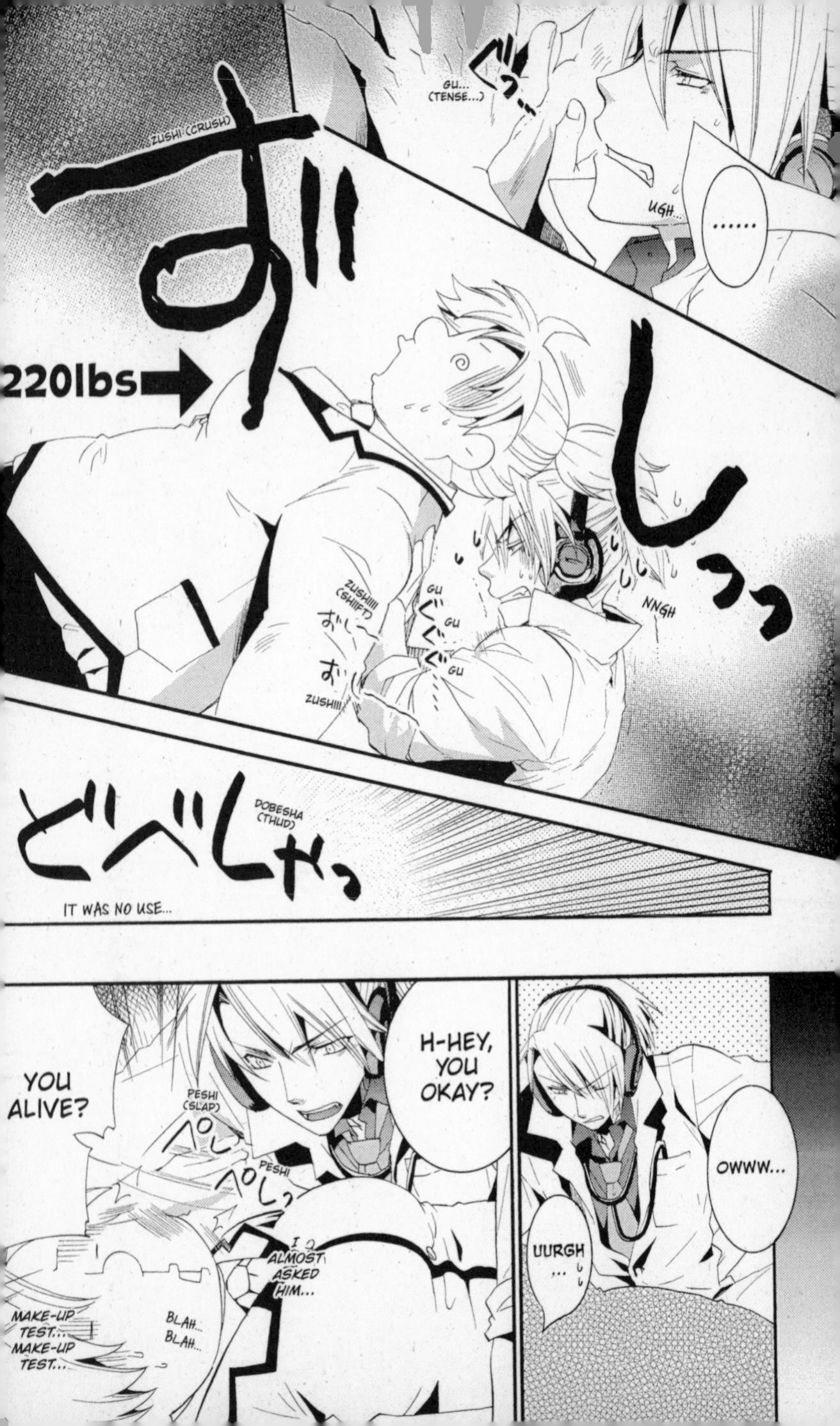
ぐっ…
GU... (TENSE...)
UGH...
......
ずしっ
ZUSHI (CRUSH)
220lbs
NNGH
ずしー
ZUSHIIII (SHIFT)
ぐぐぐ
GU GU GU
ずし
ZUSHIIII
どべしゃっ
DOBESHA (THUD)
IT WAS NO USE...
OWWW...
UURGH...
H-HEY, YOU OKAY?
YOU ALIVE?
ぺしっ
PESHI (SLAP)
ぺしっ
PESHI
I ALMOST ASKED HIM...
MAKE-UP TEST... MAKE-UP TEST...
BLAH... BLAH...

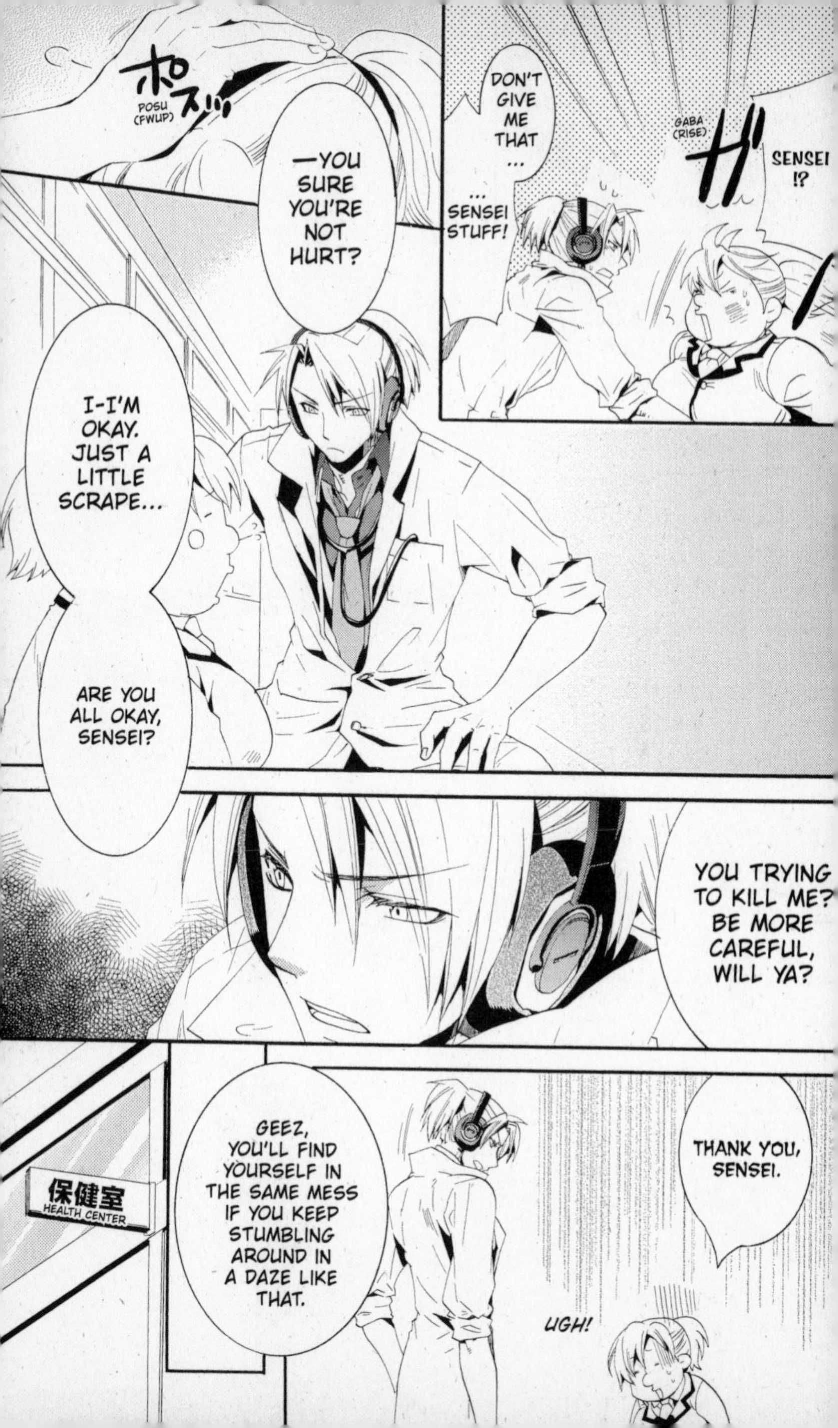

GABA (RISE)
SENSEI !?
DON'T GIVE ME THAT ...
... SENSEI STUFF!
POSU (FWUP)
—YOU SURE YOU'RE NOT HURT?
I-I'M OKAY. JUST A LITTLE SCRAPE...
ARE YOU ALL OKAY, SENSEI?
YOU TRYING TO KILL ME? BE MORE CAREFUL, WILL YA?
THANK YOU, SENSEI.
GEEZ, YOU'LL FIND YOURSELF IN THE SAME MESS IF YOU KEEP STUMBLING AROUND IN A DAZE LIKE THAT.
保健室
HEALTH CENTER
UGH!

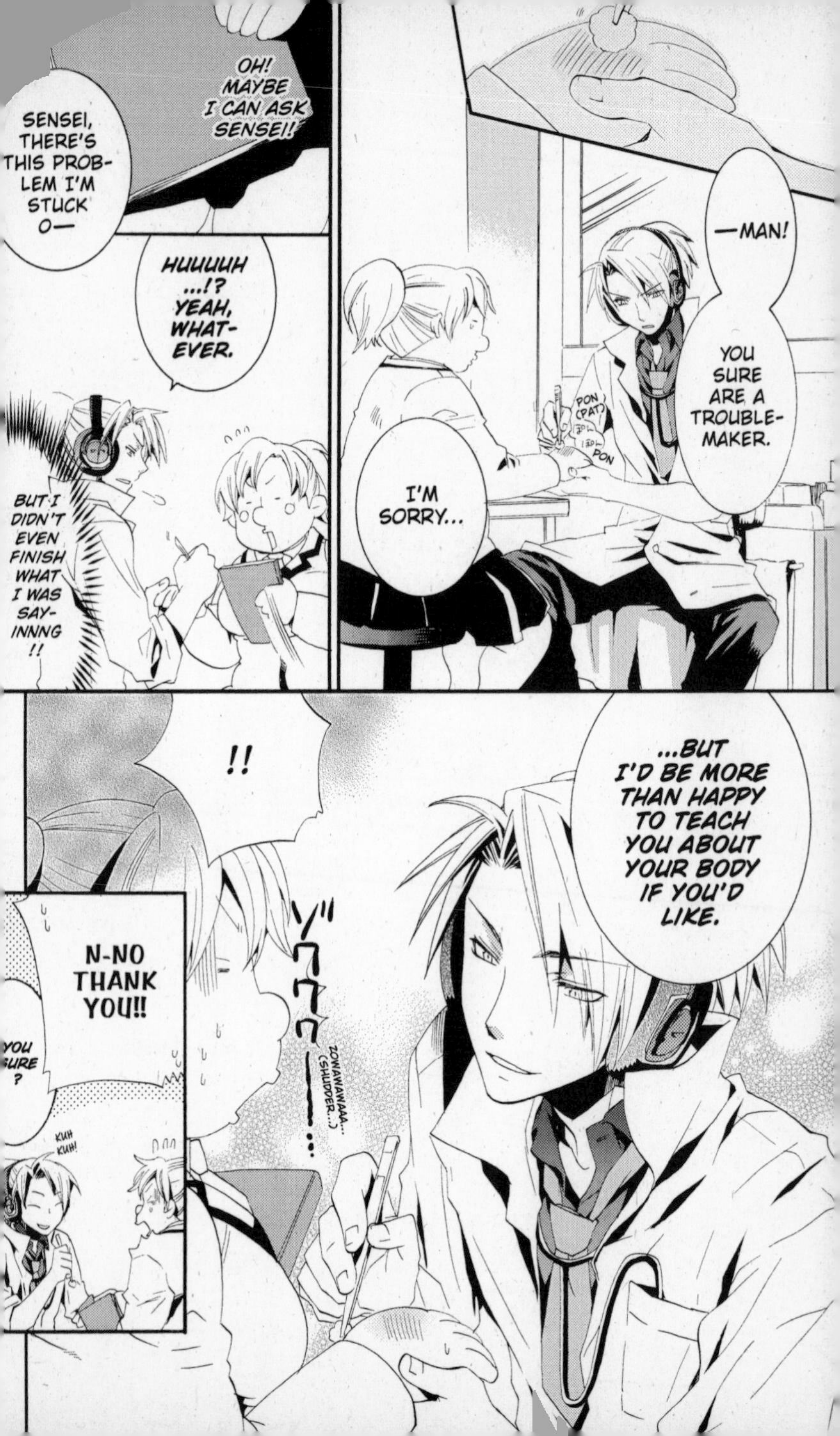
—MAN!
YOU SURE ARE A TROUBLE-MAKER.
PON (PAT) PON
I'M SORRY...
OH! MAYBE I CAN ASK SENSEI!
SENSEI, THERE'S THIS PROB-LEM I'M STUCK O—
HUUUUH ...!? YEAH, WHAT-EVER.
BUT I DIDN'T EVEN FINISH WHAT I WAS SAY-INNNG !!
...BUT I'D BE MORE THAN HAPPY TO TEACH YOU ABOUT YOUR BODY IF YOU'D LIKE.
!!
ZOWAWAWAA... (SHUDDER...)
N-NO THANK YOU!!
YOU SURE ?
KUH KUH!

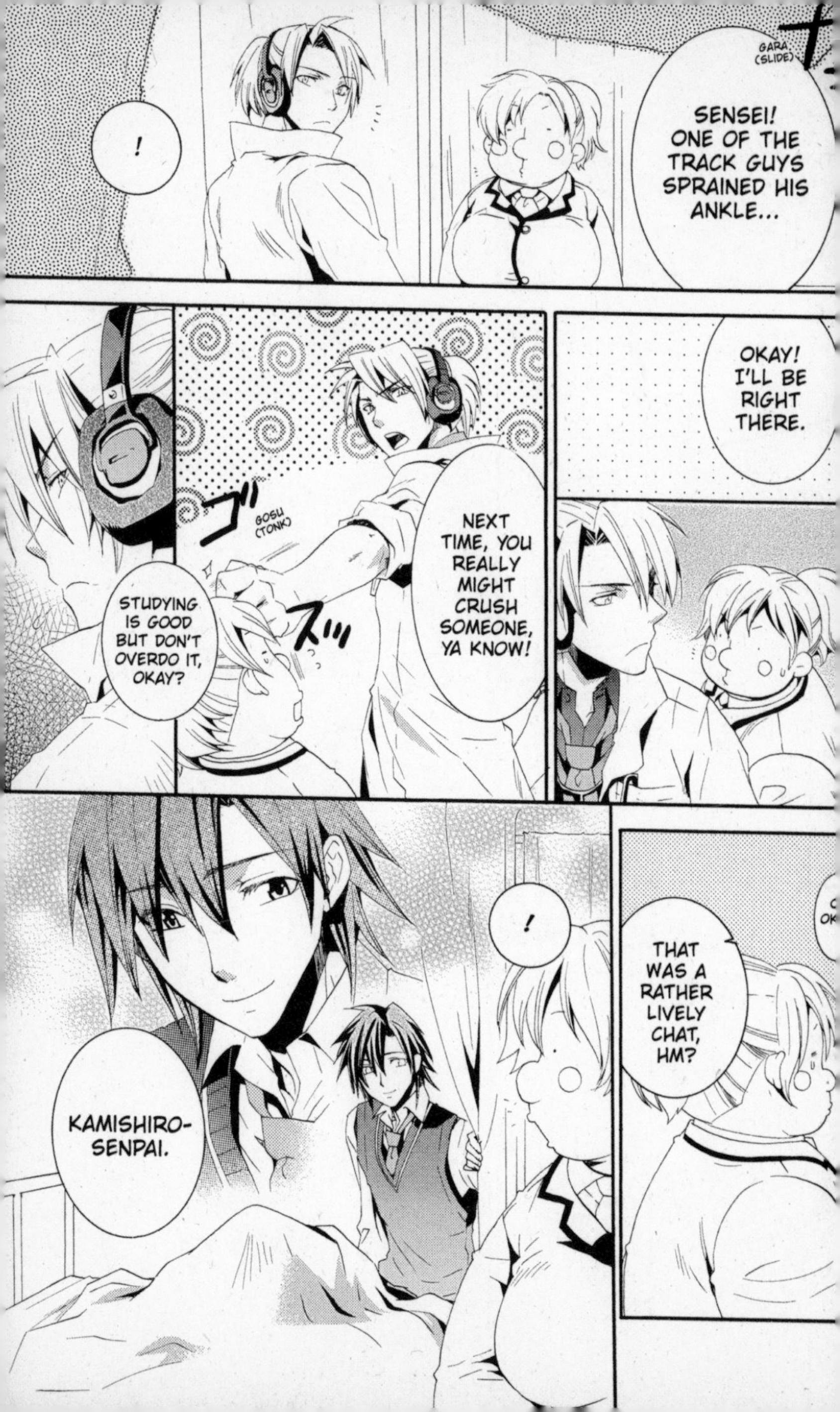
GARA (SLIDE)
SENSEI! ONE OF THE TRACK GUYS SPRAINED HIS ANKLE...
!
OKAY! I'LL BE RIGHT THERE.
GOSU (TONK)
NEXT TIME, YOU REALLY MIGHT CRUSH SOMEONE, YA KNOW!
STUDYING IS GOOD BUT DON'T OVERDO IT, OKAY?
THAT WAS A RATHER LIVELY CHAT, HM?
!
KAMISHIRO-SENPAI.

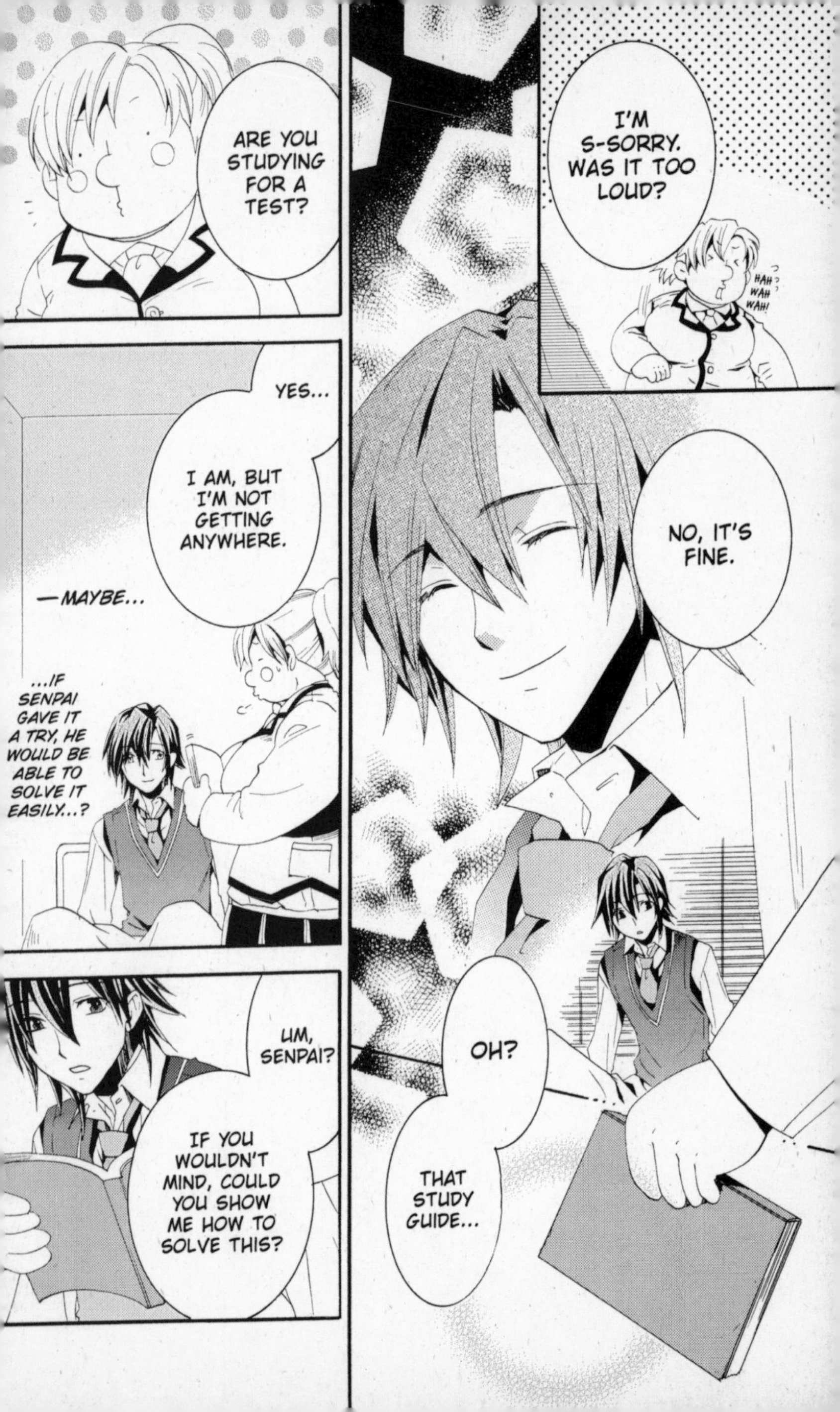
I'M S-SORRY. WAS IT TOO LOUD?
HAH WAH WAH!
NO, IT'S FINE.
OH?
THAT STUDY GUIDE...
ARE YOU STUDYING FOR A TEST?
YES...
I AM, BUT I'M NOT GETTING ANYWHERE.
—MAYBE...
...IF SENPAI GAVE IT A TRY, HE WOULD BE ABLE TO SOLVE IT EASILY...?
UM, SENPAI?
IF YOU WOULDN'T MIND, COULD YOU SHOW ME HOW TO SOLVE THIS?

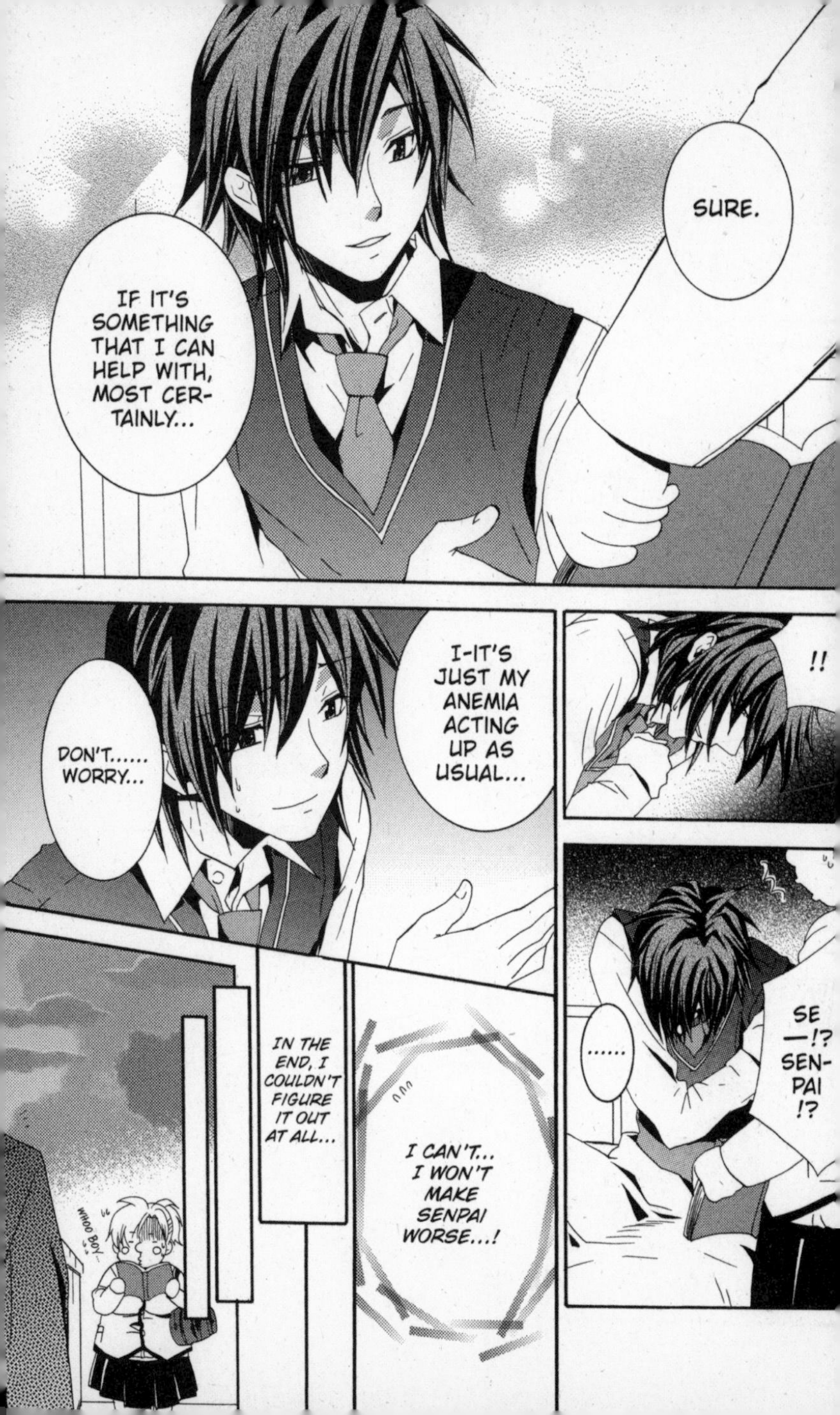
SURE.
IF IT'S SOMETHING THAT I CAN HELP WITH, MOST CER-TAINLY...
!!
I-IT'S JUST MY ANEMIA ACTING UP AS USUAL...
DON'T...... WORRY...
SE—!? SENPAI!?
......
I CAN'T... I WON'T MAKE SENPAI WORSE...!
IN THE END, I COULDN'T FIGURE IT OUT AT ALL...
WHOO BOY...

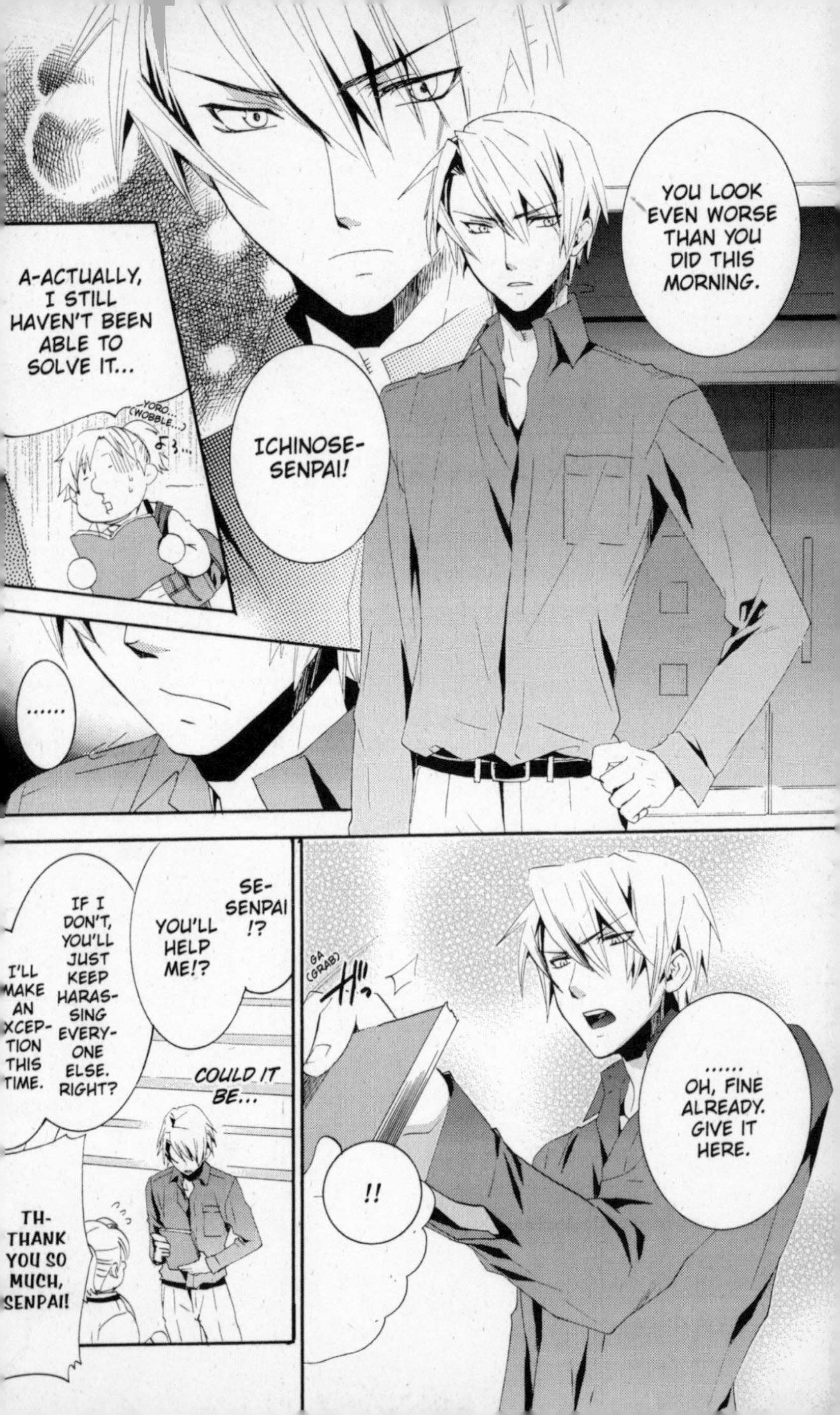
YOU LOOK EVEN WORSE THAN YOU DID THIS MORNING.
ICHINOSE-SENPAI!
A-ACTUALLY, I STILL HAVEN'T BEEN ABLE TO SOLVE IT...
YORO... (WOBBLE...)
よろ...
......
...... OH, FINE ALREADY. GIVE IT HERE.
GA (GRAB)
!!
SE-SENPAI!?
YOU'LL HELP ME!?
COULD IT BE...
IF I DON'T, YOU'LL JUST KEEP HARASSING EVERYONE ELSE. RIGHT?
I'LL MAKE AN XCEPTION THIS TIME.
TH-THANK YOU SO MUCH, SENPAI!

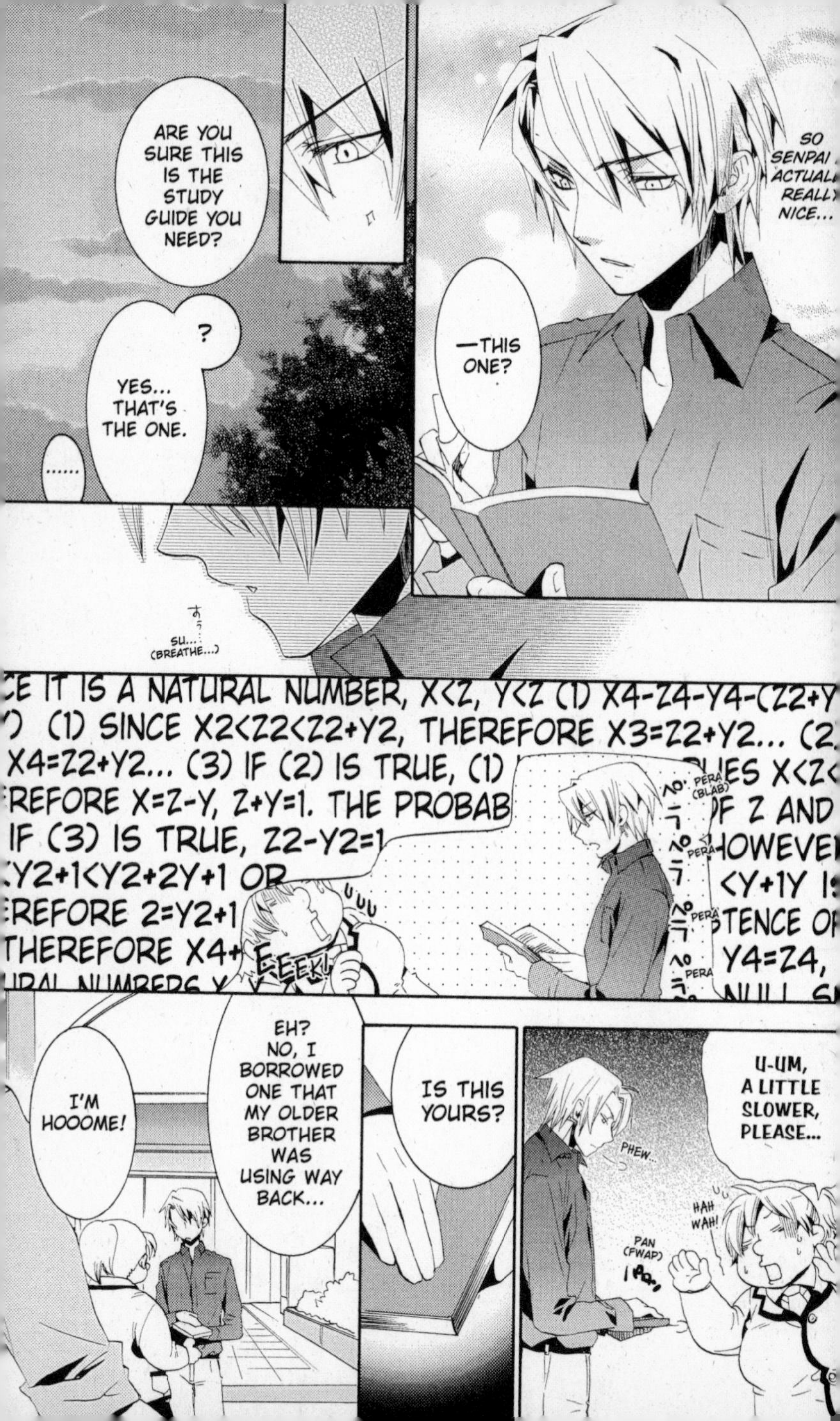

SO SENPAI ACTUAL REALL NICE...
—THIS ONE?
ARE YOU SURE THIS IS THE STUDY GUIDE YOU NEED?
?
YES... THAT'S THE ONE.
......
すう
SU... (BREATHE...)
CE IT IS A NATURAL NUMBER, X<Z, Y<Z (1) X4-Z4-Y4-(Z2+Y
) (1) SINCE X2<Z2<Z2+Y2, THEREFORE X3=Z2+Y2... (2
X4=Z2+Y2... (3) IF (2) IS TRUE, (1)
REFORE X=Z-Y, Z+Y=1. THE PROBAB
IF (3) IS TRUE, Z2-Y2=1
Y2+1<Y2+2Y+1 OR
REFORE 2=Y2+1
THEREFORE X4+
ES X<Z<
F Z AND
HOWEVE
<Y+1Y I
TENCE O
Y4=Z4,
ペラ PERA (BLAB)
ペラ PERA
ペラ PERA
ペラ PERA
EEEK!
U-UM, A LITTLE SLOWER, PLEASE...
PHEW...
HAH WAH!
PAN (FWAP)
IS THIS YOURS?
EH? NO, I BORROWED ONE THAT MY OLDER BROTHER WAS USING WAY BACK...
I'M HOOOME!

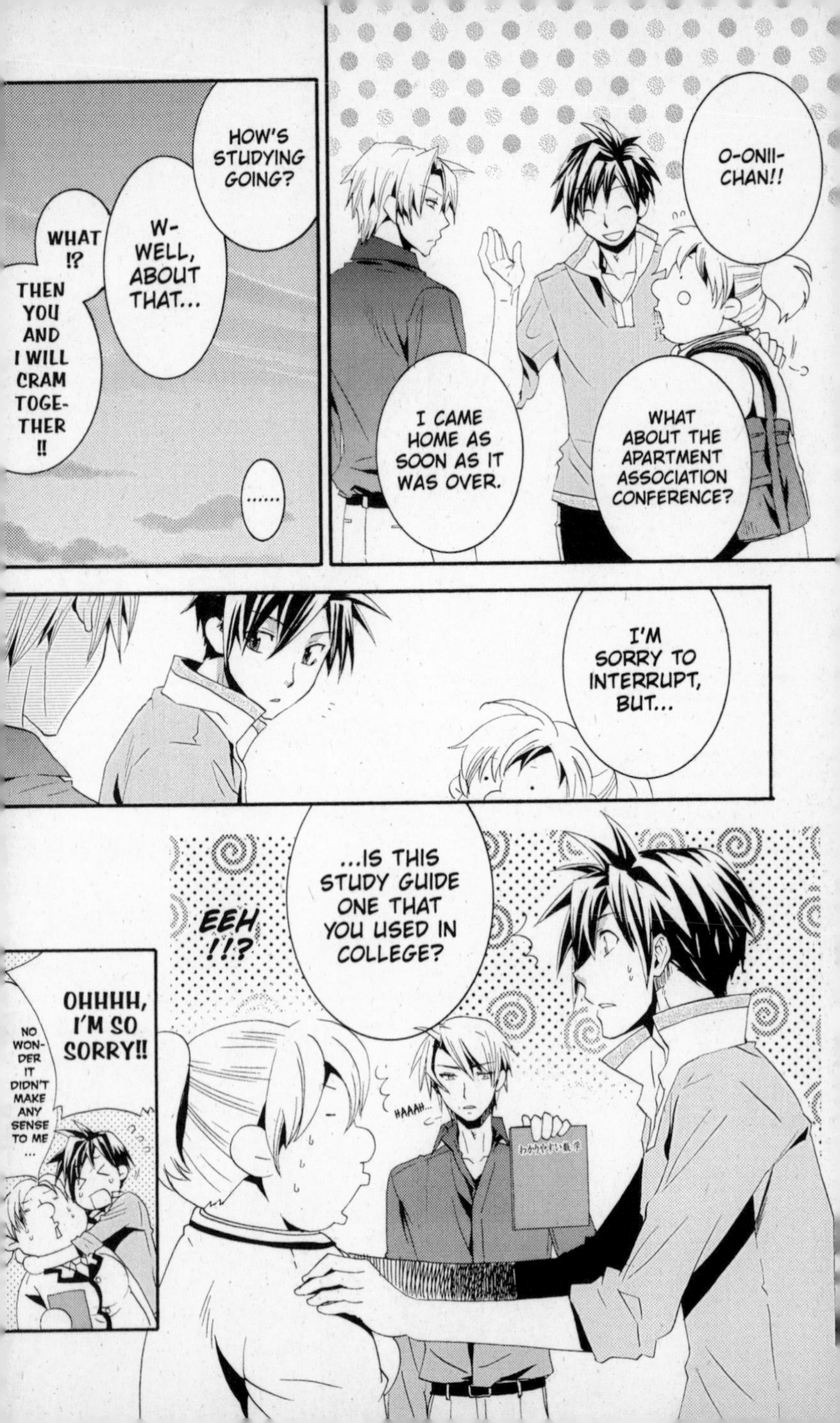
O-ONII-CHAN!!
WHAT ABOUT THE APARTMENT ASSOCIATION CONFERENCE?
I CAME HOME AS SOON AS IT WAS OVER.
HOW'S STUDYING GOING?
W-WELL, ABOUT THAT...
WHAT!? THEN YOU AND I WILL CRAM TOGE-THER!!
......
I'M SORRY TO INTERRUPT, BUT...
...IS THIS STUDY GUIDE ONE THAT YOU USED IN COLLEGE?
EEH!!?
わかりやすい数学
HAAAH...
OHHHH, I'M SO SORRY!!
NO WONDER IT DIDN'T MAKE ANY SENSE TO ME...

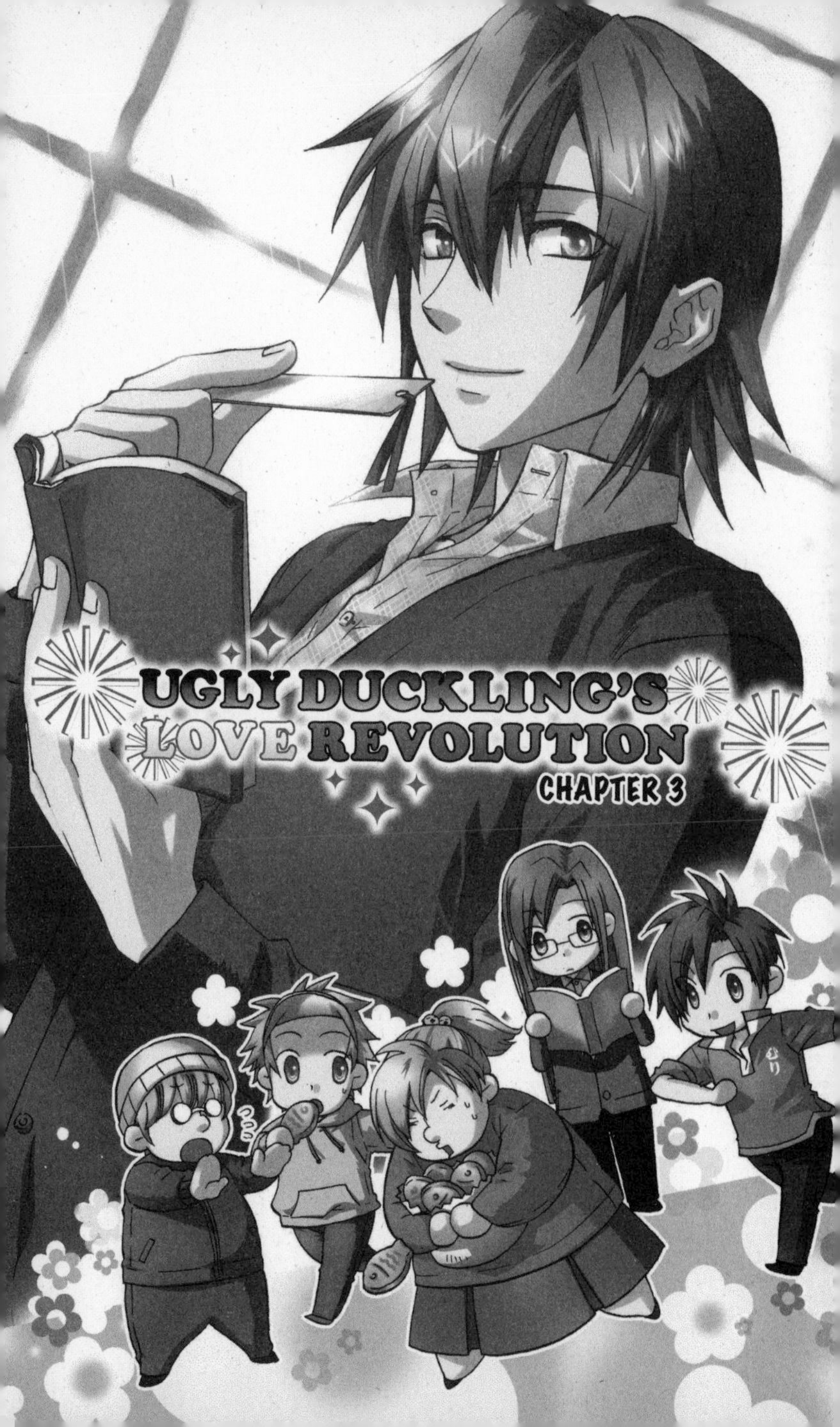
UGLY DUCKLING'S LOVE REVOLUTION
CHAPTER 3

REN

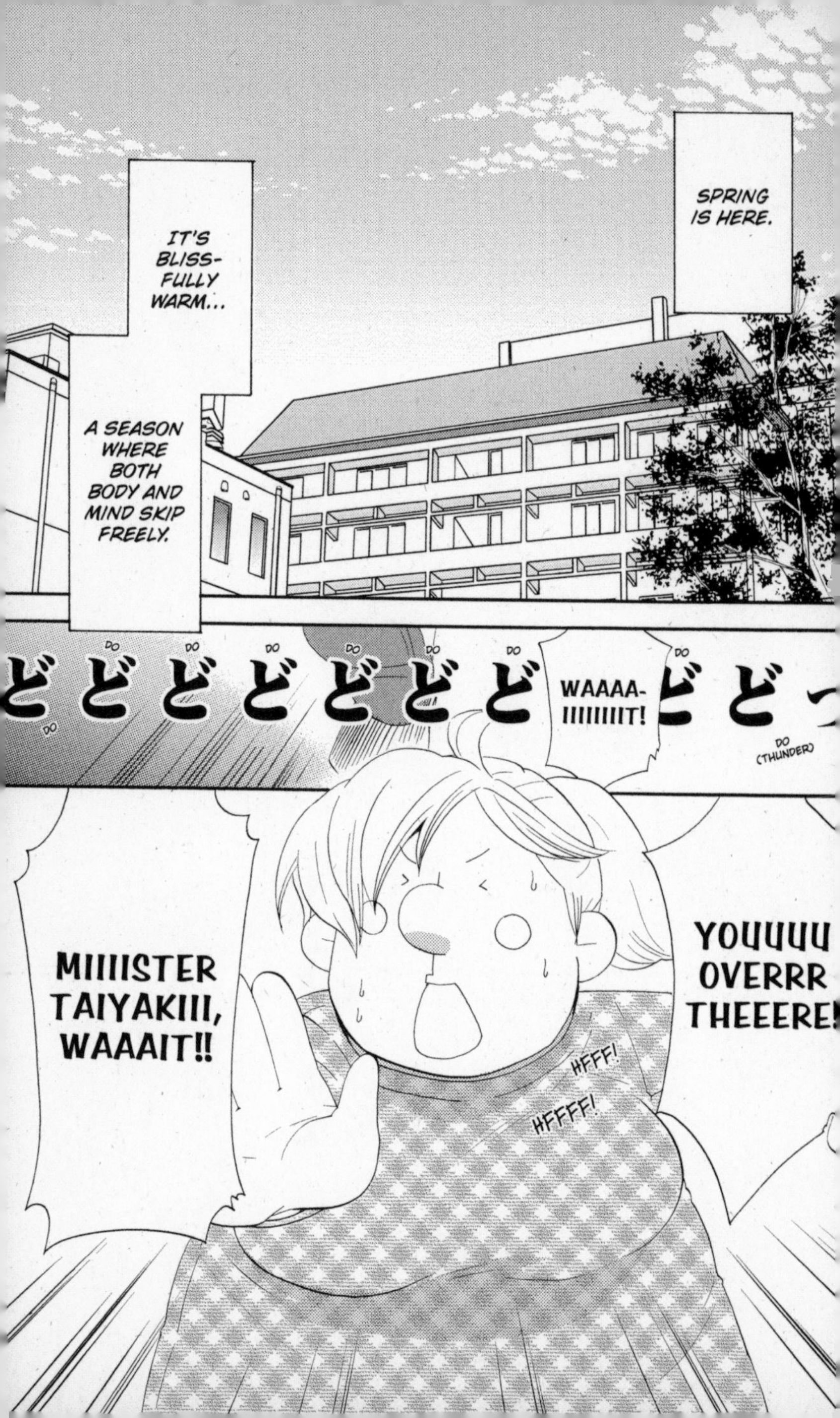
SPRING IS HERE.
IT'S BLISS-FULLY WARM...
A SEASON WHERE BOTH BODY AND MIND SKIP FREELY.
どどっ
DO DO (THUNDER)
WAAAA-IIIIIIIIIT!
どどどどどどど
DO DO DO DO DO DO DO
YOUUUU OVERRR THEEERE!
HFFF!
HFFFF!
MIIIISTER TAIYAKIII, WAAAIT!!

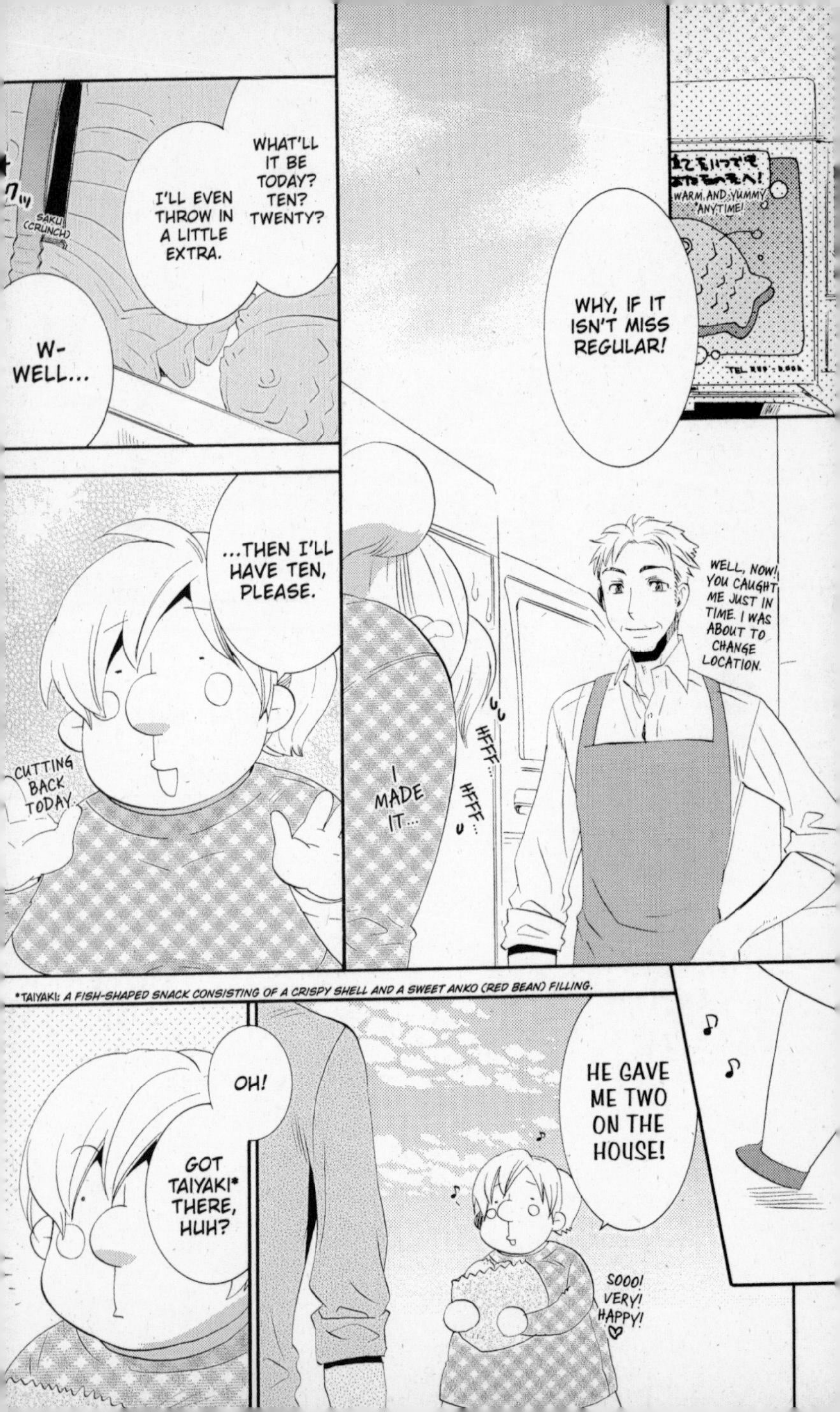
WARM AND YUMMY ANYTIME!
WHY, IF IT ISN'T MISS REGULAR!
WELL, NOW! YOU CAUGHT ME JUST IN TIME. I WAS ABOUT TO CHANGE LOCATION.
HFFF... HFFF...
I MADE IT...
WHAT'LL IT BE TODAY? TEN? TWENTY?
I'LL EVEN THROW IN A LITTLE EXTRA.
SAKU (CRUNCH)
W-WELL...
...THEN I'LL HAVE TEN, PLEASE.
CUTTING BACK TODAY.
HE GAVE ME TWO ON THE HOUSE!
SOOO! VERY! HAPPY!
OH!
GOT TAIYAKI* THERE, HUH?

*TAIYAKI: A FISH-SHAPED SNACK CONSISTING OF A CRISPY SHELL AND A SWEET ANKO (RED BEAN) FILLING.

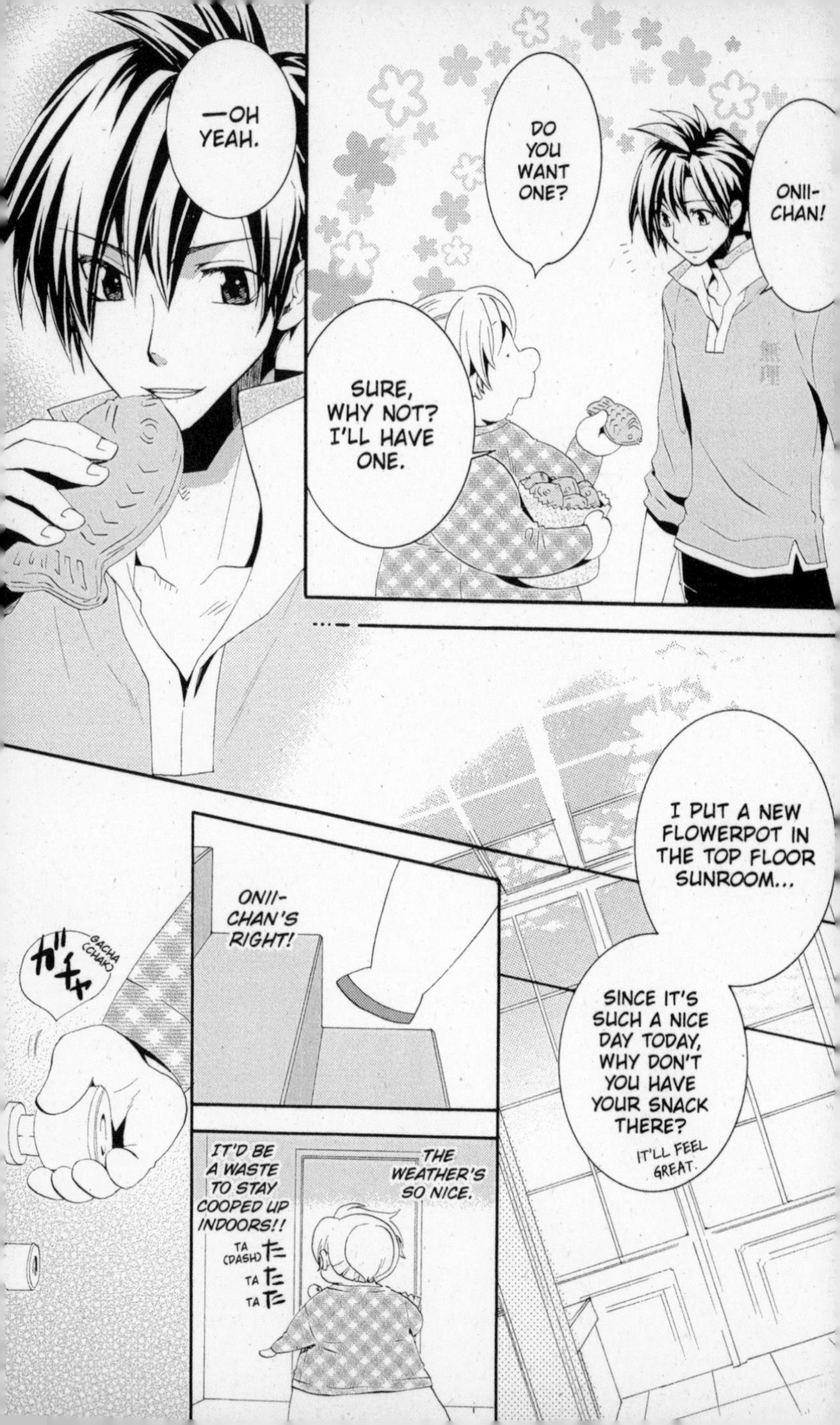
ONII-CHAN!
DO YOU WANT ONE?
SURE, WHY NOT? I'LL HAVE ONE.
—OH YEAH.
I PUT A NEW FLOWERPOT IN THE TOP FLOOR SUNROOM...
SINCE IT'S SUCH A NICE DAY TODAY, WHY DON'T YOU HAVE YOUR SNACK THERE?
IT'LL FEEL GREAT.
ONII-CHAN'S RIGHT!
THE WEATHER'S SO NICE.
IT'D BE A WASTE TO STAY COOPED UP INDOORS!!
TA (DASH) タ
TA タ
TA タ
GACHA (CHAK)
ガチャ

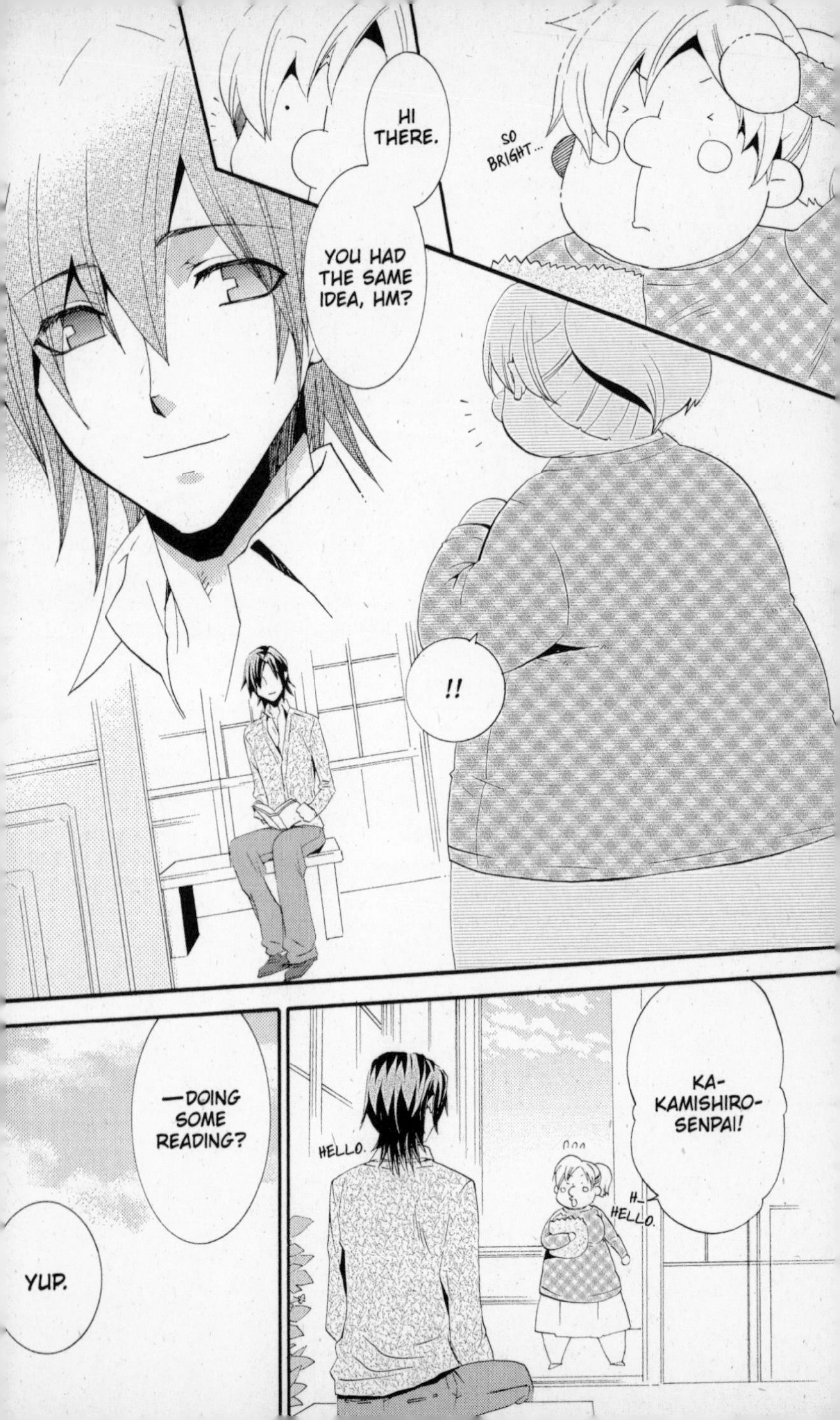
SO BRIGHT...
HI THERE.
YOU HAD THE SAME IDEA, HM?
!!
KA-KAMISHIRO-SENPAI!
H- HELLO.
HELLO.
—DOING SOME READING?
YUP.

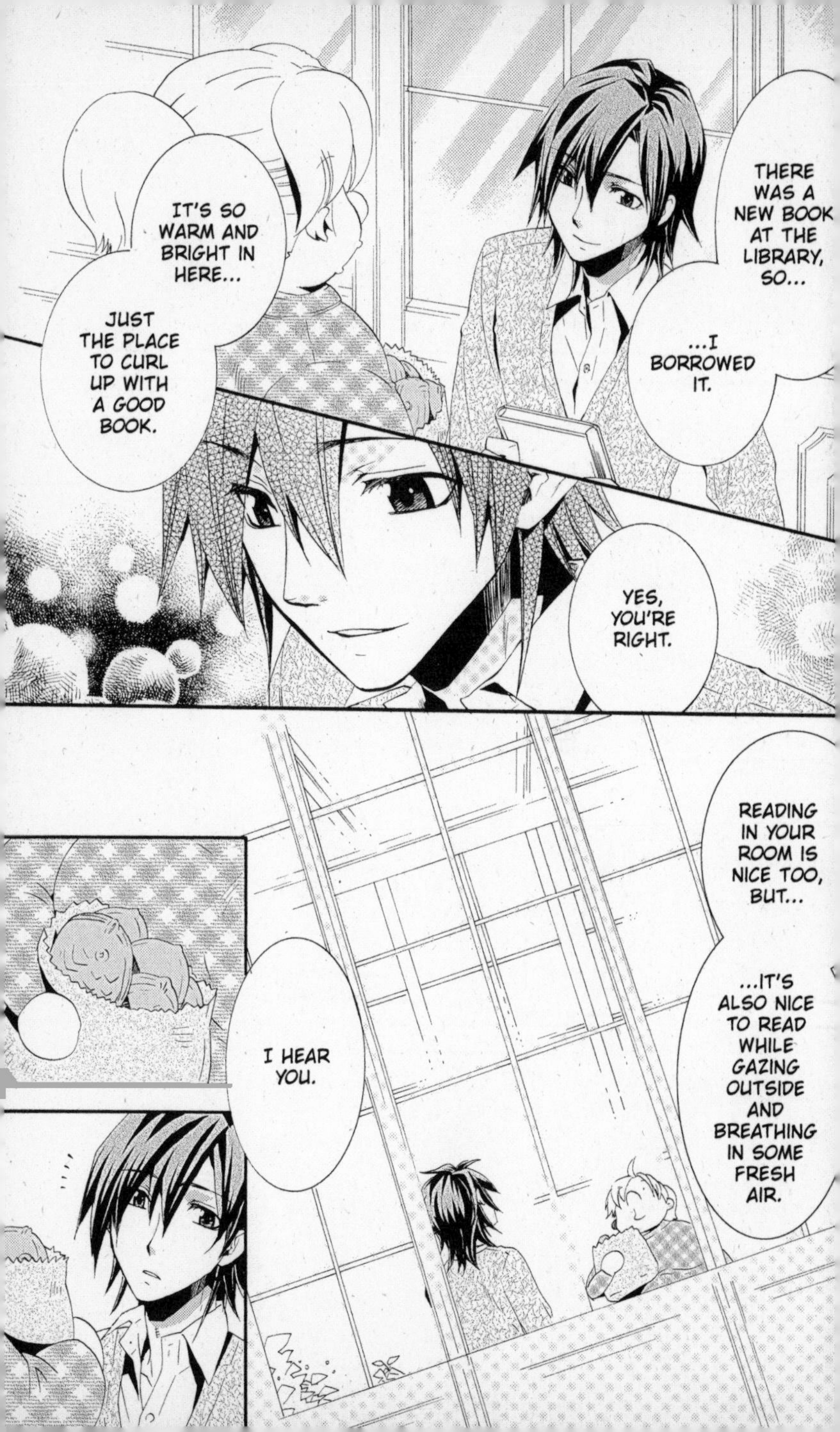
THERE WAS A NEW BOOK AT THE LIBRARY, SO...
...I BORROWED IT.
IT'S SO WARM AND BRIGHT IN HERE...
JUST THE PLACE TO CURL UP WITH A GOOD BOOK.
YES, YOU'RE RIGHT.
READING IN YOUR ROOM IS NICE TOO, BUT...
...IT'S ALSO NICE TO READ WHILE GAZING OUTSIDE AND BREATHING IN SOME FRESH AIR.
I HEAR YOU.

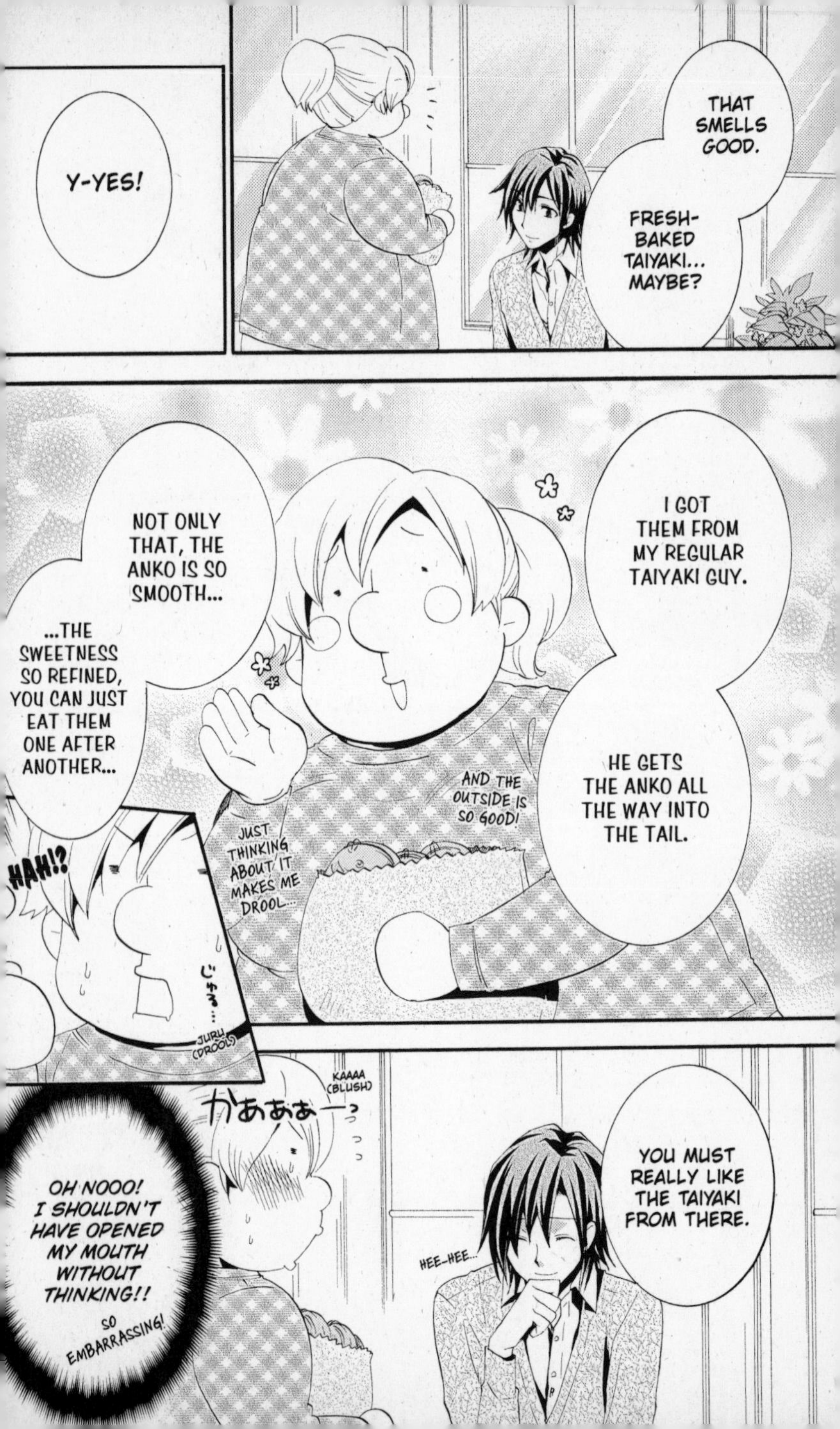
THAT SMELLS GOOD.
FRESH-BAKED TAIYAKI... MAYBE?
Y-YES!
I GOT THEM FROM MY REGULAR TAIYAKI GUY.
HE GETS THE ANKO ALL THE WAY INTO THE TAIL.
AND THE OUTSIDE IS SO GOOD!
NOT ONLY THAT, THE ANKO IS SO SMOOTH...
...THE SWEETNESS SO REFINED, YOU CAN JUST EAT THEM ONE AFTER ANOTHER...
JUST THINKING ABOUT IT MAKES ME DROOL...
HAH!?
じゅる…
JURU (DROOL)
YOU MUST REALLY LIKE THE TAIYAKI FROM THERE.
HEE-HEE...
かあああー
KAAAA (BLUSH)
OH NOOO! I SHOULDN'T HAVE OPENED MY MOUTH WITHOUT THINKING!!
SO EMBARRASSING!

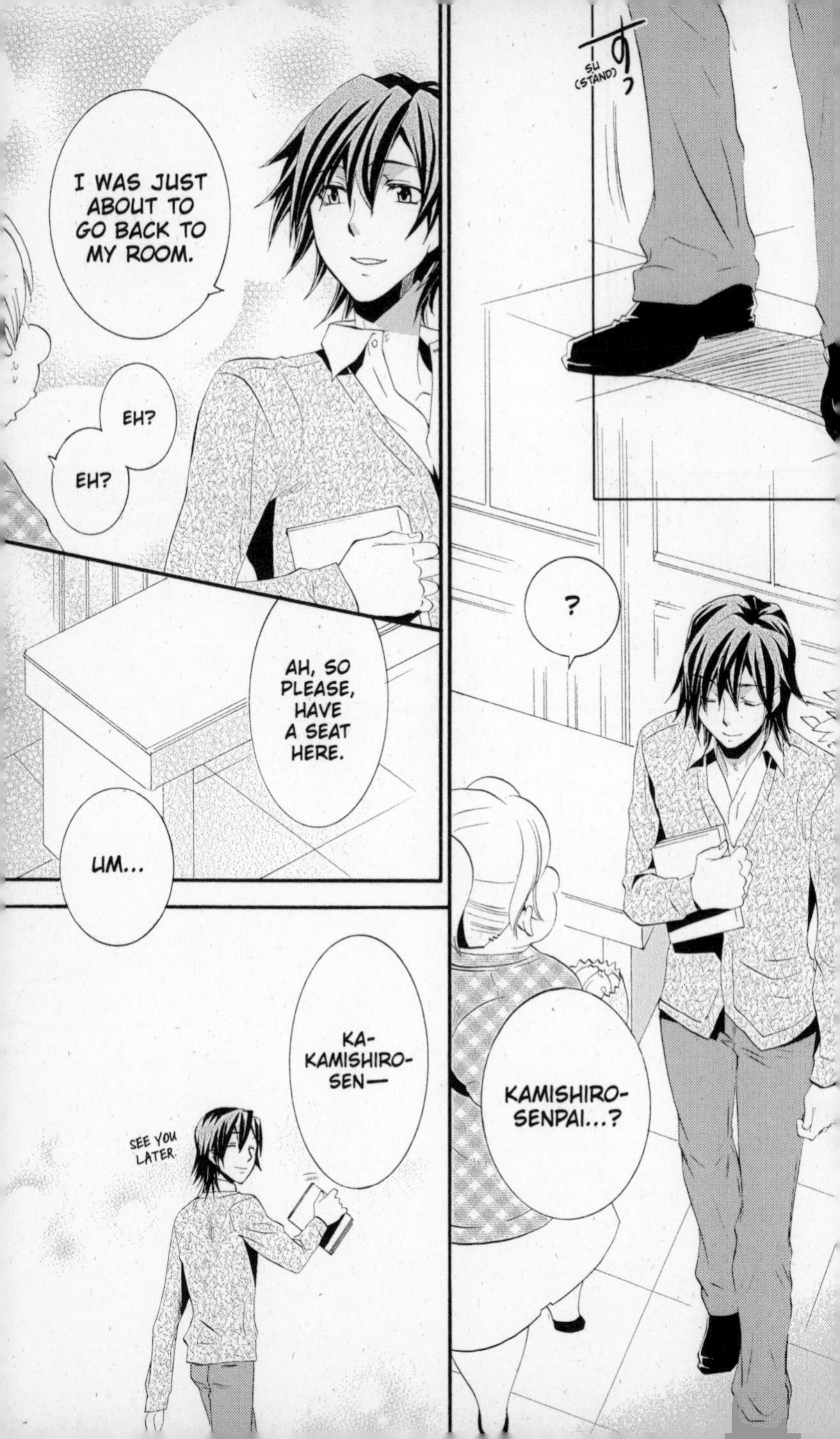
SU (STAND)
?
KAMISHIRO-SENPAI...?
I WAS JUST ABOUT TO GO BACK TO MY ROOM.
EH?
EH?
AH, SO PLEASE, HAVE A SEAT HERE.
UM...
KA-KAMISHIRO-SEN—
SEE YOU LATER.

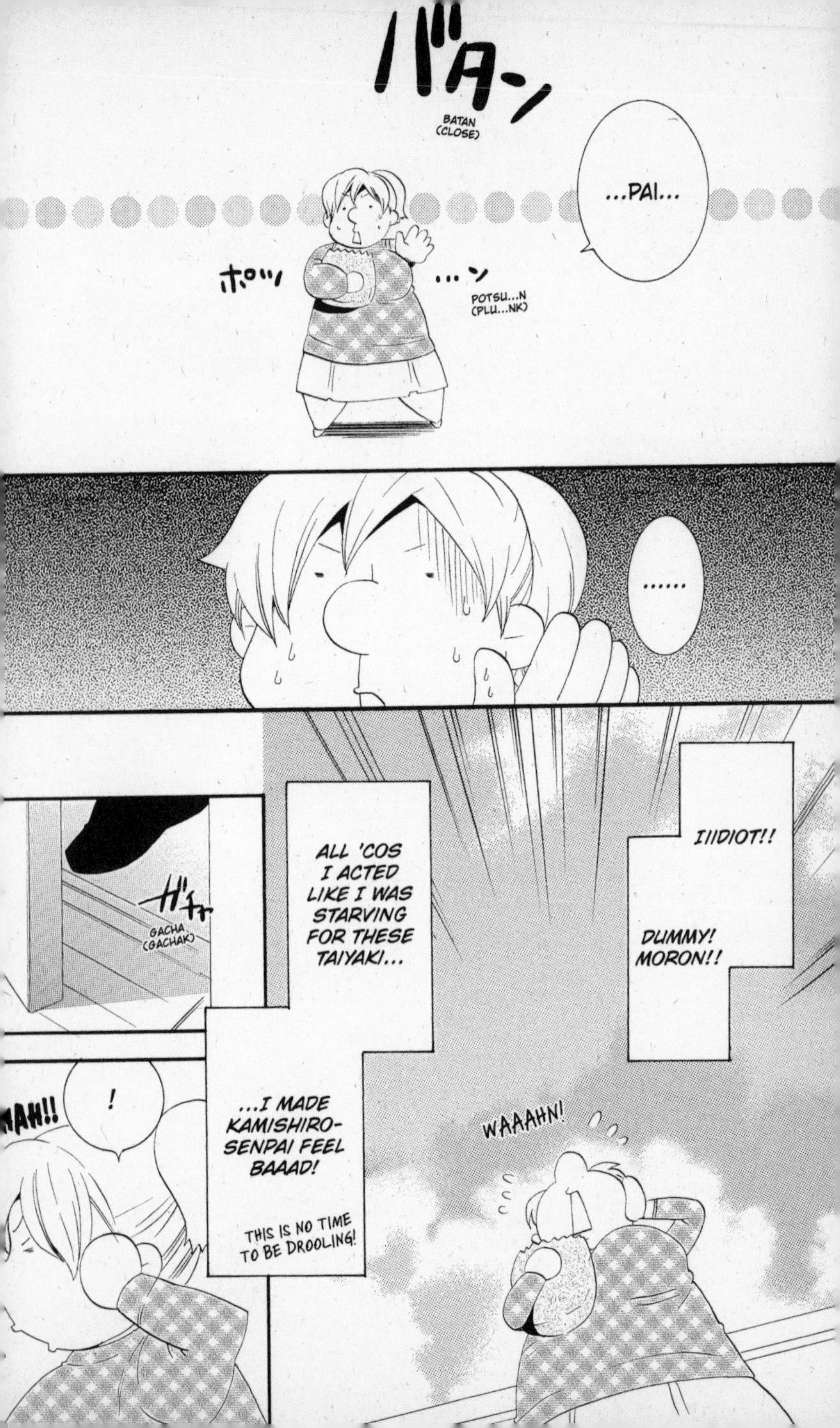

バターン
BATAN (CLOSE)
...PAI...
ポツ…ン
POTSU...N (PLU...NK)
......
IIIDIOT!!
DUMMY! MORON!!
ALL 'COS I ACTED LIKE I WAS STARVING FOR THESE TAIYAKI...
...I MADE KAMISHIRO-SENPAI FEEL BAAAD!
THIS IS NO TIME TO BE DROOLING!
WAAAHN!
ガチャ
GACHA (GACHAK)
!
AH!!

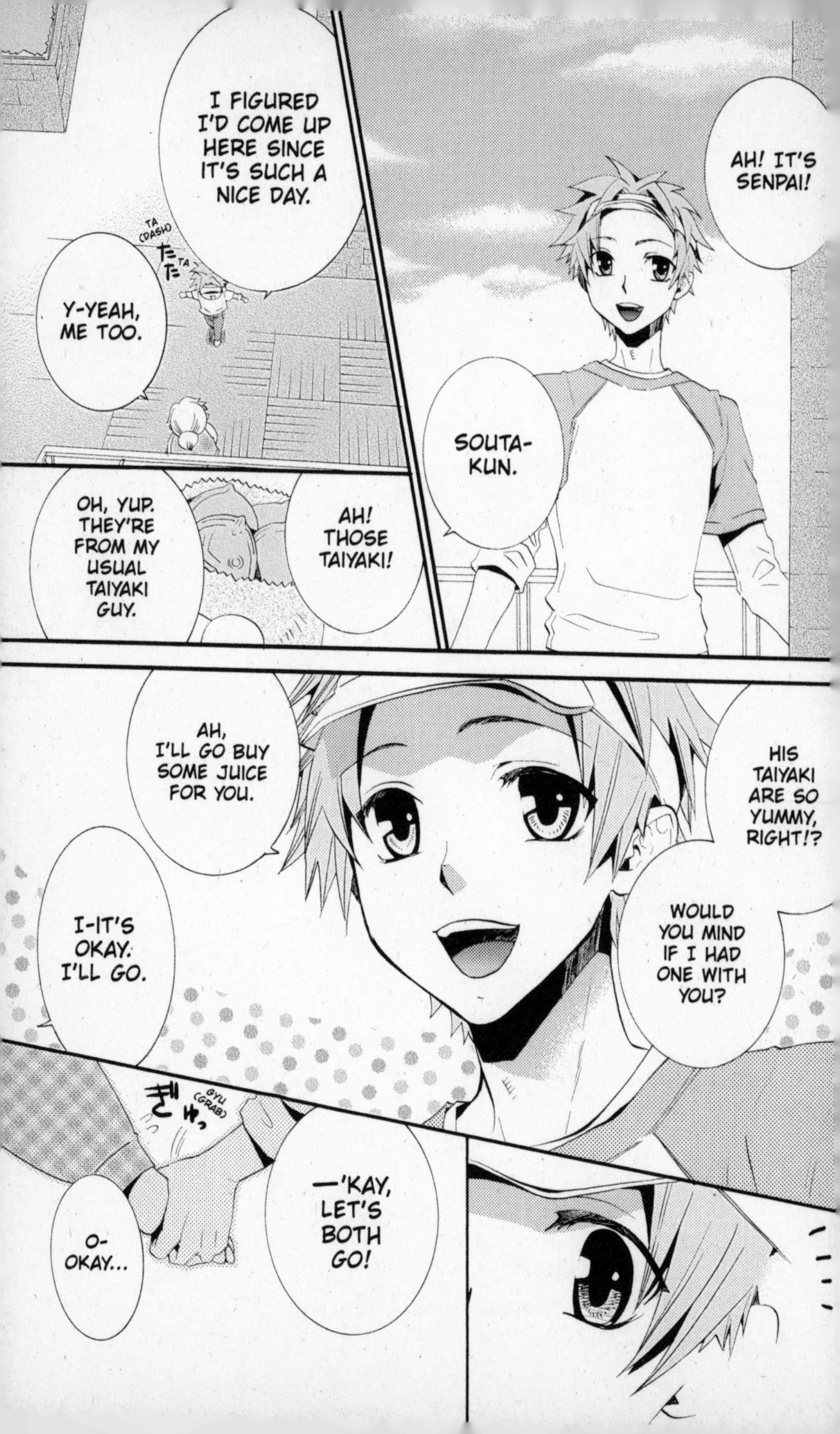
AH! IT'S SENPAI!
SOUTA-KUN.
I FIGURED I'D COME UP HERE SINCE IT'S SUCH A NICE DAY.
TA (DASH) TA
Y-YEAH, ME TOO.
AH! THOSE TAIYAKI!
OH, YUP. THEY'RE FROM MY USUAL TAIYAKI GUY.
HIS TAIYAKI ARE SO YUMMY, RIGHT!?
WOULD YOU MIND IF I HAD ONE WITH YOU?
AH, I'LL GO BUY SOME JUICE FOR YOU.
I-IT'S OKAY. I'LL GO.
...
—'KAY, LET'S BOTH GO!
GYU (GRAB)
O-OKAY...

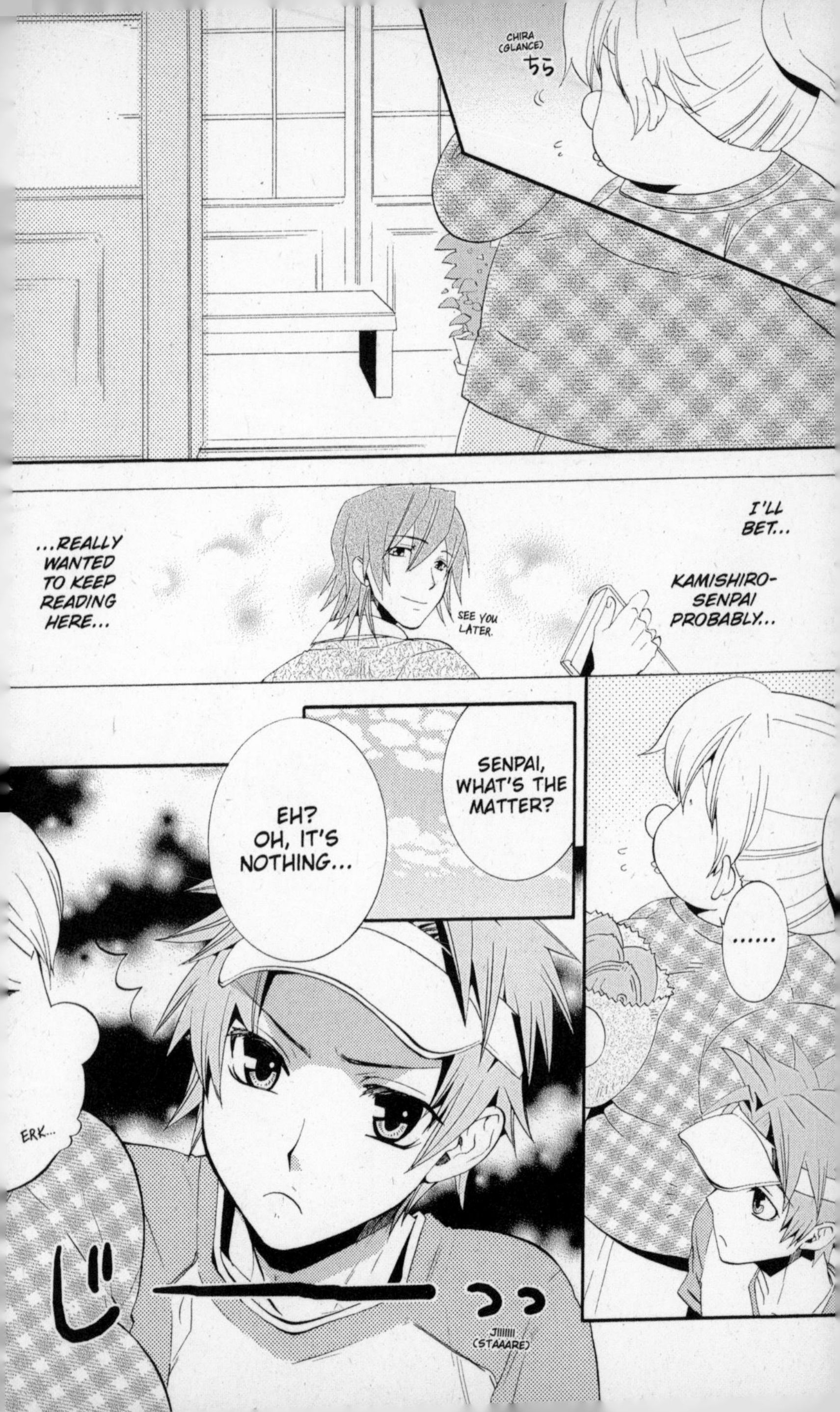
CHIRA (GLANCE)
ちら
I'LL BET...
KAMISHIRO-SENPAI PROBABLY...
SEE YOU LATER.
...REALLY WANTED TO KEEP READING HERE...
......
SENPAI, WHAT'S THE MATTER?
EH? OH, IT'S NOTHING...
ERK...
じーっっ
JIIIIII (STAAARE)

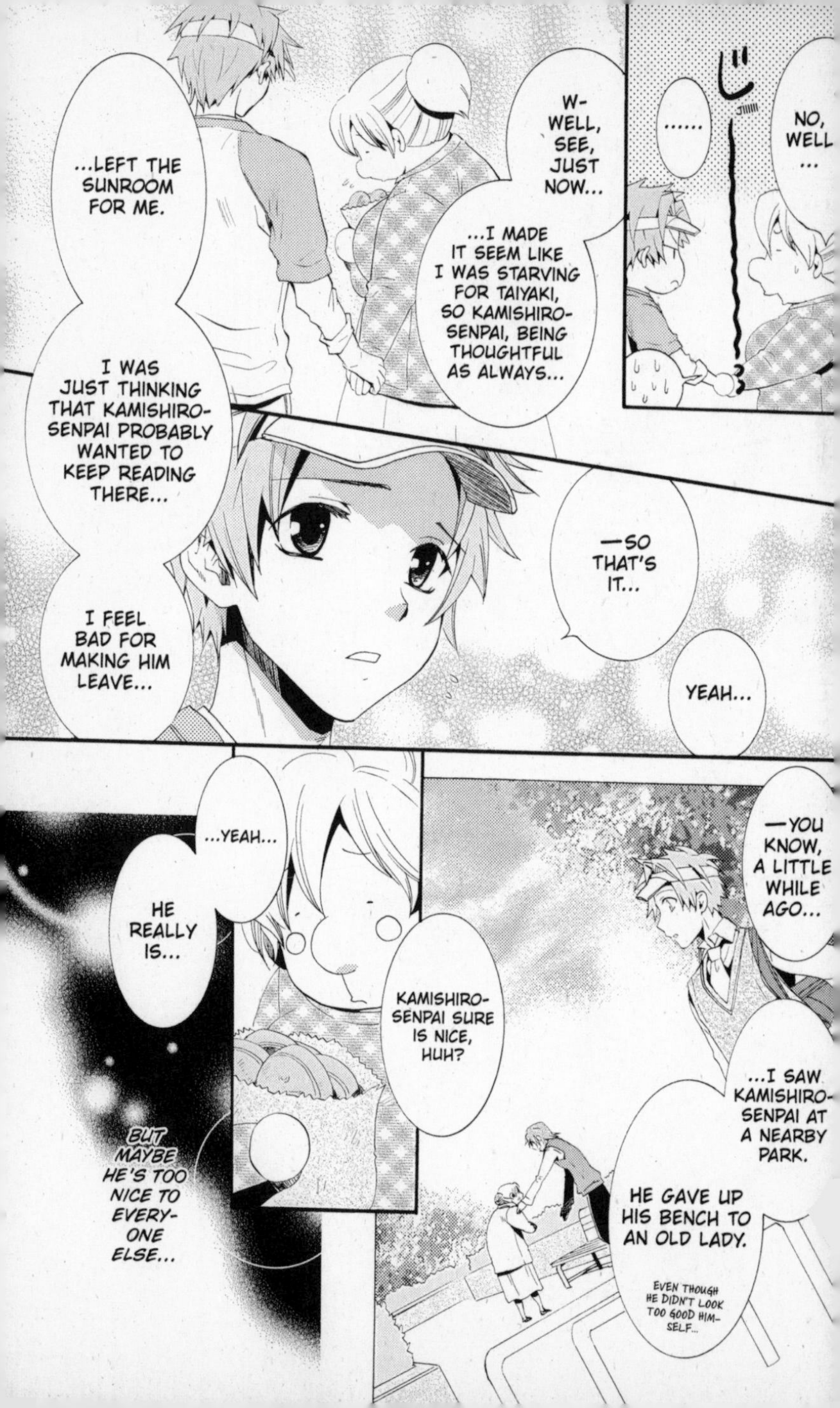

じ
JIIII
NO, WELL ...
......
W-WELL, SEE, JUST NOW...
...I MADE IT SEEM LIKE I WAS STARVING FOR TAIYAKI, SO KAMISHIRO-SENPAI, BEING THOUGHTFUL AS ALWAYS...
...LEFT THE SUNROOM FOR ME.
—SO THAT'S IT...
YEAH...
I WAS JUST THINKING THAT KAMISHIRO-SENPAI PROBABLY WANTED TO KEEP READING THERE...
I FEEL BAD FOR MAKING HIM LEAVE...
—YOU KNOW, A LITTLE WHILE AGO...
...I SAW KAMISHIRO-SENPAI AT A NEARBY PARK.
HE GAVE UP HIS BENCH TO AN OLD LADY.
EVEN THOUGH HE DIDN'T LOOK TOO GOOD HIM-SELF...
KAMISHIRO-SENPAI SURE IS NICE, HUH?
...YEAH...
HE REALLY IS...
BUT MAYBE HE'S TOO NICE TO EVERY-ONE ELSE...

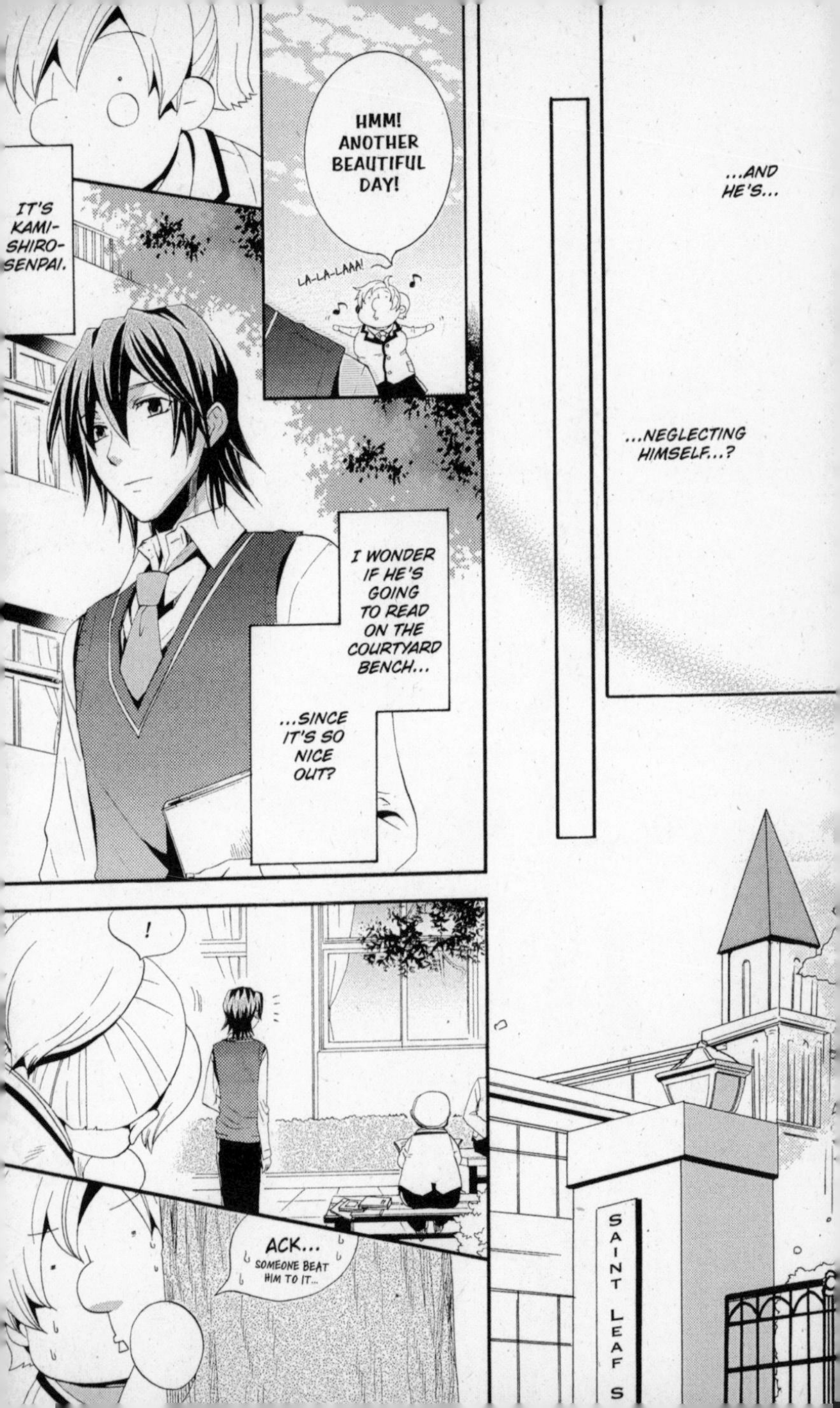

...AND HE'S...
...NEGLECTING HIMSELF...?
SAINT LEAF S
HMM! ANOTHER BEAUTIFUL DAY!
LA-LA-LAAA!
IT'S KAMI-SHIRO-SENPAI.
I WONDER IF HE'S GOING TO READ ON THE COURTYARD BENCH...
...SINCE IT'S SO NICE OUT?
!
ACK...
SOMEONE BEAT HIM TO IT...

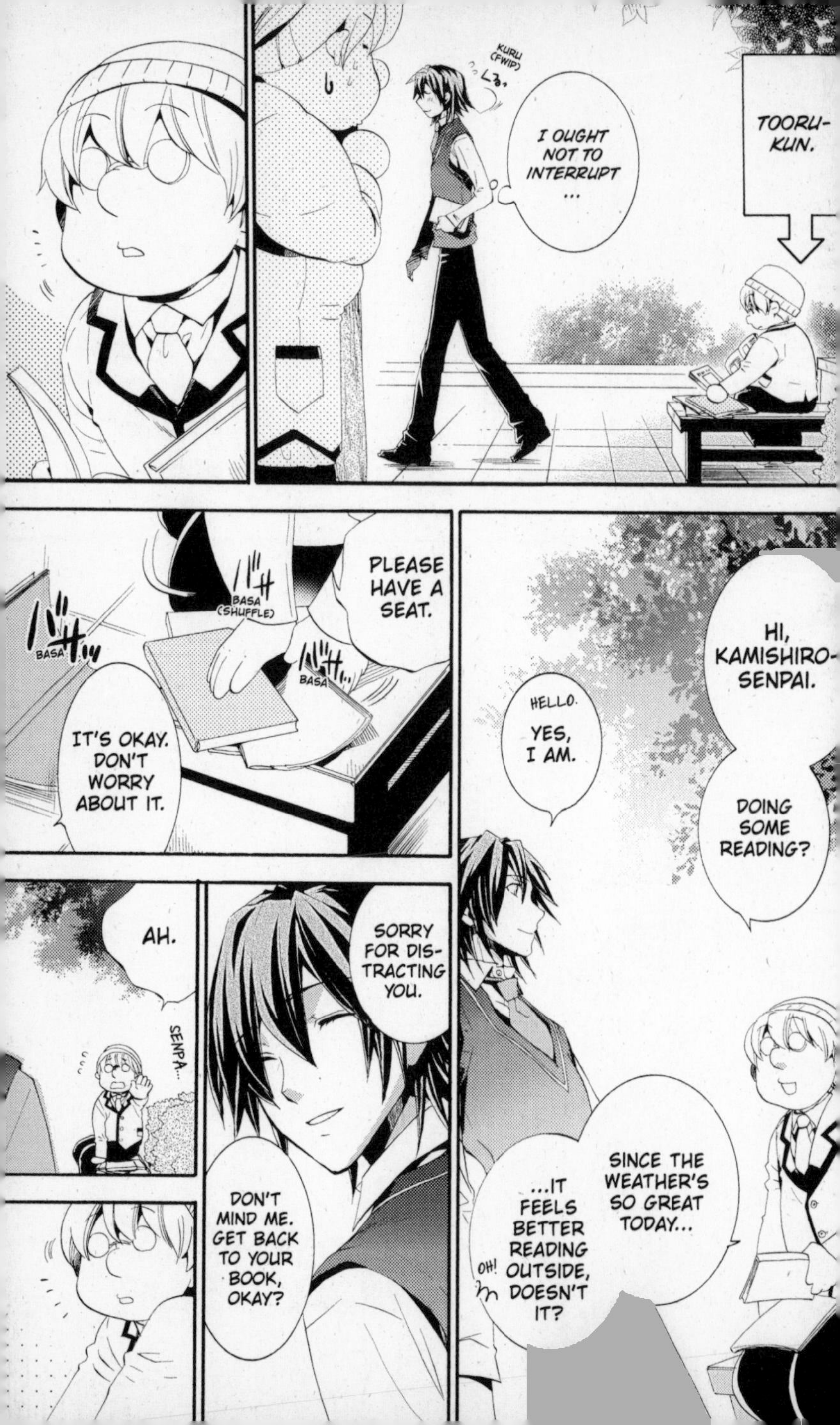
TOORU-KUN.
KURU (FWIP)
I OUGHT NOT TO INTERRUPT ...
HI, KAMISHIRO-SENPAI.
DOING SOME READING?
HELLO.
YES, I AM.
SINCE THE WEATHER'S SO GREAT TODAY...
...IT FEELS BETTER READING OUTSIDE, DOESN'T IT?
OH!
PLEASE HAVE A SEAT.
BASA (SHUFFLE)
BASA
BASA
IT'S OKAY. DON'T WORRY ABOUT IT.
SORRY FOR DIS-TRACTING YOU.
DON'T MIND ME. GET BACK TO YOUR BOOK, OKAY?
AH.
SENPA...

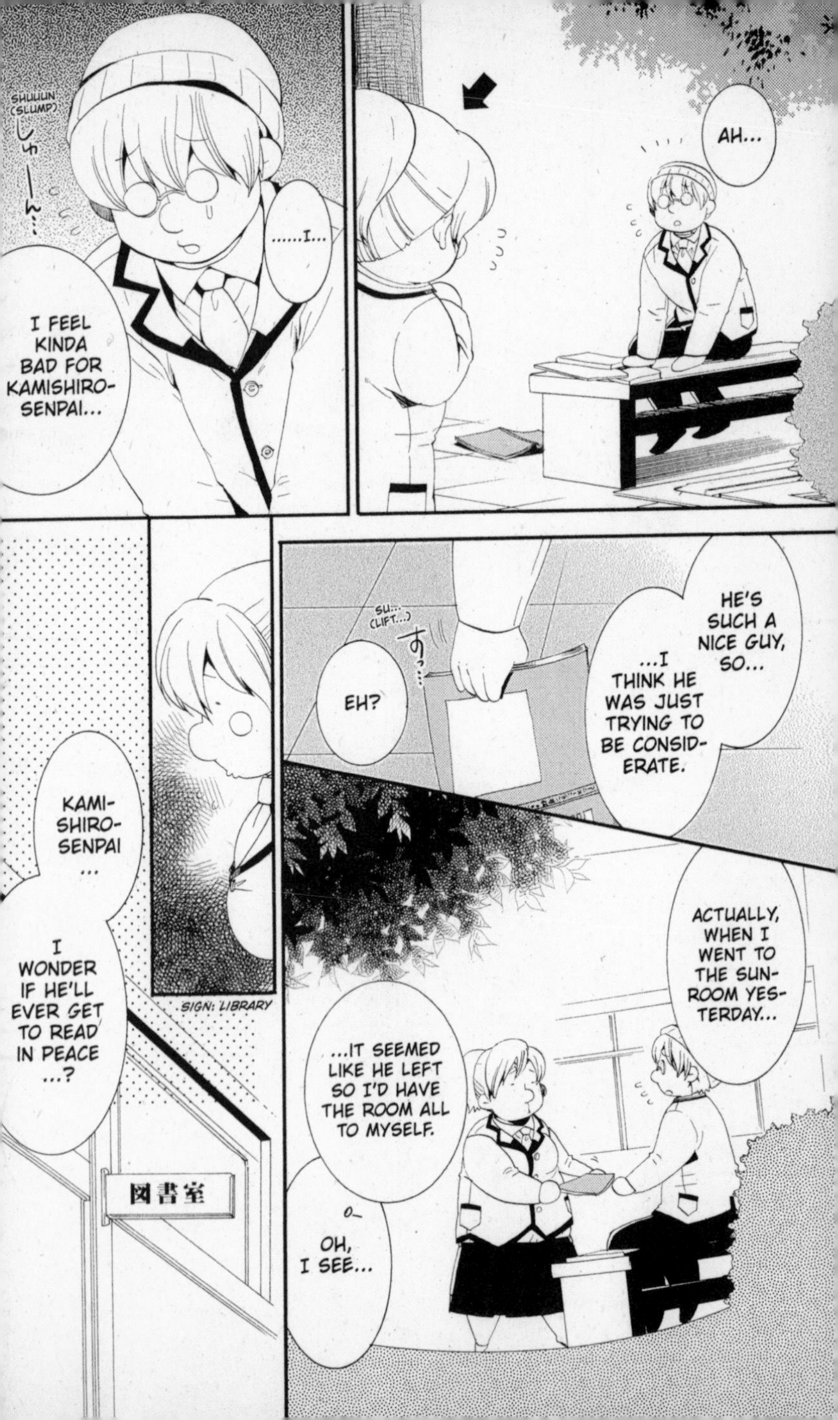
AH...
SHUUUN (SLUMP)
しゅーん…
......I...
I FEEL KINDA BAD FOR KAMISHIRO-SENPAI...
HE'S SUCH A NICE GUY, SO...
...I THINK HE WAS JUST TRYING TO BE CONSIDERATE.
SU... (LIFT...)
すっ…
EH?
ACTUALLY, WHEN I WENT TO THE SUN-ROOM YESTERDAY...
...IT SEEMED LIKE HE LEFT SO I'D HAVE THE ROOM ALL TO MYSELF.
O-
OH, I SEE...
KAMI-SHIRO-SENPAI...
I WONDER IF HE'LL EVER GET TO READ IN PEACE...?
SIGN: LIBRARY
図書室

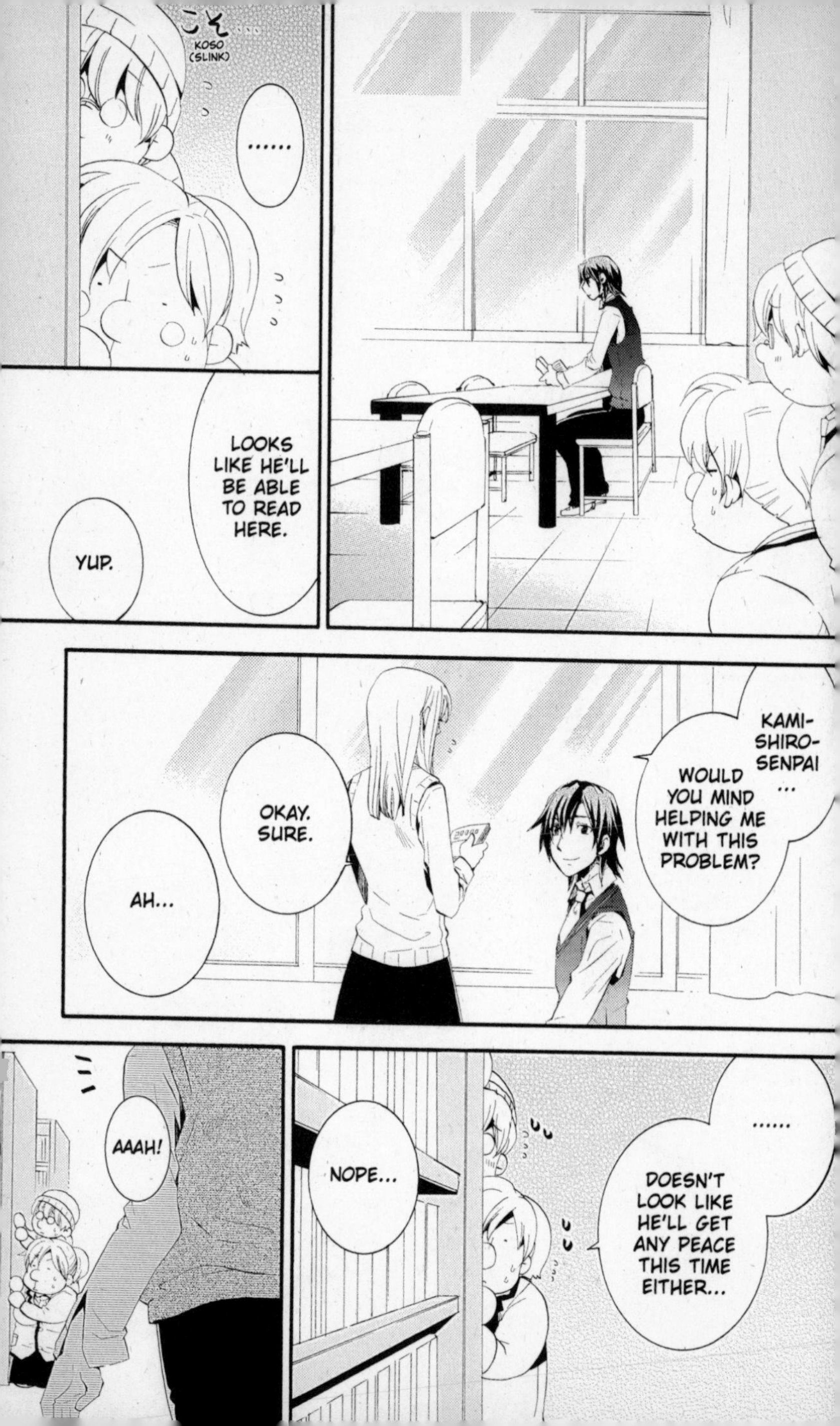
こそ…
KOSO (SLINK)
......
LOOKS LIKE HE'LL BE ABLE TO READ HERE.
YUP.
KAMI-SHIRO-SENPAI...
WOULD YOU MIND HELPING ME WITH THIS PROBLEM?
OKAY. SURE.
AH...
......
DOESN'T LOOK LIKE HE'LL GET ANY PEACE THIS TIME EITHER...
NOPE...
AAAH!

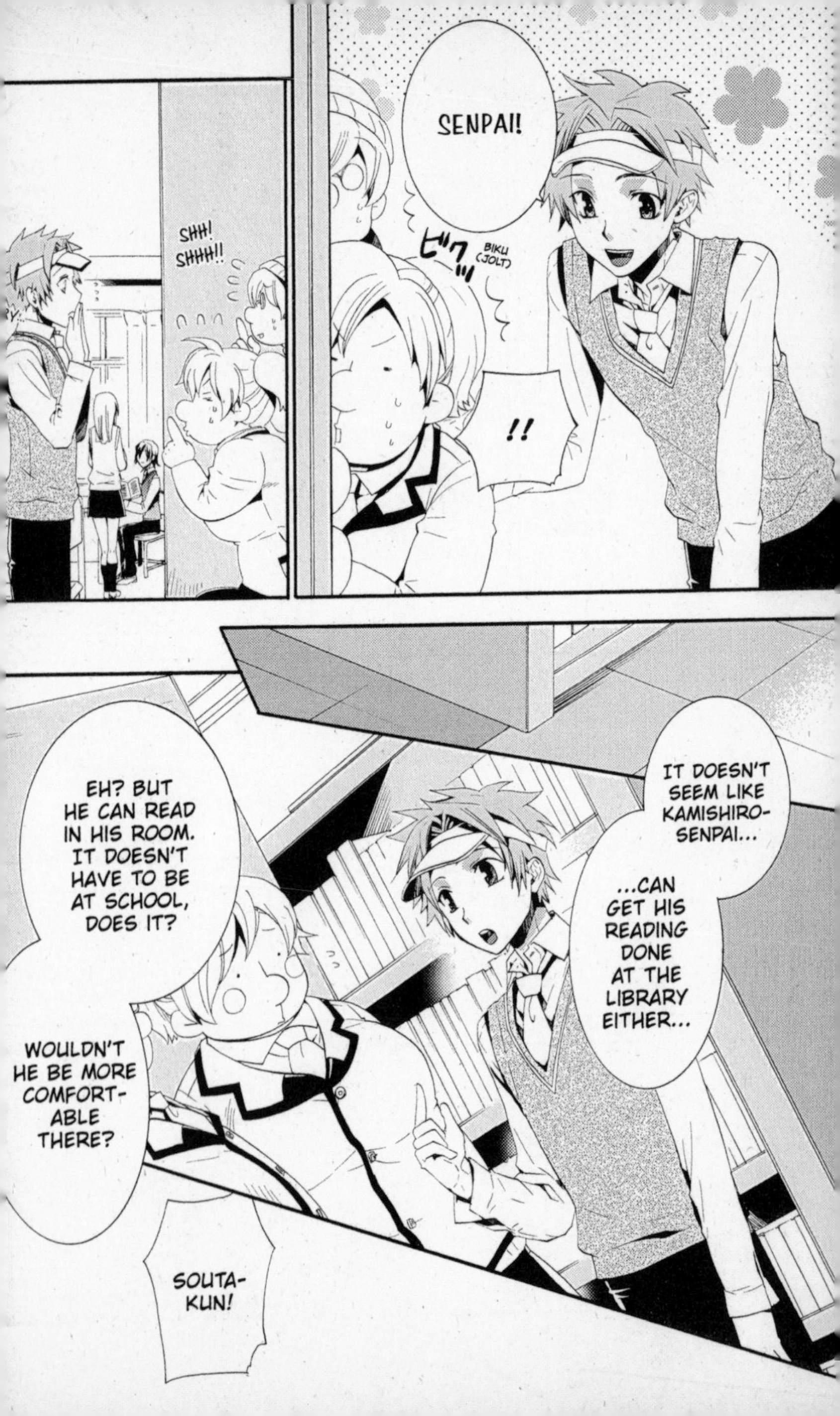
SENPAI!
ビクッ
BIKU (JOLT)
!!
SHH! SHHH!!
IT DOESN'T SEEM LIKE KAMISHIRO-SENPAI...
...CAN GET HIS READING DONE AT THE LIBRARY EITHER...
EH? BUT HE CAN READ IN HIS ROOM. IT DOESN'T HAVE TO BE AT SCHOOL, DOES IT?
WOULDN'T HE BE MORE COMFORT-ABLE THERE?
SOUTA-KUN!

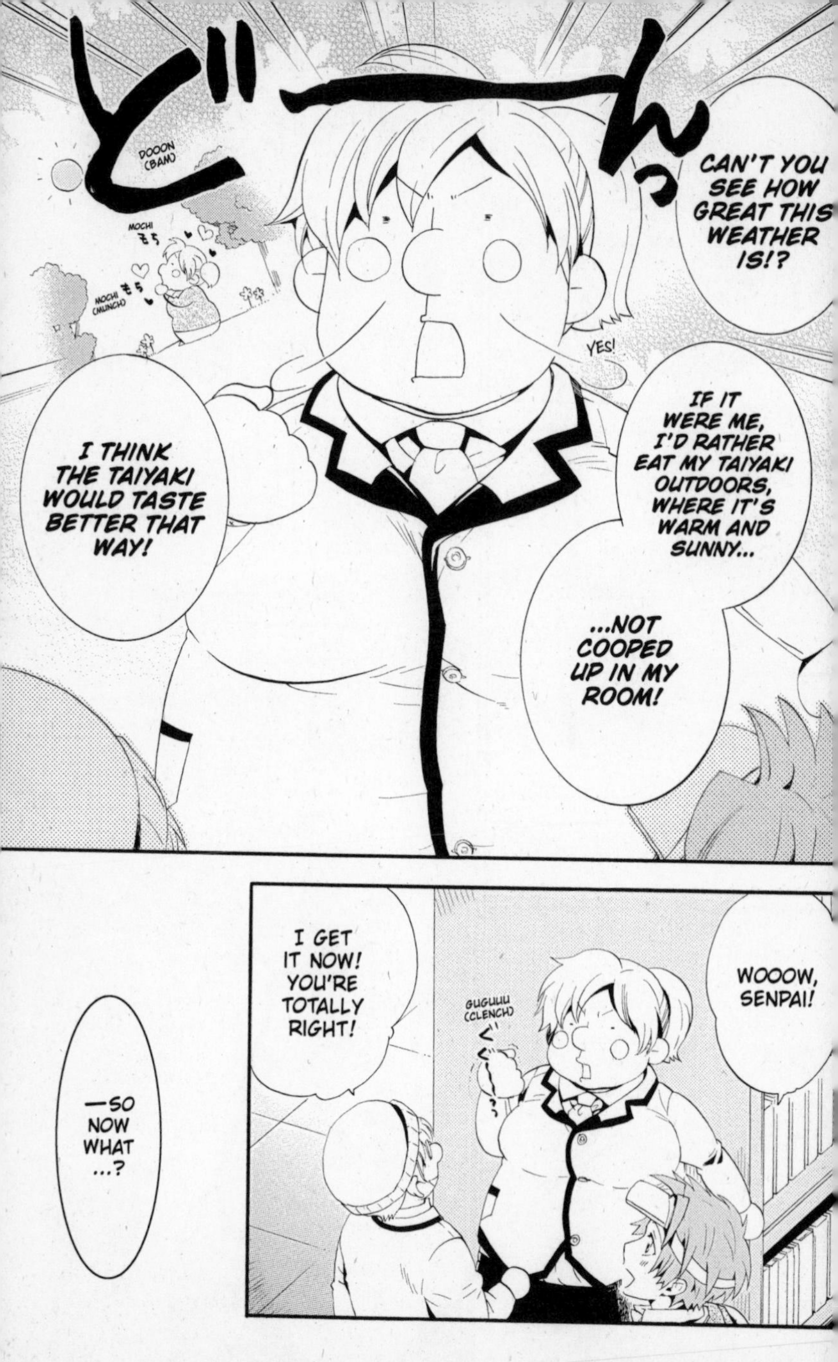
どーんっ
DOOON (BAM)
CAN'T YOU SEE HOW GREAT THIS WEATHER IS!?
MOCHI もち
MOCHI もち (MUNCH)
YES!
IF IT WERE ME, I'D RATHER EAT MY TAIYAKI OUTDOORS, WHERE IT'S WARM AND SUNNY...
...NOT COOPED UP IN MY ROOM!
I THINK THE TAIYAKI WOULD TASTE BETTER THAT WAY!
WOOOW, SENPAI!
GUGUUU (CLENCH)
I GET IT NOW! YOU'RE TOTALLY RIGHT!
—SO NOW WHAT ...?

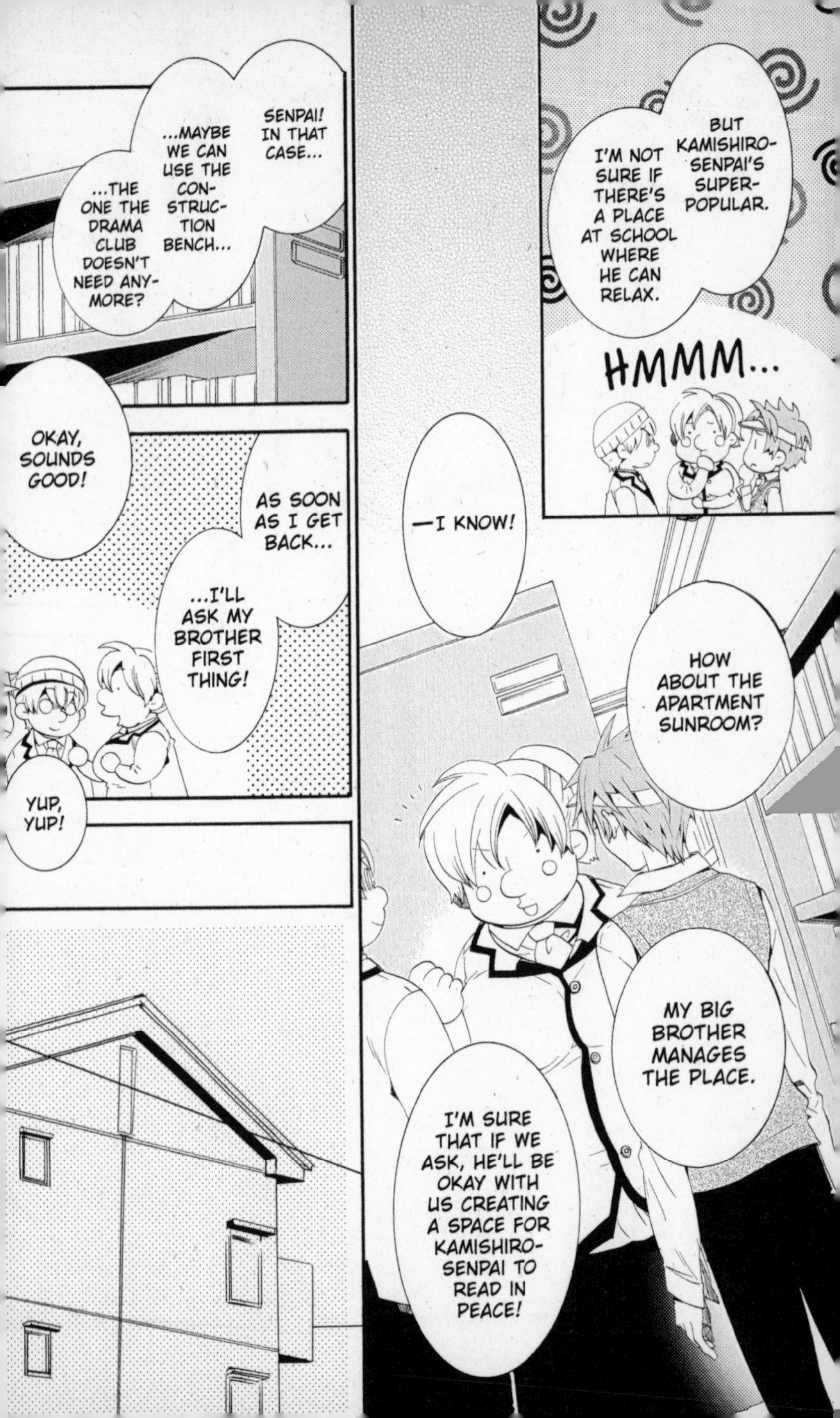
BUT KAMISHIRO-SENPAI'S SUPER-POPULAR.
I'M NOT SURE IF THERE'S A PLACE AT SCHOOL WHERE HE CAN RELAX.
HMMM...
—I KNOW!
HOW ABOUT THE APARTMENT SUNROOM?
MY BIG BROTHER MANAGES THE PLACE.
I'M SURE THAT IF WE ASK, HE'LL BE OKAY WITH US CREATING A SPACE FOR KAMISHIRO-SENPAI TO READ IN PEACE!
SENPAI! IN THAT CASE...
...MAYBE WE CAN USE THE CON-STRUC-TION BENCH...
...THE ONE THE DRAMA CLUB DOESN'T NEED ANY-MORE?
OKAY, SOUNDS GOOD!
AS SOON AS I GET BACK...
...I'LL ASK MY BROTHER FIRST THING!
YUP, YUP!

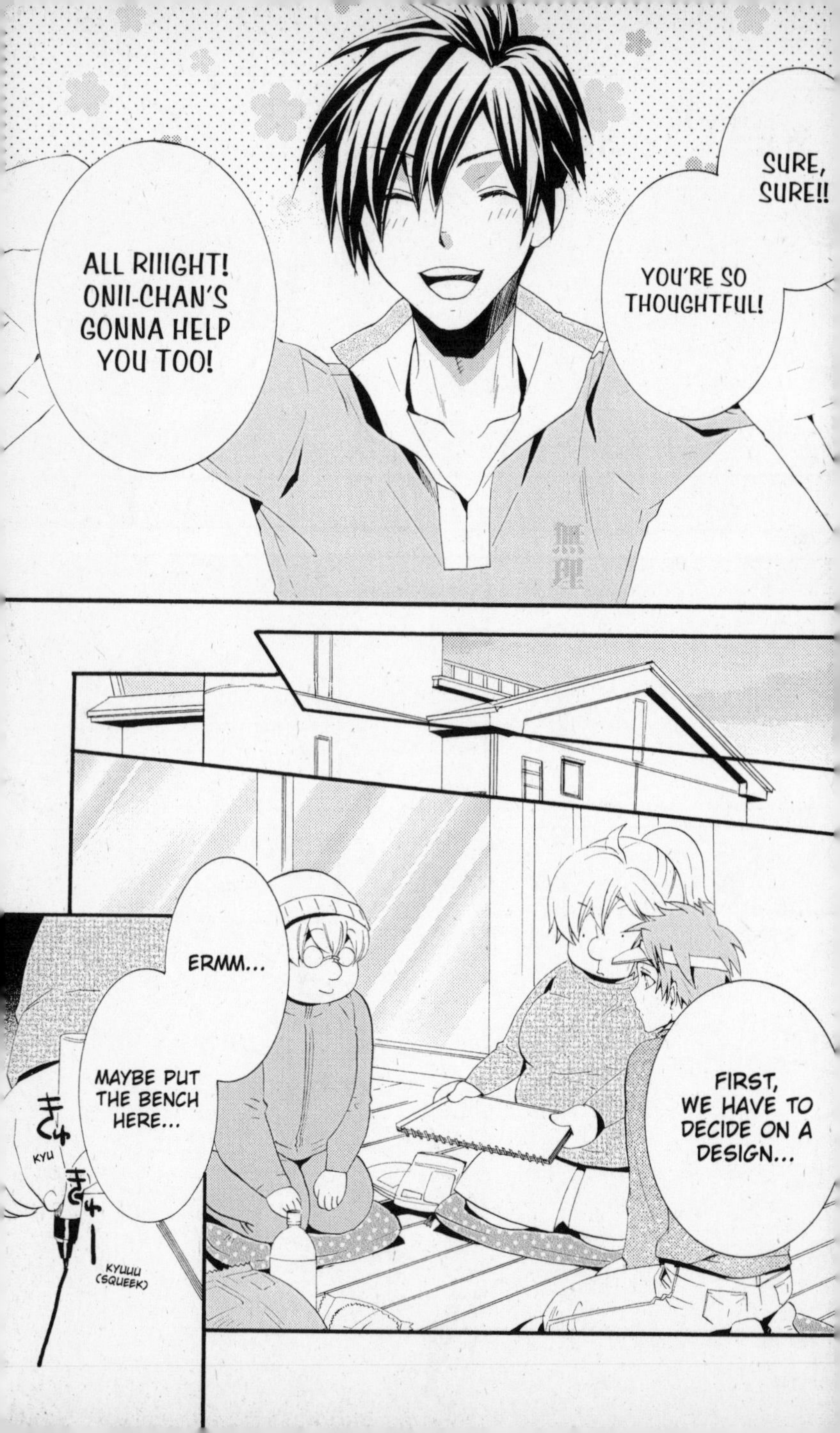
SURE, SURE!!
YOU'RE SO THOUGHTFUL!
ALL RIIIGHT! ONII-CHAN'S GONNA HELP YOU TOO!
無理
FIRST, WE HAVE TO DECIDE ON A DESIGN...
ERMM...
MAYBE PUT THE BENCH HERE...
きゅ
KYU
きゅー
KYUUU (SQUEEK)

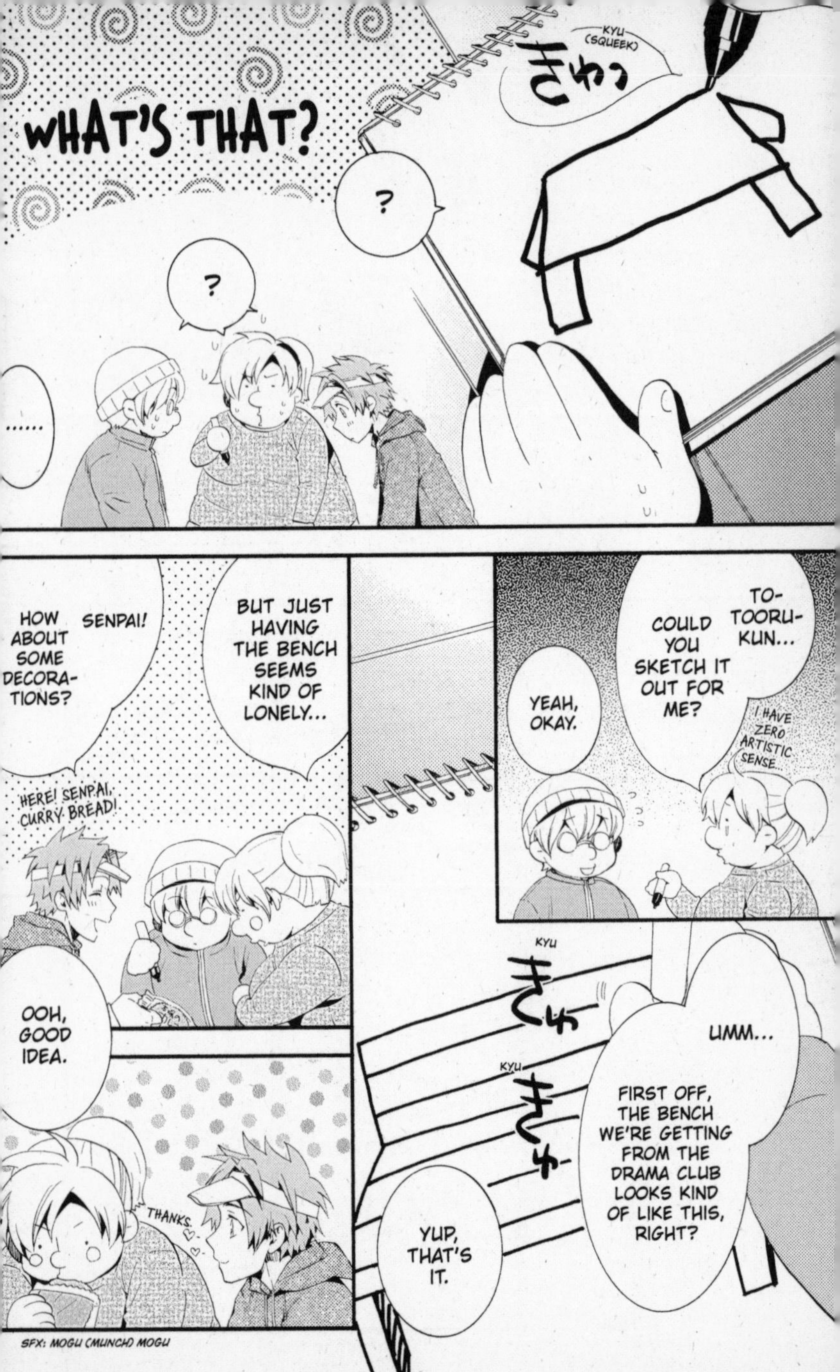
KYU (SQUEEK)
きゅっ
WHAT'S THAT?
?
?
......
TO-TOORU-KUN...
COULD YOU SKETCH IT OUT FOR ME?
I HAVE ZERO ARTISTIC SENSE...
YEAH, OKAY.
BUT JUST HAVING THE BENCH SEEMS KIND OF LONELY...
SENPAI!
HOW ABOUT SOME DECORATIONS?
HERE! SENPAI, CURRY BREAD!
OOH, GOOD IDEA.
KYU
きゅ
KYU
きゅ
UMM...
FIRST OFF, THE BENCH WE'RE GETTING FROM THE DRAMA CLUB LOOKS KIND OF LIKE THIS, RIGHT?
YUP, THAT'S IT.
THANKS.
SFX: MOGU (MUNCH) MOGU

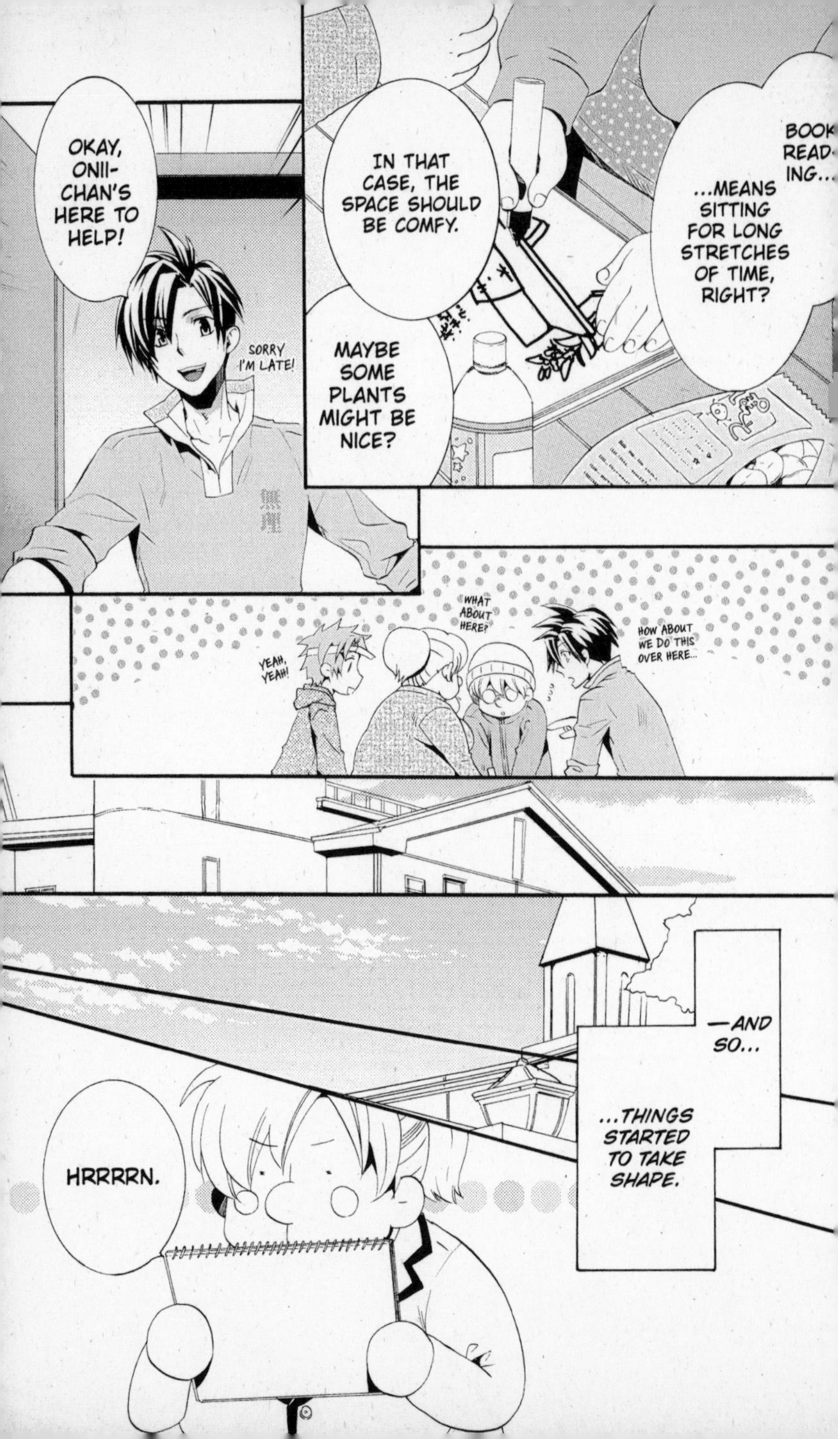
BOOK READ-ING...
...MEANS SITTING FOR LONG STRETCHES OF TIME, RIGHT?
IN THAT CASE, THE SPACE SHOULD BE COMFY.
MAYBE SOME PLANTS MIGHT BE NICE?
OKAY, ONII-CHAN'S HERE TO HELP!
SORRY I'M LATE!
HOW ABOUT WE DO THIS OVER HERE...
WHAT ABOUT HERE?
YEAH, YEAH!
—AND SO...
...THINGS STARTED TO TAKE SHAPE.
HRRRRN.

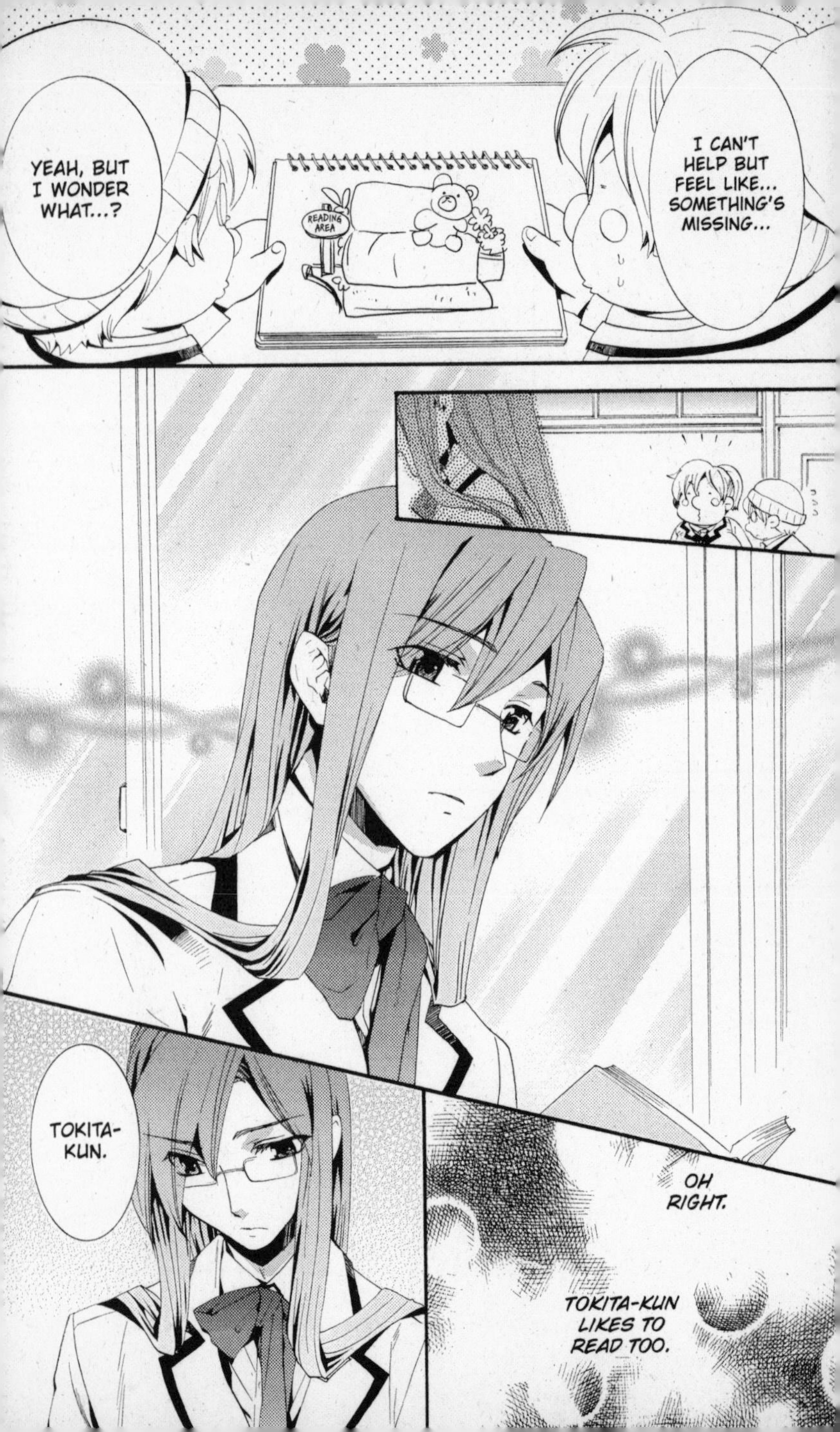
I CAN'T HELP BUT FEEL LIKE... SOMETHING'S MISSING...
READING AREA
YEAH, BUT I WONDER WHAT...?
OH RIGHT.
TOKITA-KUN LIKES TO READ TOO.
TOKITA-KUN.

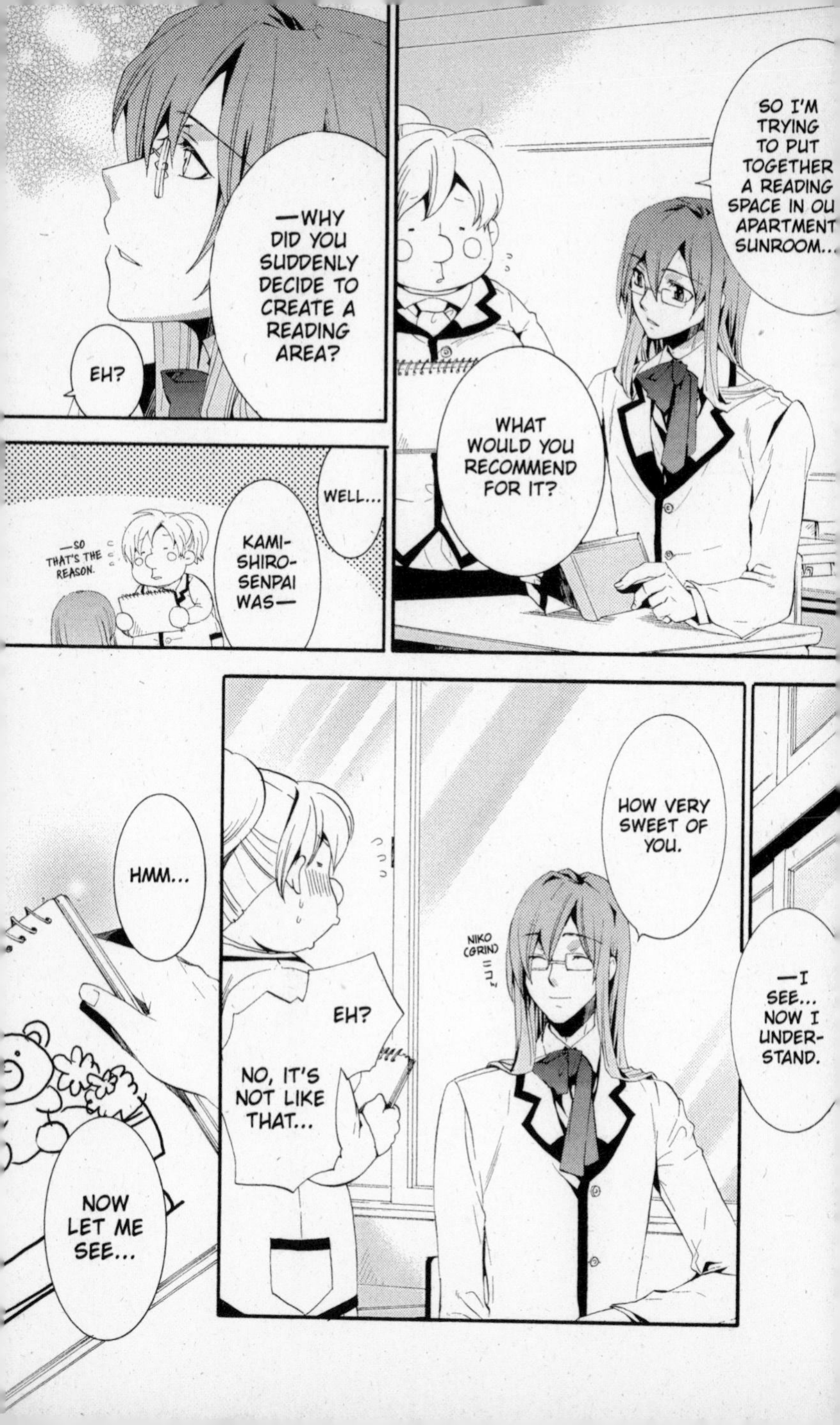
SO I'M TRYING TO PUT TOGETHER A READING SPACE IN OU APARTMENT SUNROOM...
WHAT WOULD YOU RECOMMEND FOR IT?
—WHY DID YOU SUDDENLY DECIDE TO CREATE A READING AREA?
EH?
WELL...
KAMI-SHIRO-SENPAI WAS—
—SO THAT'S THE REASON.
—I SEE... NOW I UNDER-STAND.
HOW VERY SWEET OF YOU.
NIKO (GRIN)
EH?
NO, IT'S NOT LIKE THAT...
HMM...
NOW LET ME SEE...

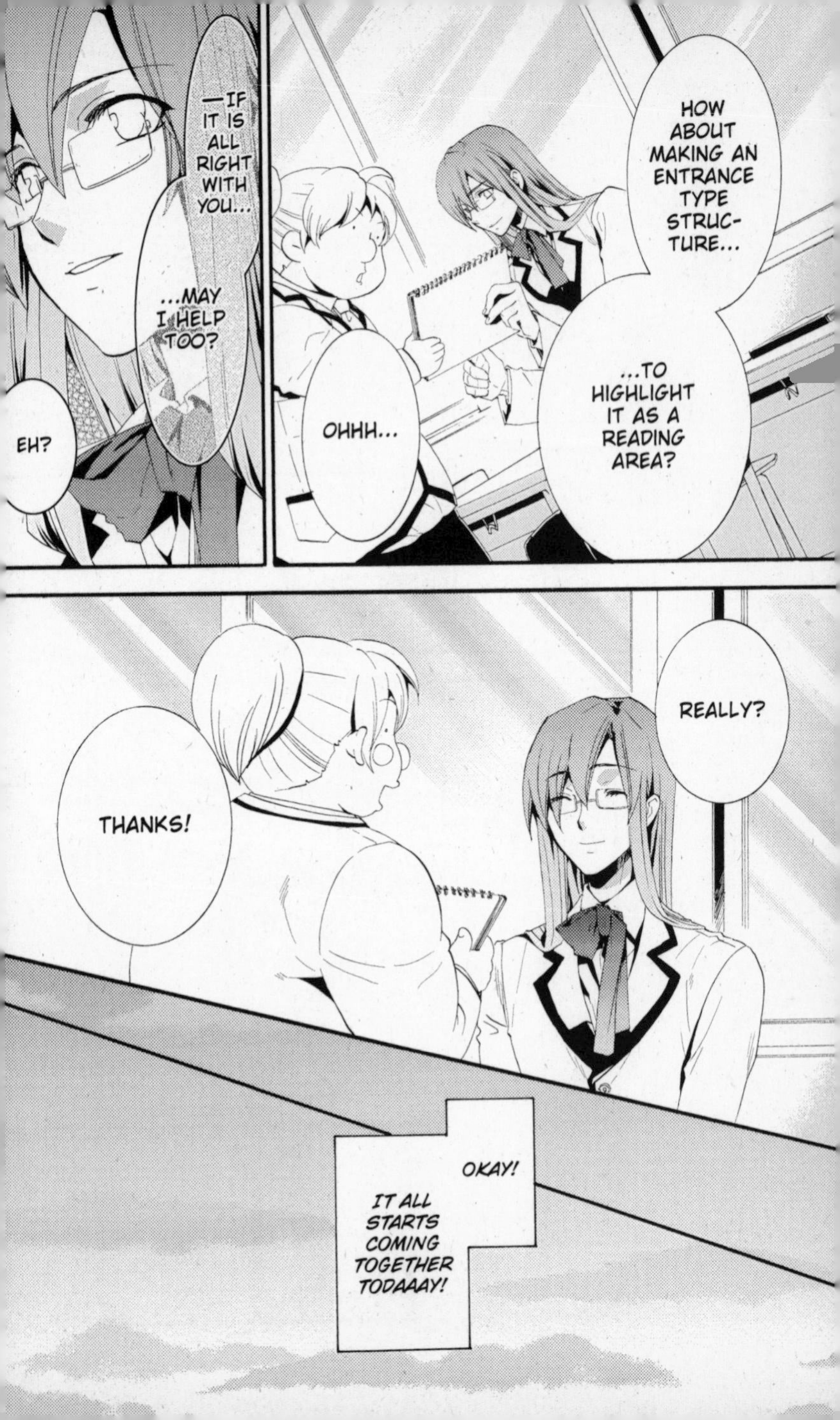
HOW ABOUT MAKING AN ENTRANCE TYPE STRUCTURE...
...TO HIGHLIGHT IT AS A READING AREA?
OHHH...
—IF IT IS ALL RIGHT WITH YOU...
...MAY I HELP TOO?
EH?
REALLY?
THANKS!
OKAY!
IT ALL STARTS COMING TOGETHER TODAAAY!

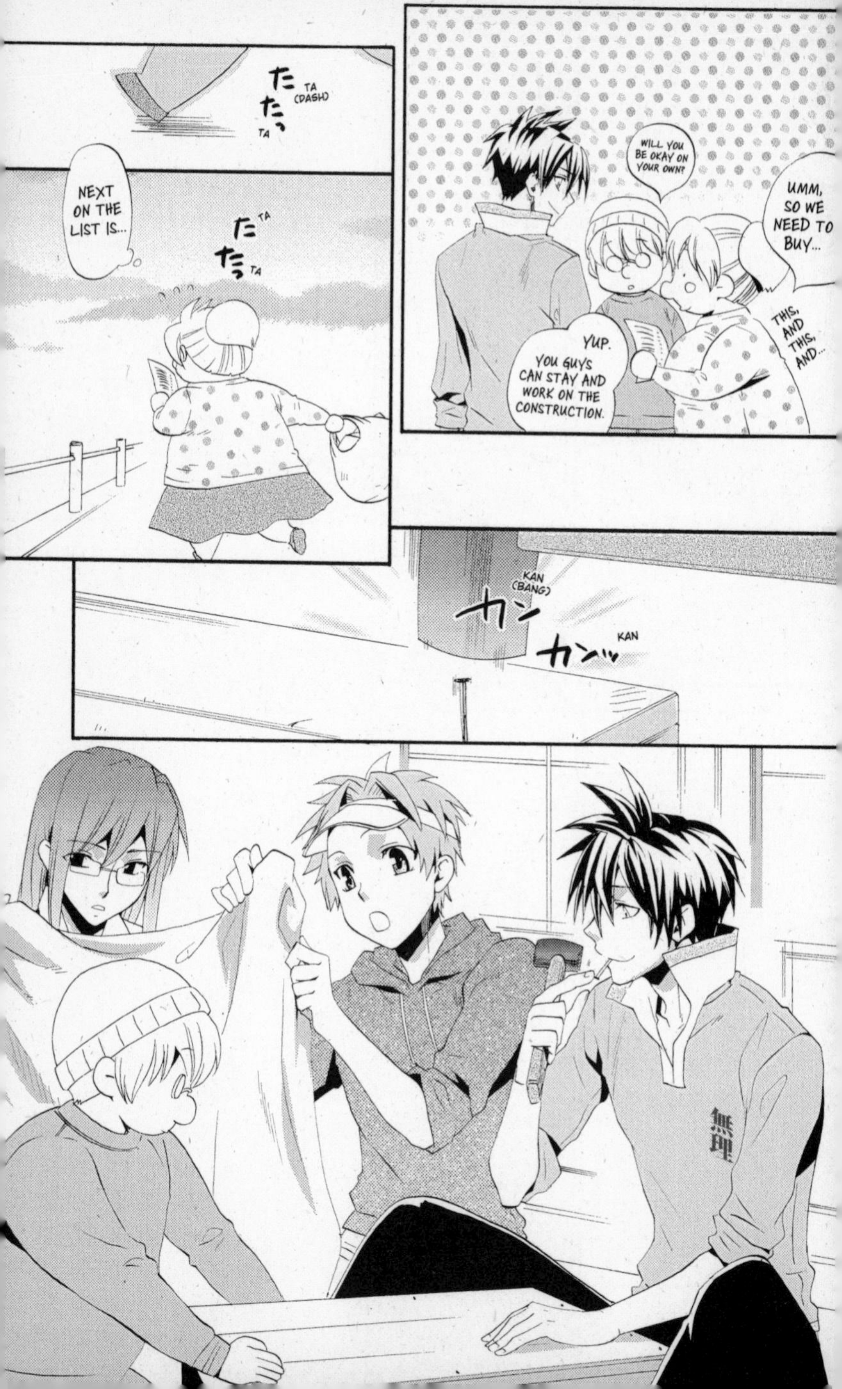
UMM, SO WE NEED TO BUY...
WILL YOU BE OKAY ON YOUR OWN?
THIS, AND THIS, AND...
YUP. YOU GUYS CAN STAY AND WORK ON THE CONSTRUCTION.
たた
TA (DASH)
TA
NEXT ON THE LIST IS...
たた
TA
TA
カン
KAN (BANG)
カンッ
KAN

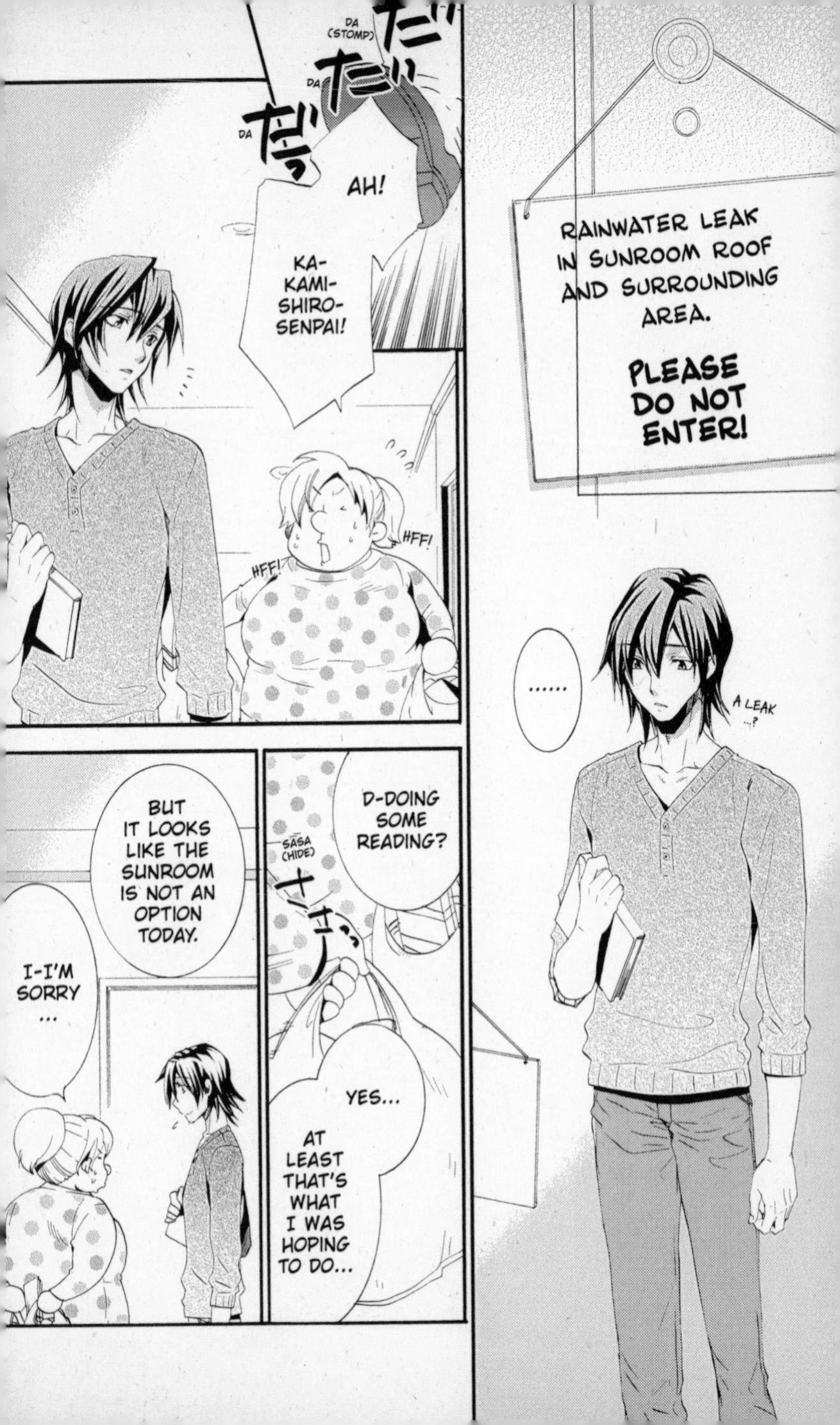

RAINWATER LEAK IN SUNROOM ROOF AND SURROUNDING AREA.
PLEASE DO NOT ENTER!
......
A LEAK ...?
DA (STOMP)
DA
DA
AH!
KA-KAMI-SHIRO-SENPAI!
HFF!
HFF!
D-DOING SOME READING?
SASA (HIDE)
YES...
AT LEAST THAT'S WHAT I WAS HOPING TO DO...
BUT IT LOOKS LIKE THE SUNROOM IS NOT AN OPTION TODAY.
I-I'M SORRY ...

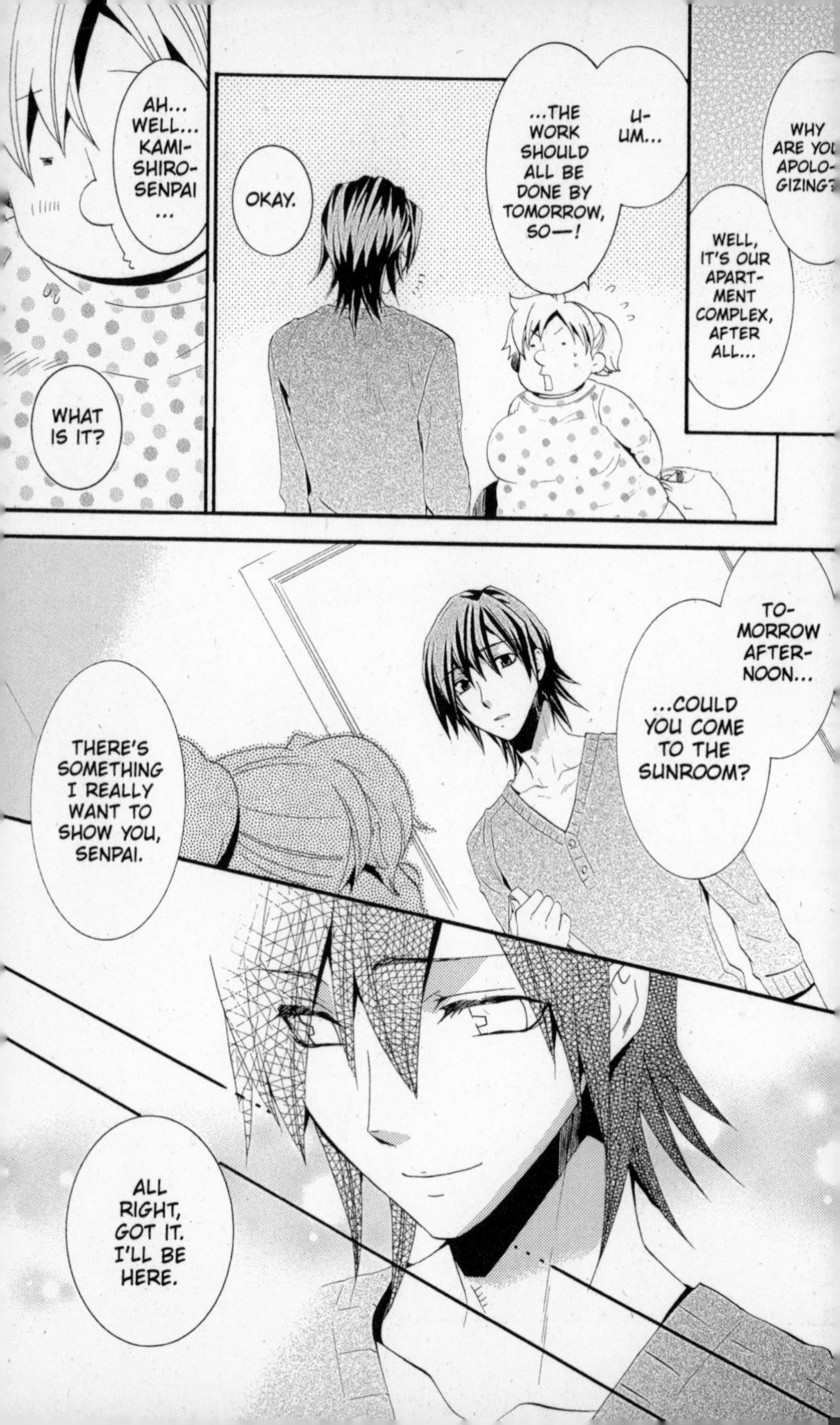
WHY ARE YOU APOLOGIZING?
WELL, IT'S OUR APARTMENT COMPLEX, AFTER ALL...
U-UM...
...THE WORK SHOULD ALL BE DONE BY TOMORROW, SO—!
OKAY.
AH... WELL... KAMISHIRO-SENPAI...
WHAT IS IT?
TOMORROW AFTERNOON...
...COULD YOU COME TO THE SUNROOM?
THERE'S SOMETHING I REALLY WANT TO SHOW YOU, SENPAI.
ALL RIGHT, GOT IT. I'LL BE HERE.

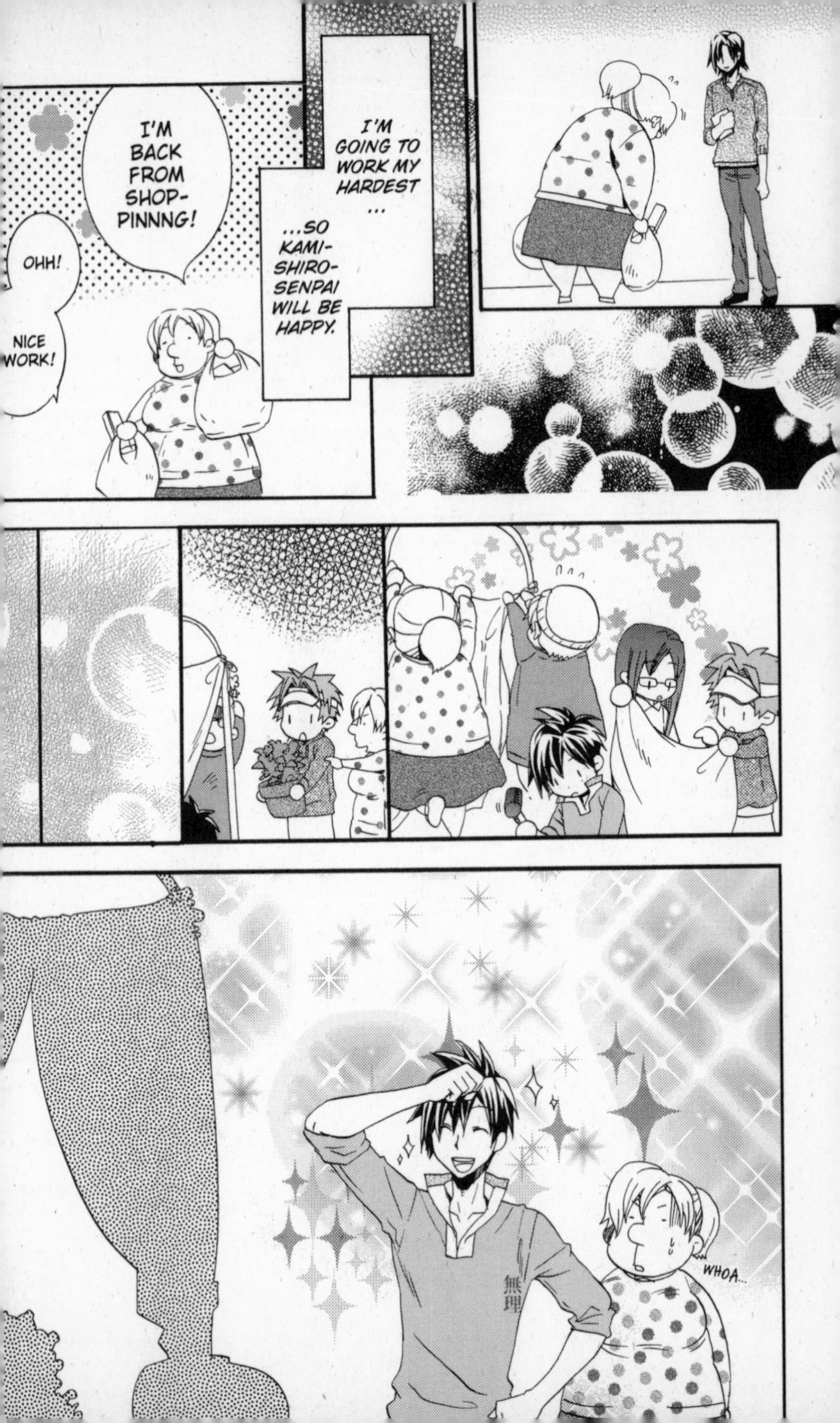
I'M GOING TO WORK MY HARDEST...
...SO KAMI-SHIRO-SENPAI WILL BE HAPPY.
I'M BACK FROM SHOP-PINNNG!
OHH!
NICE WORK!
WHOA...
無理

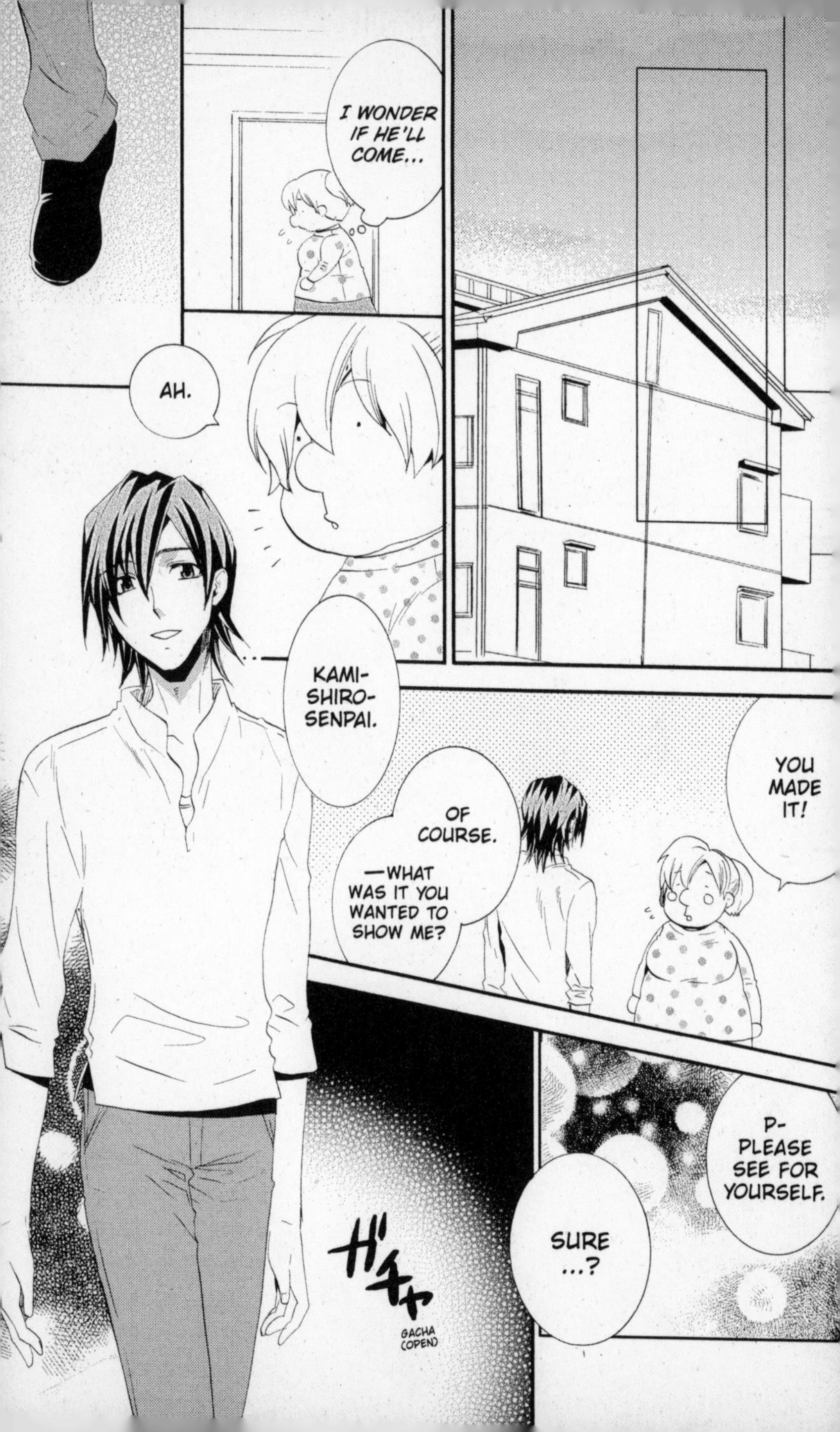
I WONDER IF HE'LL COME...
AH.
KAMI-SHIRO-SENPAI.
YOU MADE IT!
OF COURSE.
—WHAT WAS IT YOU WANTED TO SHOW ME?
P-PLEASE SEE FOR YOURSELF.
SURE ...?
ガチャ
GACHA (OPEN)

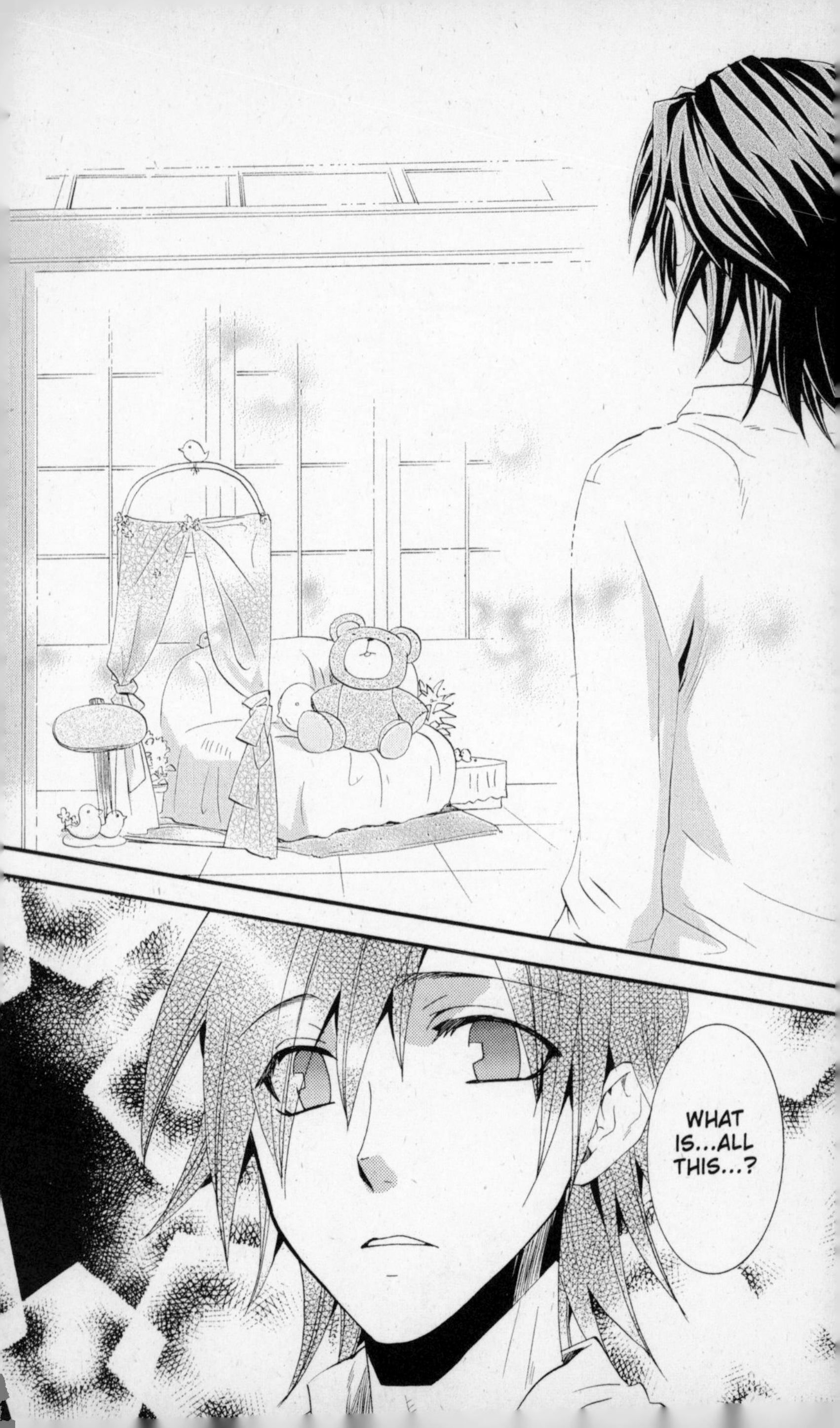
WHAT IS...ALL THIS...?

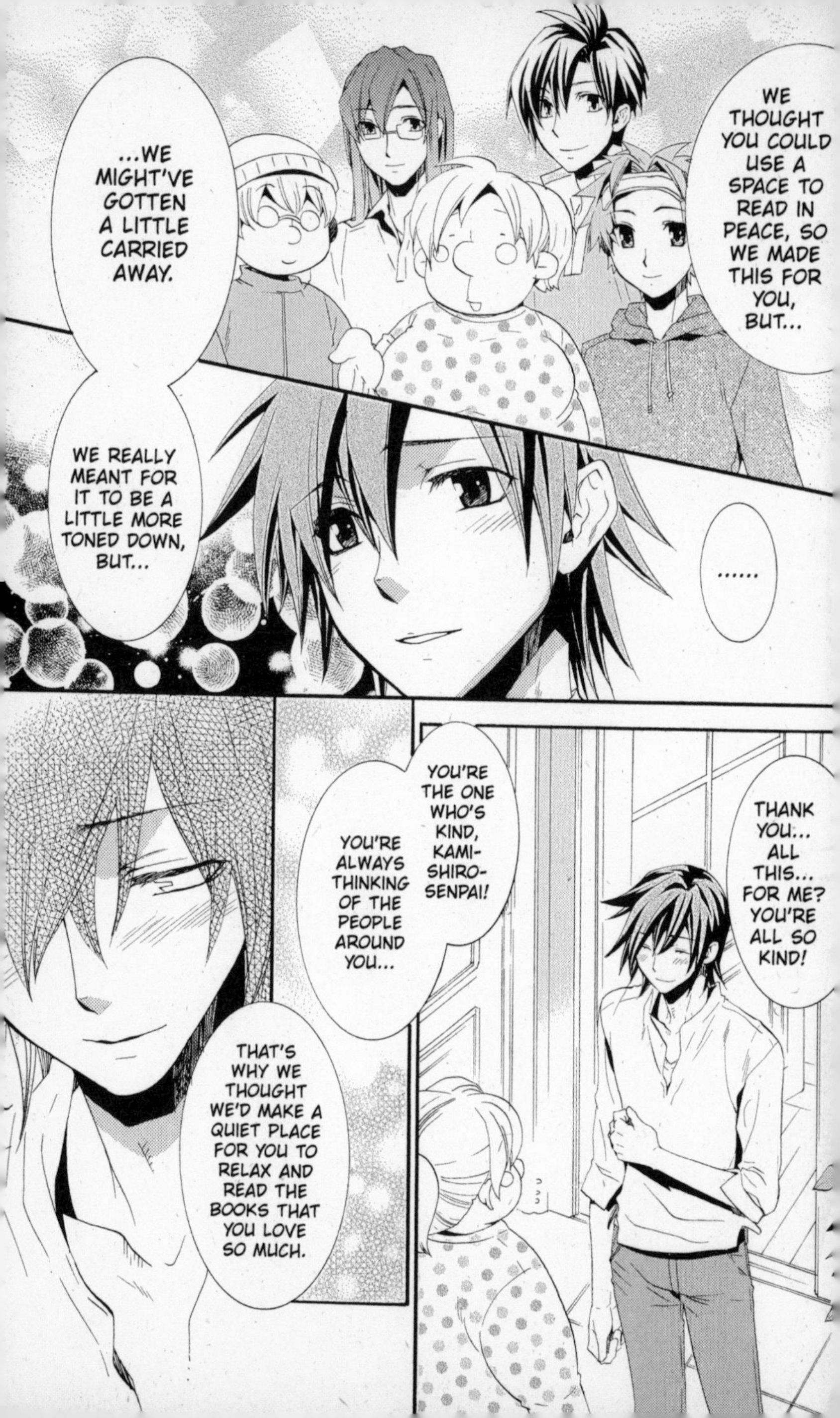
WE THOUGHT YOU COULD USE A SPACE TO READ IN PEACE, SO WE MADE THIS FOR YOU, BUT...
...WE MIGHT'VE GOTTEN A LITTLE CARRIED AWAY.
WE REALLY MEANT FOR IT TO BE A LITTLE MORE TONED DOWN, BUT...
......
THANK YOU... ALL THIS... FOR ME? YOU'RE ALL SO KIND!
YOU'RE THE ONE WHO'S KIND, KAMI-SHIRO-SENPAI!
YOU'RE ALWAYS THINKING OF THE PEOPLE AROUND YOU...
THAT'S WHY WE THOUGHT WE'D MAKE A QUIET PLACE FOR YOU TO RELAX AND READ THE BOOKS THAT YOU LOVE SO MUCH.

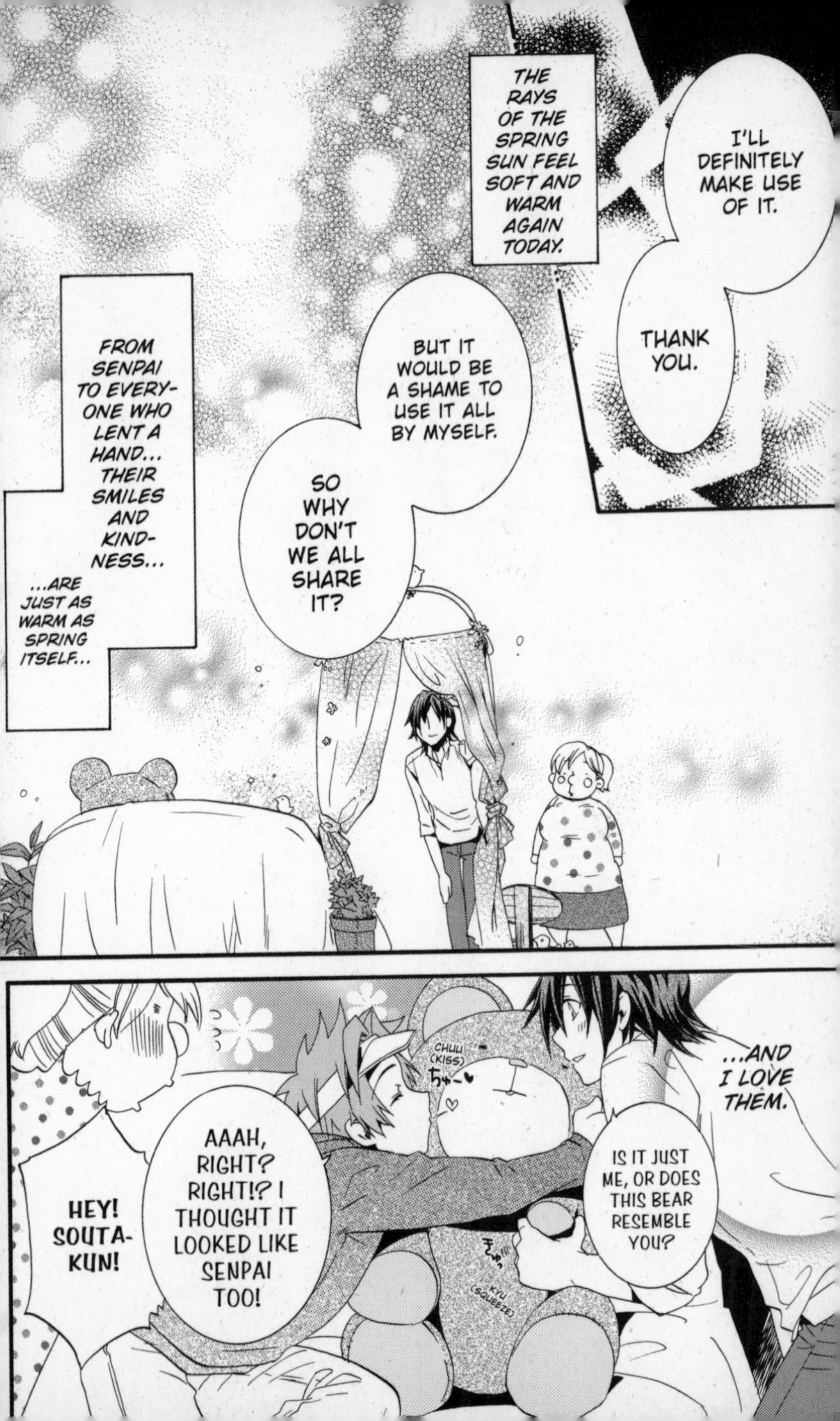
I'LL DEFINITELY MAKE USE OF IT.
THANK YOU.
THE RAYS OF THE SPRING SUN FEEL SOFT AND WARM AGAIN TODAY.
BUT IT WOULD BE A SHAME TO USE IT ALL BY MYSELF.
SO WHY DON'T WE ALL SHARE IT?
FROM SENPAI TO EVERY-ONE WHO LENT A HAND... THEIR SMILES AND KIND-NESS...
...ARE JUST AS WARM AS SPRING ITSELF...
...AND I LOVE THEM.
IS IT JUST ME, OR DOES THIS BEAR RESEMBLE YOU?
CHUU (KISS)
KYU (SQUEEZE)
AAAH, RIGHT? RIGHT!? I THOUGHT IT LOOKED LIKE SENPAI TOO!
HEY! SOUTA-KUN!

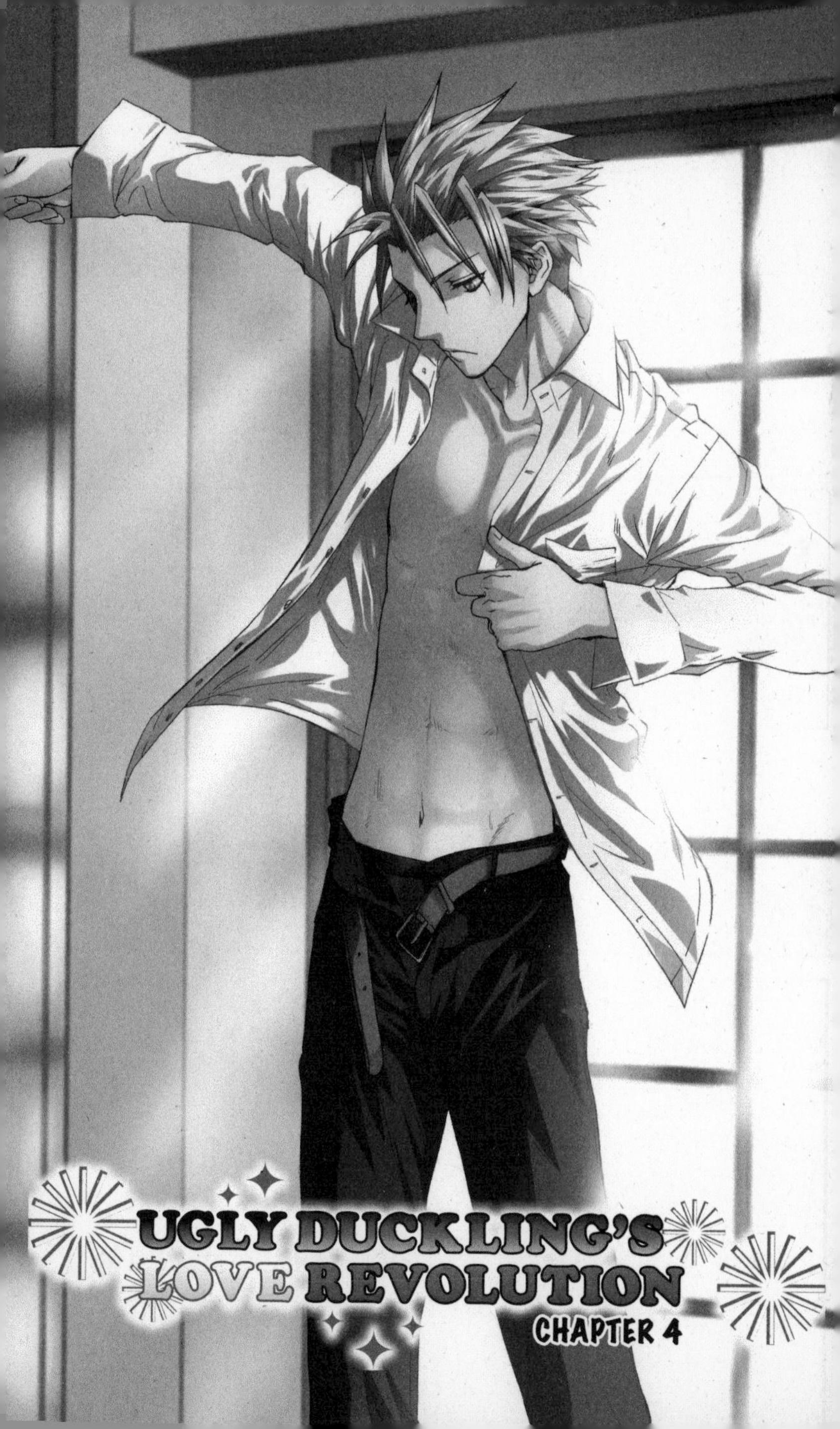
UGLY DUCKLING'S LOVE REVOLUTION
CHAPTER 4

KAEDE

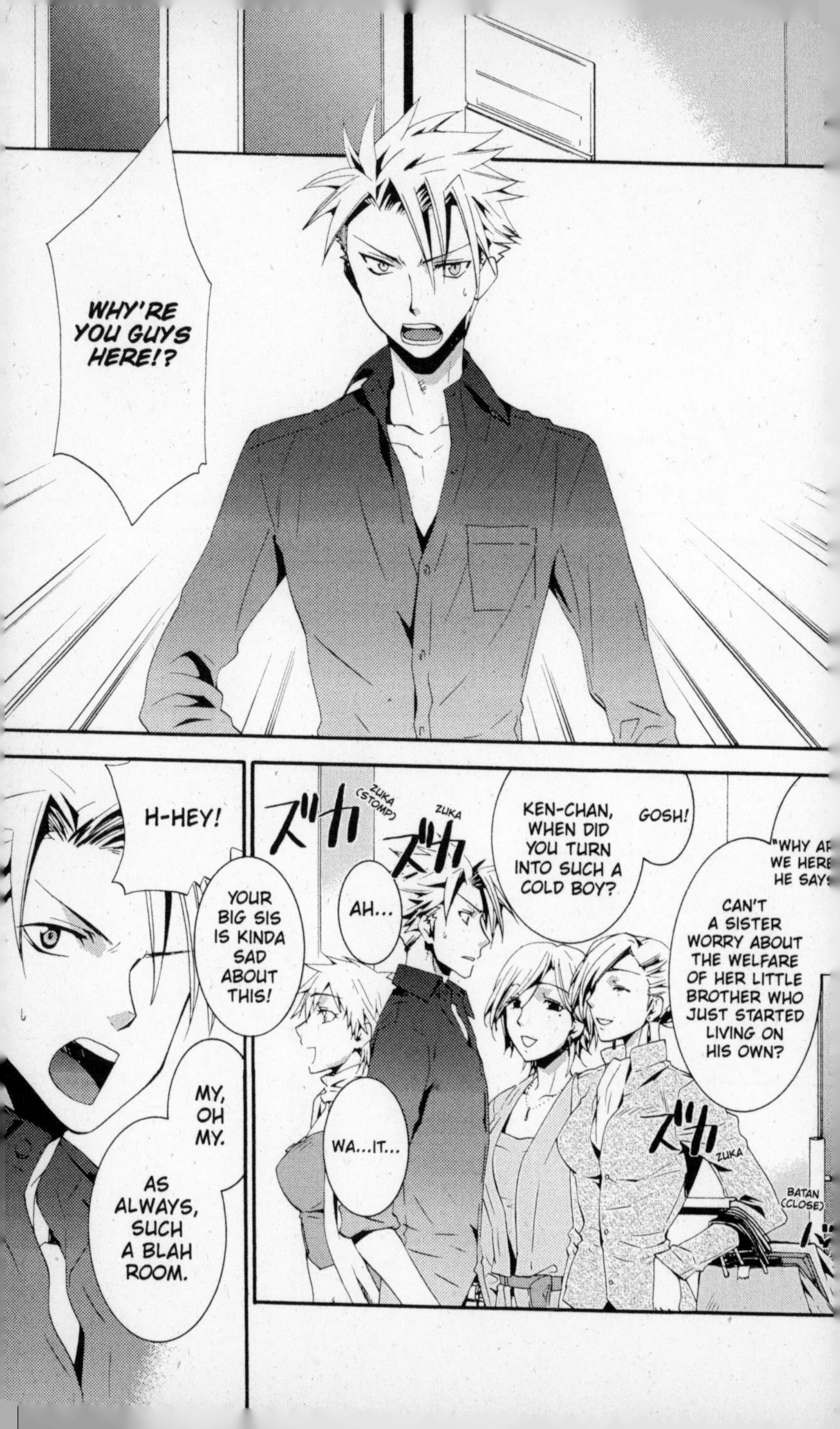

WHY'RE YOU GUYS HERE!?
"WHY AR WE HER HE SAYS
CAN'T A SISTER WORRY ABOUT THE WELFARE OF HER LITTLE BROTHER WHO JUST STARTED LIVING ON HIS OWN?
GOSH!
KEN-CHAN, WHEN DID YOU TURN INTO SUCH A COLD BOY?
ZUKA
ZUKA (STOMP)
AH...
YOUR BIG SIS IS KINDA SAD ABOUT THIS!
ZUKA
BATAN (CLOSE)
WA...IT...
H-HEY!
MY, OH MY.
AS ALWAYS, SUCH A BLAH ROOM.

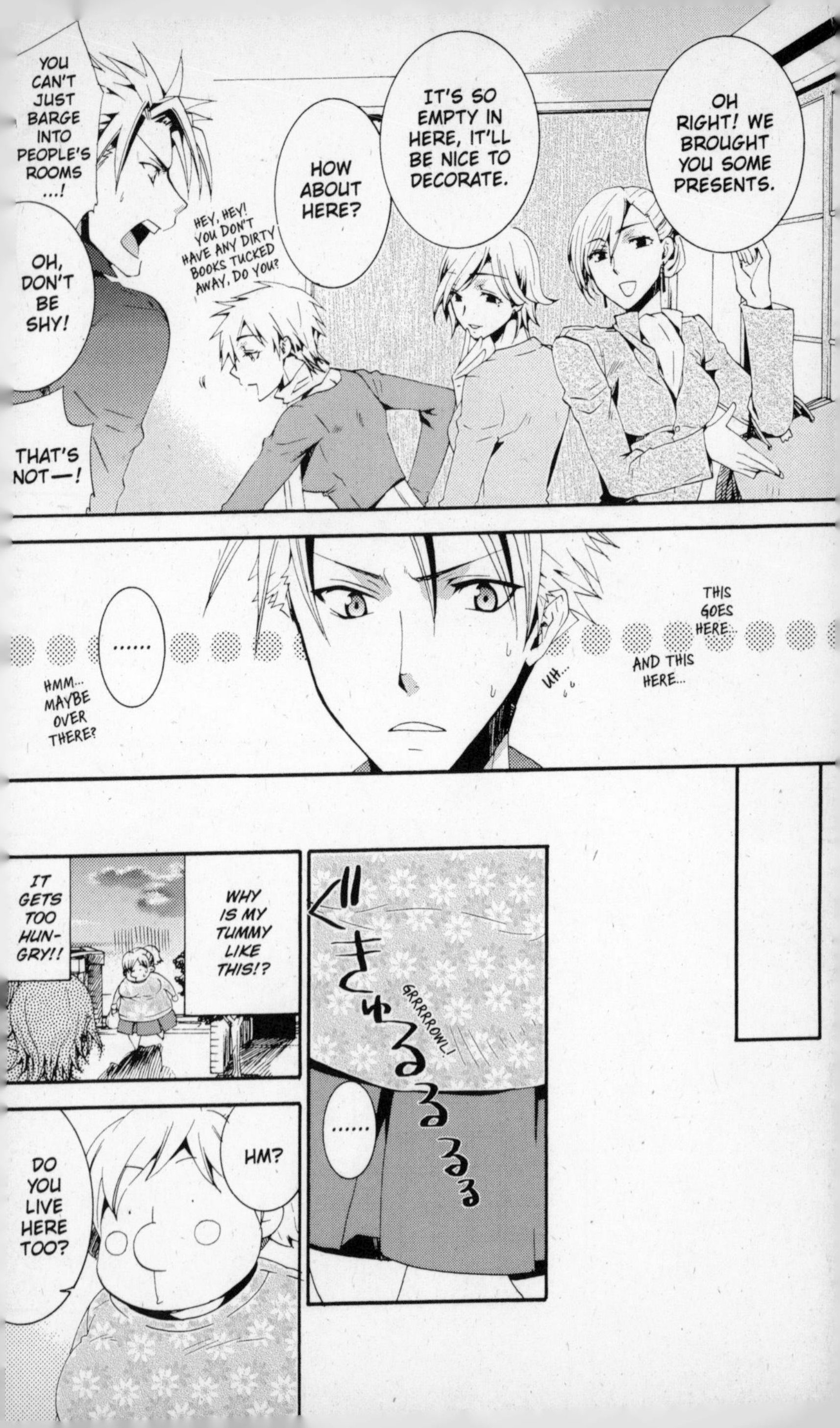
OH RIGHT! WE BROUGHT YOU SOME PRESENTS.
IT'S SO EMPTY IN HERE, IT'LL BE NICE TO DECORATE.
HOW ABOUT HERE?
HEY, HEY! YOU DON'T HAVE ANY DIRTY BOOKS TUCKED AWAY, DO YOU?
YOU CAN'T JUST BARGE INTO PEOPLE'S ROOMS ...!
OH, DON'T BE SHY!
THAT'S NOT—!
THIS GOES HERE...
AND THIS HERE...
UH...
......
HMM... MAYBE OVER THERE?
ぐきゅるるるる
GRRRRROWL!
......
WHY IS MY TUMMY LIKE THIS!?
IT GETS TOO HUN-GRY!!
HM?
DO YOU LIVE HERE TOO?

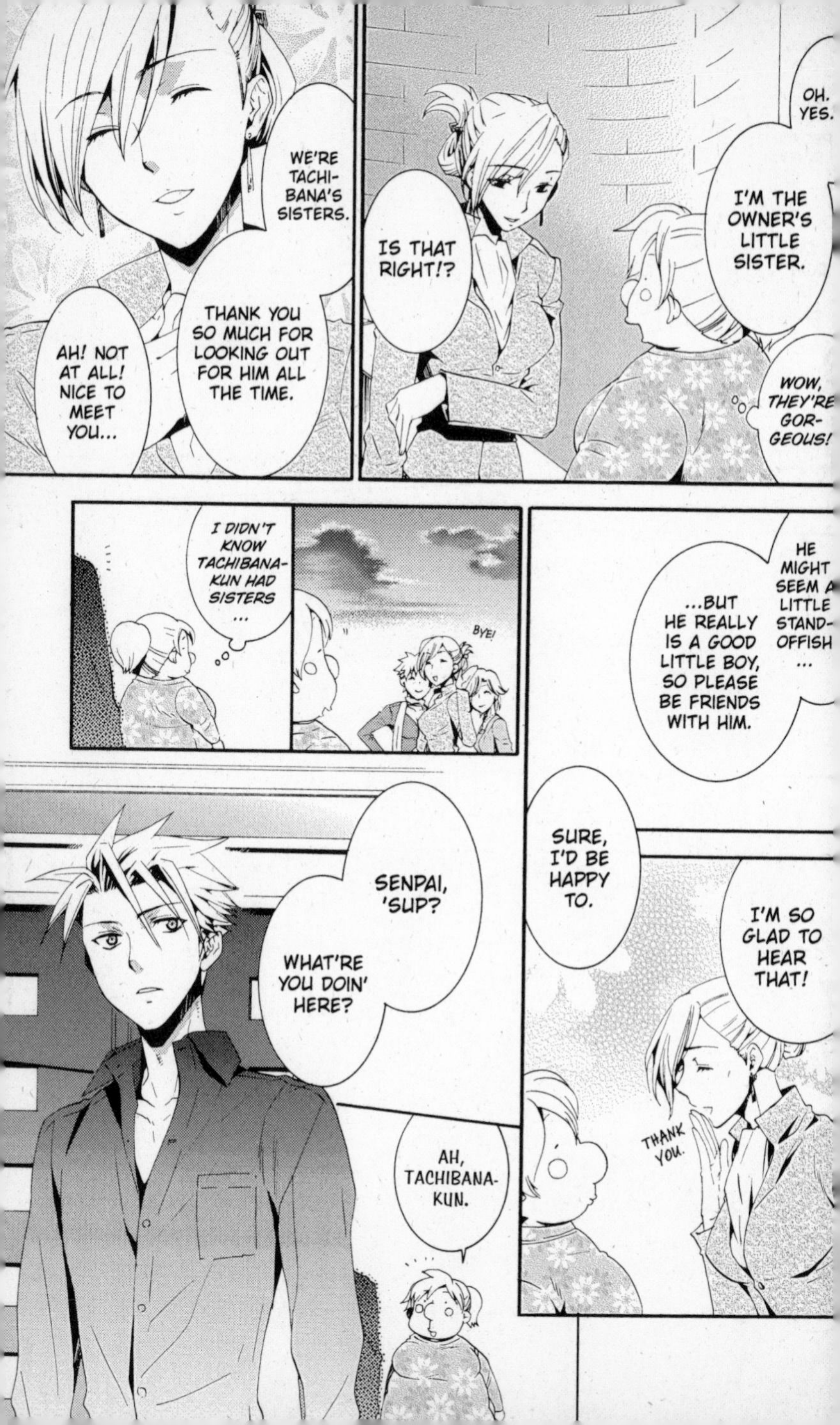
OH. YES.
I'M THE OWNER'S LITTLE SISTER.
WOW, THEY'RE GORGEOUS!
IS THAT RIGHT!?
WE'RE TACHIBANA'S SISTERS.
THANK YOU SO MUCH FOR LOOKING OUT FOR HIM ALL THE TIME.
AH! NOT AT ALL! NICE TO MEET YOU...
HE MIGHT SEEM A LITTLE STAND-OFFISH...
...BUT HE REALLY IS A GOOD LITTLE BOY, SO PLEASE BE FRIENDS WITH HIM.
SURE, I'D BE HAPPY TO.
I'M SO GLAD TO HEAR THAT!
THANK YOU.
BYE!
I DIDN'T KNOW TACHIBANA-KUN HAD SISTERS...
SENPAI, 'SUP?
WHAT'RE YOU DOIN' HERE?
AH, TACHIBANA-KUN.

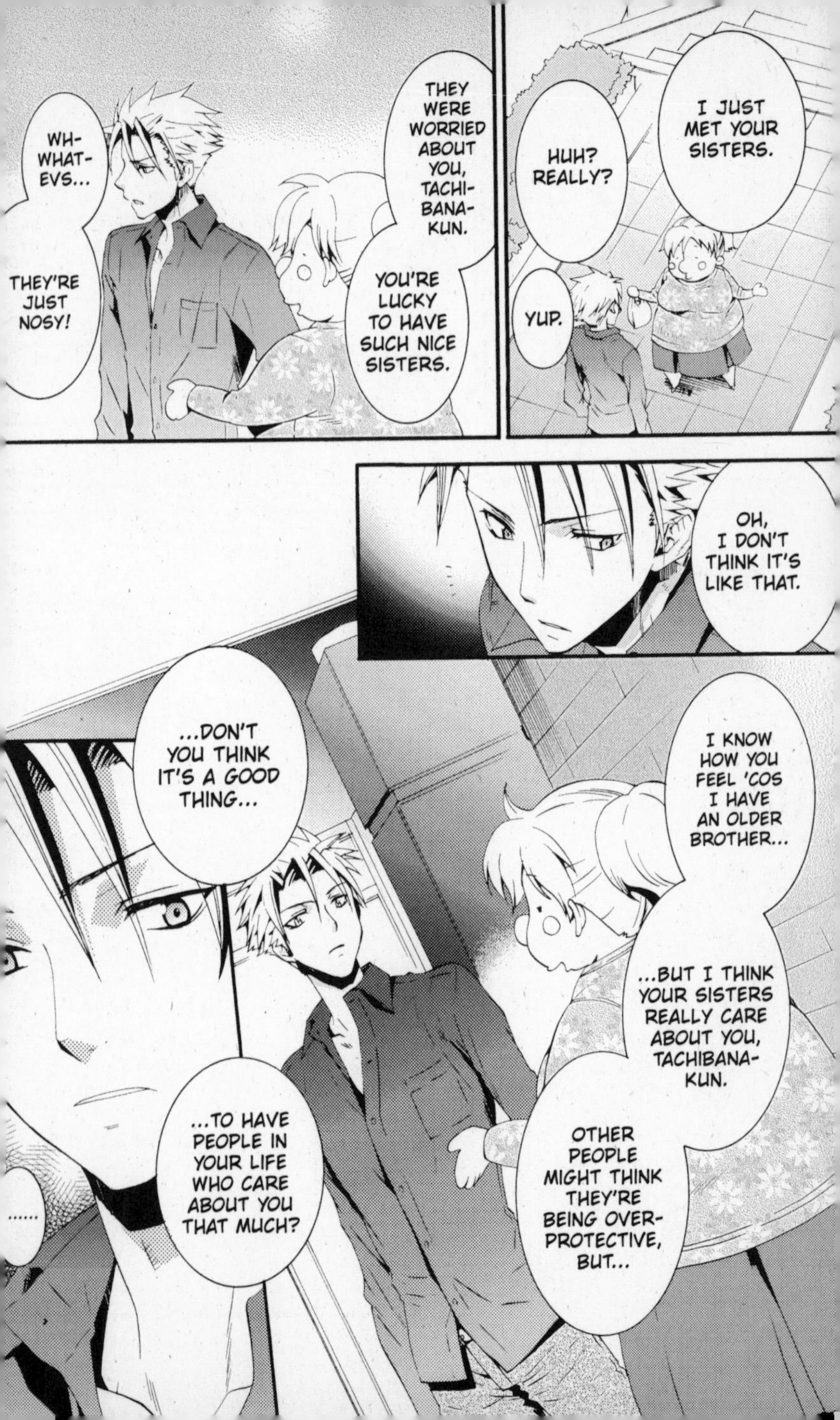
I JUST MET YOUR SISTERS.
HUH? REALLY?
YUP.
THEY WERE WORRIED ABOUT YOU, TACHIBANA-KUN.
YOU'RE LUCKY TO HAVE SUCH NICE SISTERS.
WH-WHATEVS...
THEY'RE JUST NOSY!
OH, I DON'T THINK IT'S LIKE THAT.
I KNOW HOW YOU FEEL 'COS I HAVE AN OLDER BROTHER...
...BUT I THINK YOUR SISTERS REALLY CARE ABOUT YOU, TACHIBANA-KUN.
OTHER PEOPLE MIGHT THINK THEY'RE BEING OVER-PROTECTIVE, BUT...
...DON'T YOU THINK IT'S A GOOD THING...
...TO HAVE PEOPLE IN YOUR LIFE WHO CARE ABOUT YOU THAT MUCH?
......

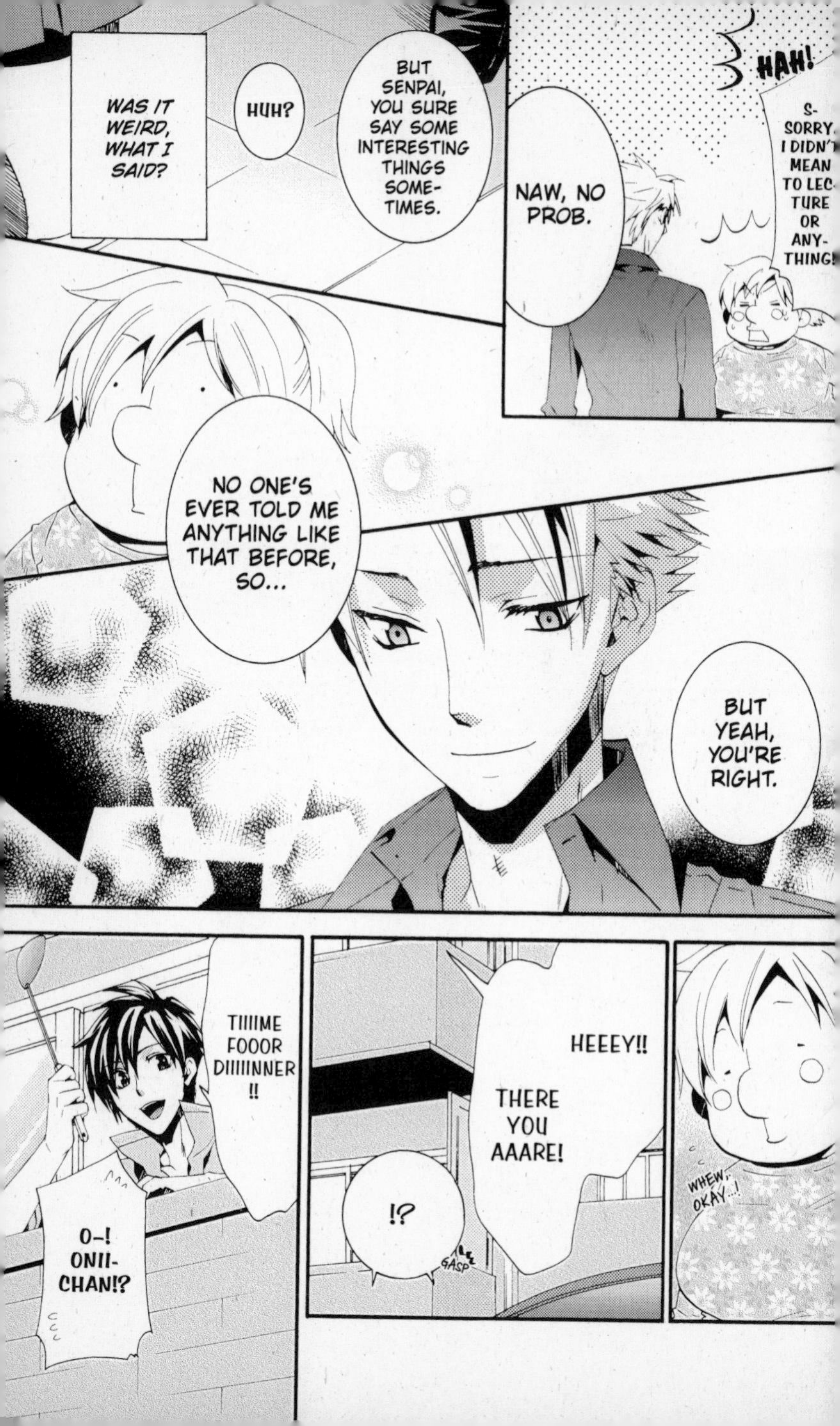
HAH!
S-SORRY. I DIDN'T MEAN TO LECTURE OR ANYTHING!
NAW, NO PROB.
BUT SENPAI, YOU SURE SAY SOME INTERESTING THINGS SOME-TIMES.
HUH?
WAS IT WEIRD, WHAT I SAID?
NO ONE'S EVER TOLD ME ANYTHING LIKE THAT BEFORE, SO...
BUT YEAH, YOU'RE RIGHT.
WHEW, OKAY...!
HEEEY!!
THERE YOU AAARE!
!?
GASP
TIIIIME FOOOR DIIIIINNER!!
O-! ONII-CHAN!?

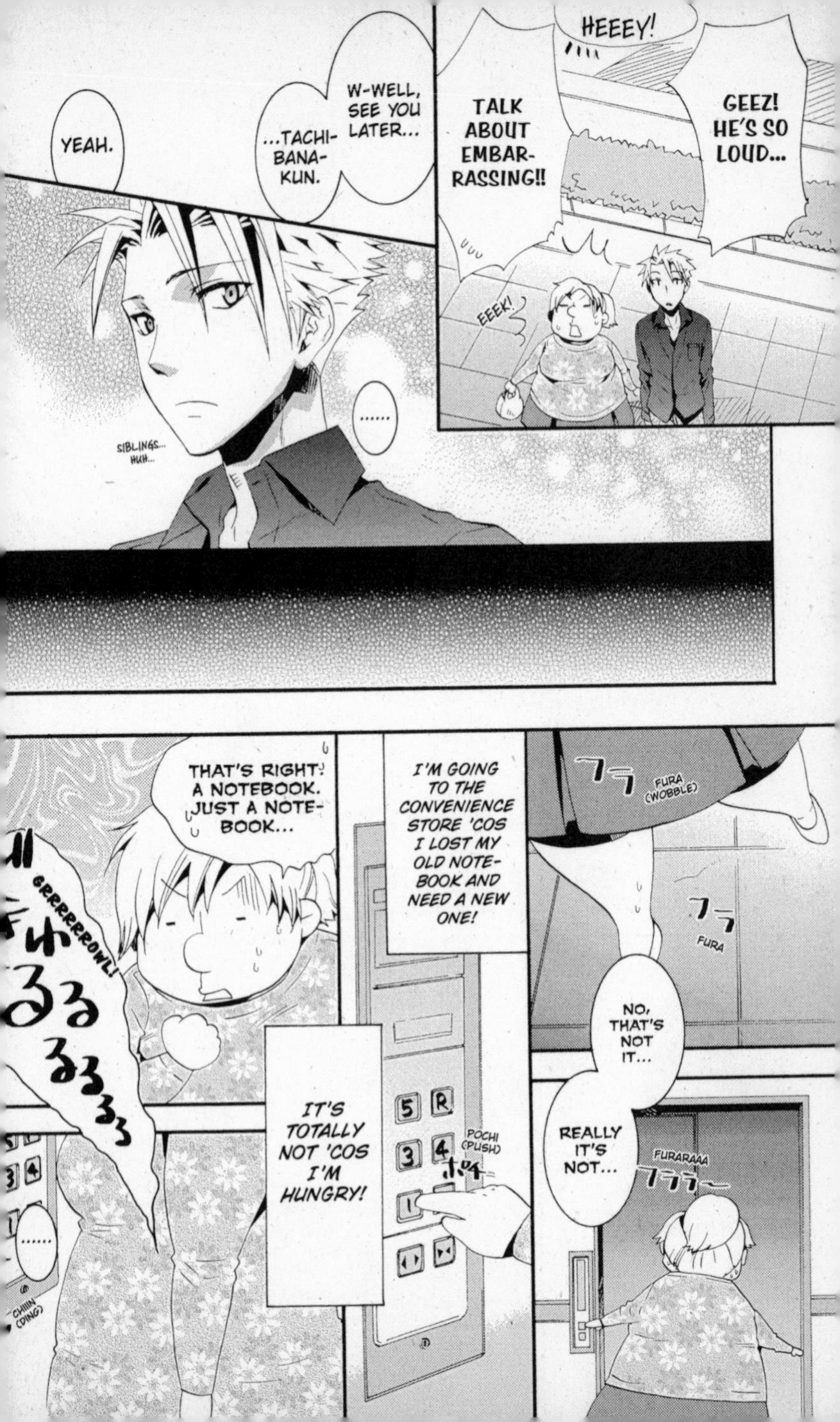
HEEEY!
GEEZ! HE'S SO LOUD...
TALK ABOUT EMBARRASSING!!
EEEK!
W-WELL, SEE YOU LATER...
...TACHIBANA-KUN.
YEAH.
......
SIBLINGS... HUH...
FURA (WOBBLE)
FURA
NO, THAT'S NOT IT...
REALLY IT'S NOT...
FURARAAA
I'M GOING TO THE CONVENIENCE STORE 'COS I LOST MY OLD NOTEBOOK AND NEED A NEW ONE!
IT'S TOTALLY NOT 'COS I'M HUNGRY!
POCHI (PUSH)
THAT'S RIGHT. A NOTEBOOK. JUST A NOTEBOOK...
GRRRRRROWL!
......
CHIIIN (DING)

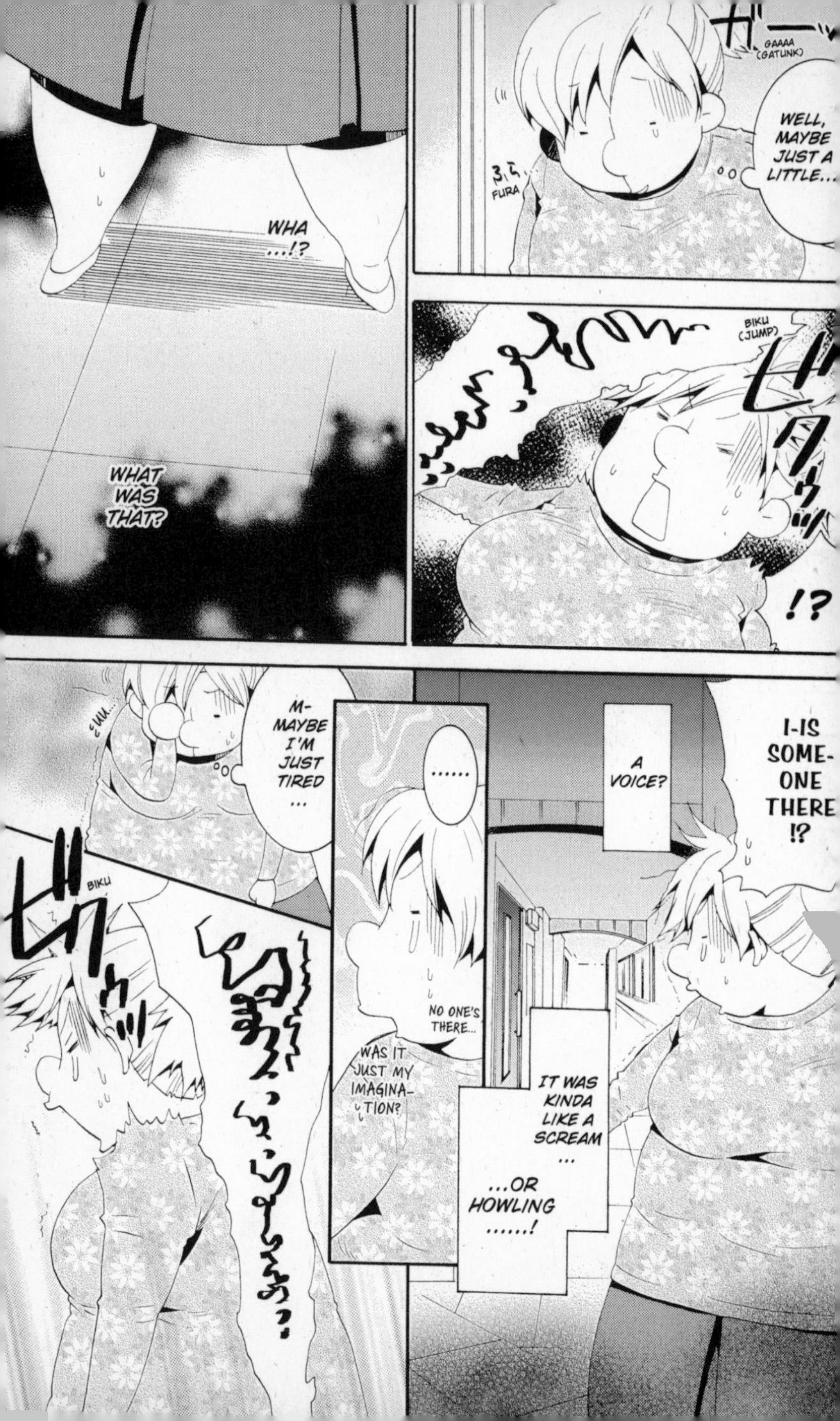
GAAAA (GATUNK)
WELL, MAYBE JUST A LITTLE...
FURA
BIKU (JUMP)
!?
WHA ...!?
WHAT WAS THAT?
I-IS SOMEONE THERE!?
A VOICE?
IT WAS KINDA LIKE A SCREAM...
...OR HOWLING......!
......
NO ONE'S THERE...
WAS IT JUST MY IMAGINATION?
UUU...
M-MAYBE I'M JUST TIRED...
BIKU

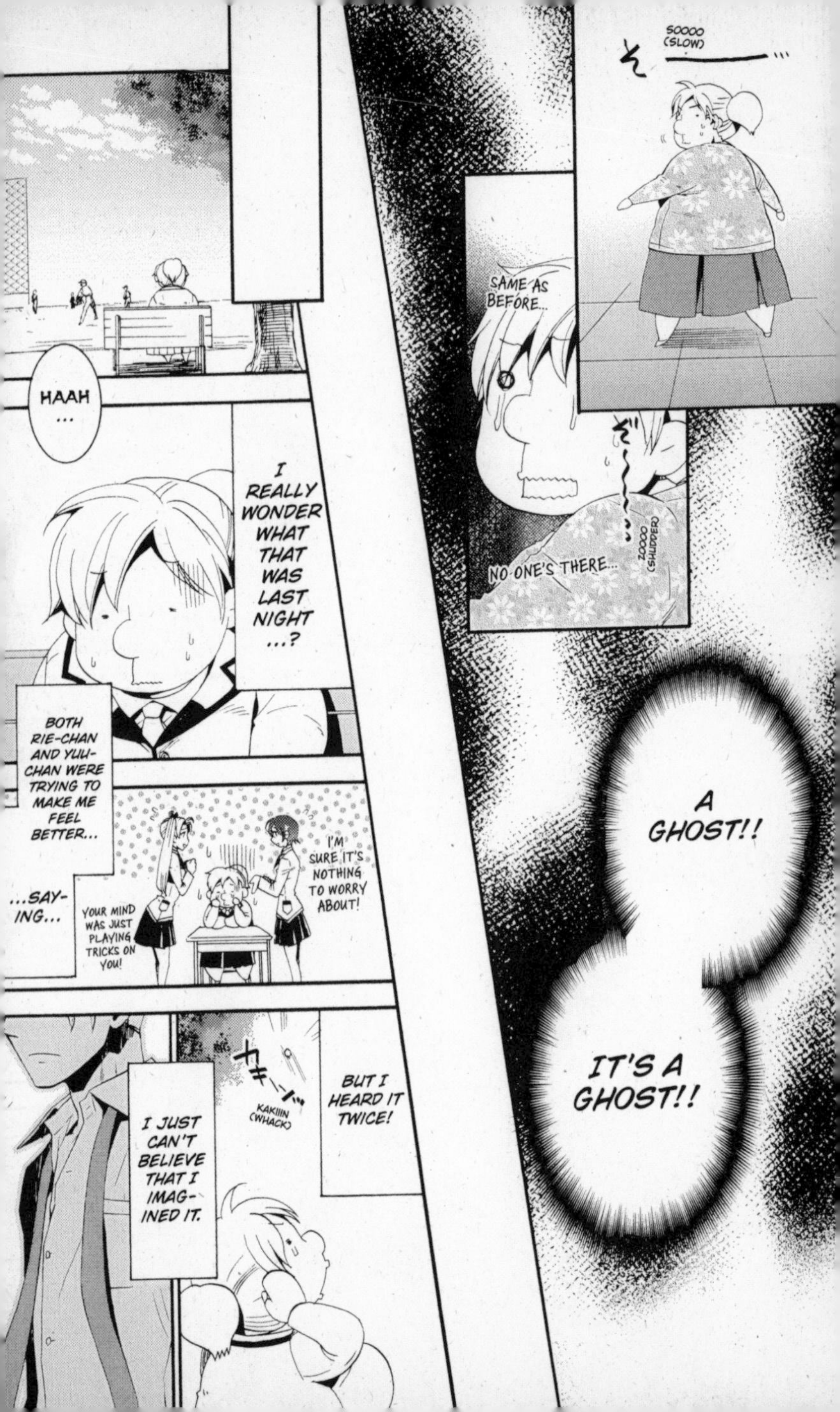
SOOOO (SLOW)
SAME AS BEFORE...
NO ONE'S THERE...
ZOOOO (SHUDDER)
A GHOST!!
IT'S A GHOST!!
HAAH ...
I REALLY WONDER WHAT THAT WAS LAST NIGHT ...?
BOTH RIE-CHAN AND YUU-CHAN WERE TRYING TO MAKE ME FEEL BETTER...
...SAY-ING...
I'M SURE IT'S NOTHING TO WORRY ABOUT!
YOUR MIND WAS JUST PLAYING TRICKS ON YOU!
BUT I HEARD IT TWICE!
KAKIIIN (WHACK)
I JUST CAN'T BELIEVE THAT I IMAG-INED IT.

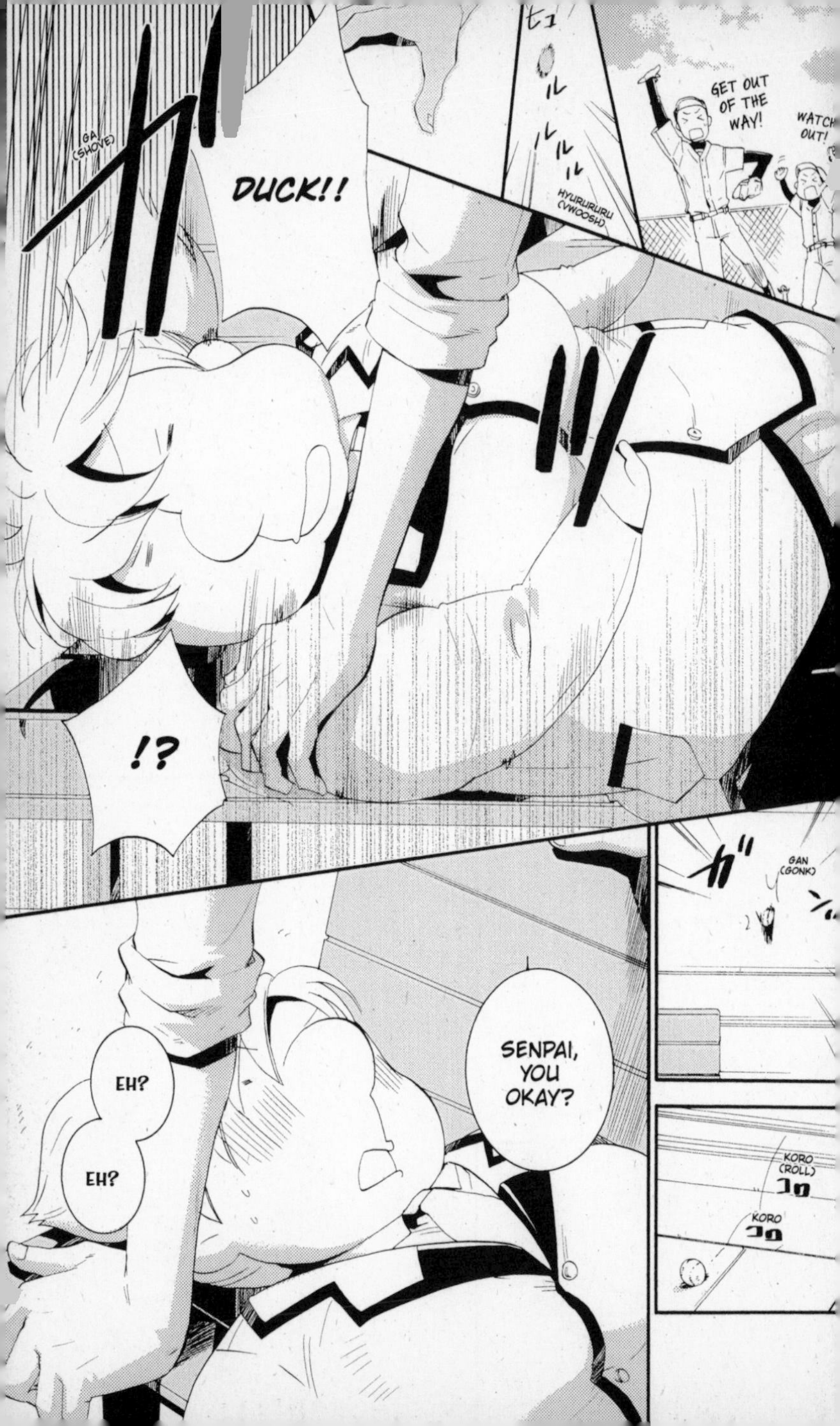

WATCH OUT!
GET OUT OF THE WAY!
HYURURURU (VWOOSH)
DUCK!!
GA (SHOVE)
!?
GAN (GONK)
KORO (ROLL)
コロ
KORO
コロ
SENPAI, YOU OKAY?
EH?
EH?

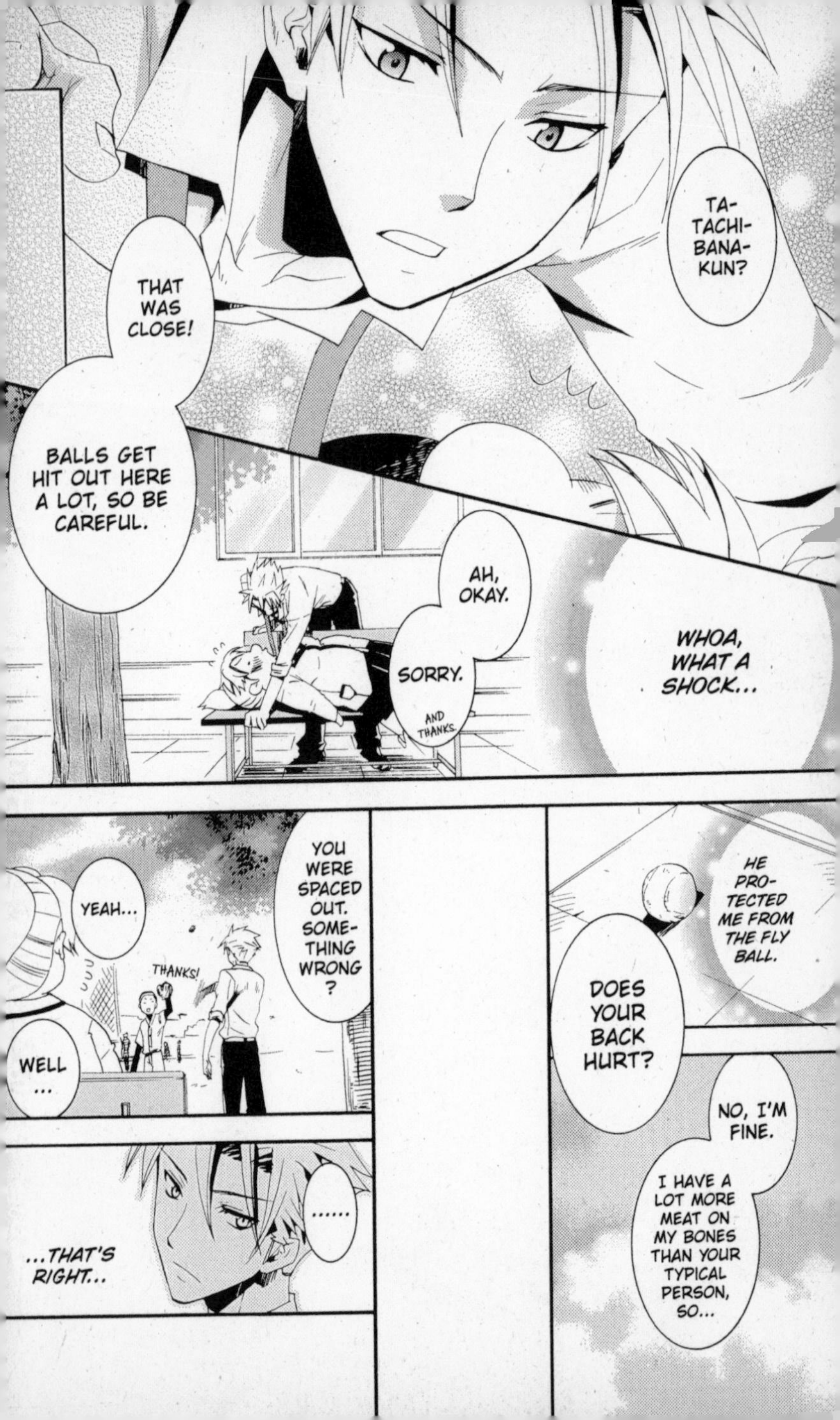
TA-TACHI-BANA-KUN?
THAT WAS CLOSE!
BALLS GET HIT OUT HERE A LOT, SO BE CAREFUL.
WHOA, WHAT A SHOCK...
AH, OKAY.
SORRY.
AND THANKS.
HE PROTECTED ME FROM THE FLY BALL.
DOES YOUR BACK HURT?
NO, I'M FINE.
I HAVE A LOT MORE MEAT ON MY BONES THAN YOUR TYPICAL PERSON, SO...
YOU WERE SPACED OUT. SOMETHING WRONG?
THANKS!
YEAH...
WELL...
......
...THAT'S RIGHT...

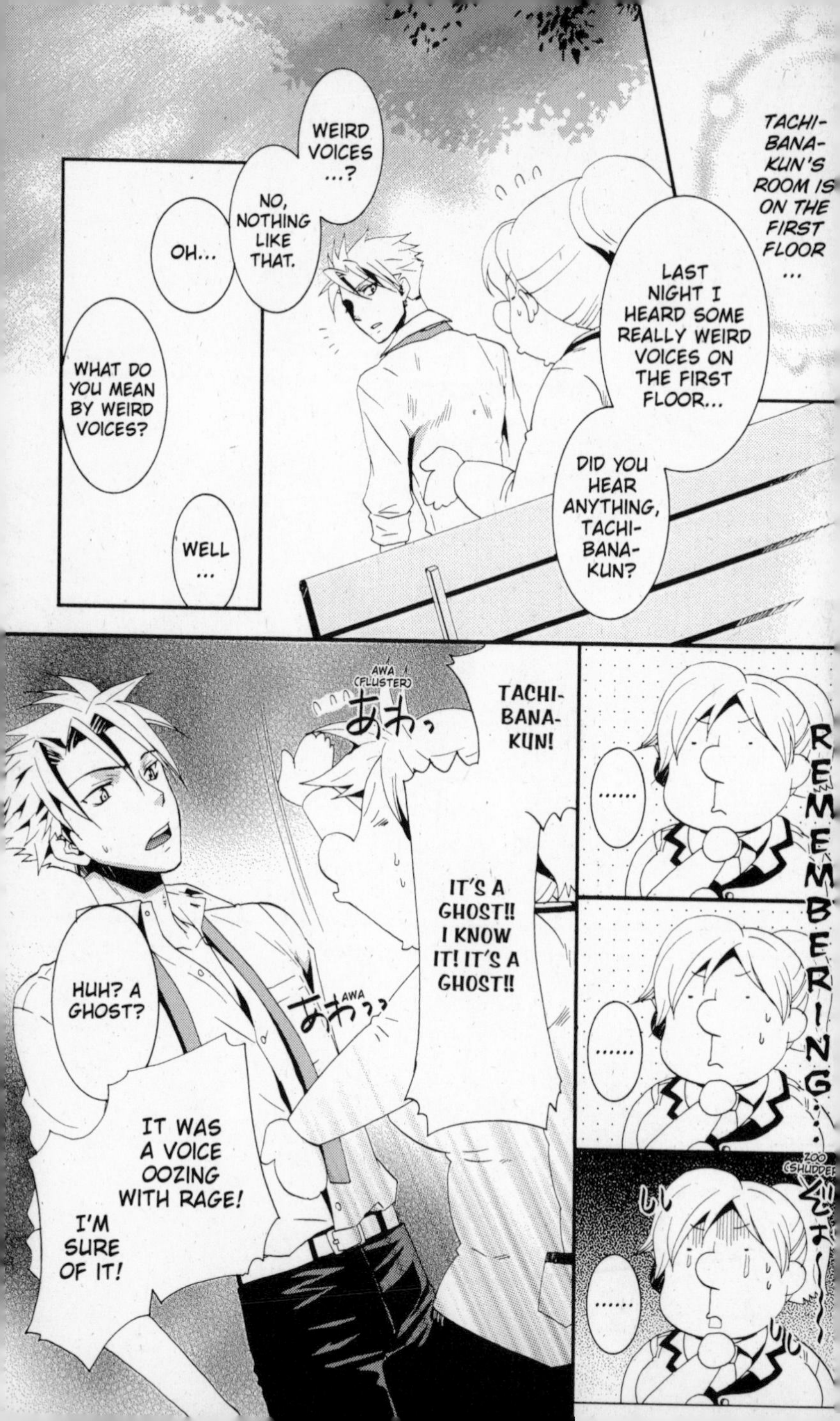
TACHI-BANA-KUN'S ROOM IS ON THE FIRST FLOOR...
LAST NIGHT I HEARD SOME REALLY WEIRD VOICES ON THE FIRST FLOOR...
DID YOU HEAR ANYTHING, TACHI-BANA-KUN?
WEIRD VOICES ...?
NO, NOTHING LIKE THAT.
OH...
WHAT DO YOU MEAN BY WEIRD VOICES?
WELL ...
......
REMEMBERING...
......
ZOO (SHUDDER)
......
TACHI-BANA-KUN!
AWA (FLUSTER)
あわっ
IT'S A GHOST!! I KNOW IT! IT'S A GHOST!!
AWA
あわっ
HUH? A GHOST?
IT WAS A VOICE OOZING WITH RAGE! I'M SURE OF IT!

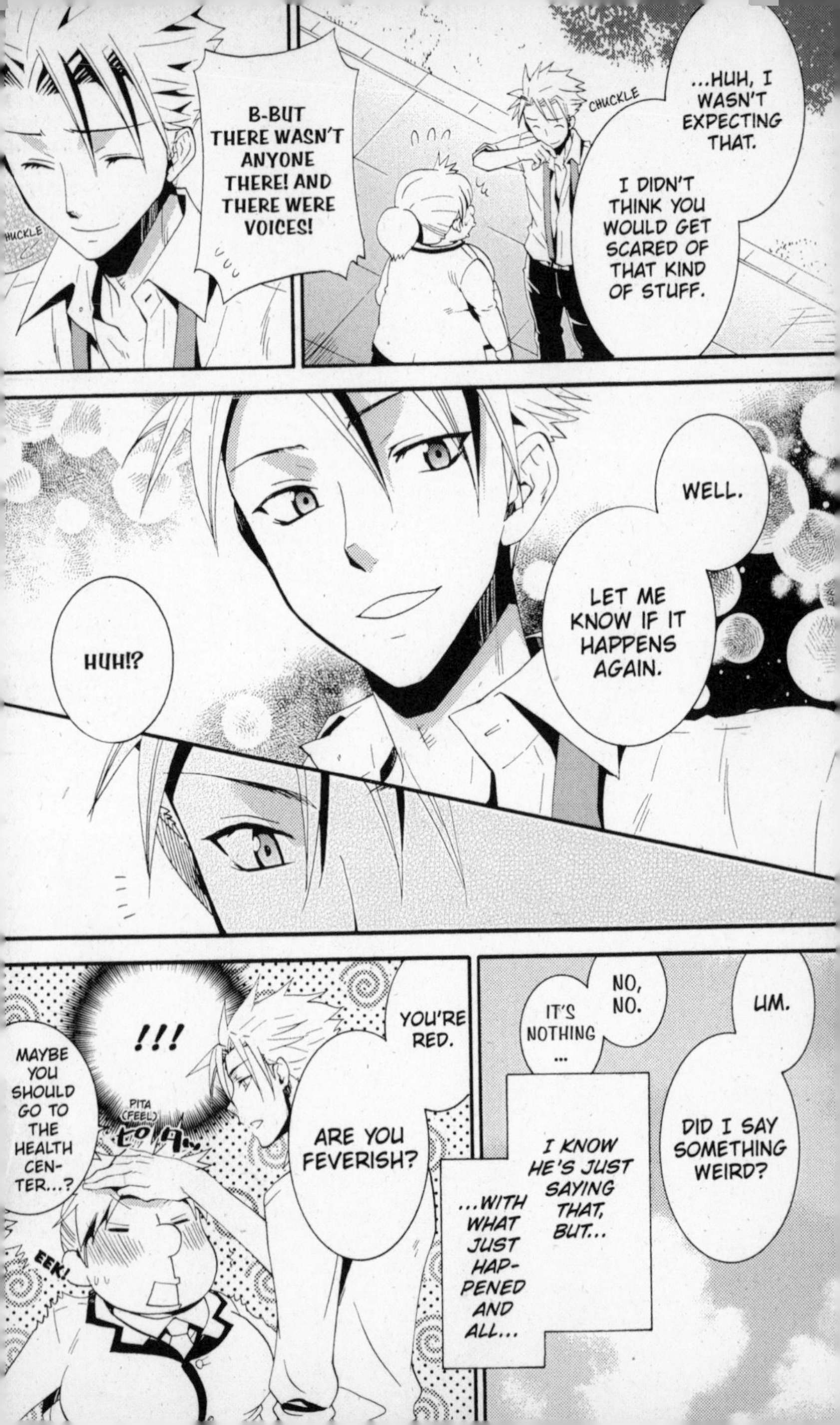
CHUCKLE
...HUH, I WASN'T EXPECTING THAT.
I DIDN'T THINK YOU WOULD GET SCARED OF THAT KIND OF STUFF.
B-BUT THERE WASN'T ANYONE THERE! AND THERE WERE VOICES!
HUCKLE
WELL.
LET ME KNOW IF IT HAPPENS AGAIN.
HUH!?
UM.
DID I SAY SOMETHING WEIRD?
NO, NO.
IT'S NOTHING ...
I KNOW HE'S JUST SAYING THAT, BUT...
...WITH WHAT JUST HAPPENED AND ALL...
YOU'RE RED.
ARE YOU FEVERISH?
!!!
PITA (FEEL)
MAYBE YOU SHOULD GO TO THE HEALTH CENTER...?
EEK!

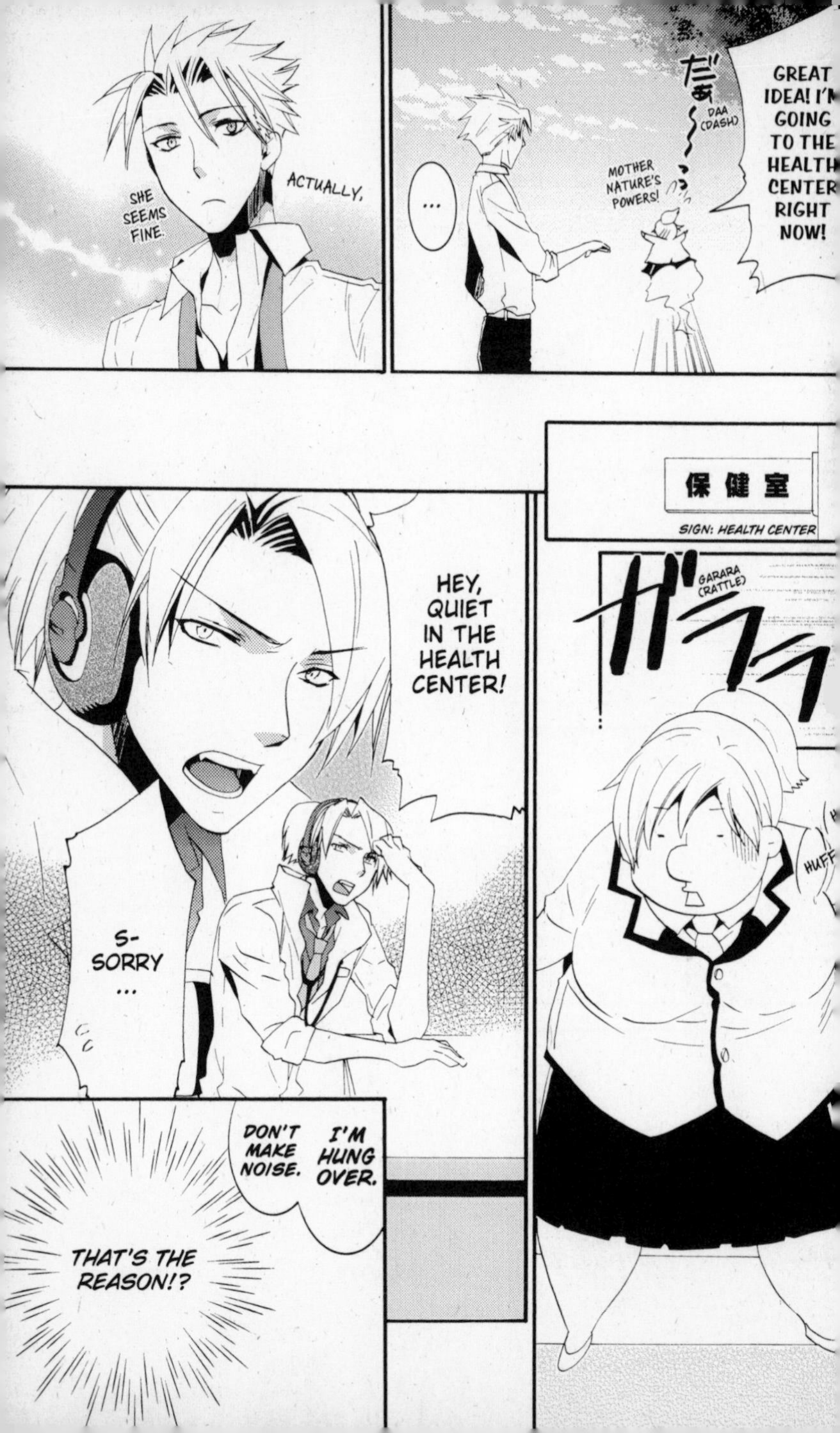

GREAT IDEA! I'M GOING TO THE HEALTH CENTER RIGHT NOW!
だぁ~
DAA (DASH)
MOTHER NATURE'S POWERS!
...
ACTUALLY,
SHE SEEMS FINE.
保健室
SIGN: HEALTH CENTER
ガララ
GARARA (RATTLE)
HUFF
HEY, QUIET IN THE HEALTH CENTER!
S- SORRY ...
I'M HUNG OVER.
DON'T MAKE NOISE.
THAT'S THE REASON!?

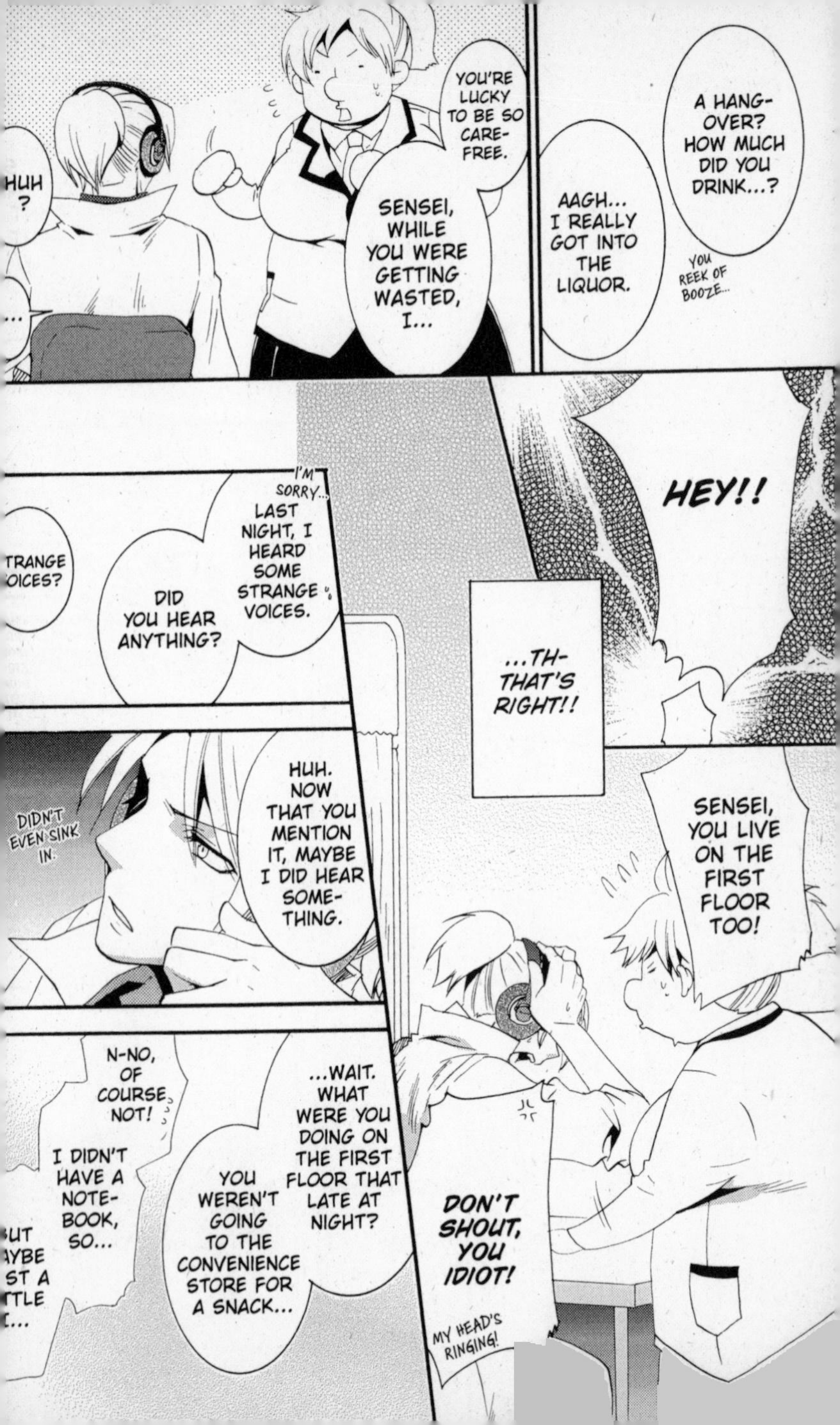
A HANG-OVER? HOW MUCH DID YOU DRINK...?
YOU REEK OF BOOZE...
AAGH... I REALLY GOT INTO THE LIQUOR.
YOU'RE LUCKY TO BE SO CAREFREE.
SENSEI, WHILE YOU WERE GETTING WASTED, I...
HUH?
...
HEY!!
...TH-THAT'S RIGHT!!
SENSEI, YOU LIVE ON THE FIRST FLOOR TOO!
DON'T SHOUT, YOU IDIOT!
MY HEAD'S RINGING!
I'M SORRY...
LAST NIGHT, I HEARD SOME STRANGE VOICES.
DID YOU HEAR ANYTHING?
TRANGE OICES?
HUH. NOW THAT YOU MENTION IT, MAYBE I DID HEAR SOMETHING.
DIDN'T EVEN SINK IN.
...WAIT. WHAT WERE YOU DOING ON THE FIRST FLOOR THAT LATE AT NIGHT?
YOU WEREN'T GOING TO THE CONVENIENCE STORE FOR A SNACK...
N-NO, OF COURSE NOT!
I DIDN'T HAVE A NOTEBOOK, SO...
UT AYBE ST A TLE ...

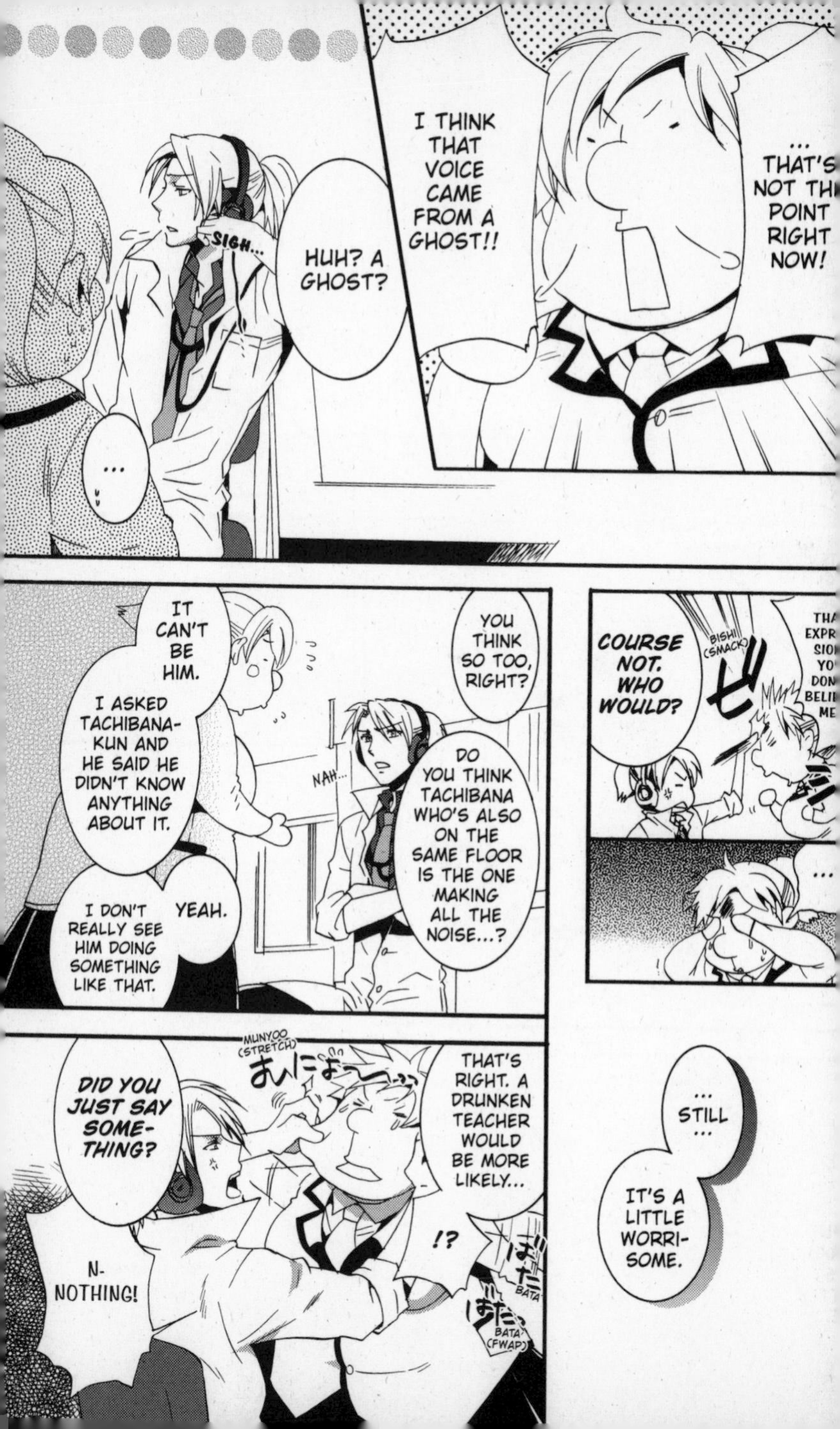

... THAT'S NOT TH POINT RIGHT NOW!
I THINK THAT VOICE CAME FROM A GHOST!!
HUH? A GHOST?
SIGH...
...
THA EXPR SIO YO DON BELI ME
BISHI (SMACK)
COURSE NOT. WHO WOULD?
...
YOU THINK SO TOO, RIGHT?
IT CAN'T BE HIM.
I ASKED TACHIBANA-KUN AND HE SAID HE DIDN'T KNOW ANYTHING ABOUT IT.
DO YOU THINK TACHIBANA WHO'S ALSO ON THE SAME FLOOR IS THE ONE MAKING ALL THE NOISE...?
NAH...
YEAH.
I DON'T REALLY SEE HIM DOING SOMETHING LIKE THAT.
... STILL ...
IT'S A LITTLE WORRI-SOME.
THAT'S RIGHT. A DRUNKEN TEACHER WOULD BE MORE LIKELY...
MUNYOO (STRETCH)
DID YOU JUST SAY SOME-THING?
!?
BATA
BATA (FWAP)
N-NOTHING!

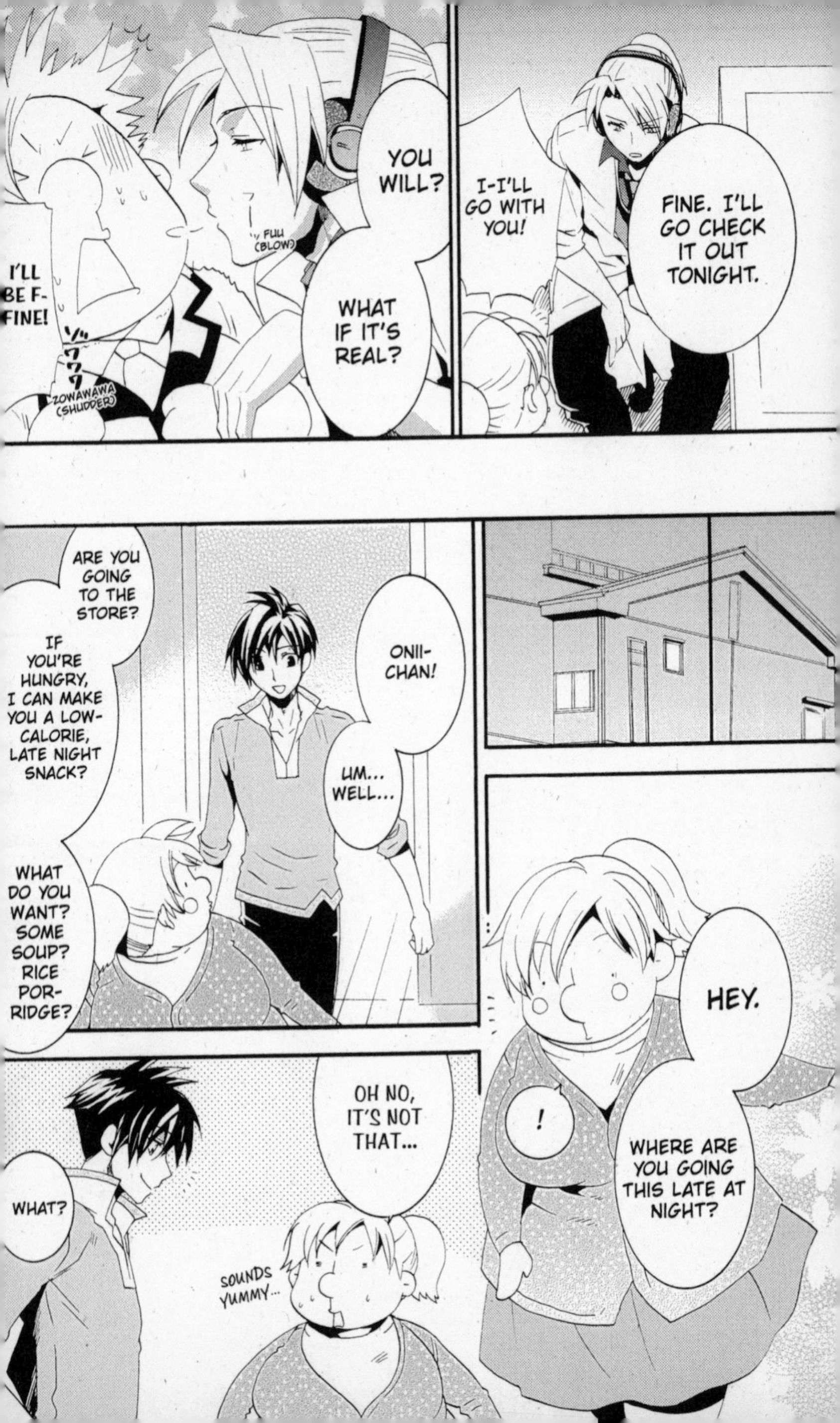
FINE. I'LL GO CHECK IT OUT TONIGHT.
I-I'LL GO WITH YOU!
YOU WILL?
WHAT IF IT'S REAL?
FUU (BLOW)
I'LL BE F-FINE!
ゾワワワ
ZOWAWAWA (SHUDDER)
HEY.
!
WHERE ARE YOU GOING THIS LATE AT NIGHT?
ONII-CHAN!
UM... WELL...
ARE YOU GOING TO THE STORE?
IF YOU'RE HUNGRY, I CAN MAKE YOU A LOW-CALORIE, LATE NIGHT SNACK?
WHAT DO YOU WANT? SOME SOUP? RICE POR-RIDGE?
OH NO, IT'S NOT THAT...
WHAT?
SOUNDS YUMMY...

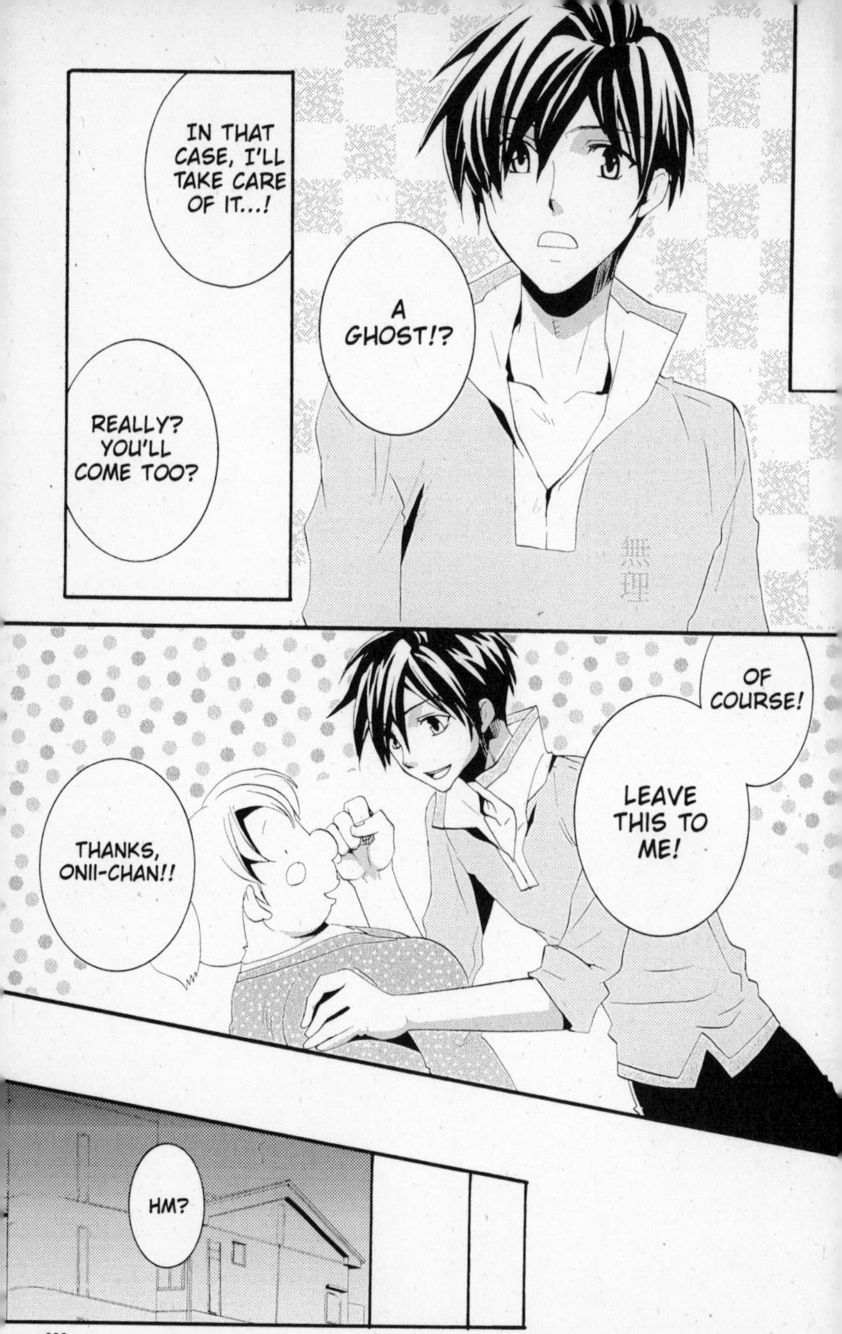
A GHOST!?
無理
IN THAT CASE, I'LL TAKE CARE OF IT...!
REALLY? YOU'LL COME TOO?
OF COURSE!
LEAVE THIS TO ME!
THANKS, ONII-CHAN!!
HM?

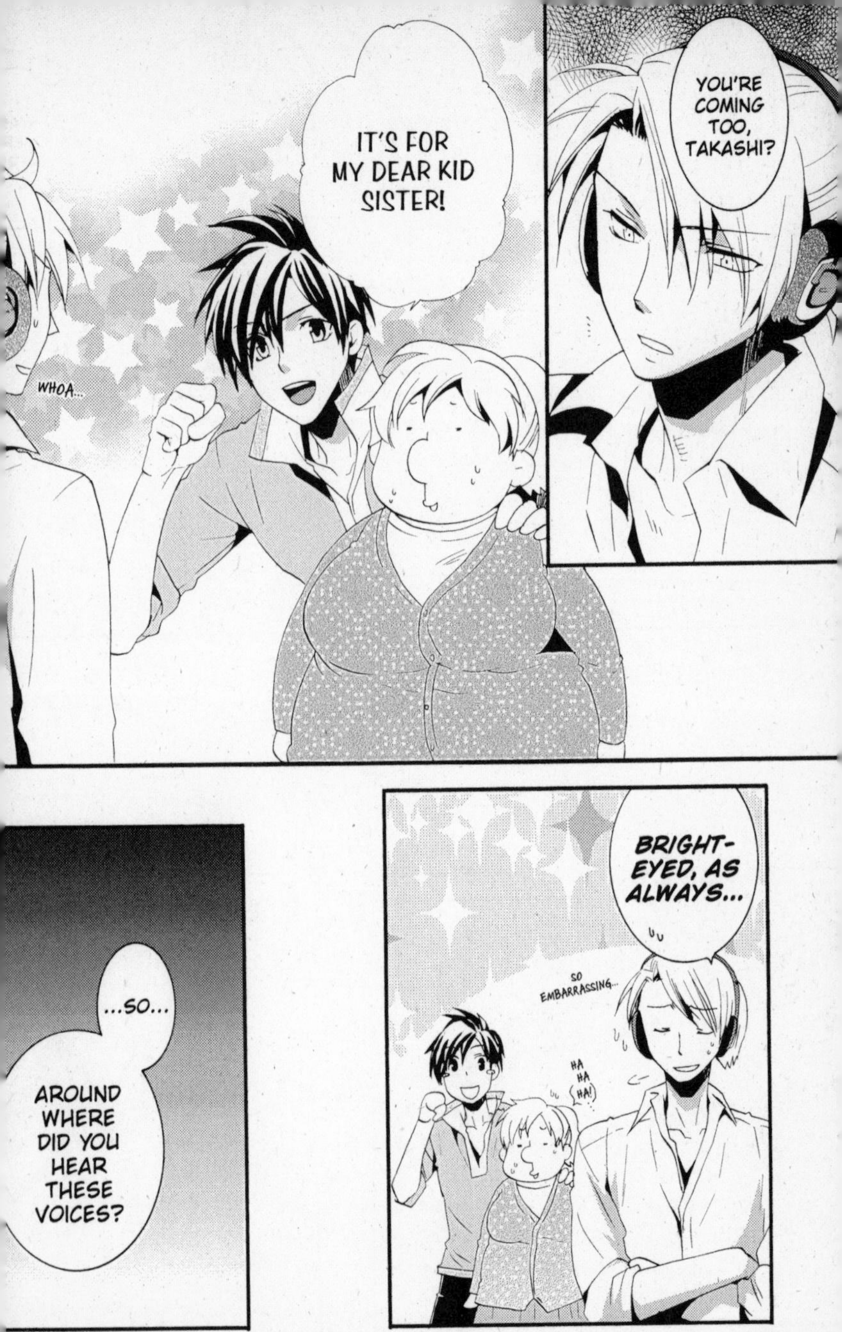
YOU'RE COMING TOO, TAKASHI?
IT'S FOR MY DEAR KID SISTER!
WHOA...
BRIGHT-EYED, AS ALWAYS...
SO EMBARRASSING...
HA HA HA!
...SO...
AROUND WHERE DID YOU HEAR THESE VOICES?

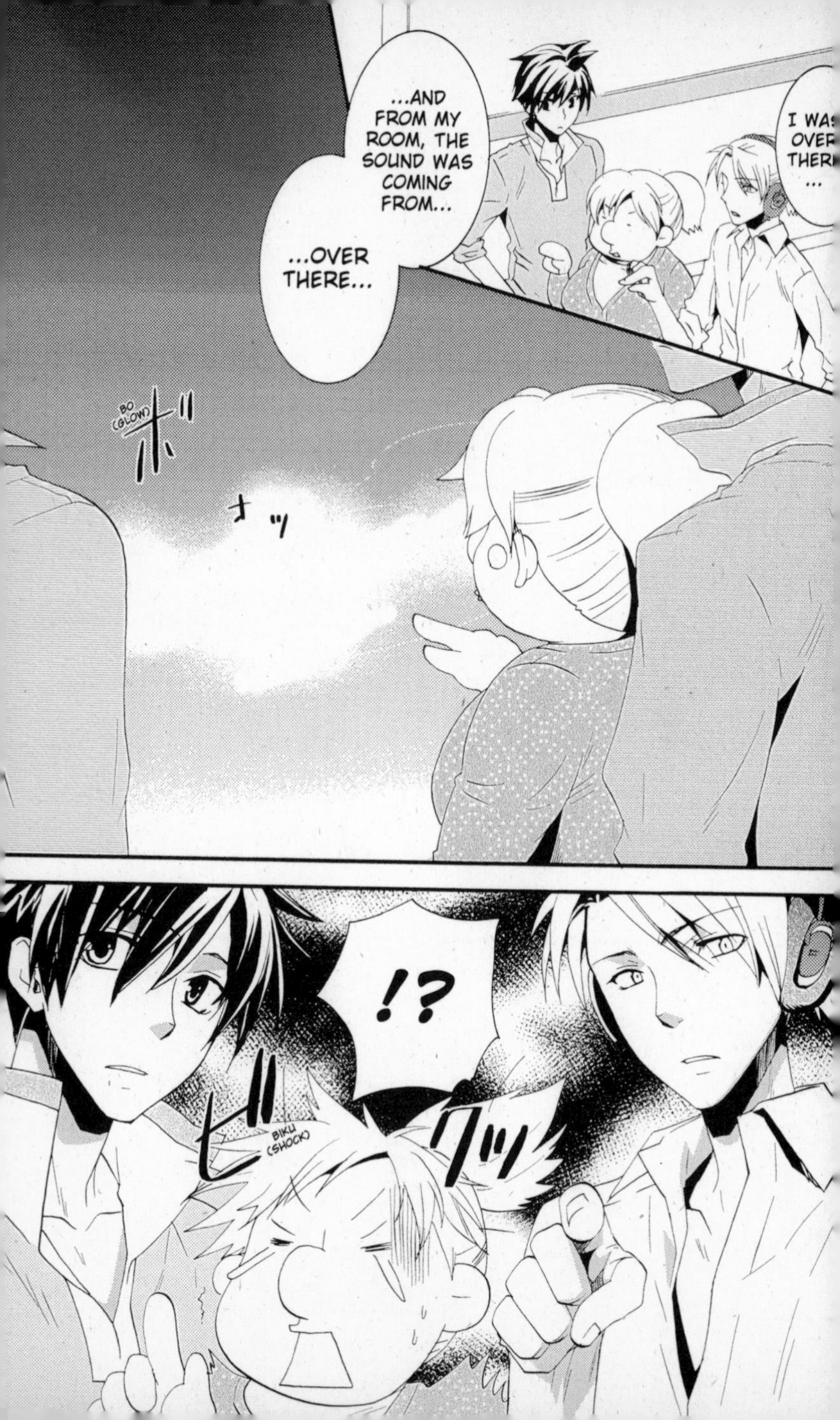
I WAS OVER THER …
...AND FROM MY ROOM, THE SOUND WAS COMING FROM...
...OVER THERE...
BO (GLOW)
ボッ
!?
ビクッ
BIKU (SHOCK)

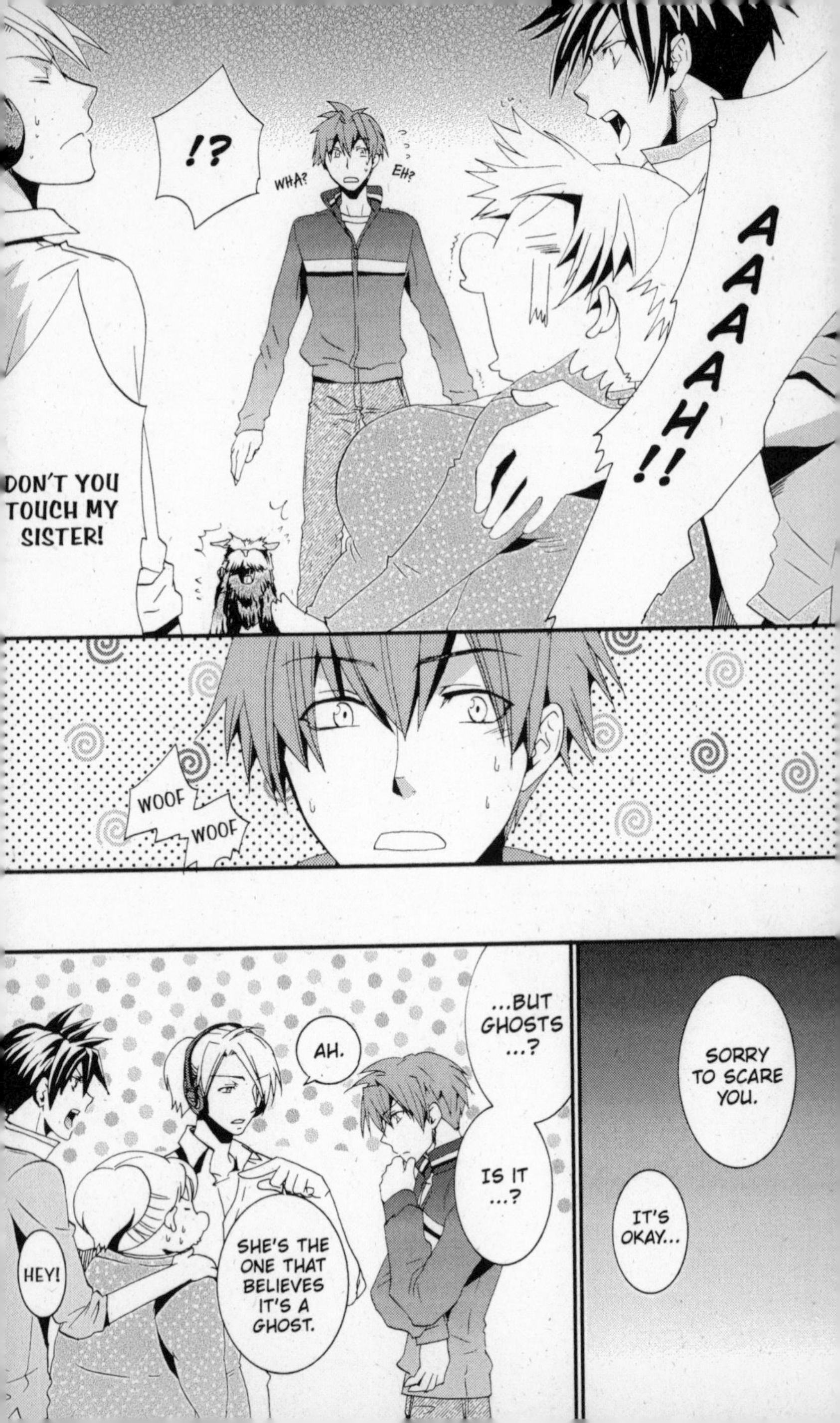
AAAAAH!!
EH?
WHA?
!?
DON'T YOU TOUCH MY SISTER!
WOOF
WOOF
SORRY TO SCARE YOU.
IT'S OKAY...
...BUT GHOSTS ...?
IS IT ...?
AH.
SHE'S THE ONE THAT BELIEVES IT'S A GHOST.
HEY!

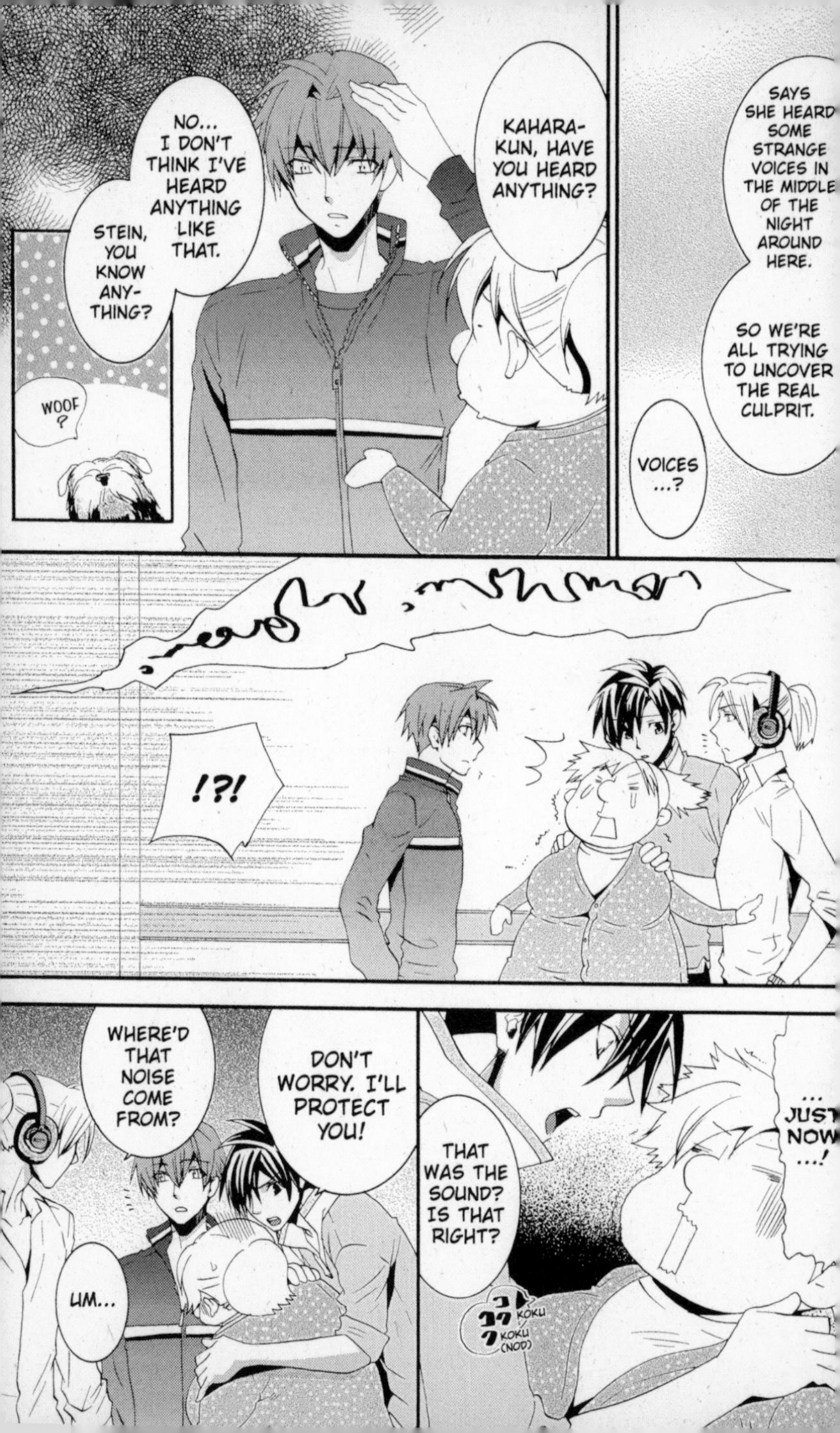
SAYS SHE HEARD SOME STRANGE VOICES IN THE MIDDLE OF THE NIGHT AROUND HERE.
SO WE'RE ALL TRYING TO UNCOVER THE REAL CULPRIT.
VOICES ...?
KAHARA-KUN, HAVE YOU HEARD ANYTHING?
NO... I DON'T THINK I'VE HEARD ANYTHING LIKE THAT.
STEIN, YOU KNOW ANYTHING?
WOOF ?
!?!
... JUST NOW ...!
THAT WAS THE SOUND? IS THAT RIGHT?
コク コク KOKU / KOKU (NOD)
DON'T WORRY. I'LL PROTECT YOU!
WHERE'D THAT NOISE COME FROM?
UM...

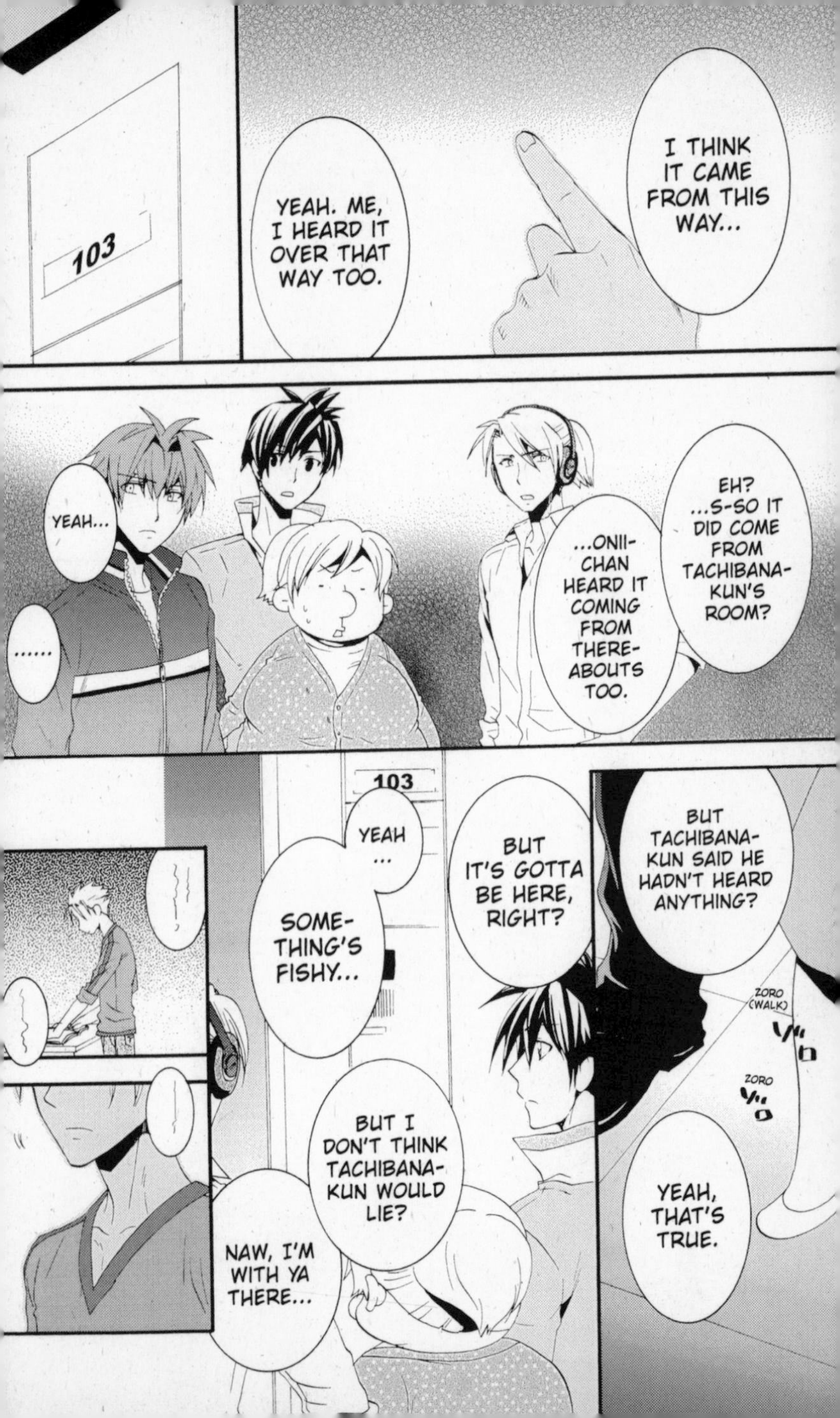
I THINK IT CAME FROM THIS WAY...
YEAH. ME, I HEARD IT OVER THAT WAY TOO.
103
EH? ...S-SO IT DID COME FROM TACHIBANA-KUN'S ROOM?
...ONII-CHAN HEARD IT COMING FROM THERE-ABOUTS TOO.
YEAH...
......
BUT TACHIBANA-KUN SAID HE HADN'T HEARD ANYTHING?
ZORO (WALK)
ゾロ
ZORO
ゾロ
YEAH, THAT'S TRUE.
BUT IT'S GOTTA BE HERE, RIGHT?
103
YEAH ...
SOME-THING'S FISHY...
BUT I DON'T THINK TACHIBANA-KUN WOULD LIE?
NAW, I'M WITH YA THERE...

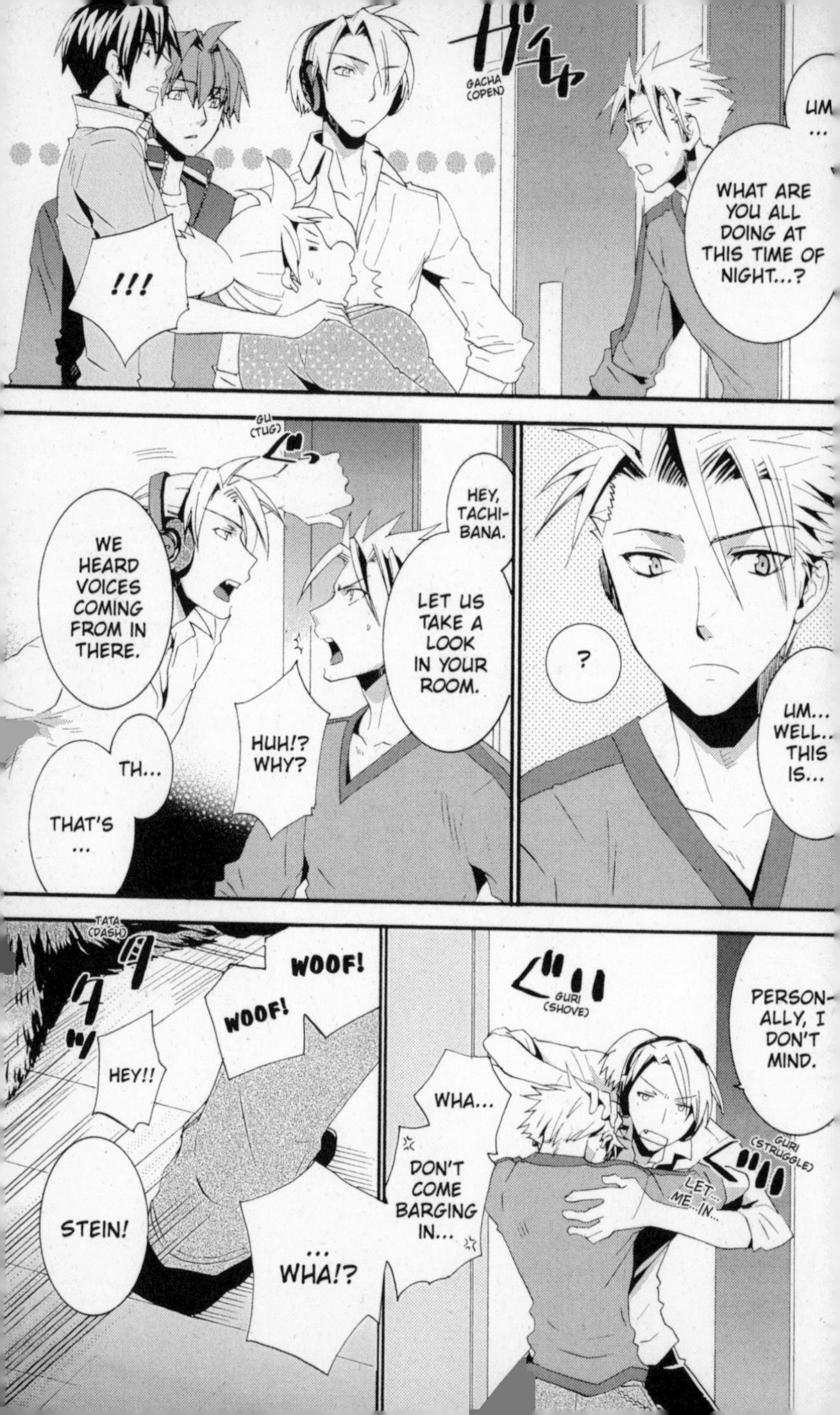
UM ...
WHAT ARE YOU ALL DOING AT THIS TIME OF NIGHT...?
GACHA (OPEND)
!!!
UM... WELL.. THIS IS...
?
HEY, TACHI-BANA.
LET US TAKE A LOOK IN YOUR ROOM.
GU (TUG)
WE HEARD VOICES COMING FROM IN THERE.
HUH!? WHY?
TH...
THAT'S ...
PERSON-ALLY, I DON'T MIND.
GURI (SHOVE)
GURI (STRUGGLE)
LET... ME...IN...
WHA...
DON'T COME BARGING IN...
WOOF!
WOOF!
TATA (DASH)
HEY!!
STEIN!
... WHA!?

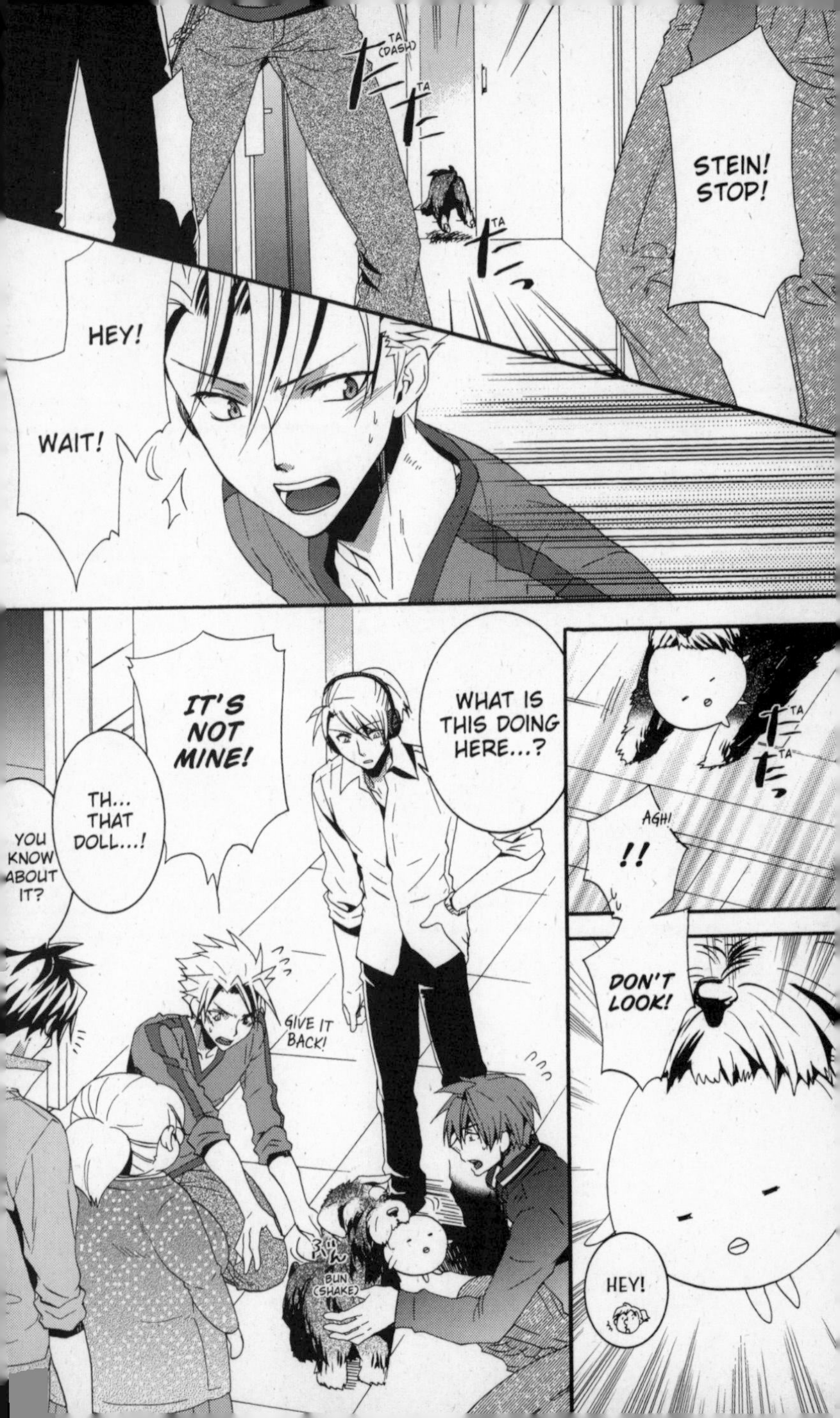
STEIN! STOP!
TA (DASH)
TA
TA
HEY!
WAIT!
TA
TA
AGH!
!!
DON'T LOOK!
HEY!
WHAT IS THIS DOING HERE...?
IT'S NOT MINE!
TH... THAT DOLL...!
YOU KNOW ABOUT IT?
GIVE IT BACK!
BUN (SHAKE)

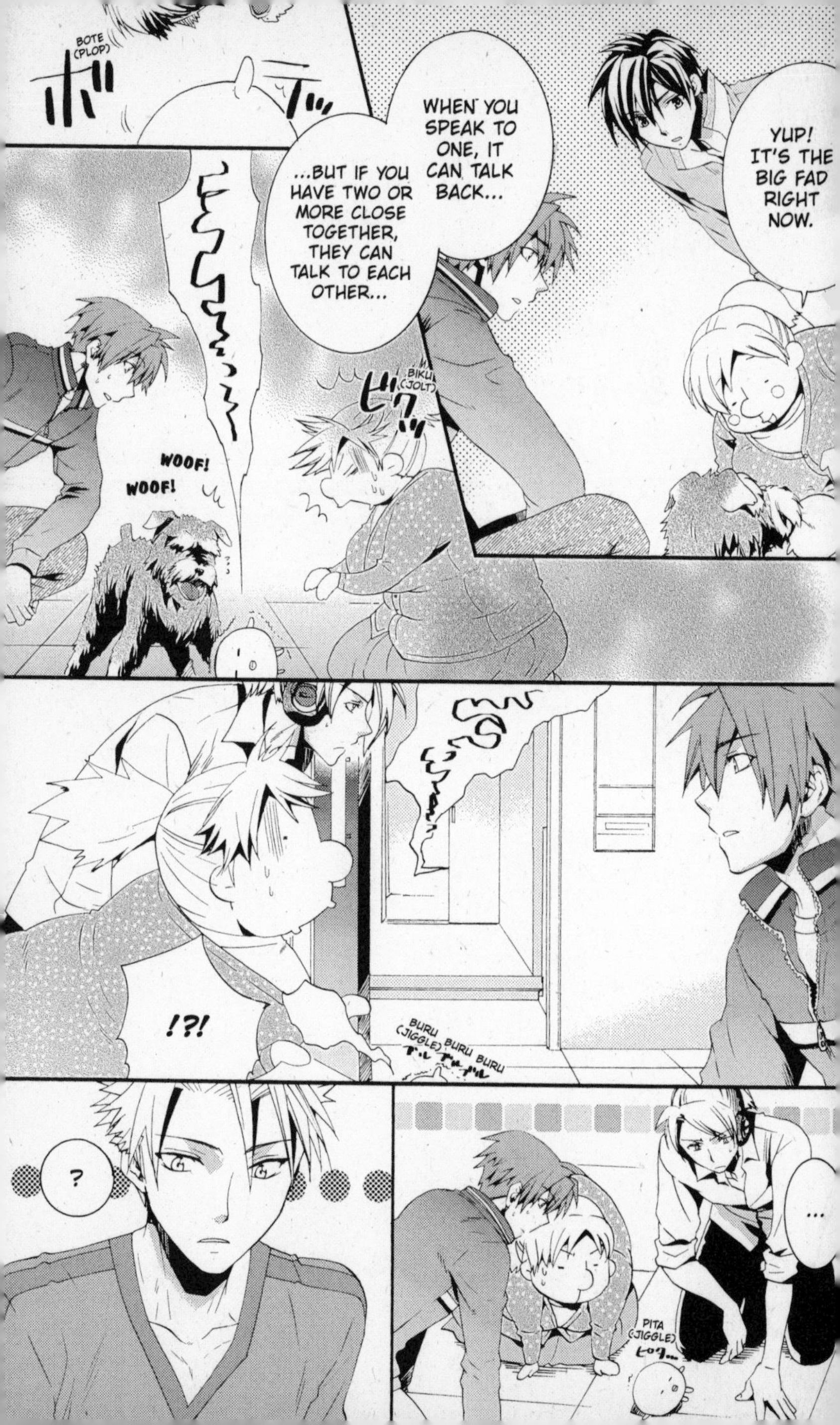
YUP! IT'S THE BIG FAD RIGHT NOW.
WHEN YOU SPEAK TO ONE, IT CAN TALK BACK...
...BUT IF YOU HAVE TWO OR MORE CLOSE TOGETHER, THEY CAN TALK TO EACH OTHER...
BOTE (PLOP)
BIKU (JOLT)
WOOF!
WOOF!
BURU (JIGGLE) BURU BURU
!?!
...
PITA (JIGGLE)
?

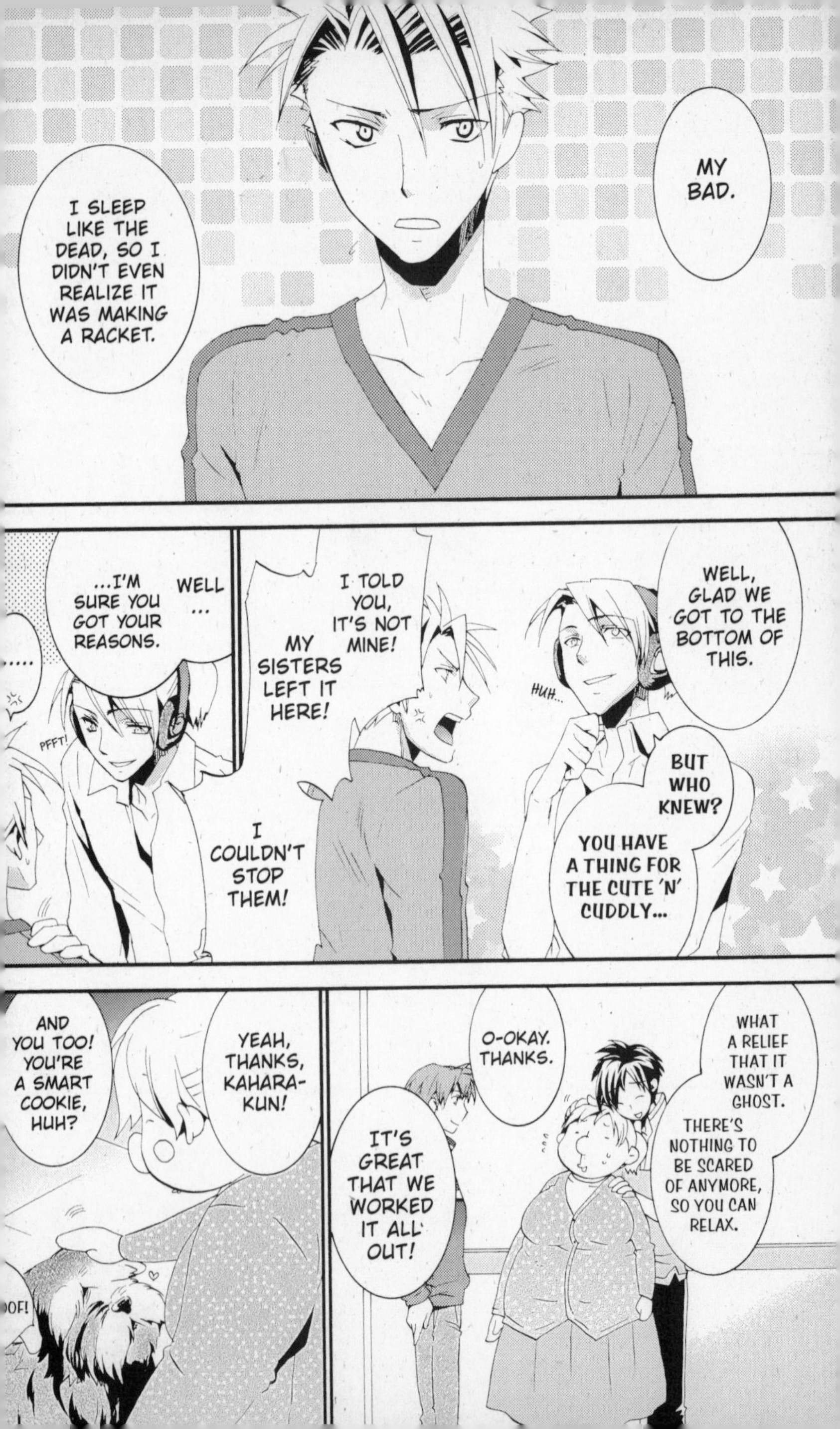
MY BAD.
I SLEEP LIKE THE DEAD, SO I DIDN'T EVEN REALIZE IT WAS MAKING A RACKET.
WELL, GLAD WE GOT TO THE BOTTOM OF THIS.
HUH...
BUT WHO KNEW?
YOU HAVE A THING FOR THE CUTE 'N' CUDDLY...
I TOLD YOU, IT'S NOT MINE!
MY SISTERS LEFT IT HERE!
I COULDN'T STOP THEM!
WELL ...
...I'M SURE YOU GOT YOUR REASONS.
PFFT!
.....
WHAT A RELIEF THAT IT WASN'T A GHOST.
THERE'S NOTHING TO BE SCARED OF ANYMORE, SO YOU CAN RELAX.
O-OKAY. THANKS.
IT'S GREAT THAT WE WORKED IT ALL OUT!
YEAH, THANKS, KAHARA-KUN!
AND YOU TOO! YOU'RE A SMART COOKIE, HUH?

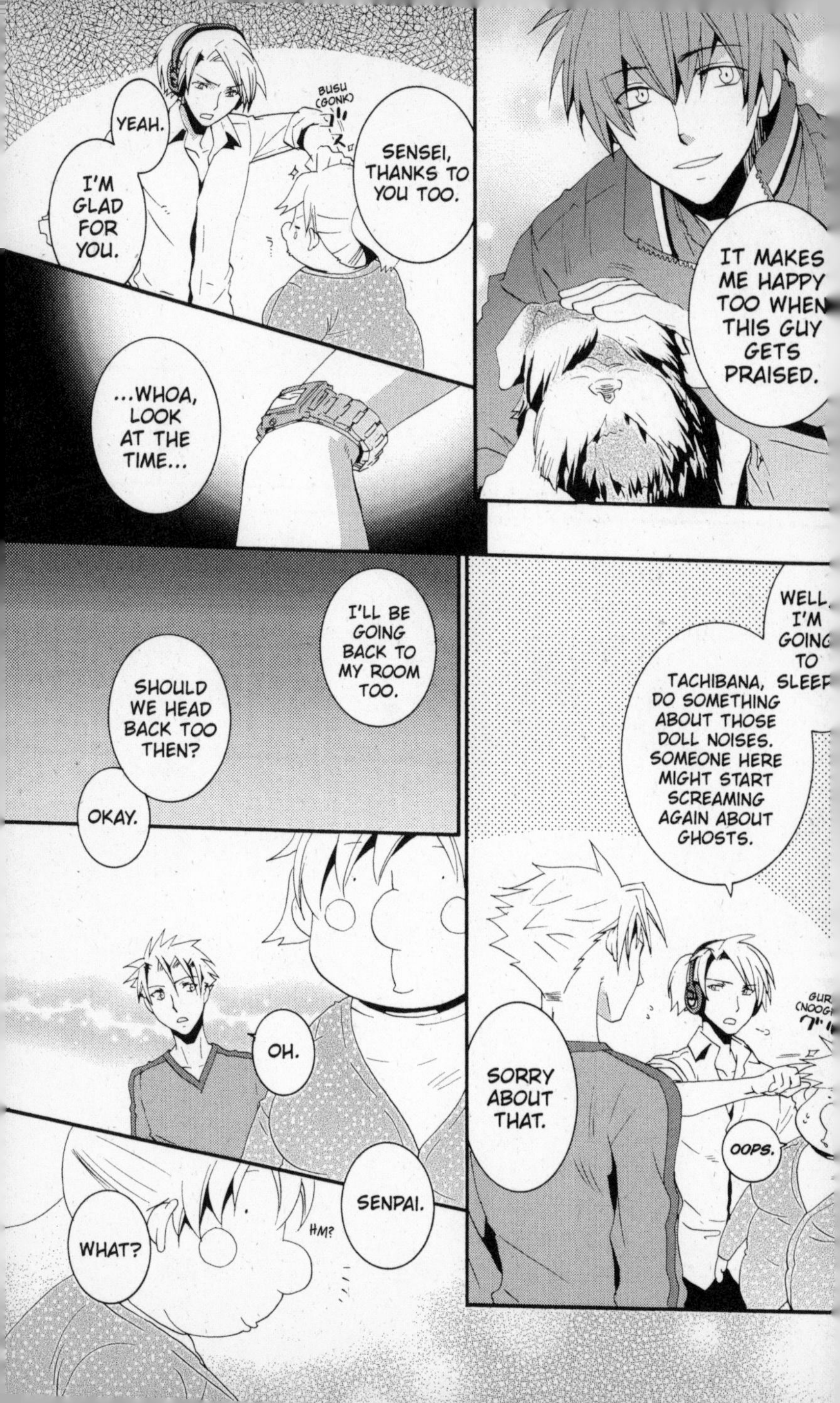
IT MAKES ME HAPPY TOO WHEN THIS GUY GETS PRAISED.
SENSEI, THANKS TO YOU TOO.
BUSU (GONK)
YEAH.
I'M GLAD FOR YOU.
...WHOA, LOOK AT THE TIME...
WELL, I'M GOING TO SLEEP.
TACHIBANA, DO SOMETHING ABOUT THOSE DOLL NOISES. SOMEONE HERE MIGHT START SCREAMING AGAIN ABOUT GHOSTS.
OOPS.
SORRY ABOUT THAT.
I'LL BE GOING BACK TO MY ROOM TOO.
SHOULD WE HEAD BACK TOO THEN?
OKAY.
OH.
SENPAI.
HM?
WHAT?

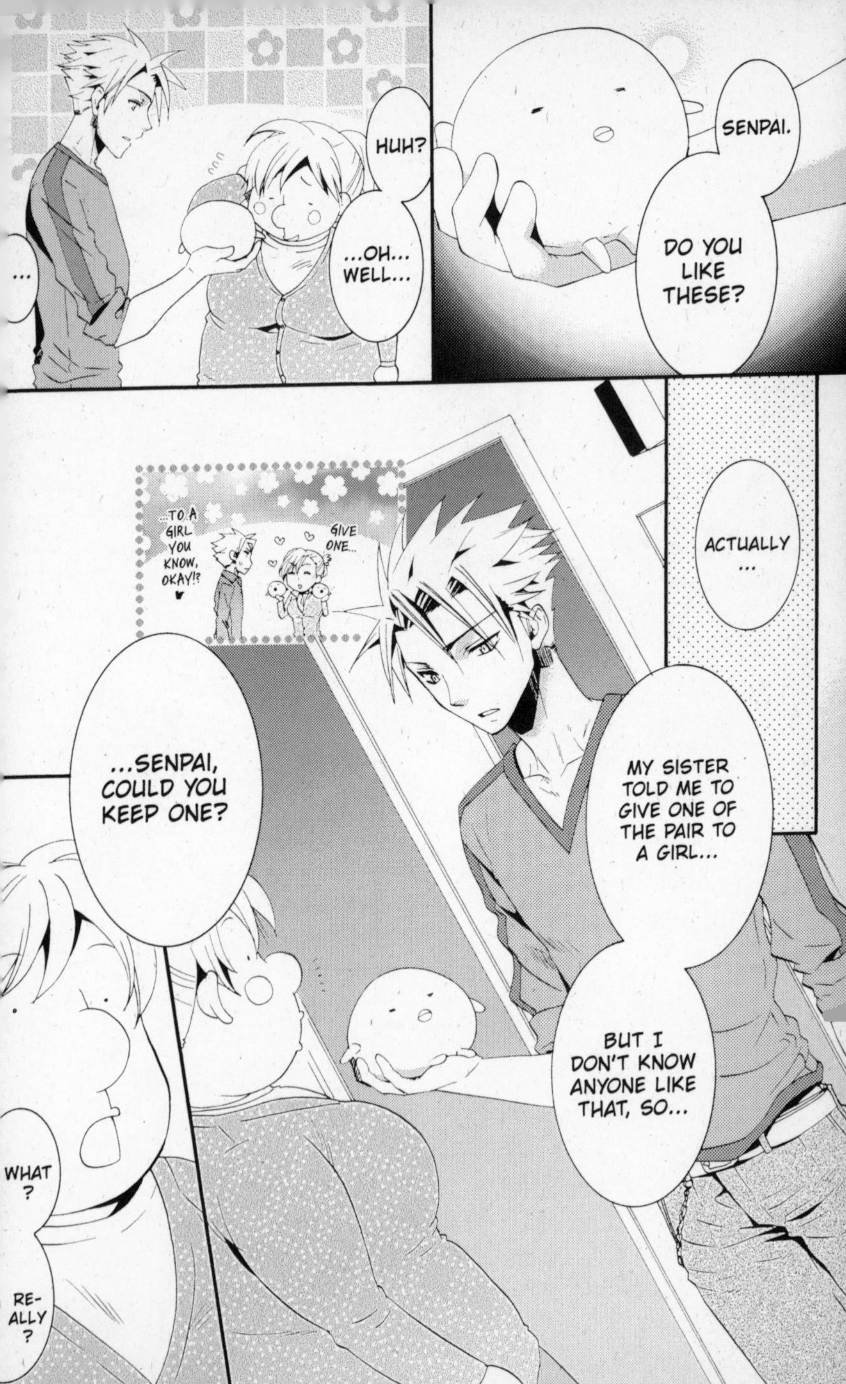
SENPAI.
DO YOU LIKE THESE?
HUH?
...OH... WELL...
...
ACTUALLY ...
MY SISTER TOLD ME TO GIVE ONE OF THE PAIR TO A GIRL...
GIVE ONE...
...TO A GIRL YOU KNOW, OKAY!?
BUT I DON'T KNOW ANYONE LIKE THAT, SO...
...SENPAI, COULD YOU KEEP ONE?
WHAT?
RE-ALLY?

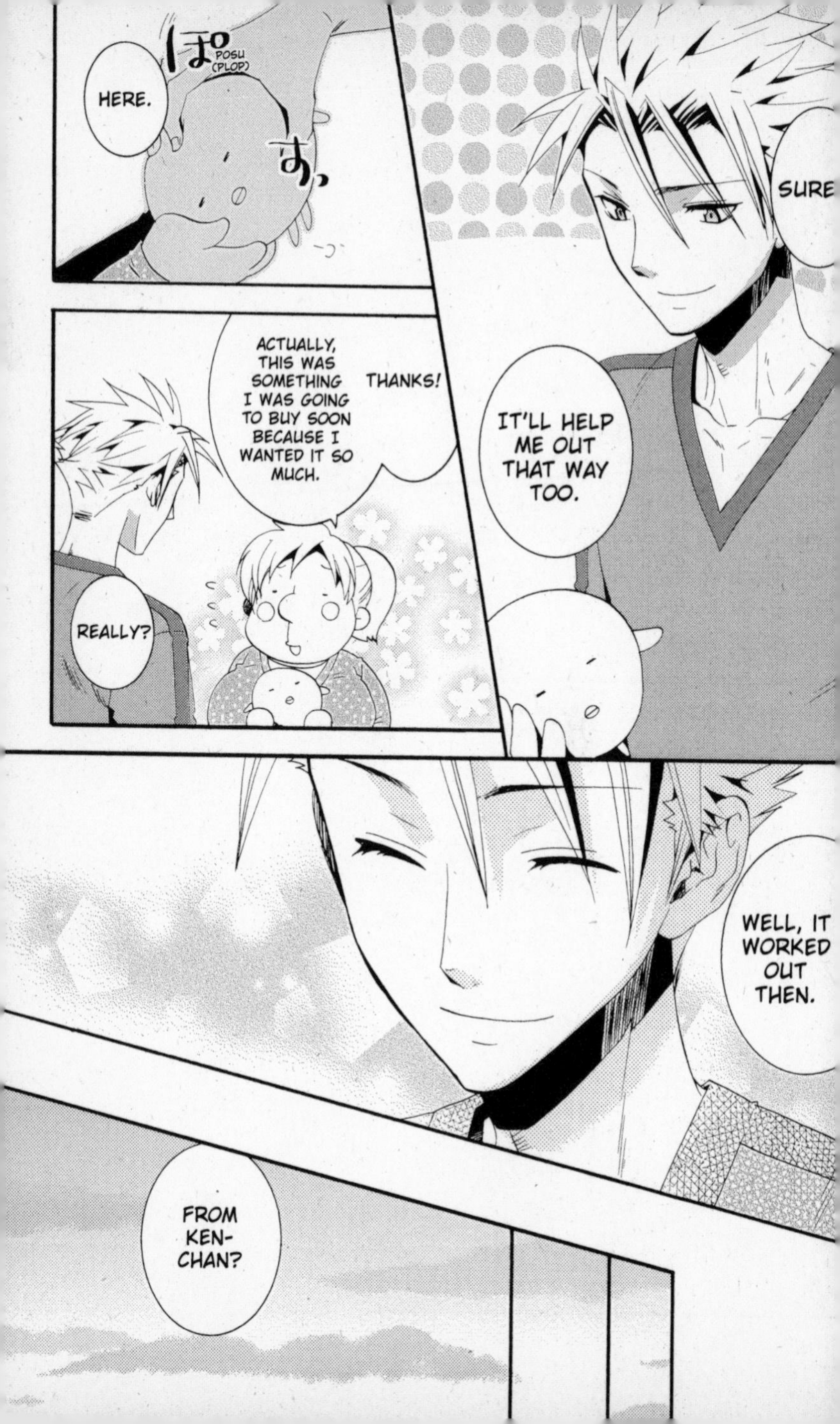
SURE
IT'LL HELP ME OUT THAT WAY TOO.
ぽ POSU (PLOP)
HERE.
あっ
THANKS!
ACTUALLY, THIS WAS SOMETHING I WAS GOING TO BUY SOON BECAUSE I WANTED IT SO MUCH.
REALLY?
WELL, IT WORKED OUT THEN.
FROM KEN-CHAN?

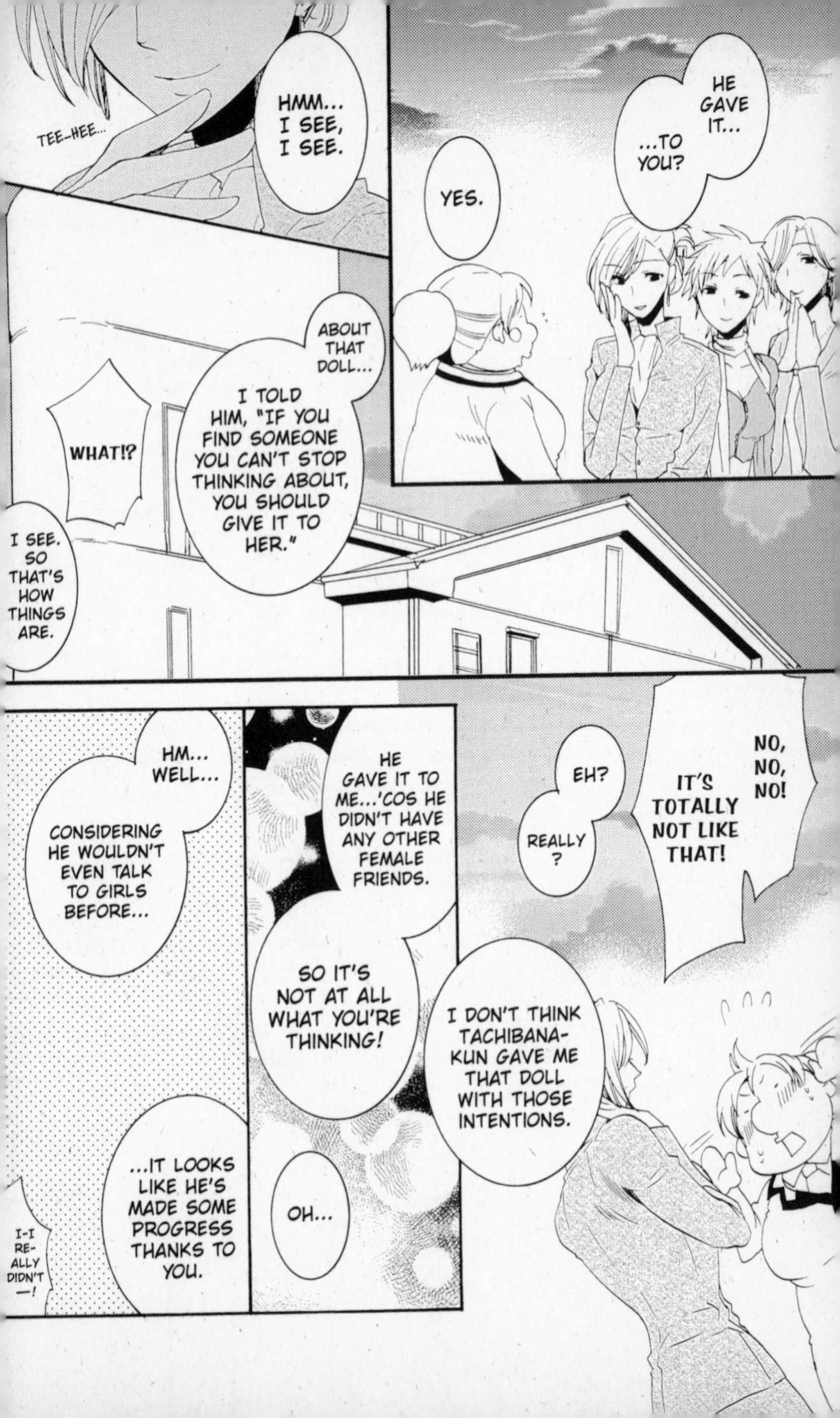
HE GAVE IT...
...TO YOU?
YES.
TEE-HEE...
HMM... I SEE, I SEE.
ABOUT THAT DOLL...
I TOLD HIM, "IF YOU FIND SOMEONE YOU CAN'T STOP THINKING ABOUT, YOU SHOULD GIVE IT TO HER."
WHAT!?
I SEE. SO THAT'S HOW THINGS ARE.
NO, NO, NO!
IT'S TOTALLY NOT LIKE THAT!
EH?
REALLY?
I DON'T THINK TACHIBANA-KUN GAVE ME THAT DOLL WITH THOSE INTENTIONS.
HE GAVE IT TO ME...'COS HE DIDN'T HAVE ANY OTHER FEMALE FRIENDS.
SO IT'S NOT AT ALL WHAT YOU'RE THINKING!
OH...
HM... WELL...
CONSIDERING HE WOULDN'T EVEN TALK TO GIRLS BEFORE...
...IT LOOKS LIKE HE'S MADE SOME PROGRESS THANKS TO YOU.
I-I RE-ALLY DIDN'T—!

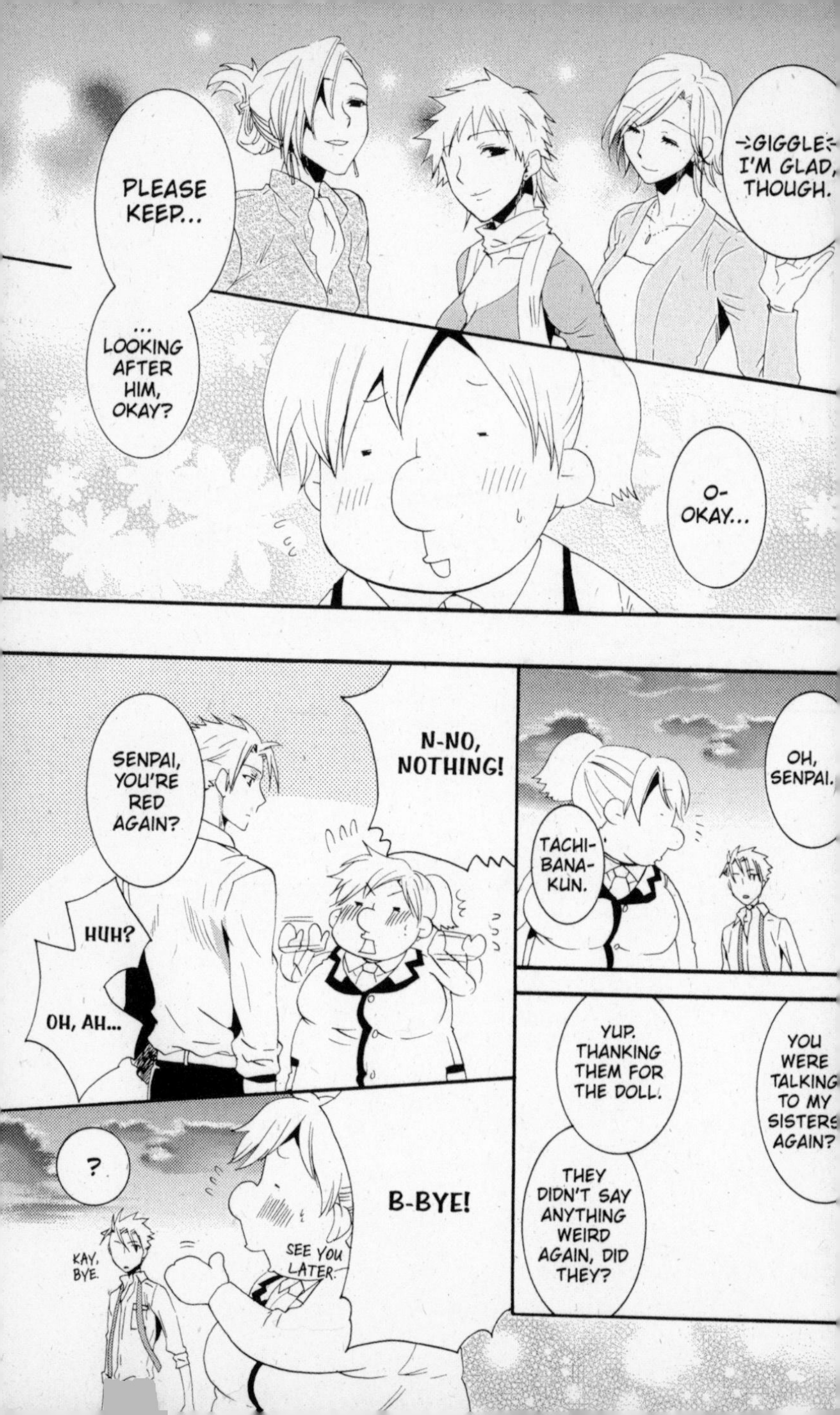

⇒GIGGLE⇐ I'M GLAD, THOUGH.
PLEASE KEEP...
...LOOKING AFTER HIM, OKAY?
O-OKAY...
OH, SENPAI.
TACHIBANA-KUN.
YOU WERE TALKING TO MY SISTERS AGAIN?
YUP. THANKING THEM FOR THE DOLL.
THEY DIDN'T SAY ANYTHING WEIRD AGAIN, DID THEY?
HUH?
OH, AH...
SENPAI, YOU'RE RED AGAIN?
N-NO, NOTHING!
B-BYE!
SEE YOU LATER.
?
KAY, BYE.

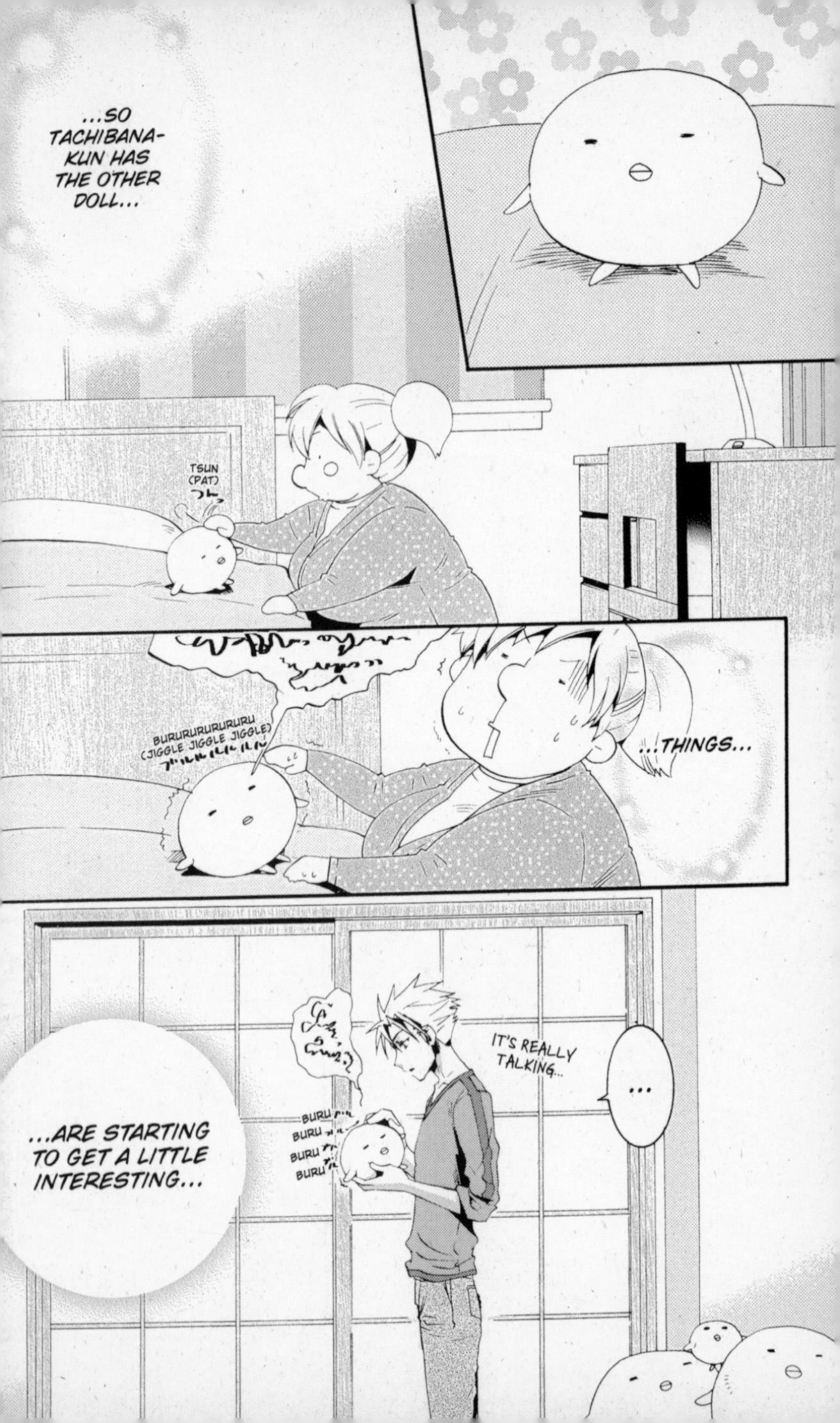
...SO TACHIBANA-KUN HAS THE OTHER DOLL...
TSUN (PAT)
...THINGS...
BURURURURURURU (JIGGLE JIGGLE JIGGLE)
...
IT'S REALLY TALKING...
BURU BURU BURU BURU
...ARE STARTING TO GET A LITTLE INTERESTING...

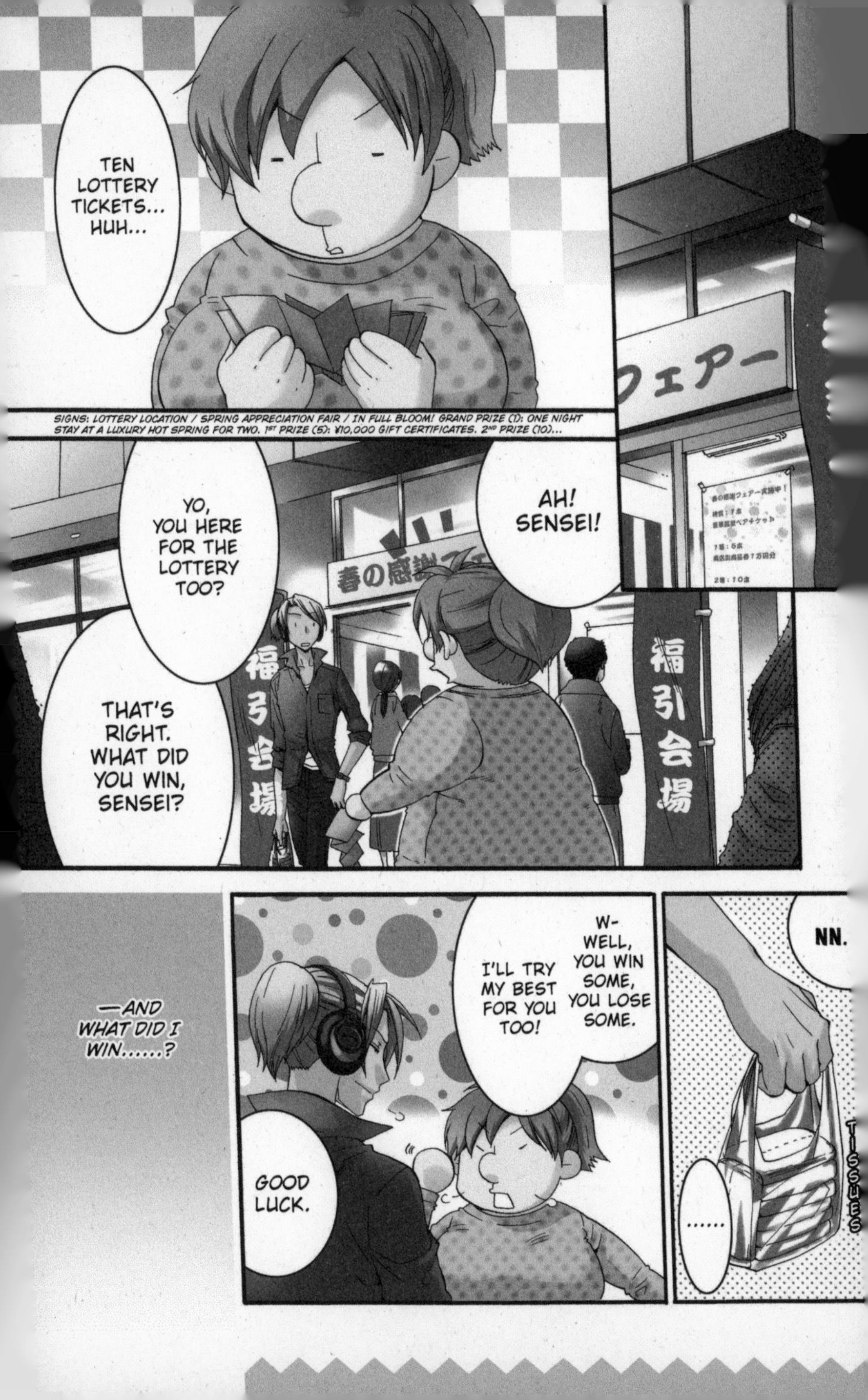
フェアー
TEN LOTTERY TICKETS... HUH...
SIGNS: LOTTERY LOCATION / SPRING APPRECIATION FAIR / IN FULL BLOOM! GRAND PRIZE (1): ONE NIGHT STAY AT A LUXURY HOT SPRING FOR TWO. 1ST PRIZE (5): ¥10,000 GIFT CERTIFICATES. 2ND PRIZE (10)...
AH! SENSEI!
YO, YOU HERE FOR THE LOTTERY TOO?
福引会場
THAT'S RIGHT. WHAT DID YOU WIN, SENSEI?
NN.
......
TISSUES
W-WELL, YOU WIN SOME, YOU LOSE SOME.
I'LL TRY MY BEST FOR YOU TOO!
GOOD LUCK.
—AND WHAT DID I WIN......?

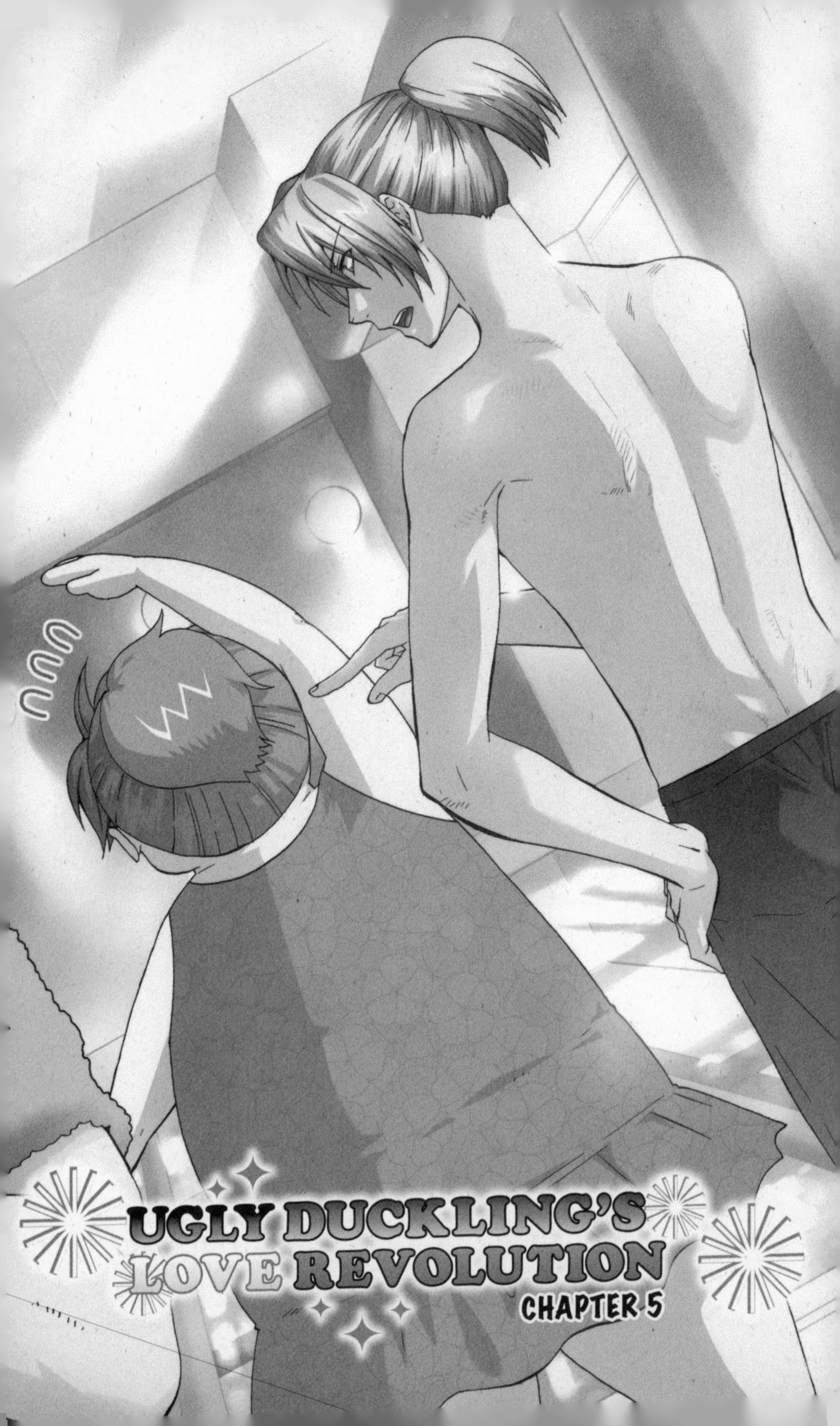
UGLY DUCKLING'S LOVE REVOLUTION
CHAPTER 5

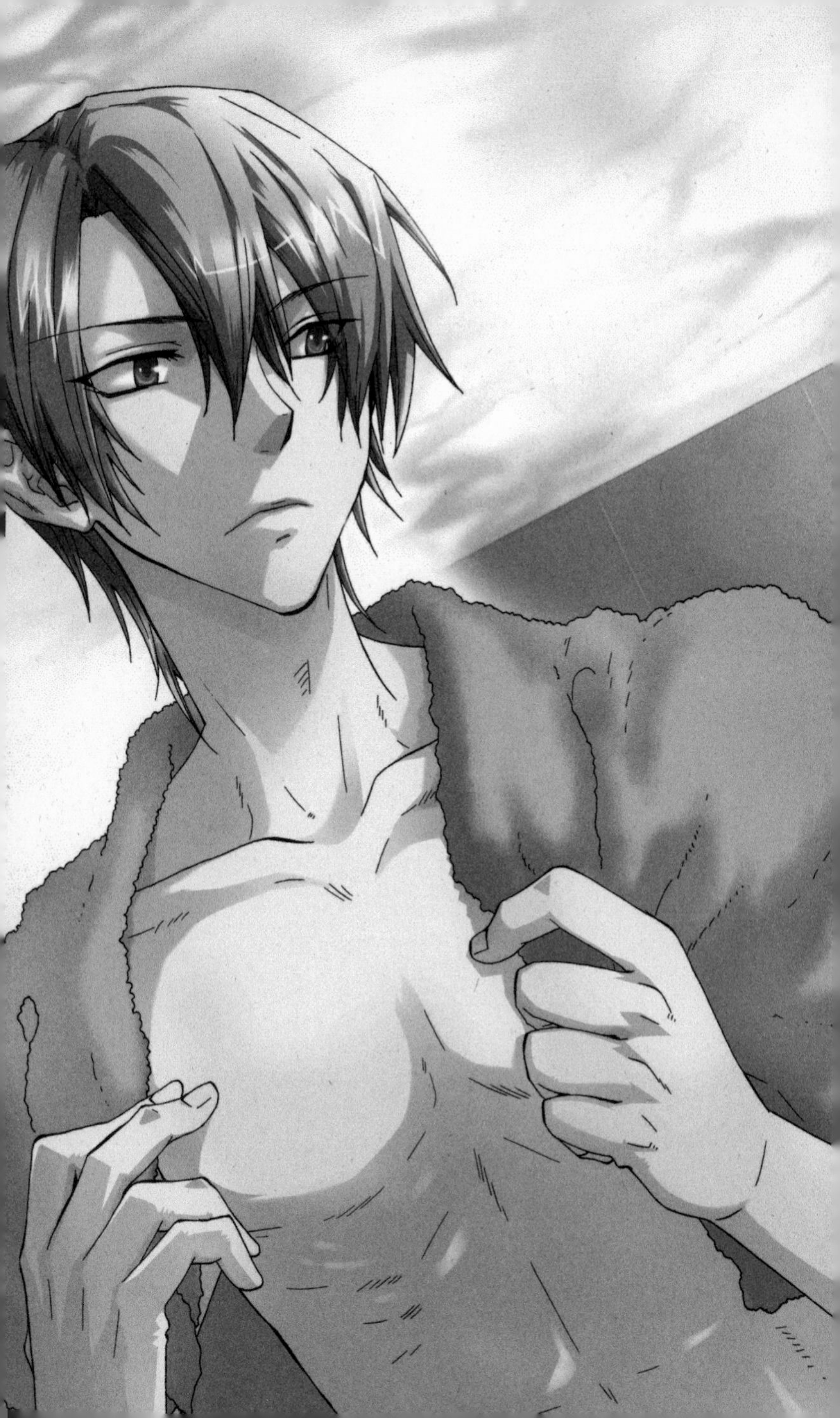

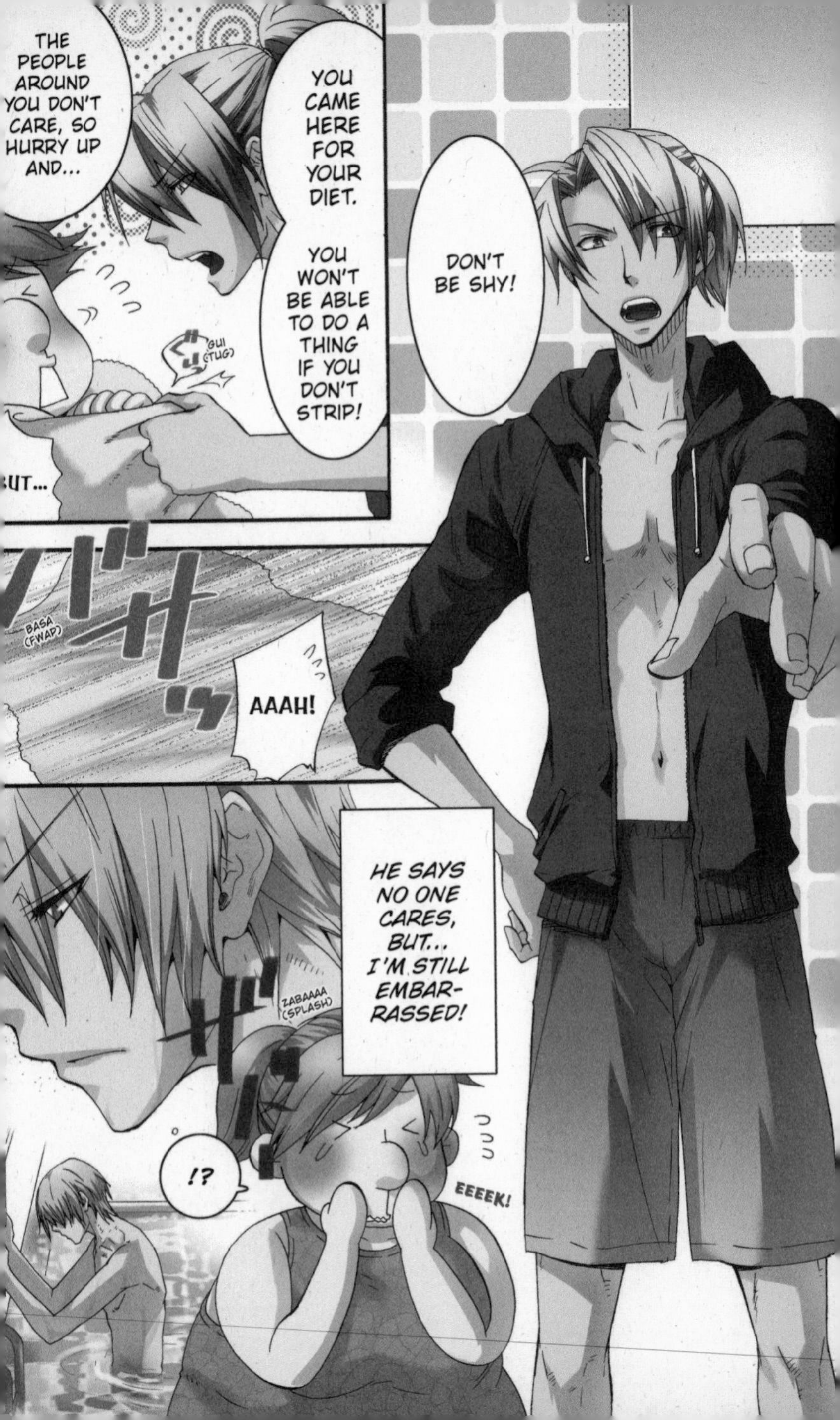
DON'T BE SHY!
YOU CAME HERE FOR YOUR DIET.
YOU WON'T BE ABLE TO DO A THING IF YOU DON'T STRIP!
THE PEOPLE AROUND YOU DON'T CARE, SO HURRY UP AND...
GUI (TUG)
BUT...
BASA (FWAP)
AAAH!
HE SAYS NO ONE CARES, BUT... I'M STILL EMBARRASSED!
ZABAAAA (SPLASH)
!?
EEEEK!

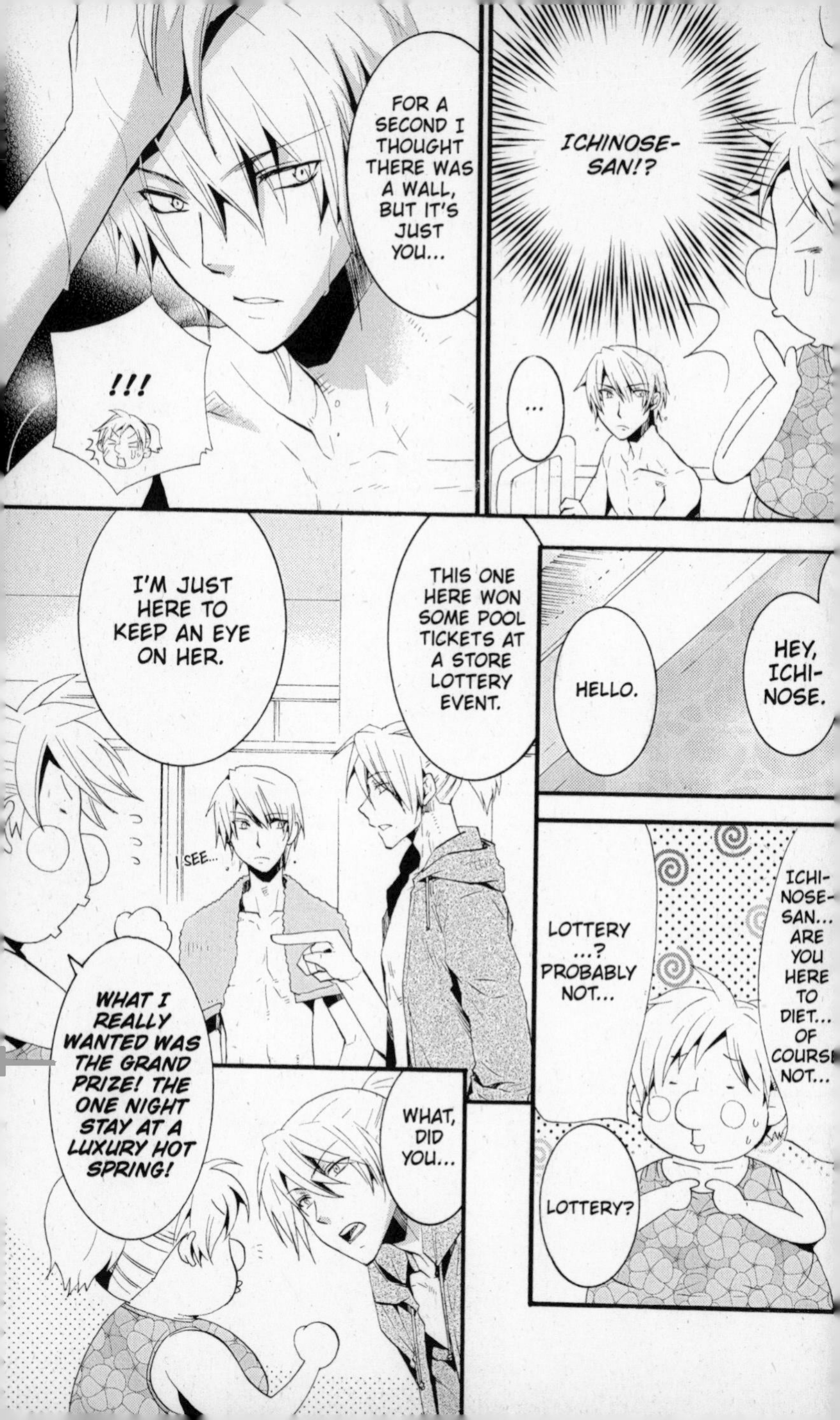
ICHINOSE-SAN!?
...
FOR A SECOND I THOUGHT THERE WAS A WALL, BUT IT'S JUST YOU...
!!!
HEY, ICHINOSE.
HELLO.
ICHINOSE-SAN... ARE YOU HERE TO DIET... OF COURSE NOT...
LOTTERY ...? PROBABLY NOT...
LOTTERY?
THIS ONE HERE WON SOME POOL TICKETS AT A STORE LOTTERY EVENT.
I'M JUST HERE TO KEEP AN EYE ON HER.
I SEE...
WHAT, DID YOU...
WHAT I REALLY WANTED WAS THE GRAND PRIZE! THE ONE NIGHT STAY AT A LUXURY HOT SPRING!

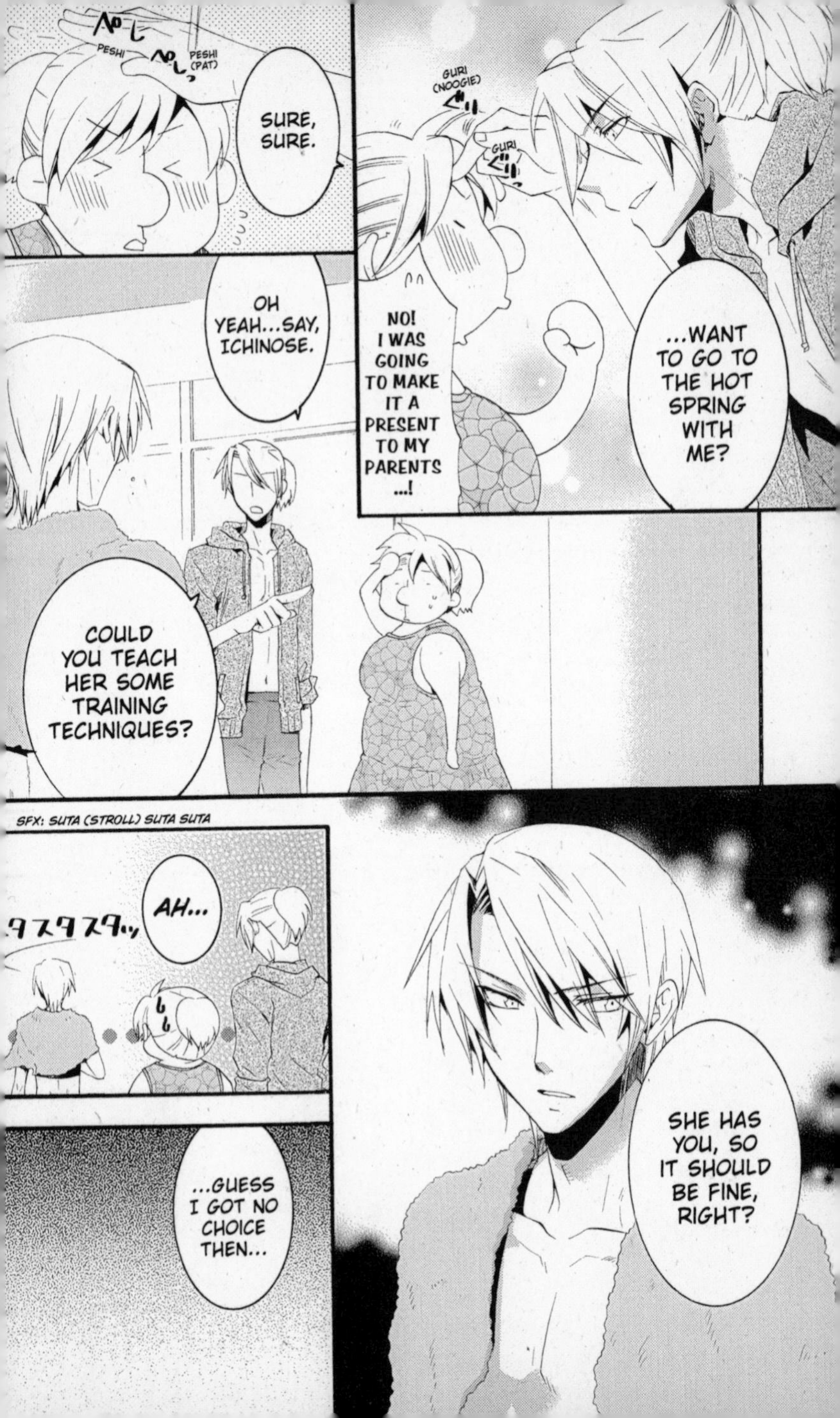
GURI (NOOGIE)
GURI
...WANT TO GO TO THE HOT SPRING WITH ME?
NO! I WAS GOING TO MAKE IT A PRESENT TO MY PARENTS ...!
PESHI (PAT)
PESHI
SURE, SURE.
OH YEAH...SAY, ICHINOSE.
COULD YOU TEACH HER SOME TRAINING TECHNIQUES?
SFX: SUTA (STROLL) SUTA SUTA
SHE HAS YOU, SO IT SHOULD BE FINE, RIGHT?
AH...
...GUESS I GOT NO CHOICE THEN...

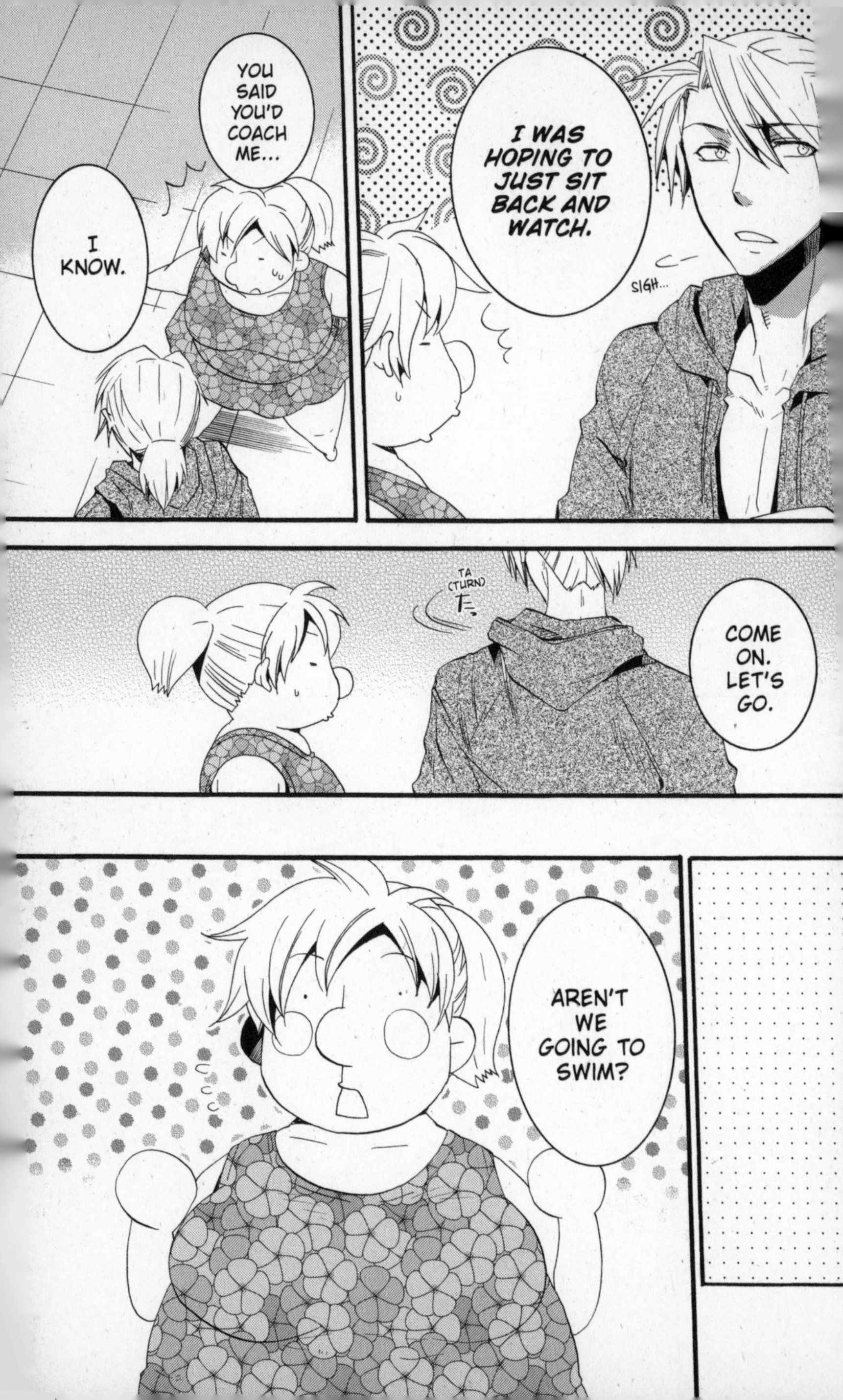
I WAS HOPING TO JUST SIT BACK AND WATCH.
SIGH...
YOU SAID YOU'D COACH ME...
I KNOW.
TA (TURN)
COME ON. LET'S GO.
AREN'T WE GOING TO SWIM?

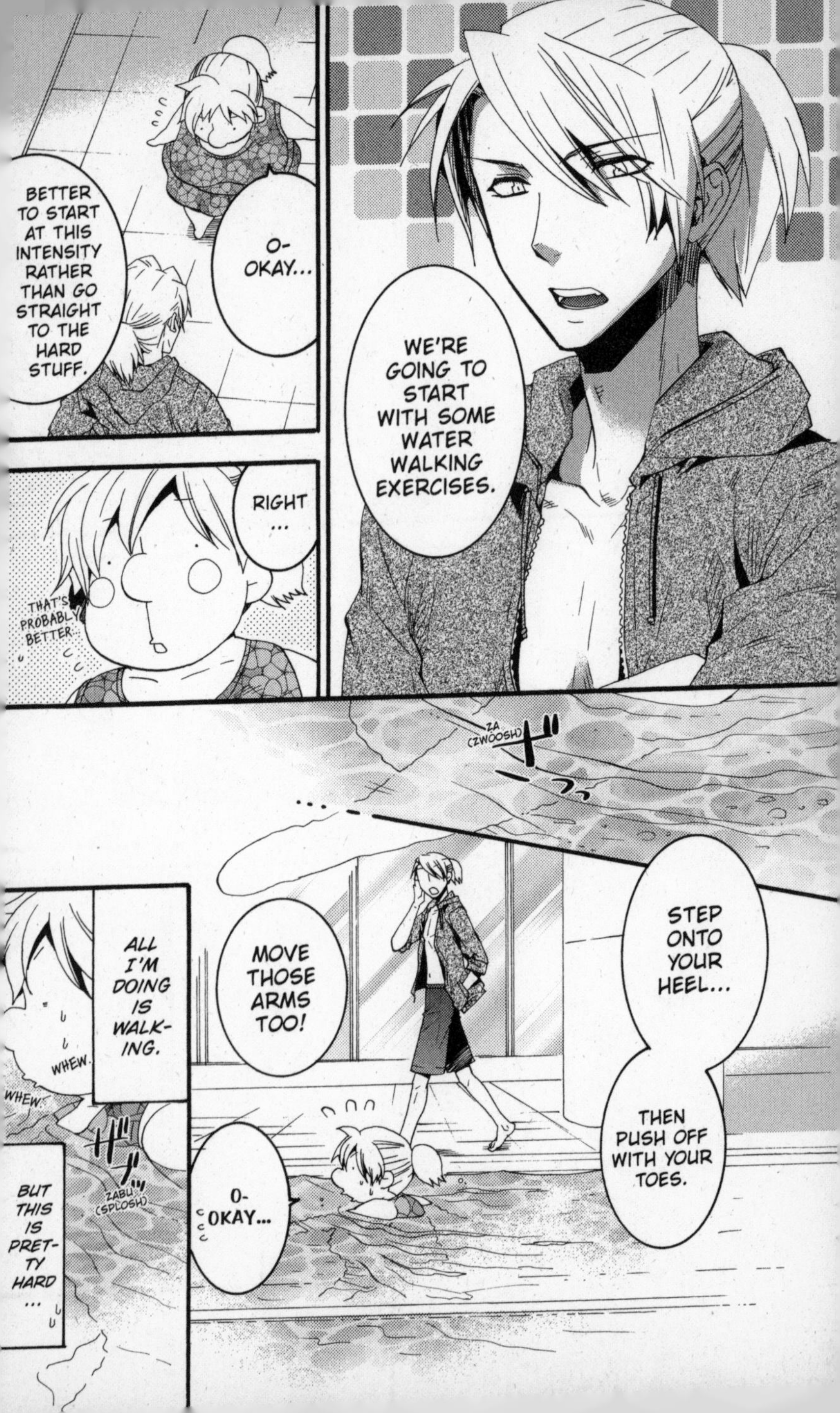
WE'RE GOING TO START WITH SOME WATER WALKING EXERCISES.
O-OKAY...
BETTER TO START AT THIS INTENSITY RATHER THAN GO STRAIGHT TO THE HARD STUFF.
RIGHT ...
THAT'S PROBABLY BETTER...
ZA (ZWOOSH)
STEP ONTO YOUR HEEL...
THEN PUSH OFF WITH YOUR TOES.
MOVE THOSE ARMS TOO!
O-OKAY...
ALL I'M DOING IS WALK-ING.
WHEW. WHEW.
ZABU (SPLOSH)
BUT THIS IS PRETTY HARD ...

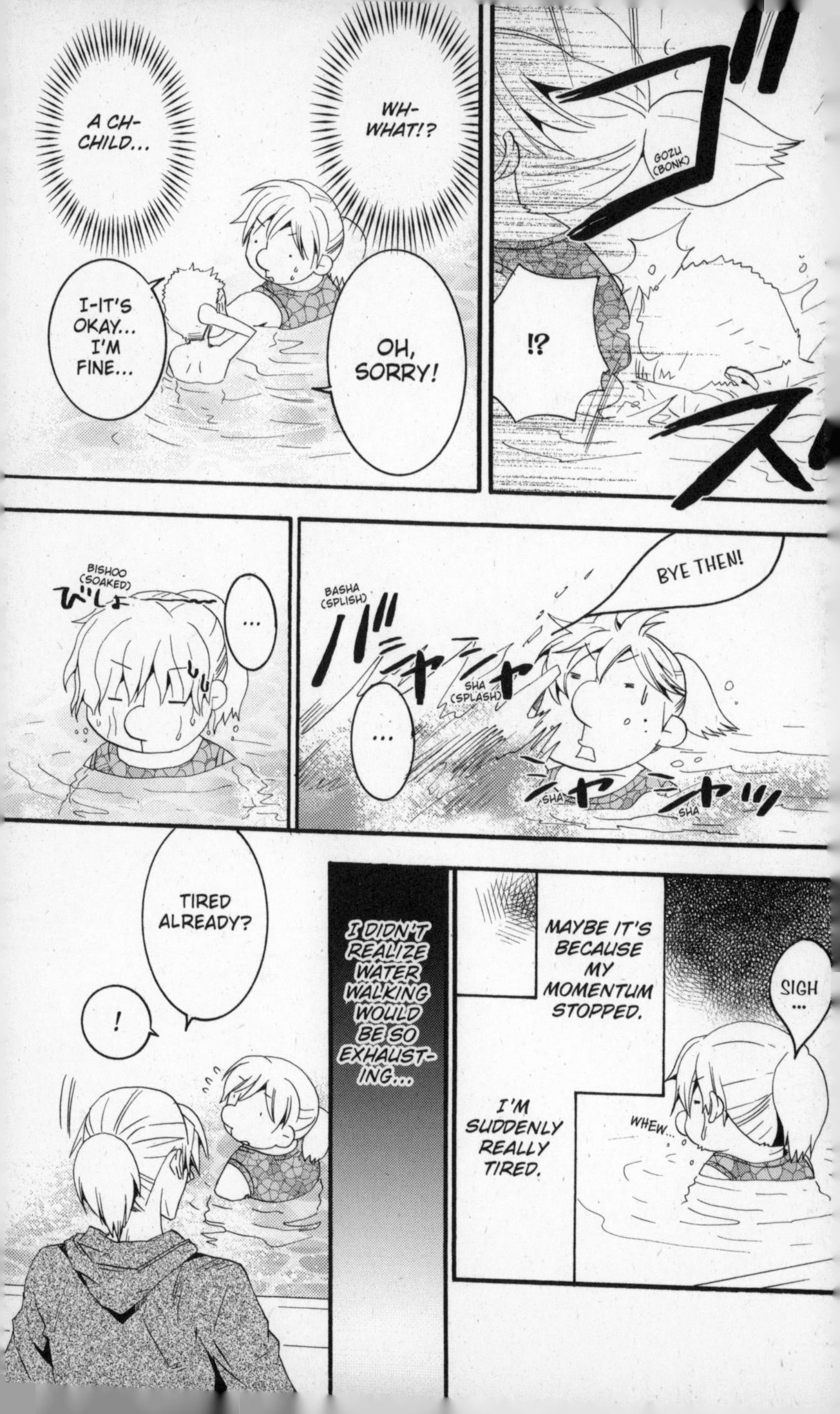
GOZU (BONK)
!?
WH-WHAT!?
A CH-CHILD...
OH, SORRY!
I-IT'S OKAY... I'M FINE...
BYE THEN!
BASHA (SPLISH)
SHA (SPLASH)
SHA
SHA
...
BISHOO (SOAKED)
...
SIGH...
WHEW...
MAYBE IT'S BECAUSE MY MOMENTUM STOPPED.
I'M SUDDENLY REALLY TIRED.
I DIDN'T REALIZE WATER WALKING WOULD BE SO EXHAUSTING...
TIRED ALREADY?
!

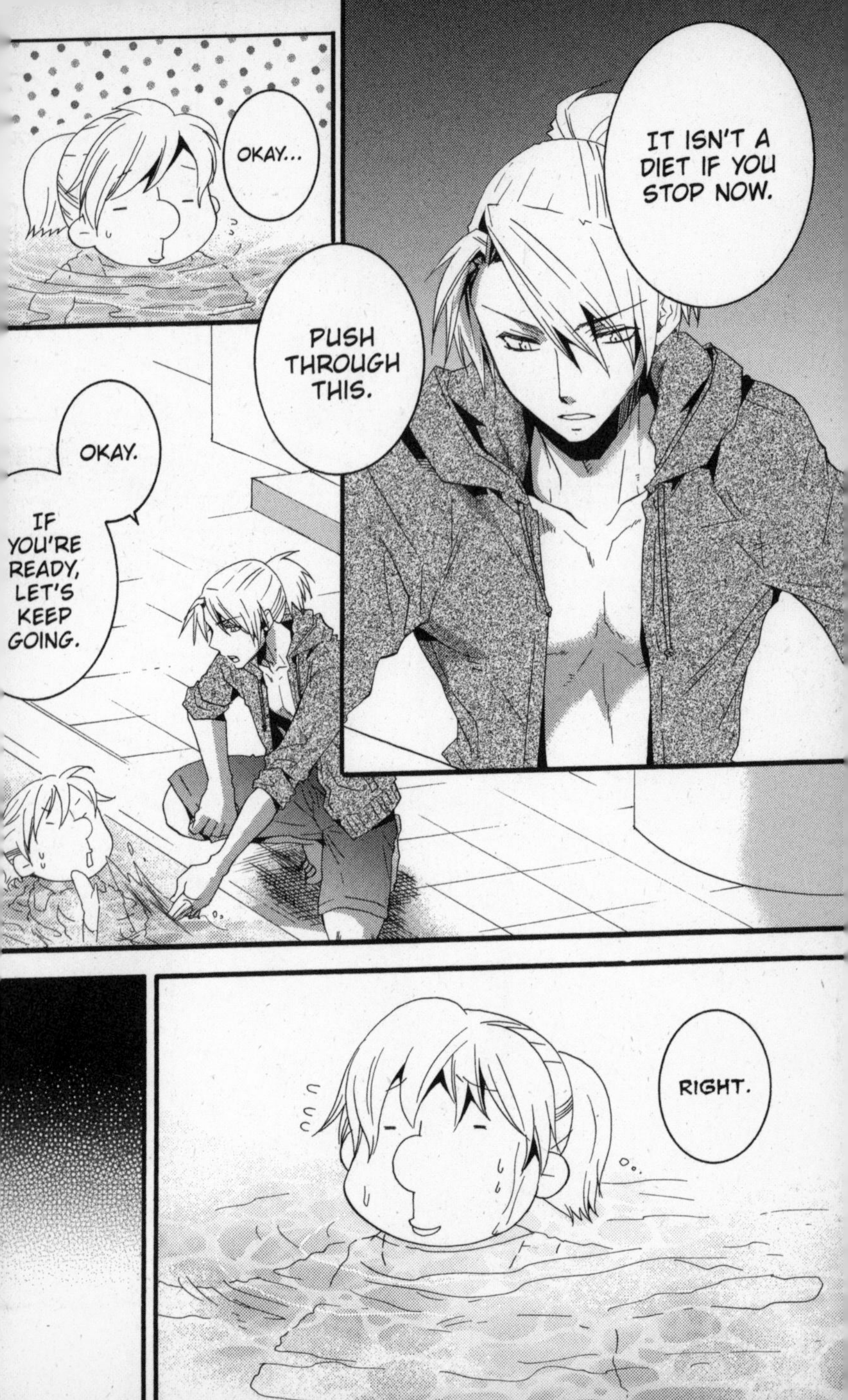
IT ISN'T A DIET IF YOU STOP NOW.
PUSH THROUGH THIS.
OKAY...
OKAY.
IF YOU'RE READY, LET'S KEEP GOING.
RIGHT.

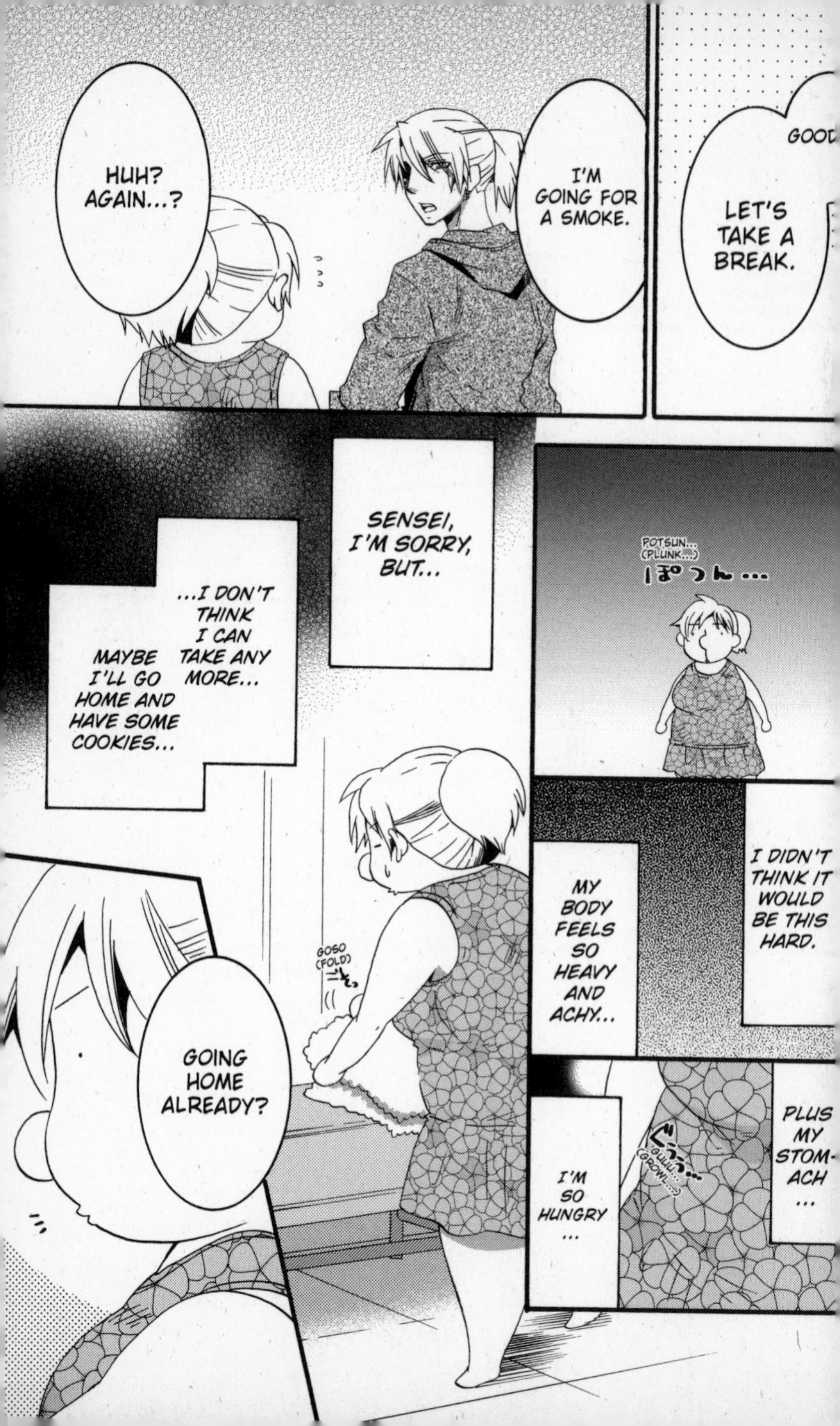

GOOD
LET'S TAKE A BREAK.
I'M GOING FOR A SMOKE.
HUH? AGAIN...?
POTSUN... (PLUNK...)
ぽつん...
SENSEI, I'M SORRY, BUT...
...I DON'T THINK I CAN TAKE ANY MORE...
MAYBE I'LL GO HOME AND HAVE SOME COOKIES...
I DIDN'T THINK IT WOULD BE THIS HARD.
MY BODY FEELS SO HEAVY AND ACHY...
PLUS MY STOM-ACH...
GUUU... (GROWL...)
I'M SO HUNGRY...
GOSO (FOLD)
GOING HOME ALREADY?

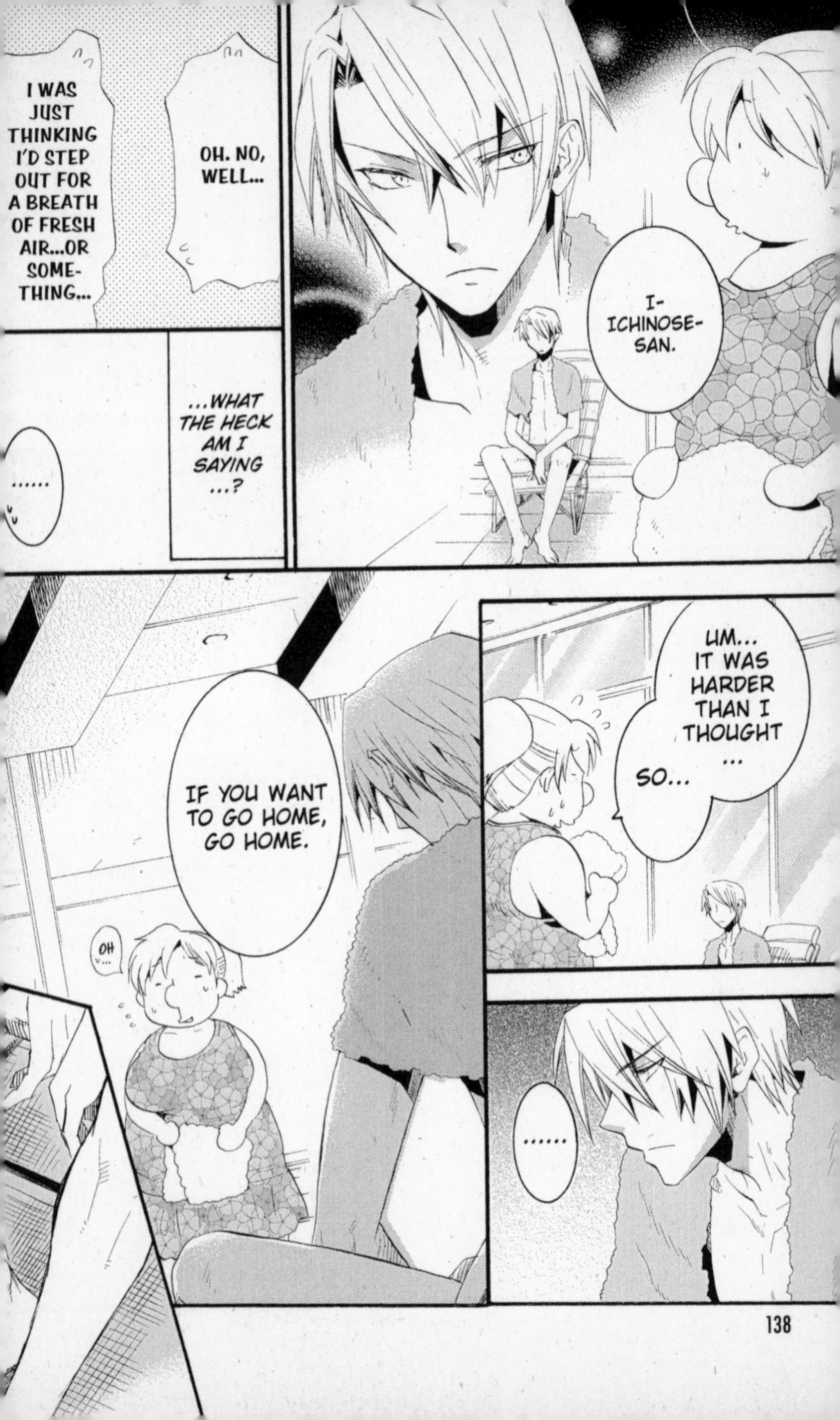
I- ICHINOSE-SAN.
OH. NO, WELL...
I WAS JUST THINKING I'D STEP OUT FOR A BREATH OF FRESH AIR...OR SOME-THING...
...WHAT THE HECK AM I SAYING ...?
......
UM... IT WAS HARDER THAN I THOUGHT ...
SO...
......
IF YOU WANT TO GO HOME, GO HOME.
OH...

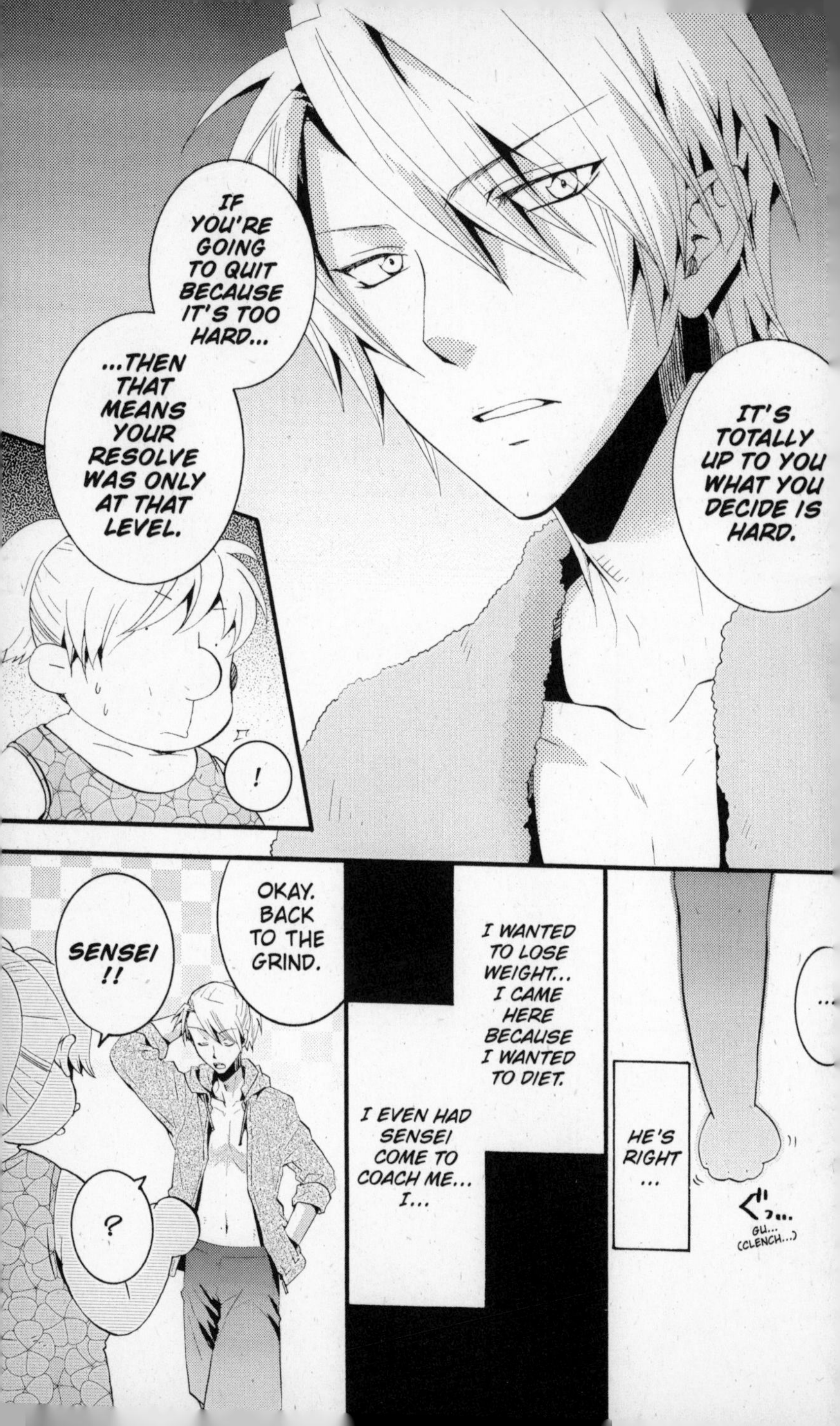
IT'S TOTALLY UP TO YOU WHAT YOU DECIDE IS HARD.
IF YOU'RE GOING TO QUIT BECAUSE IT'S TOO HARD...
...THEN THAT MEANS YOUR RESOLVE WAS ONLY AT THAT LEVEL.
!
...
HE'S RIGHT ...
ぐっ...
GU... (CLENCH...)
I WANTED TO LOSE WEIGHT... I CAME HERE BECAUSE I WANTED TO DIET.
I EVEN HAD SENSEI COME TO COACH ME... I...
OKAY. BACK TO THE GRIND.
SENSEI !!
?

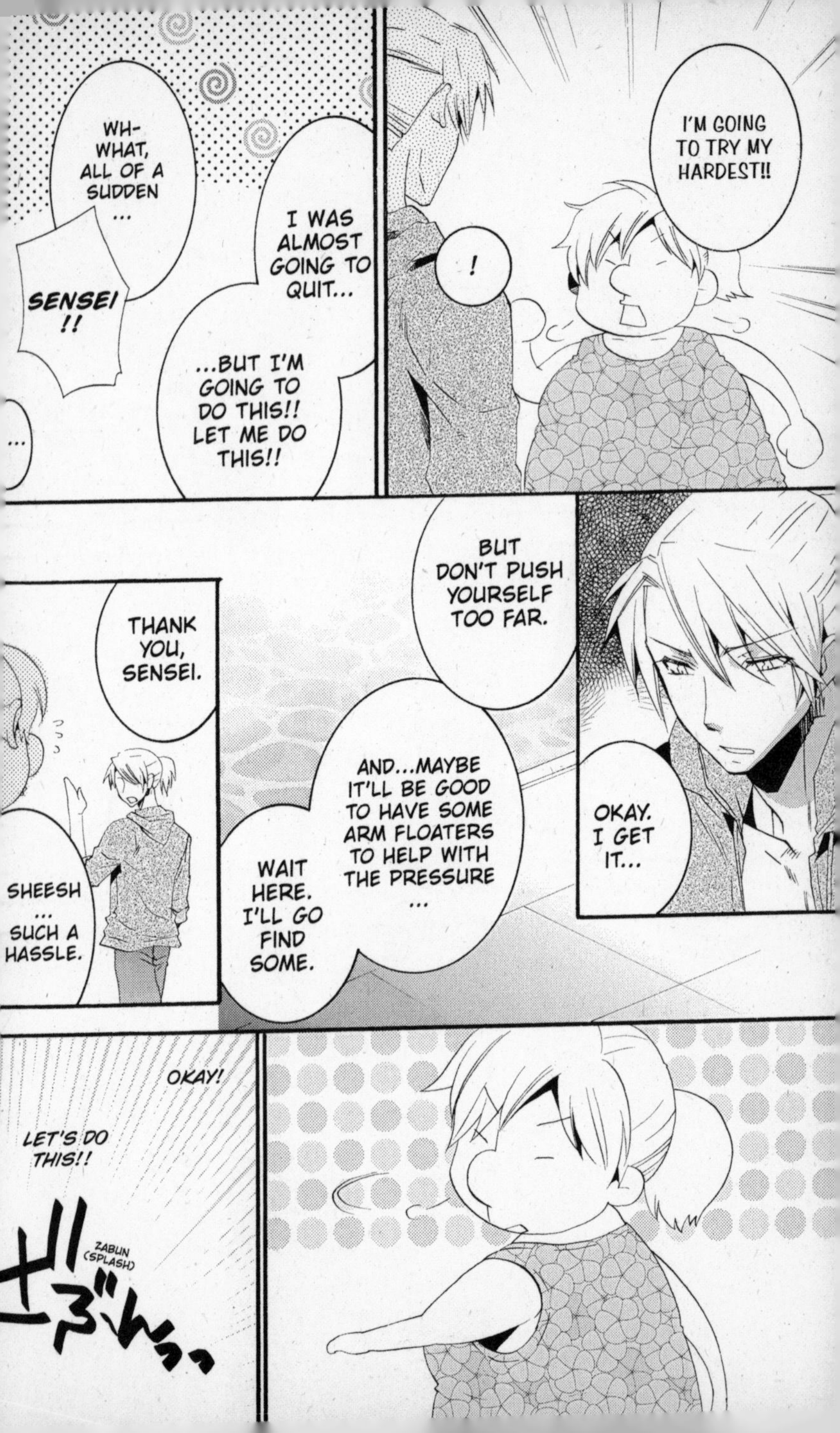
I'M GOING TO TRY MY HARDEST!!
!
I WAS ALMOST GOING TO QUIT...
...BUT I'M GOING TO DO THIS!! LET ME DO THIS!!
WH- WHAT, ALL OF A SUDDEN ...
SENSEI !!
...
BUT DON'T PUSH YOURSELF TOO FAR.
OKAY. I GET IT...
AND...MAYBE IT'LL BE GOOD TO HAVE SOME ARM FLOATERS TO HELP WITH THE PRESSURE ...
WAIT HERE. I'LL GO FIND SOME.
THANK YOU, SENSEI.
SHEESH ... SUCH A HASSLE.
OKAY!
LET'S DO THIS!!
ZABUN (SPLASH)

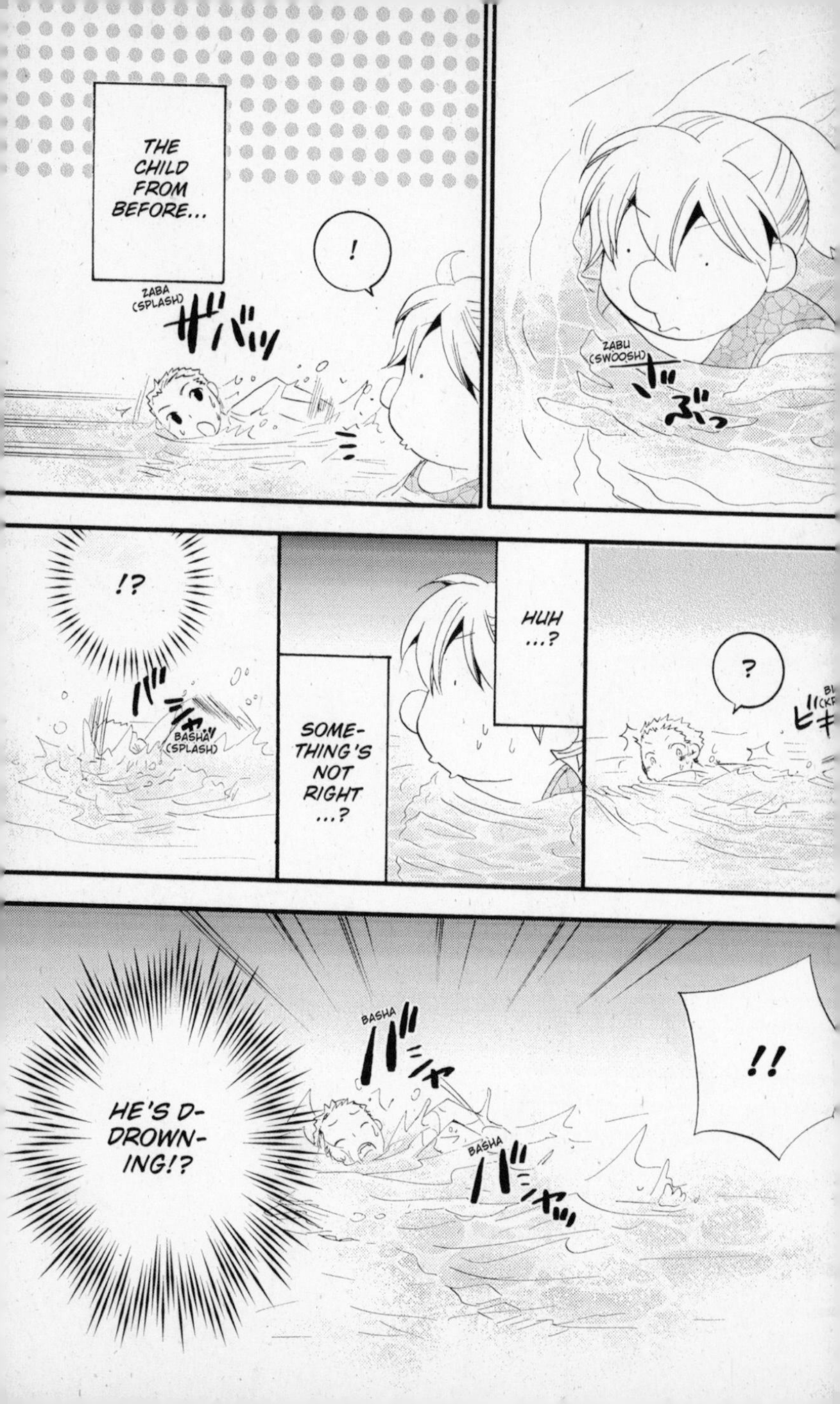
ZABU (SWOOSH)
ざぶっ
THE CHILD FROM BEFORE...
!
ZABA (SPLASH)
ザバッ
?
ビキ
HUH ...?
SOME-THING'S NOT RIGHT ...?
!?
BASHA (SPLASH)
バシャ
!!
BASHA
バシャ
BASHA
バシャッ
HE'S D-DROWN-ING!?

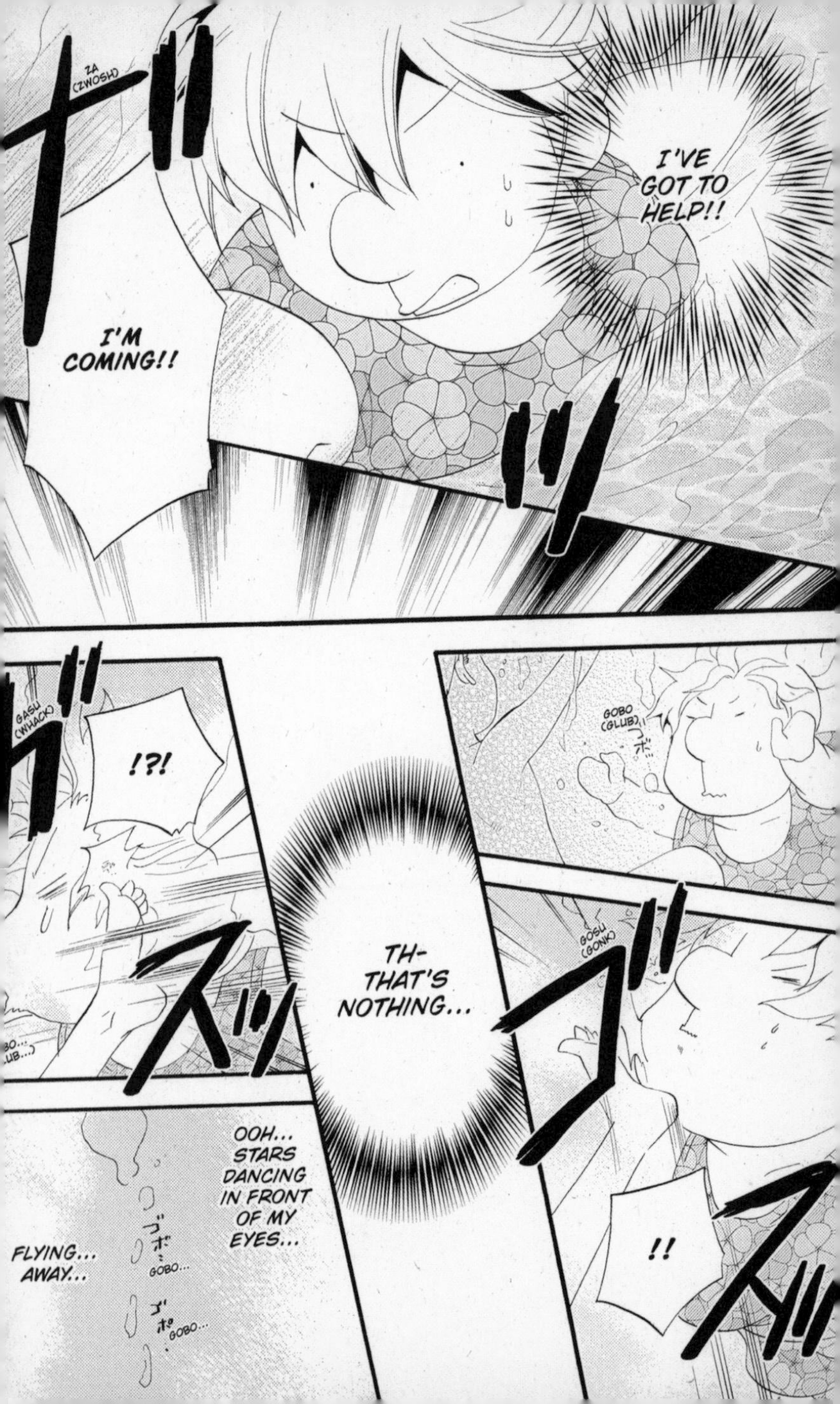
I'VE GOT TO HELP!!
ZA (ZWOSH)
I'M COMING!!
GOBO (GLUB)
GOSU (GONK)
!!
TH- THAT'S NOTHING...
GASU (WHACK)
!?!
OOH... STARS DANCING IN FRONT OF MY EYES...
GOBO...
GOBO...
FLYING... AWAY...

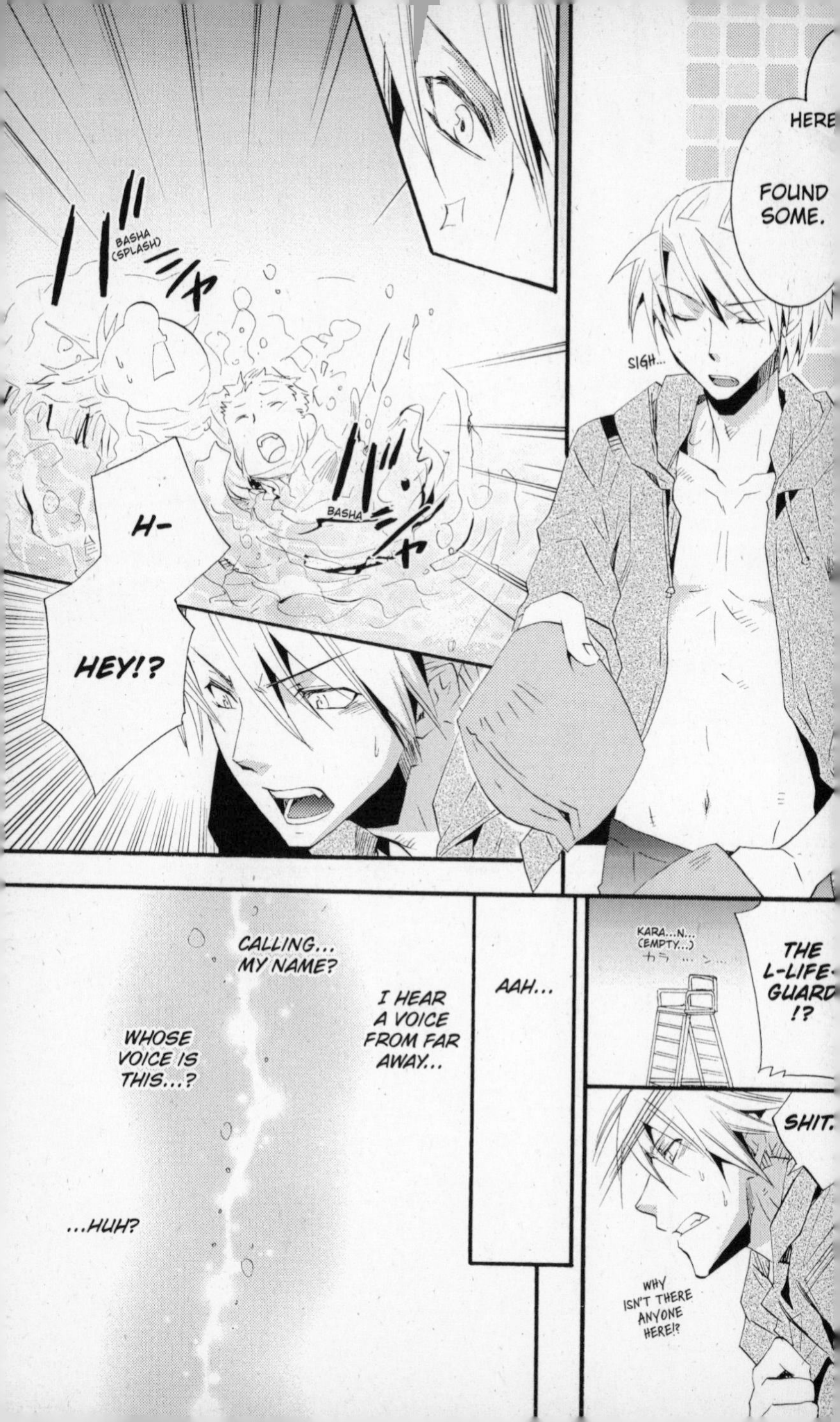
HERE FOUND SOME.
SIGH...
BASHA (SPLASH)
バシャ
BASHA
バシャ
H-
HEY!?
THE L-LIFE-GUARD!?
KARA...N... (EMPTY...)
SHIT.
WHY ISN'T THERE ANYONE HERE!?
AAH...
I HEAR A VOICE FROM FAR AWAY...
CALLING... MY NAME?
WHOSE VOICE IS THIS...?
...HUH?

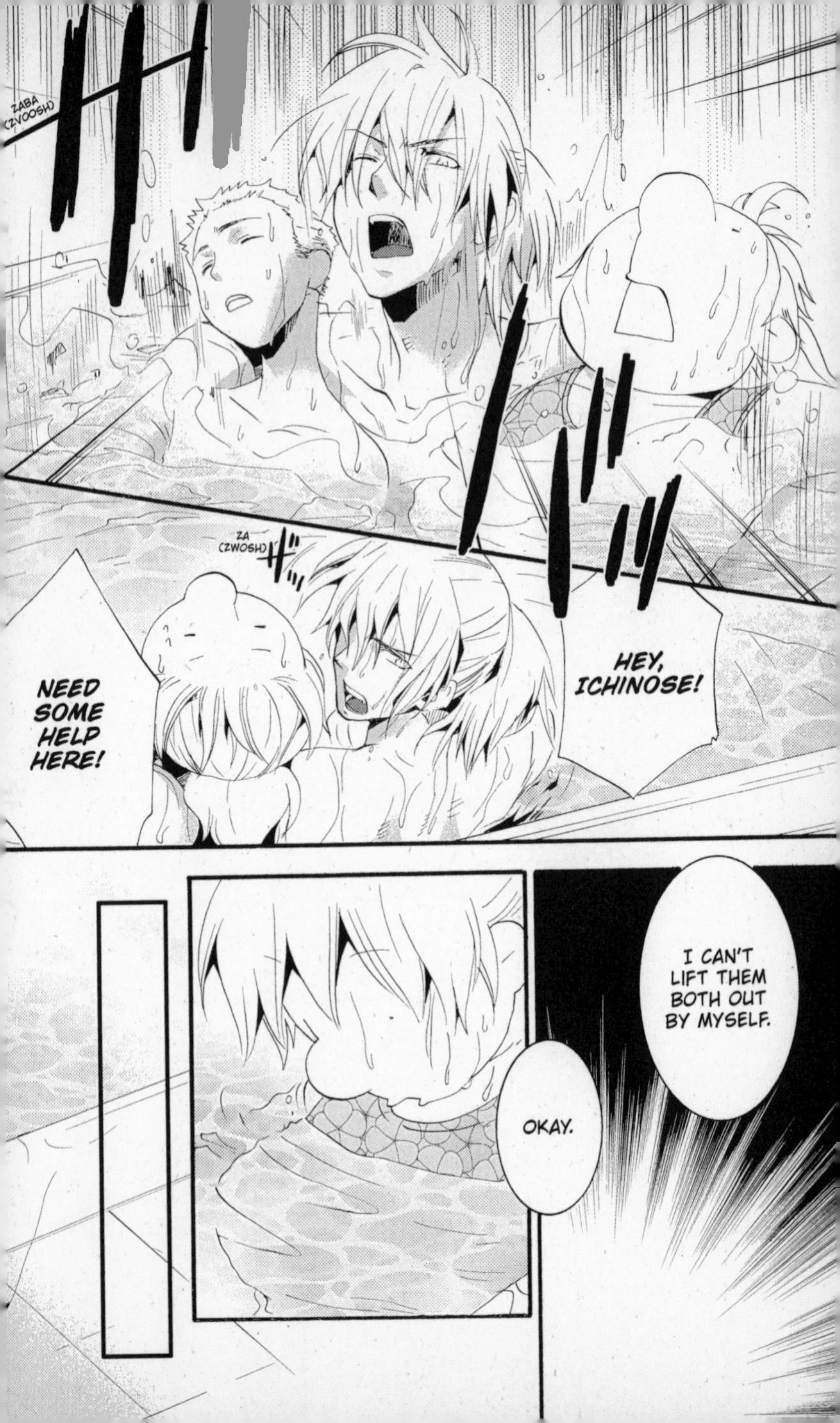
ZABA (ZVOOSH)
HEY, ICHINOSE!
ZA (ZWOSH)
NEED SOME HELP HERE!
I CAN'T LIFT THEM BOTH OUT BY MYSELF.
OKAY.

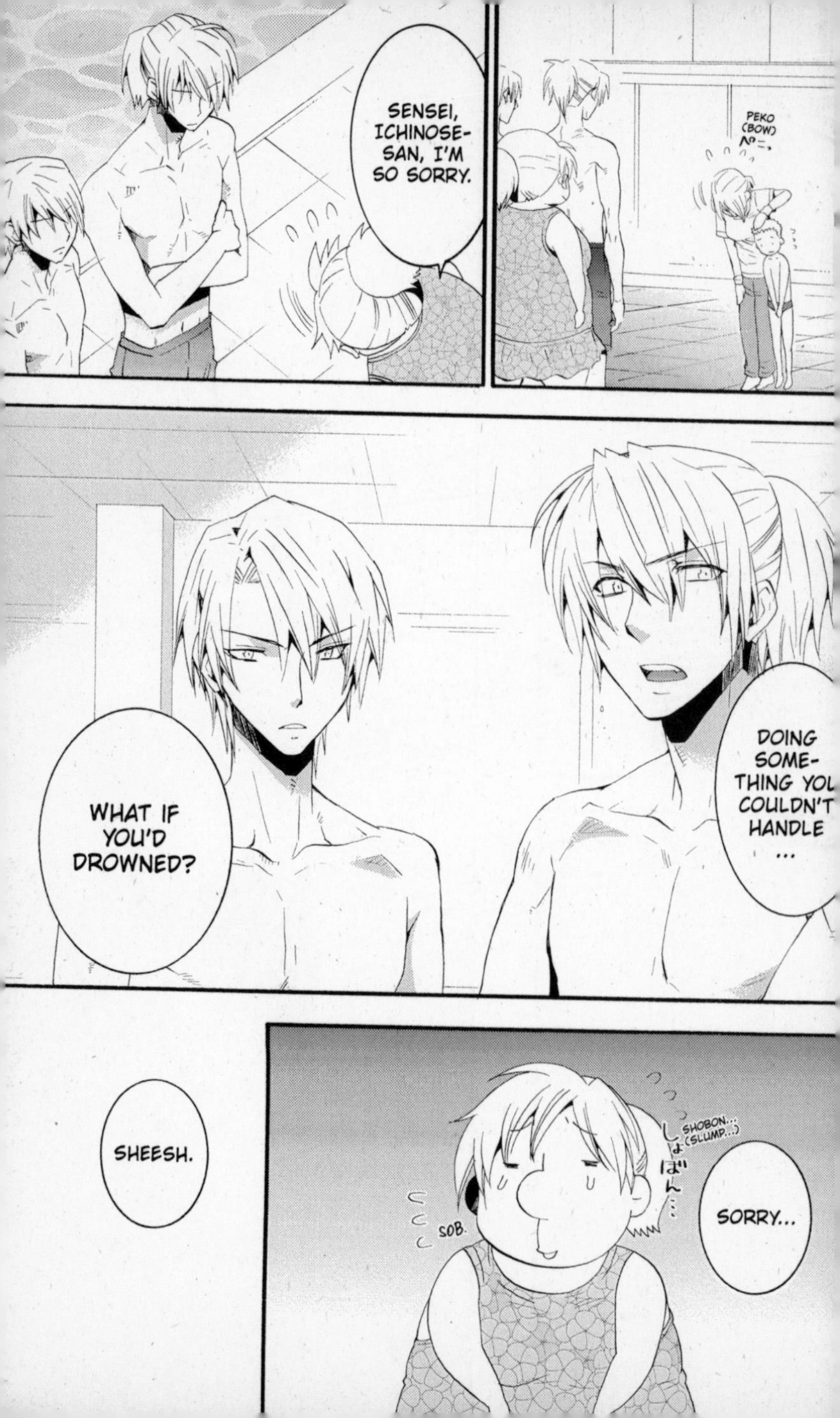
PEKO (BOW)
ぺこ
SENSEI, ICHINOSE-SAN, I'M SO SORRY.
DOING SOMETHING YOU COULDN'T HANDLE...
WHAT IF YOU'D DROWNED?
SORRY...
SHOBON... (SLUMP...)
しょぼん…
SOB.
SHEESH.

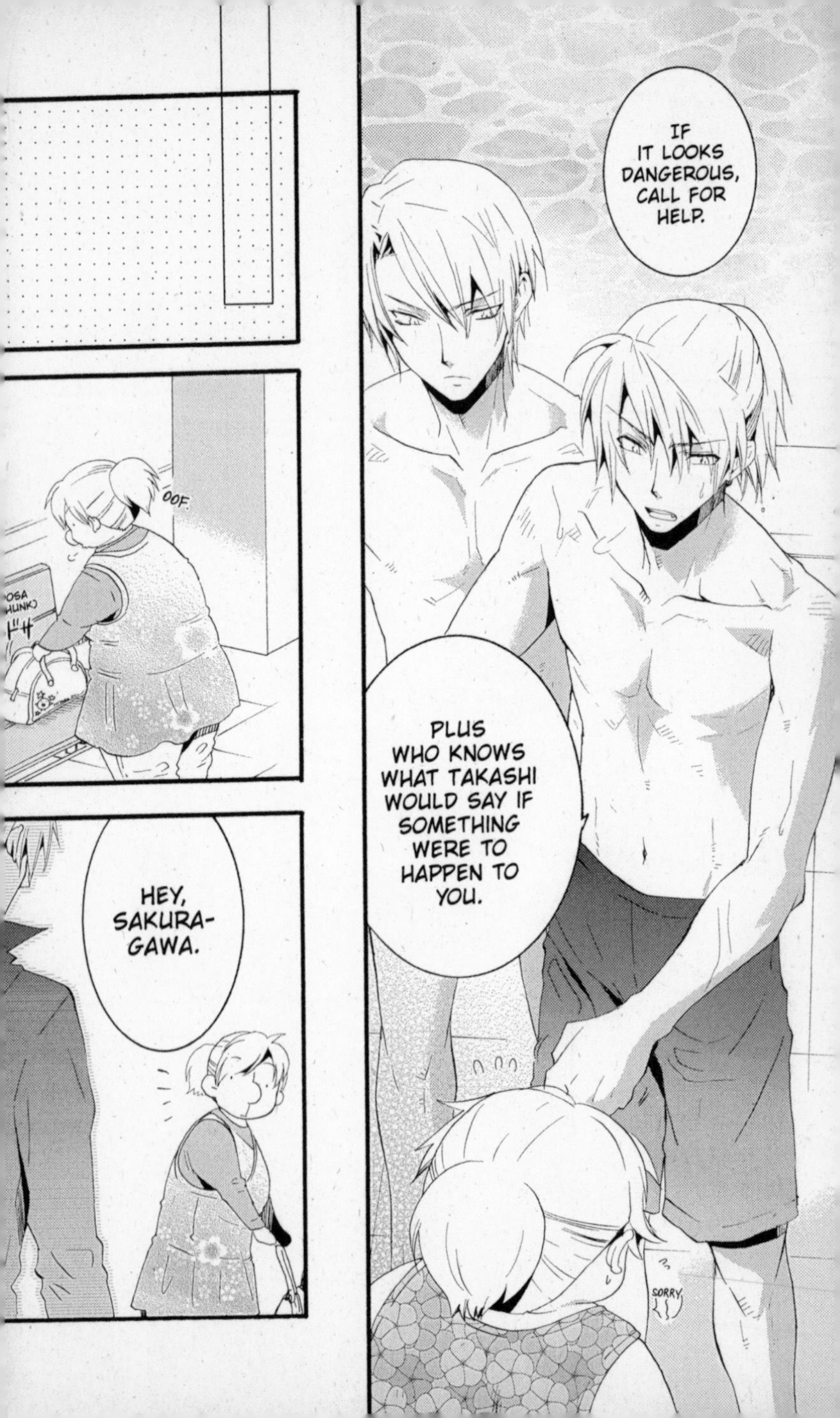

IF IT LOOKS DANGEROUS, CALL FOR HELP.
PLUS WHO KNOWS WHAT TAKASHI WOULD SAY IF SOMETHING WERE TO HAPPEN TO YOU.
SORRY
OOF.
HEY, SAKURA-GAWA.

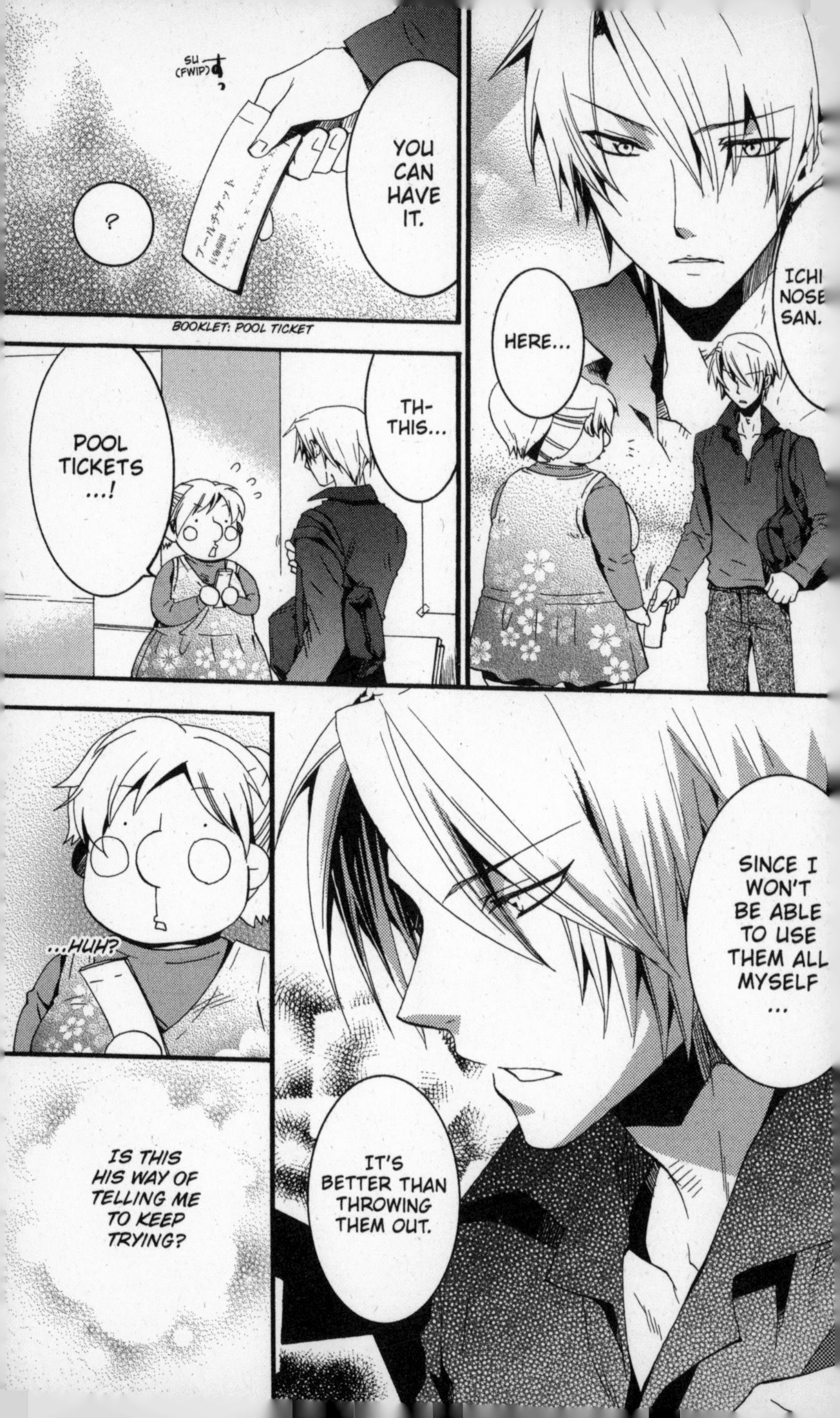
ICHINOSE SAN.
HERE...
YOU CAN HAVE IT.
SU (FWIP)
?
BOOKLET: POOL TICKET
TH-THIS...
POOL TICKETS ...!
SINCE I WON'T BE ABLE TO USE THEM ALL MYSELF ...
IT'S BETTER THAN THROWING THEM OUT.
...HUH?
IS THIS HIS WAY OF TELLING ME TO KEEP TRYING?

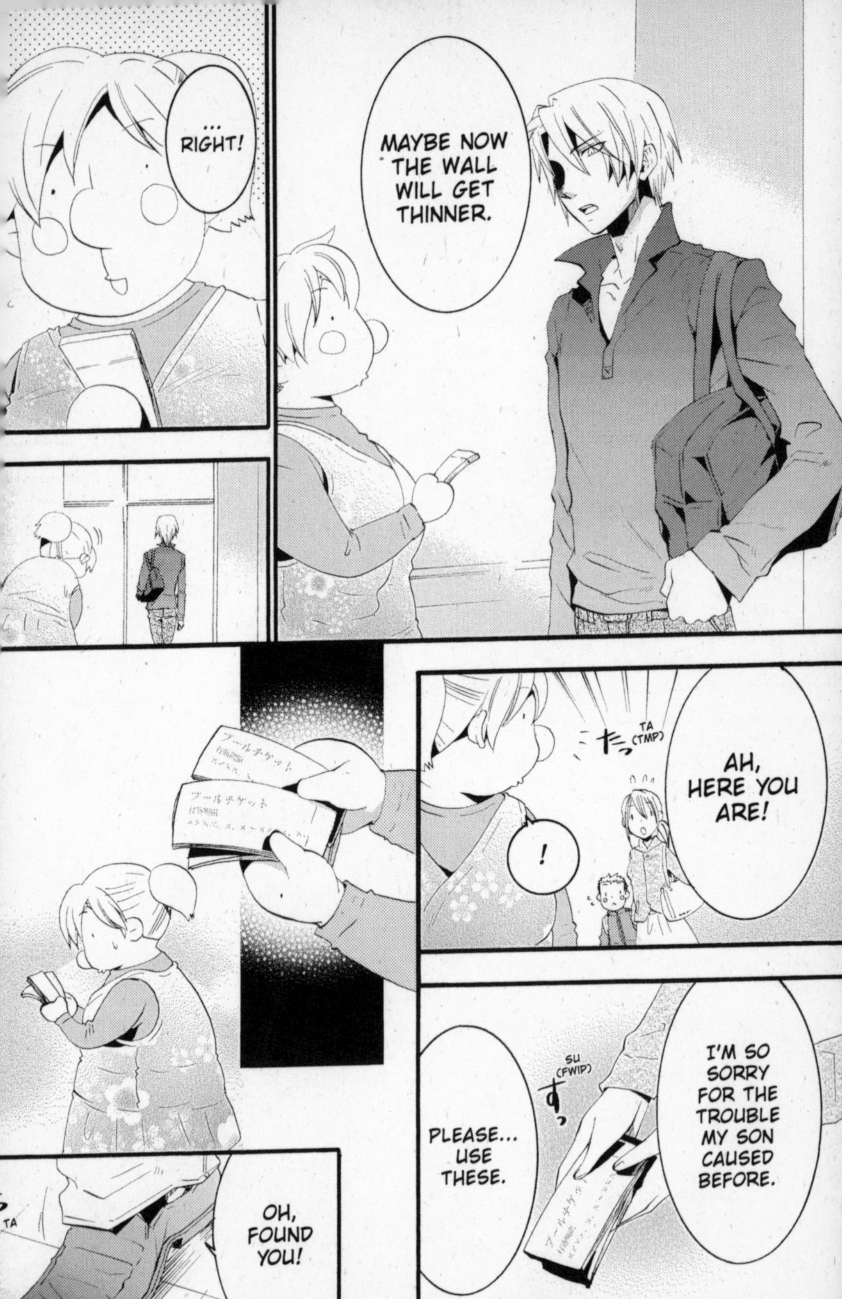
MAYBE NOW THE WALL WILL GET THINNER.
... RIGHT!
TA (TMP)
AH, HERE YOU ARE!
!
I'M SO SORRY FOR THE TROUBLE MY SON CAUSED BEFORE.
SU (FWIP)
PLEASE... USE THESE.
TA
OH, FOUND YOU!

BOOKLET: POOL TICKET

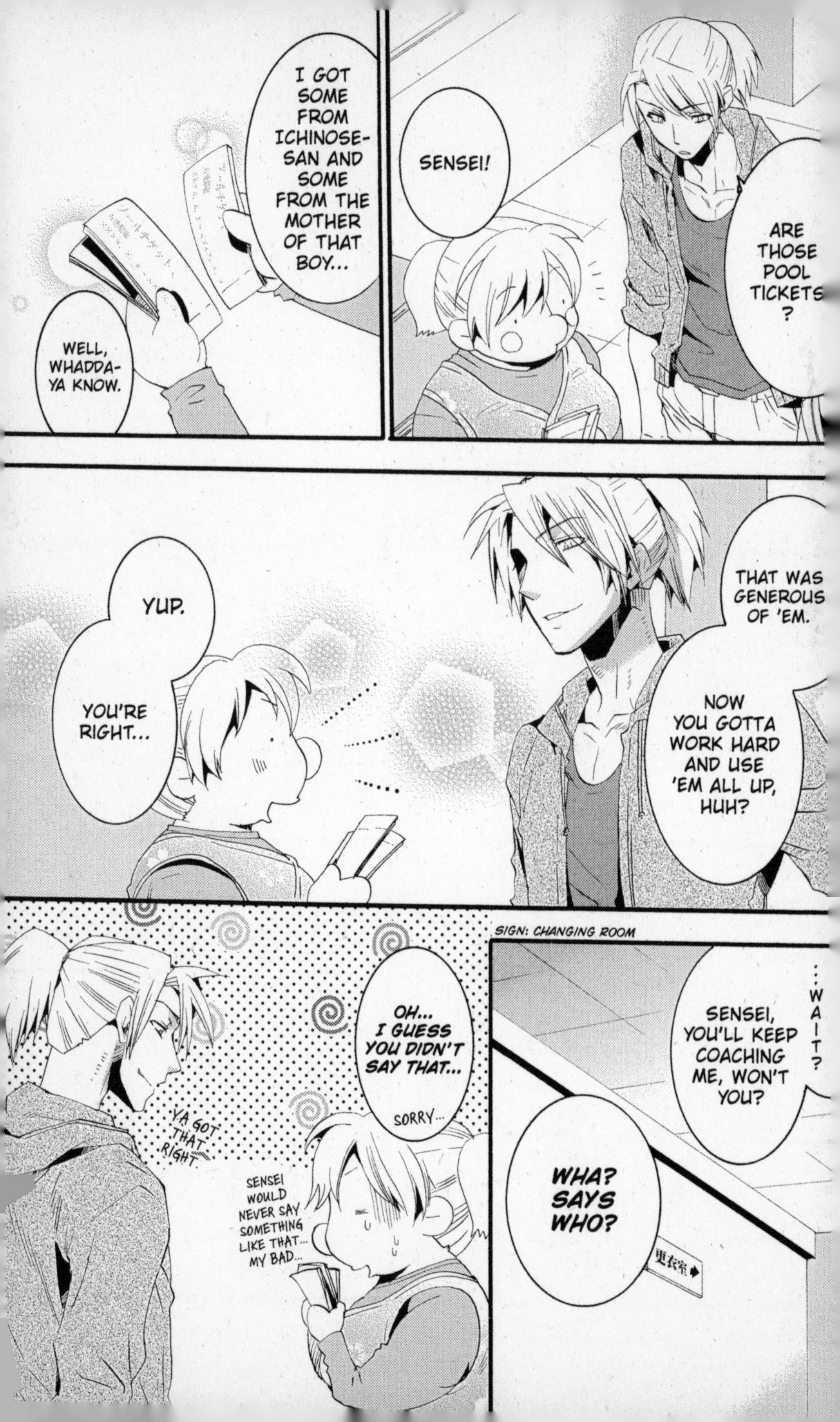
ARE THOSE POOL TICKETS?
SENSEI!
I GOT SOME FROM ICHINOSE-SAN AND SOME FROM THE MOTHER OF THAT BOY...
WELL, WHADDA-YA KNOW.
THAT WAS GENEROUS OF 'EM.
NOW YOU GOTTA WORK HARD AND USE 'EM ALL UP, HUH?
YUP.
YOU'RE RIGHT...
SIGN: CHANGING ROOM
...WAIT?
SENSEI, YOU'LL KEEP COACHING ME, WON'T YOU?
WHA? SAYS WHO?
更衣室
OH... I GUESS YOU DIDN'T SAY THAT...
SORRY...
YA GOT THAT RIGHT.
SENSEI WOULD NEVER SAY SOMETHING LIKE THAT... MY BAD...

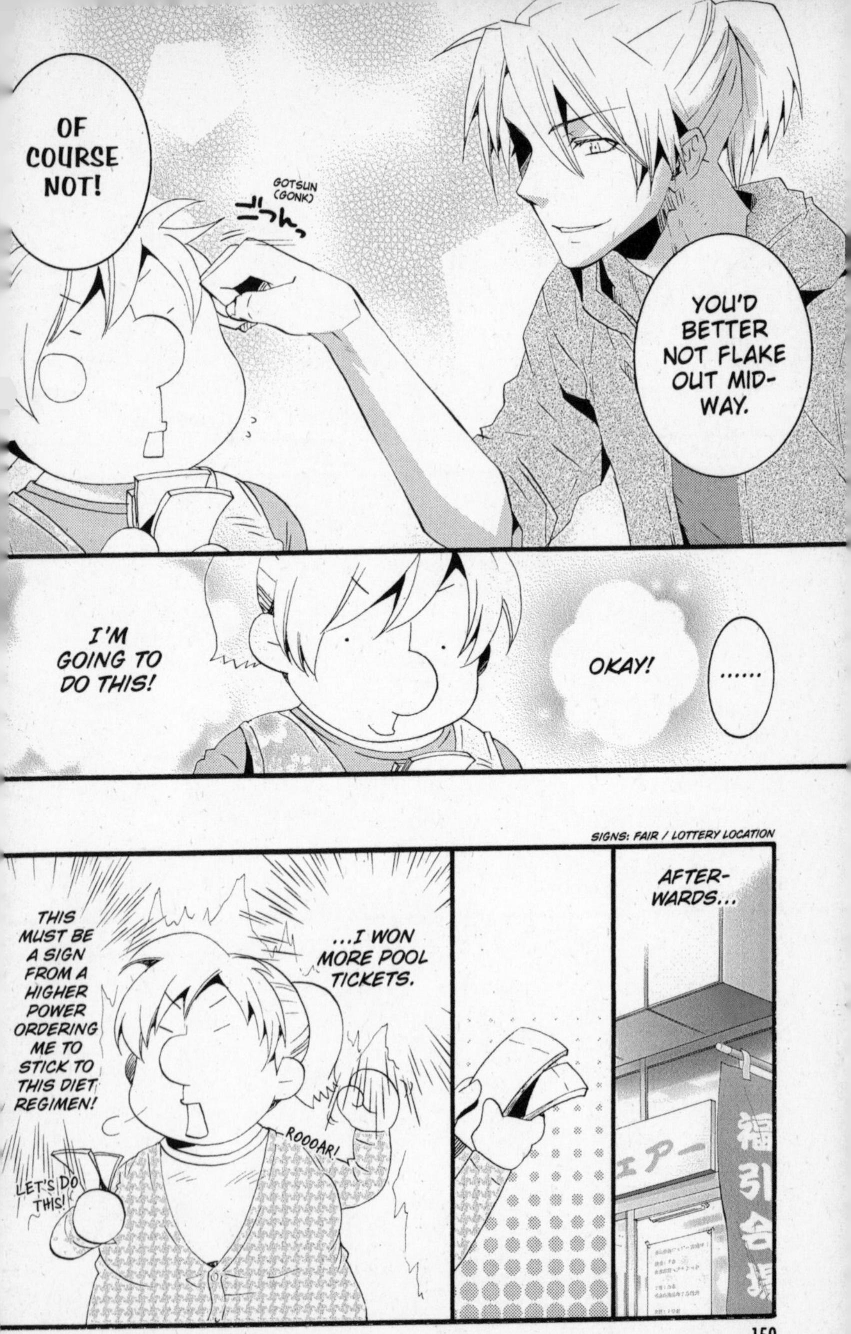
YOU'D BETTER NOT FLAKE OUT MID-WAY.
OF COURSE NOT!
GOTSUN (GONK)
......
OKAY!
I'M GOING TO DO THIS!
SIGNS: FAIR / LOTTERY LOCATION
AFTER-WARDS...
...I WON MORE POOL TICKETS.
THIS MUST BE A SIGN FROM A HIGHER POWER ORDERING ME TO STICK TO THIS DIET REGIMEN!
ROOOAR!
LET'S DO THIS!

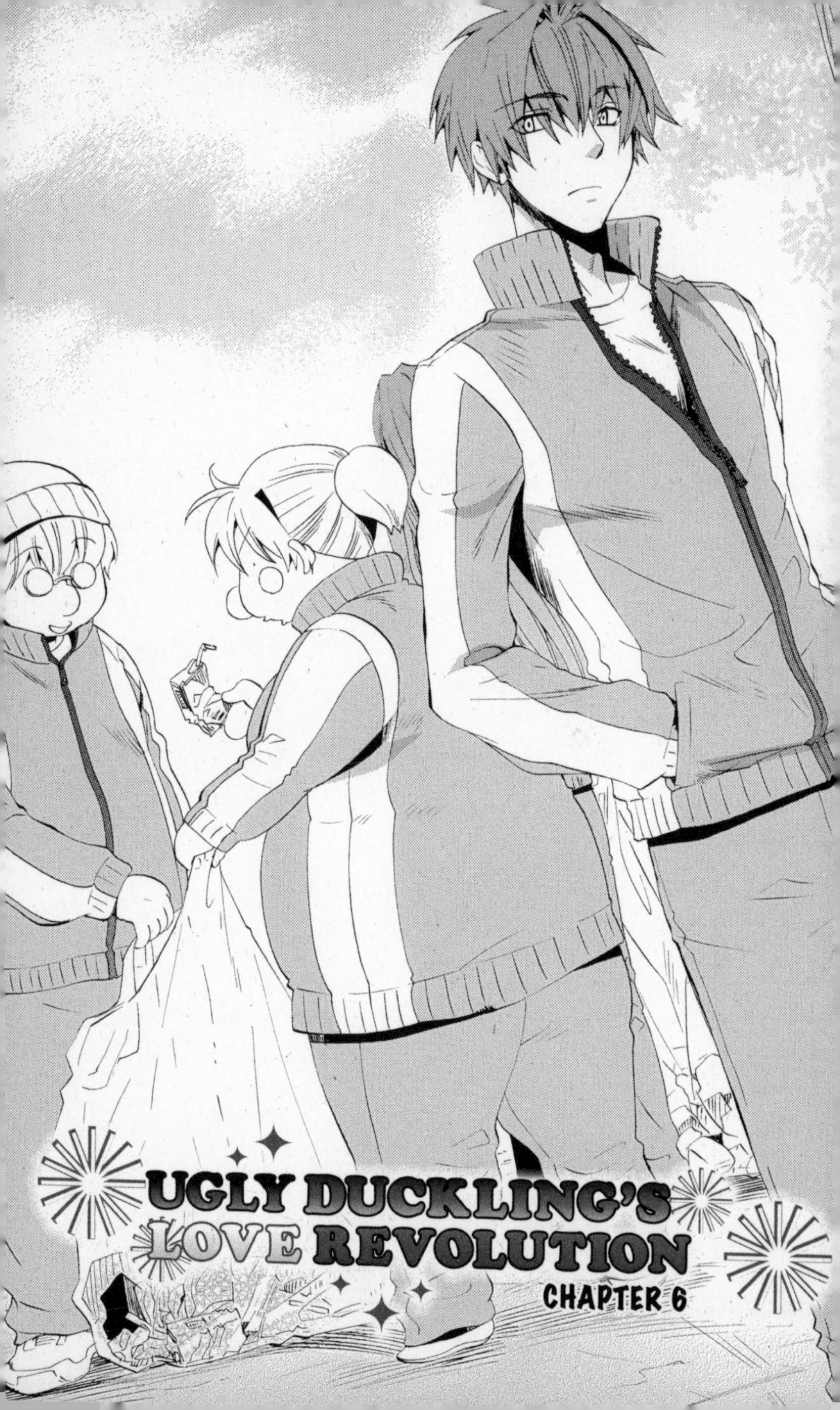
UGLY DUCKLING'S LOVE REVOLUTION
CHAPTER 6

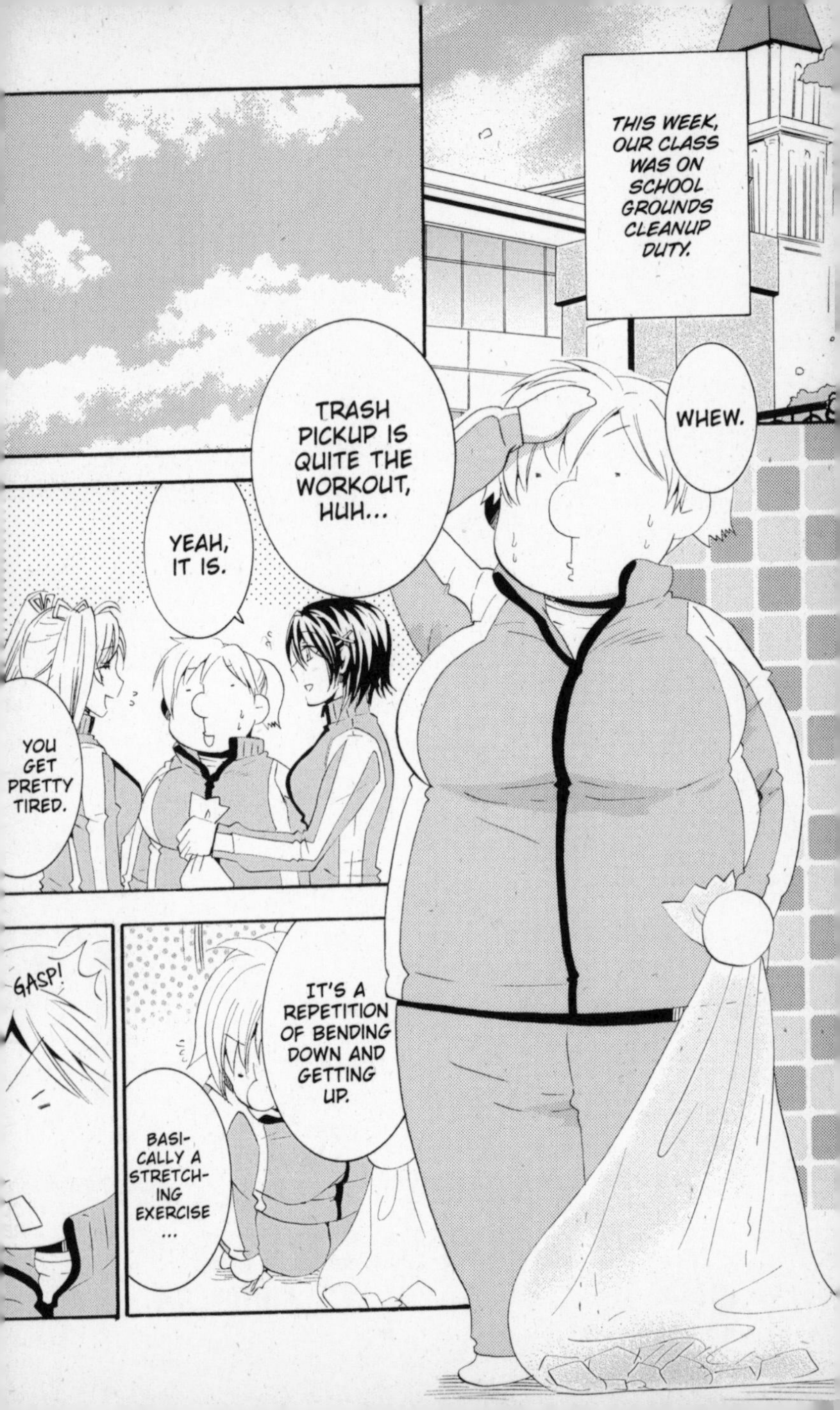
THIS WEEK, OUR CLASS WAS ON SCHOOL GROUNDS CLEANUP DUTY.
WHEW.
TRASH PICKUP IS QUITE THE WORKOUT, HUH...
YEAH, IT IS.
YOU GET PRETTY TIRED.
IT'S A REPETITION OF BENDING DOWN AND GETTING UP.
BASI-CALLY A STRETCH-ING EXERCISE ...
GASP!

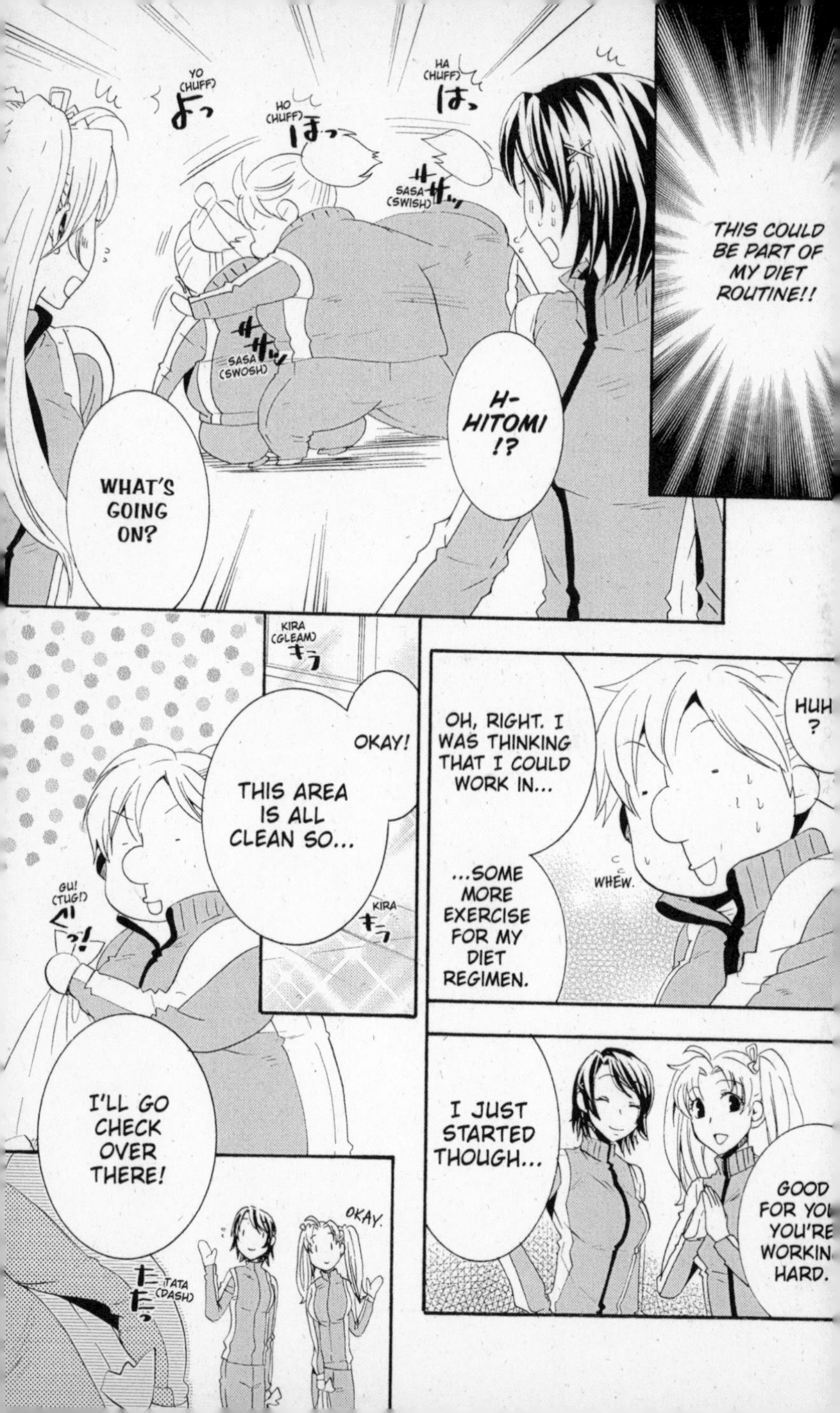
THIS COULD BE PART OF MY DIET ROUTINE!!
HA (HUFF) はっ
SASA (SWISH) ササッ
H-HITOMI!?
HO (HUFF) ほっ
YO (HUFF) よっ
SASA (SWOSH) ササッ
WHAT'S GOING ON?
HUH?
OH, RIGHT. I WAS THINKING THAT I COULD WORK IN...
WHEW.
...SOME MORE EXERCISE FOR MY DIET REGIMEN.
KIRA (GLEAM) キラ
OKAY!
THIS AREA IS ALL CLEAN SO...
KIRA キラ
GU! (TUG!) ぐっ!
I'LL GO CHECK OVER THERE!
GOOD FOR YOU YOU'RE WORKIN HARD.
I JUST STARTED THOUGH...
OKAY.
TATA (DASH) たたっ

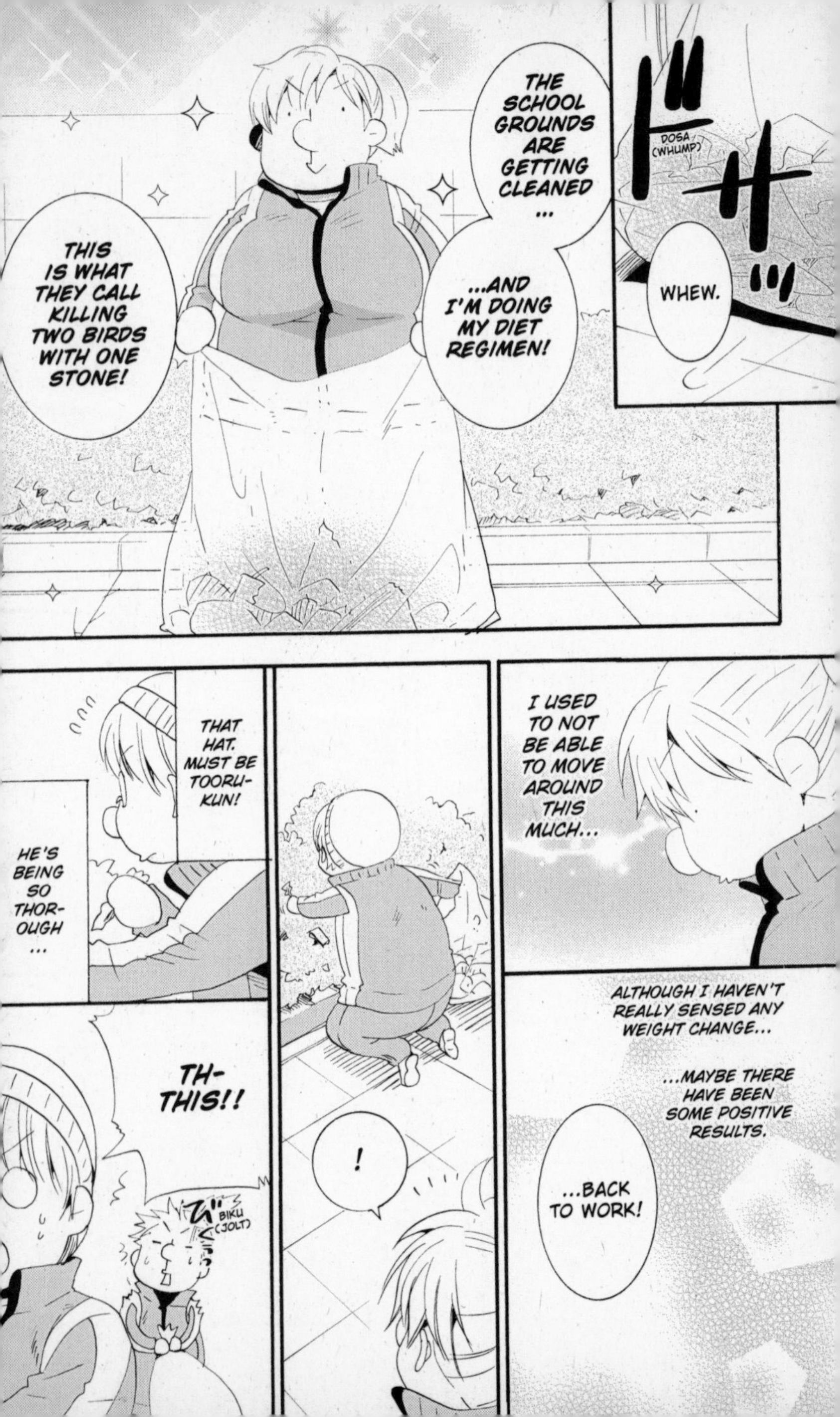
DOSA (WHUMP)
WHEW.
THE SCHOOL GROUNDS ARE GETTING CLEANED ...
...AND I'M DOING MY DIET REGIMEN!
THIS IS WHAT THEY CALL KILLING TWO BIRDS WITH ONE STONE!
I USED TO NOT BE ABLE TO MOVE AROUND THIS MUCH...
ALTHOUGH I HAVEN'T REALLY SENSED ANY WEIGHT CHANGE...
...MAYBE THERE HAVE BEEN SOME POSITIVE RESULTS.
...BACK TO WORK!
!
THAT HAT. MUST BE TOORU-KUN!
HE'S BEING SO THOR-OUGH ...
TH-THIS!!
BIKU (JOLT)

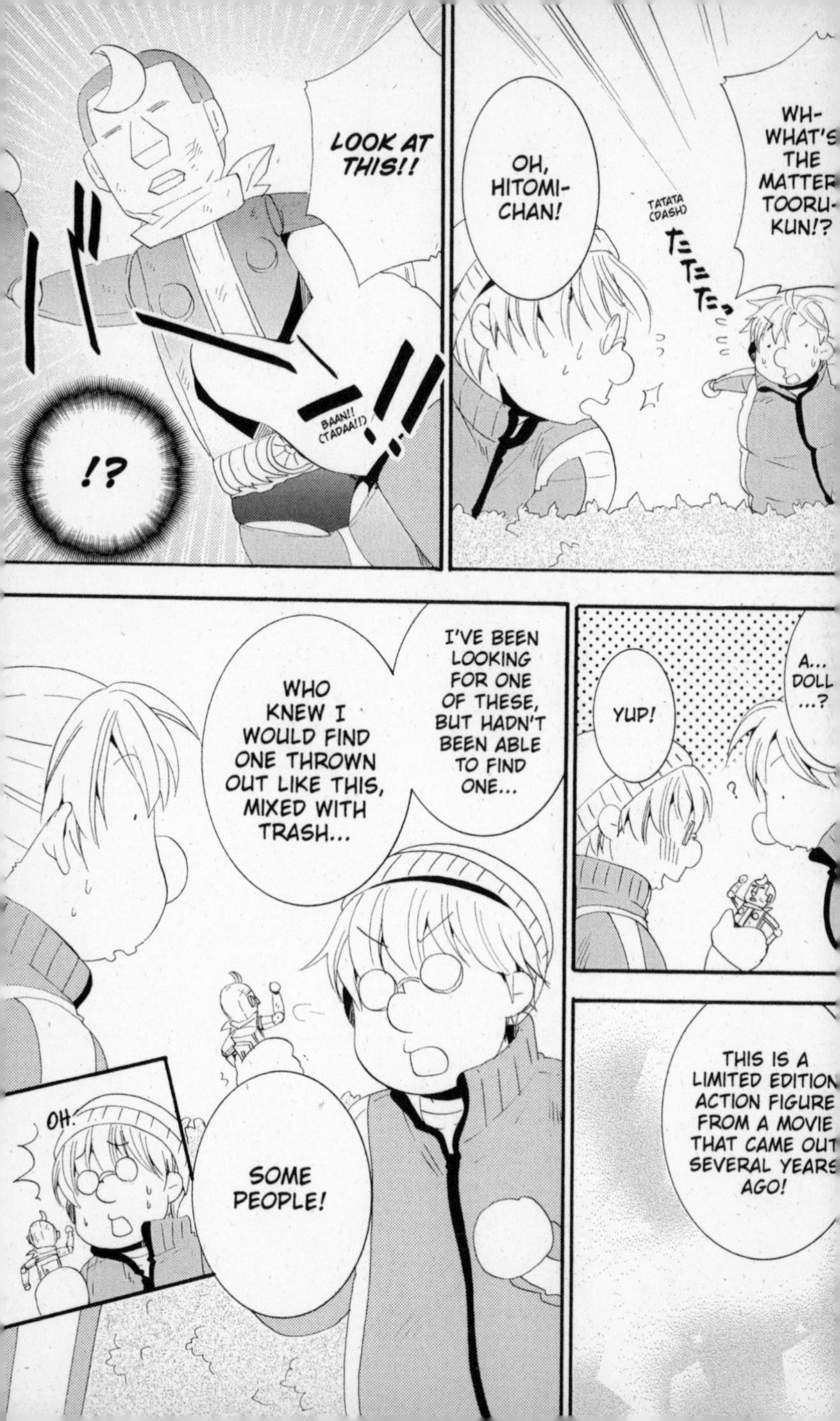

WH- WHAT'S THE MATTER TOORU-KUN!?
TATATA (DASH)
OH, HITOMI-CHAN!
LOOK AT THIS!!
BAAN!! (TADAA!!)
!?
A... DOLL ...?
YUP!
THIS IS A LIMITED EDITION ACTION FIGURE FROM A MOVIE THAT CAME OUT SEVERAL YEARS AGO!
I'VE BEEN LOOKING FOR ONE OF THESE, BUT HADN'T BEEN ABLE TO FIND ONE...
WHO KNEW I WOULD FIND ONE THROWN OUT LIKE THIS, MIXED WITH TRASH...
SOME PEOPLE!
OH.

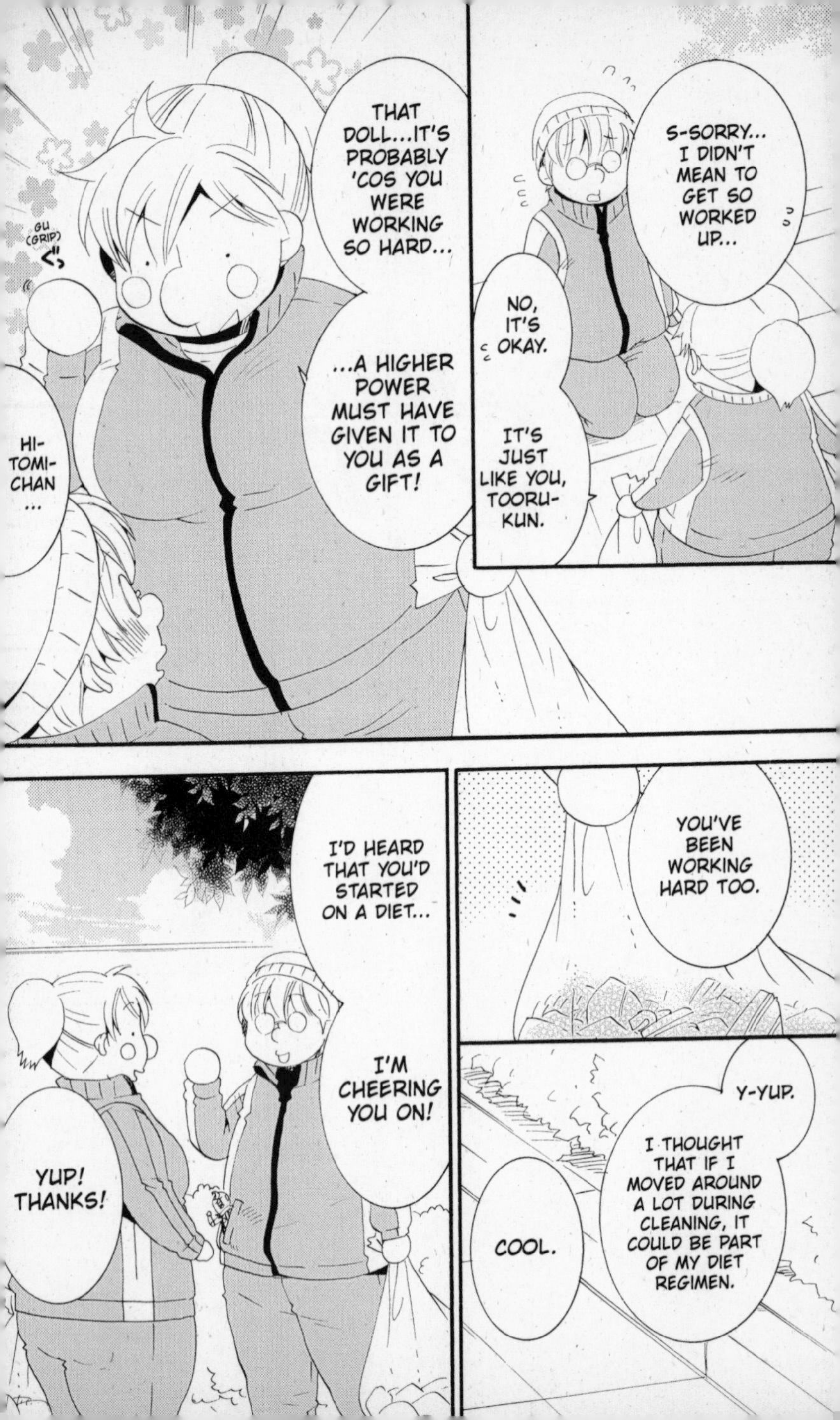
S-SORRY... I DIDN'T MEAN TO GET SO WORKED UP...
NO, IT'S OKAY.
IT'S JUST LIKE YOU, TOORU-KUN.
THAT DOLL...IT'S PROBABLY 'COS YOU WERE WORKING SO HARD...
...A HIGHER POWER MUST HAVE GIVEN IT TO YOU AS A GIFT!
GU (GRIP)
HI-TOMI-CHAN ...
YOU'VE BEEN WORKING HARD TOO.
Y-YUP.
I THOUGHT THAT IF I MOVED AROUND A LOT DURING CLEANING, IT COULD BE PART OF MY DIET REGIMEN.
COOL.
I'D HEARD THAT YOU'D STARTED ON A DIET...
I'M CHEERING YOU ON!
YUP! THANKS!

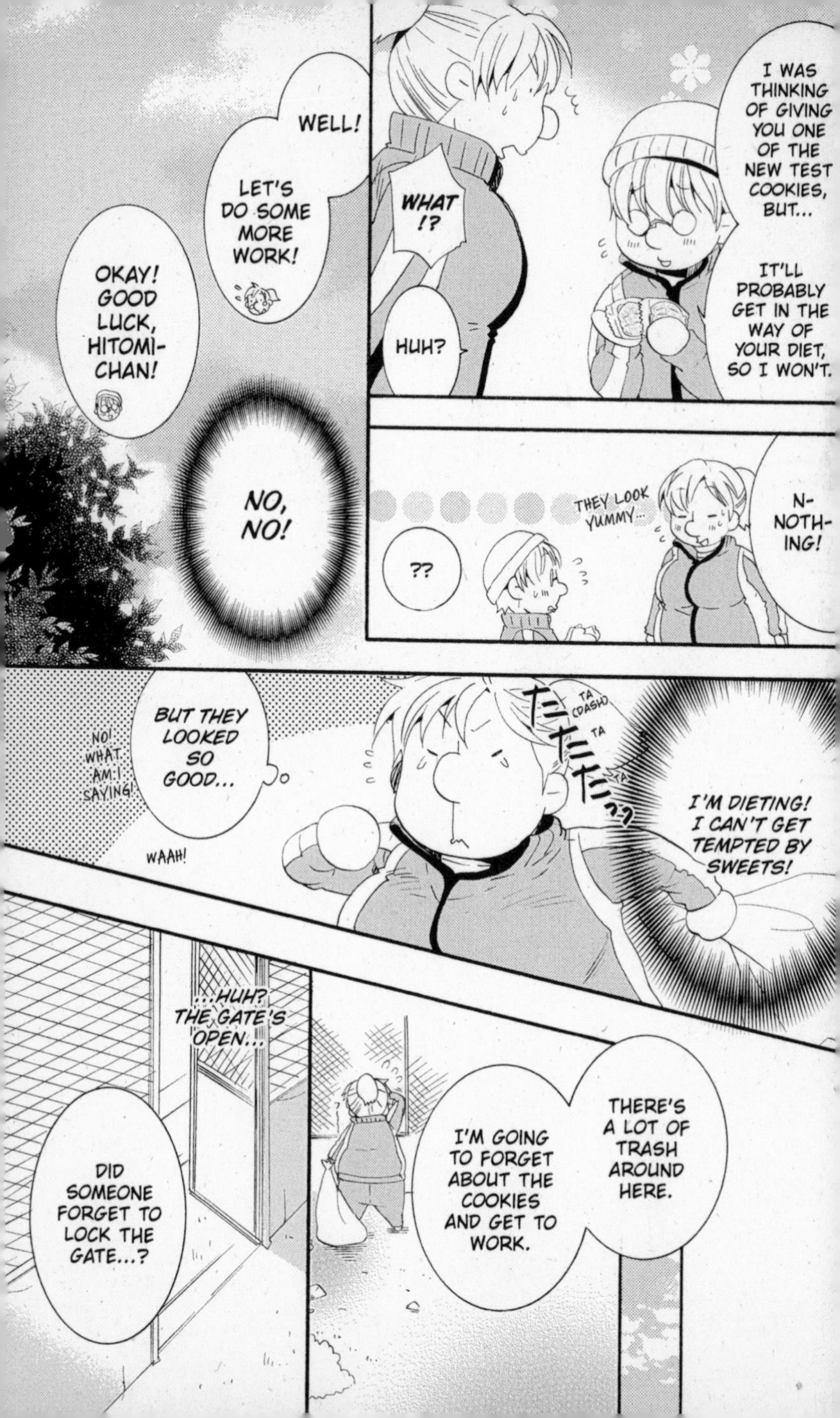
I WAS THINKING OF GIVING YOU ONE OF THE NEW TEST COOKIES, BUT...
IT'LL PROBABLY GET IN THE WAY OF YOUR DIET, SO I WON'T.
WHAT!?
HUH?
N-NOTHING!
THEY LOOK YUMMY...
??
WELL!
LET'S DO SOME MORE WORK!
OKAY! GOOD LUCK, HITOMI-CHAN!
NO, NO!
I'M DIETING! I CAN'T GET TEMPTED BY SWEETS!
TA (DASH)
TA
TA
BUT THEY LOOKED SO GOOD...
NO! WHAT AM I SAYING!
WAAH!
THERE'S A LOT OF TRASH AROUND HERE.
I'M GOING TO FORGET ABOUT THE COOKIES AND GET TO WORK.
...HUH? THE GATE'S OPEN...
DID SOMEONE FORGET TO LOCK THE GATE...?

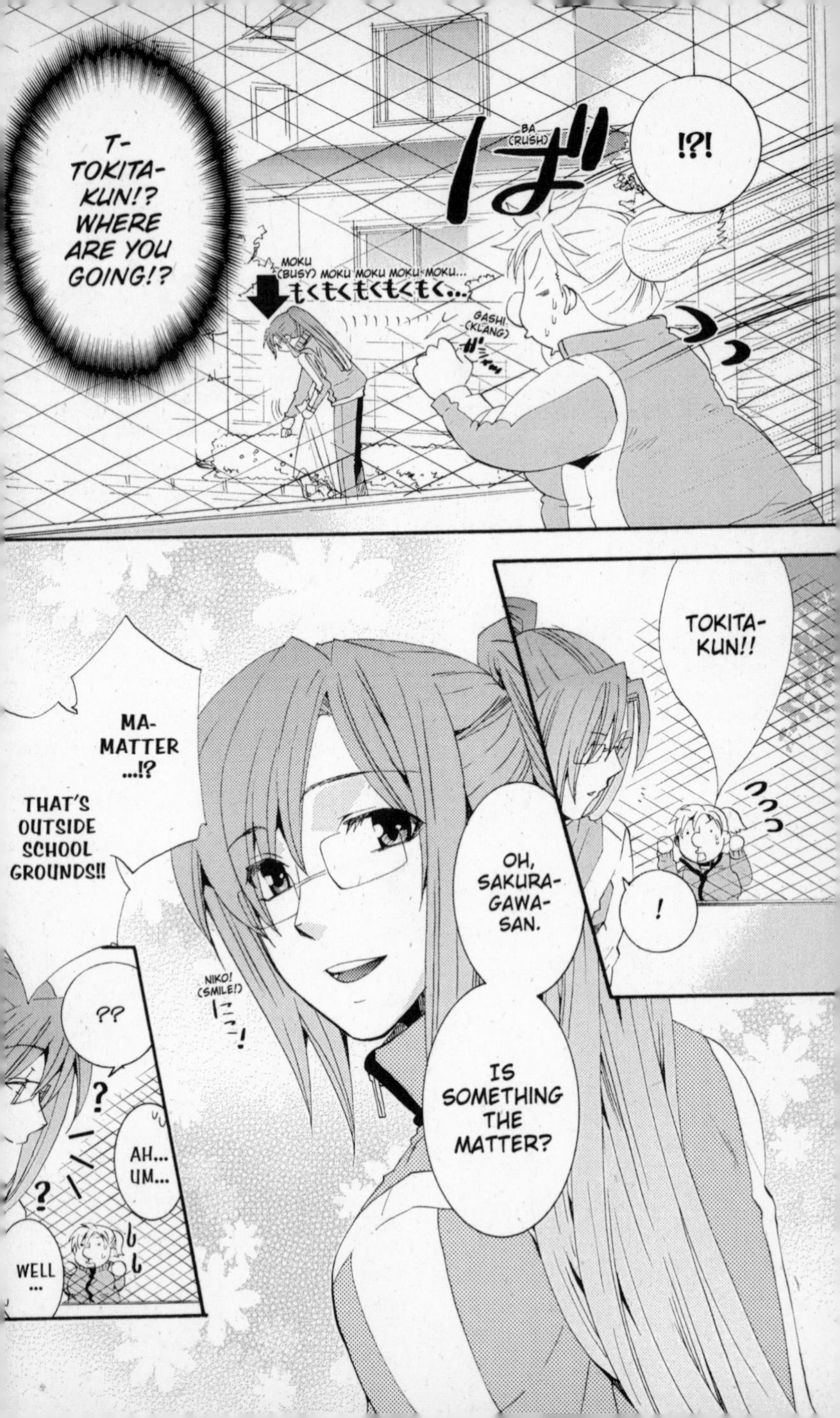
!?!
ば
BA (RUSH)
GASHI (KLANG)
MOKU (BUSY) MOKU MOKU MOKU MOKU...
もくもくもくもくもく...
T-TOKITA-KUN!? WHERE ARE YOU GOING!?
TOKITA-KUN!!
!
OH, SAKURA-GAWA-SAN.
IS SOMETHING THE MATTER?
NIKO! (SMILE!)
MA-MATTER ...!? THAT'S OUTSIDE SCHOOL GROUNDS!!
??
AH... UM...
WELL ...

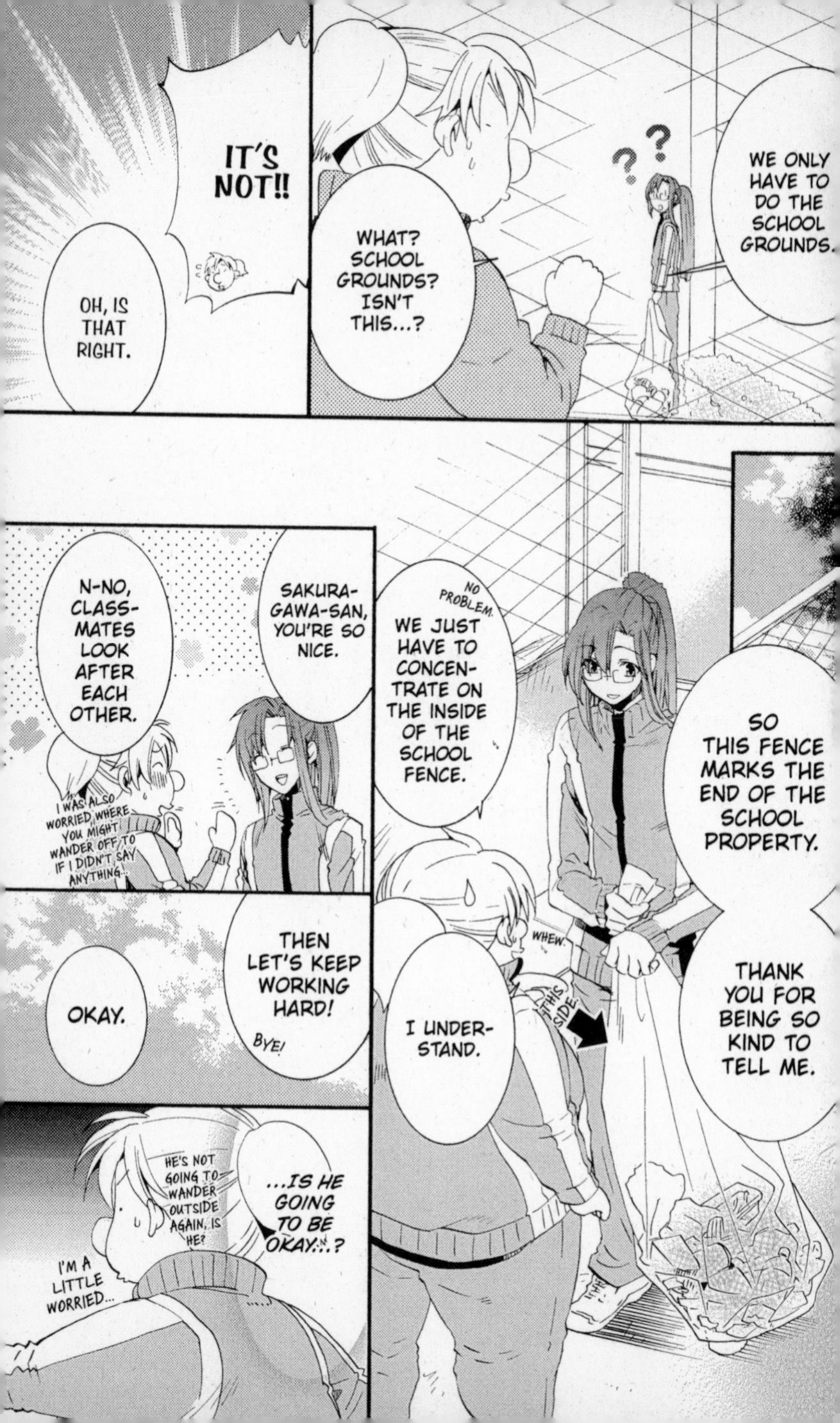
WE ONLY HAVE TO DO THE SCHOOL GROUNDS.
?
?
WHAT? SCHOOL GROUNDS? ISN'T THIS...?
IT'S NOT!!
OH, IS THAT RIGHT.
SO THIS FENCE MARKS THE END OF THE SCHOOL PROPERTY.
NO PROBLEM.
WE JUST HAVE TO CONCENTRATE ON THE INSIDE OF THE SCHOOL FENCE.
THANK YOU FOR BEING SO KIND TO TELL ME.
WHEW.
THIS SIDE
I UNDERSTAND.
SAKURA-GAWA-SAN, YOU'RE SO NICE.
N-NO, CLASSMATES LOOK AFTER EACH OTHER.
I WAS ALSO WORRIED WHERE YOU MIGHT WANDER OFF TO IF I DIDN'T SAY ANYTHING...
THEN LET'S KEEP WORKING HARD!
BYE!
OKAY.
...IS HE GOING TO BE OKAY...?
HE'S NOT GOING TO WANDER OUTSIDE AGAIN, IS HE?
I'M A LITTLE WORRIED...

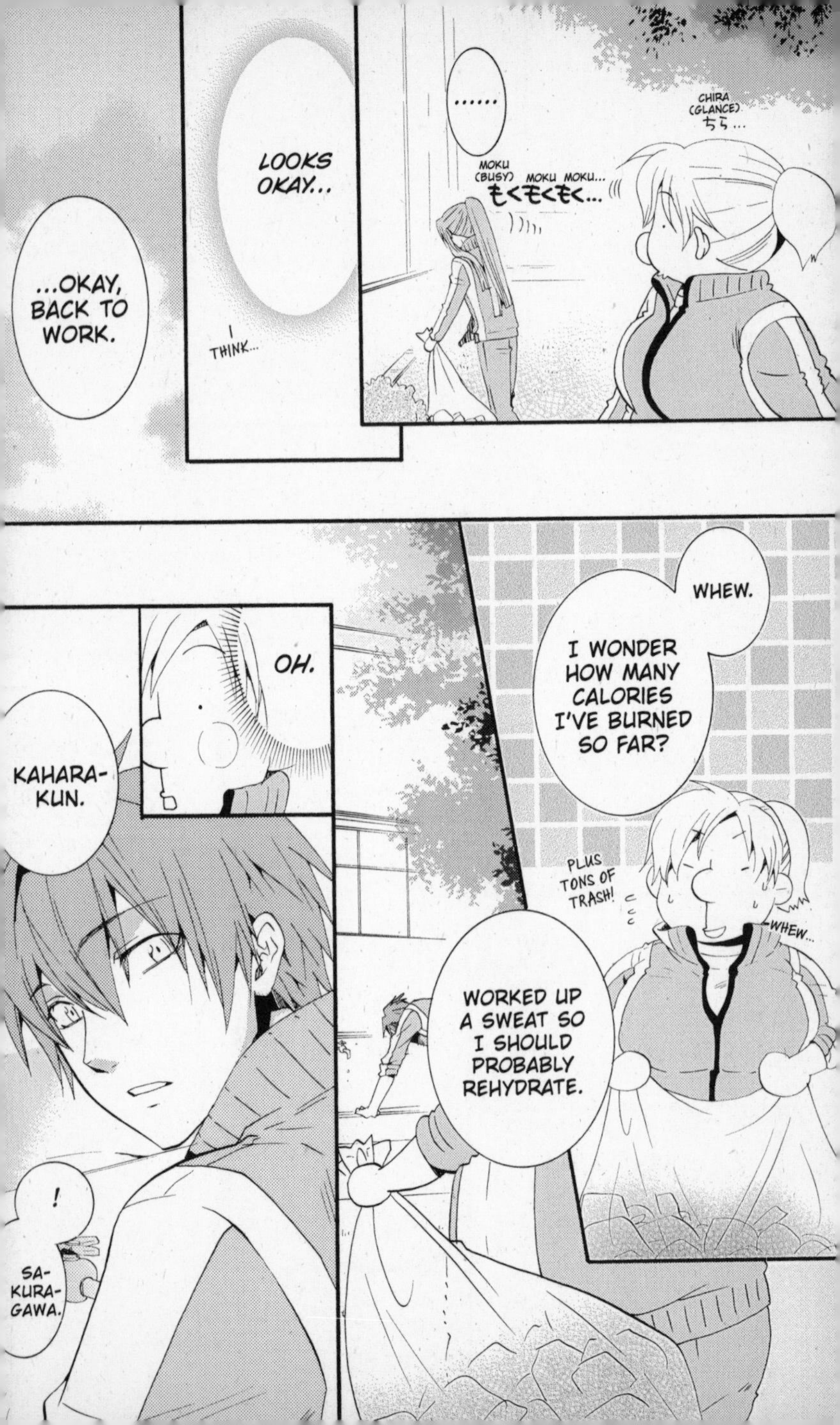

CHIRA (GLANCE) ちら...
......
MOKU (BUSY) MOKU MOKU... もくもくもく...
LOOKS OKAY...
I THINK...
...OKAY, BACK TO WORK.
WHEW.
I WONDER HOW MANY CALORIES I'VE BURNED SO FAR?
PLUS TONS OF TRASH!
WHEW...
WORKED UP A SWEAT SO I SHOULD PROBABLY REHYDRATE.
OH.
KAHARA-KUN.
!
SA-KURA-GAWA.

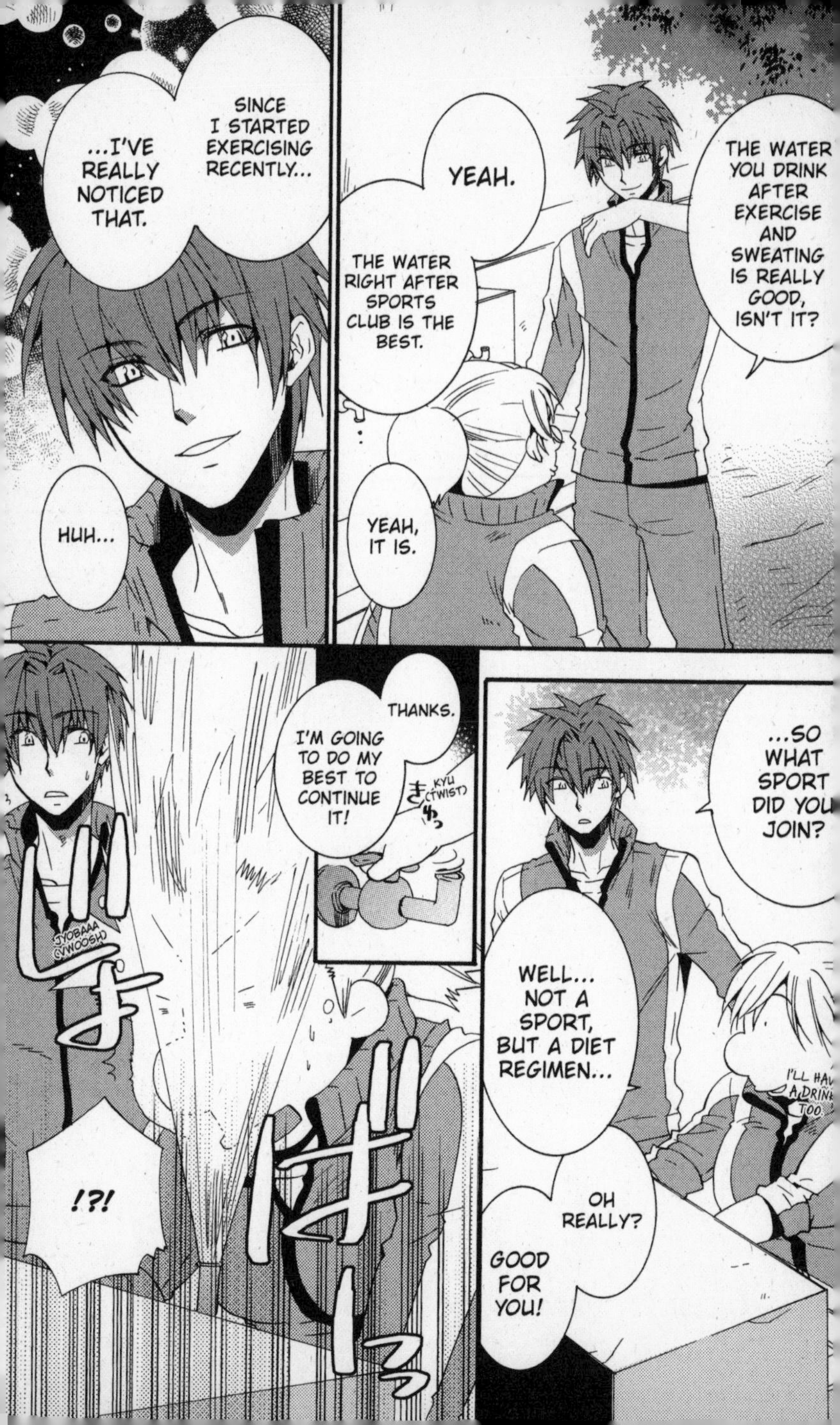
THE WATER YOU DRINK AFTER EXERCISE AND SWEATING IS REALLY GOOD, ISN'T IT?
YEAH.
THE WATER RIGHT AFTER SPORTS CLUB IS THE BEST.
YEAH, IT IS.
SINCE I STARTED EXERCISING RECENTLY...
...I'VE REALLY NOTICED THAT.
HUH...
...SO WHAT SPORT DID YOU JOIN?
I'LL HAV A DRINK TOO.
WELL... NOT A SPORT, BUT A DIET REGIMEN...
OH REALLY?
GOOD FOR YOU!
THANKS.
I'M GOING TO DO MY BEST TO CONTINUE IT!
KYU (TWIST)
JYOBAAA (VWOOSH)
!?!

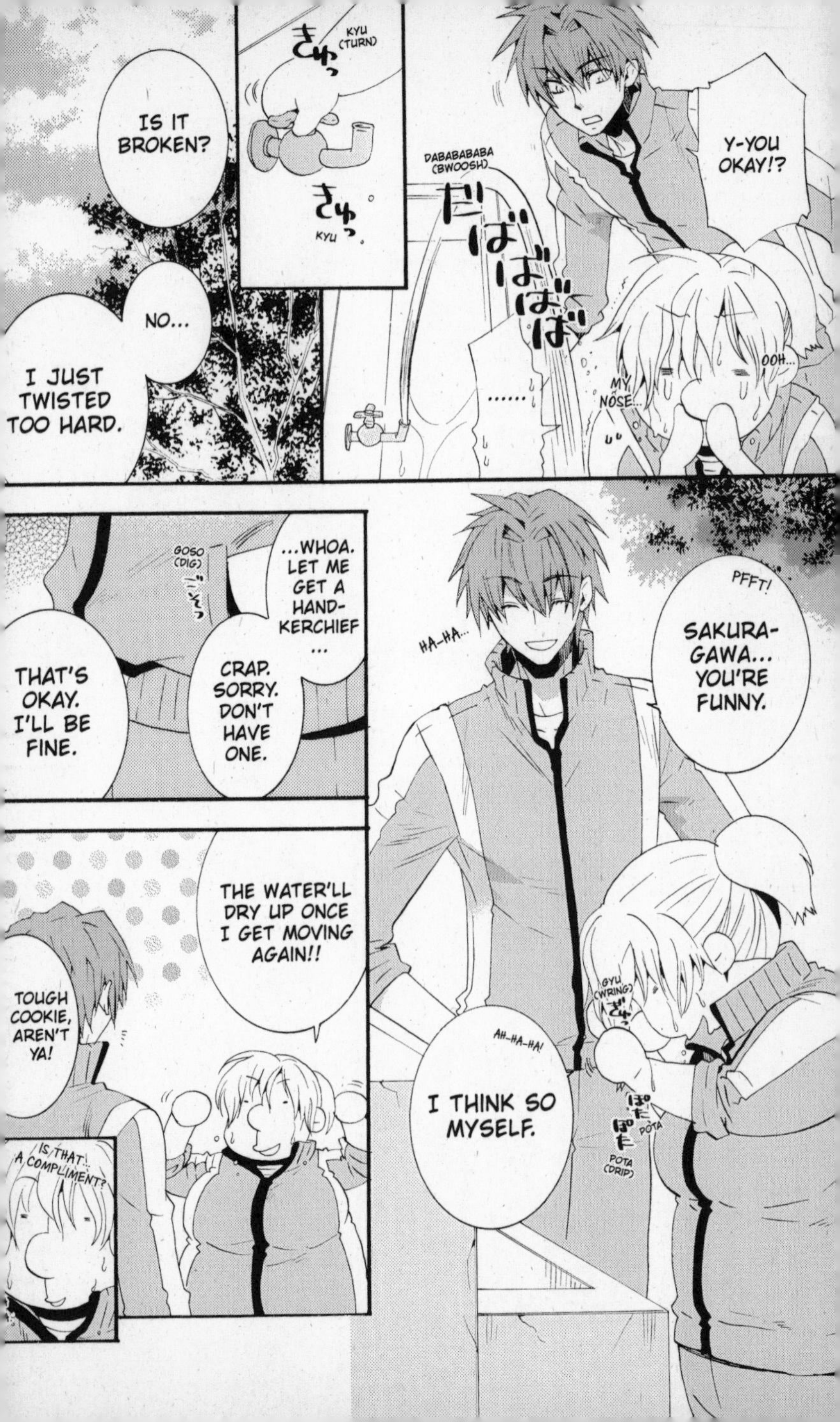
Y-YOU OKAY!?
DABABABABA (BWOOSH)
だばばばば
......
MY NOSE...
OOH...
KYU (TURN)
きゅっ
きゅっ
KYU
IS IT BROKEN?
NO...
I JUST TWISTED TOO HARD.
PFFT!
SAKURA-GAWA... YOU'RE FUNNY.
HA-HA...
GYU (WRING)
AH-HA-HA!
I THINK SO MYSELF.
POTA
POTA (DRIP)
...WHOA. LET ME GET A HAND-KERCHIEF...
GOSO (DIG)
CRAP. SORRY. DON'T HAVE ONE.
THAT'S OKAY. I'LL BE FINE.
THE WATER'LL DRY UP ONCE I GET MOVING AGAIN!!
TOUGH COOKIE, AREN'T YA!
IS THAT... A COMPLIMENT?

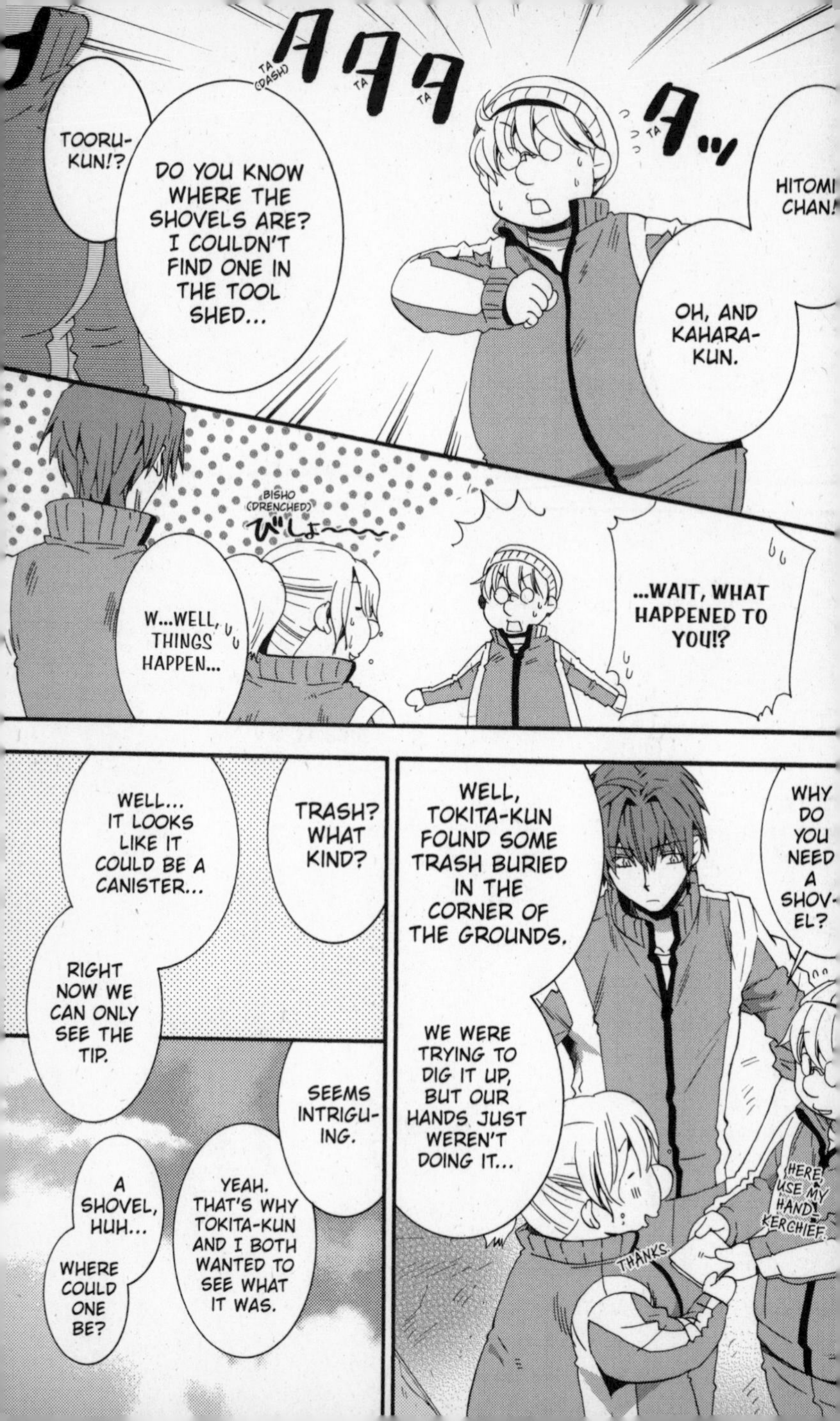
HITOMI CHAN!
OH, AND KAHARA-KUN.
タッ
TA
タタタ
TA (DASH) TA TA
DO YOU KNOW WHERE THE SHOVELS ARE? I COULDN'T FIND ONE IN THE TOOL SHED...
TOORU-KUN!?
...WAIT, WHAT HAPPENED TO YOU!?
びしょ～～
BISHO (DRENCHED)
W...WELL, THINGS HAPPEN...
WHY DO YOU NEED A SHOV-EL?
WELL, TOKITA-KUN FOUND SOME TRASH BURIED IN THE CORNER OF THE GROUNDS.
WE WERE TRYING TO DIG IT UP, BUT OUR HANDS JUST WEREN'T DOING IT...
HERE, USE MY HAND-KERCHIEF.
THANKS.
TRASH? WHAT KIND?
WELL... IT LOOKS LIKE IT COULD BE A CANISTER...
RIGHT NOW WE CAN ONLY SEE THE TIP.
SEEMS INTRIGU-ING.
YEAH. THAT'S WHY TOKITA-KUN AND I BOTH WANTED TO SEE WHAT IT WAS.
A SHOVEL, HUH...
WHERE COULD ONE BE?

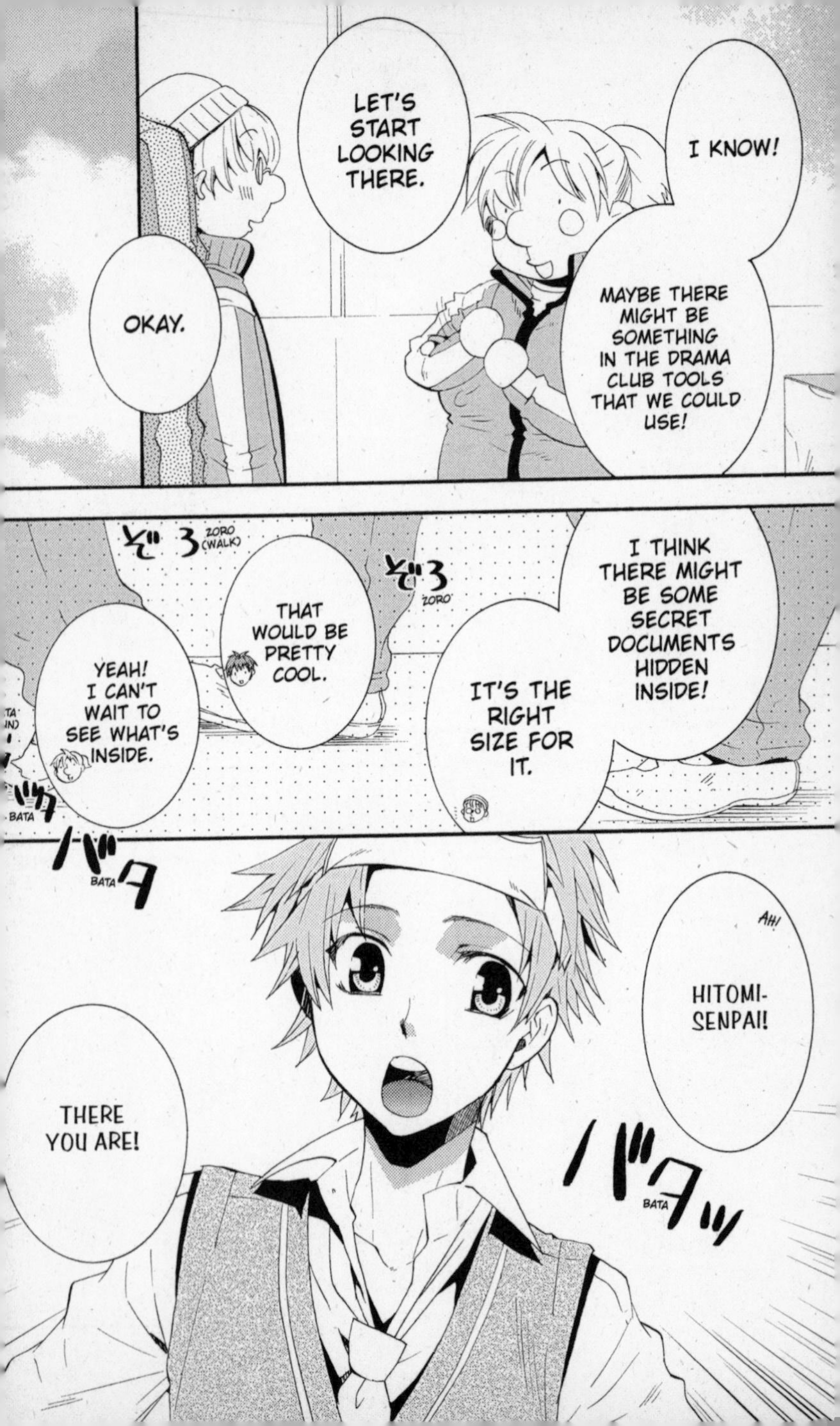
I KNOW!
MAYBE THERE MIGHT BE SOMETHING IN THE DRAMA CLUB TOOLS THAT WE COULD USE!
LET'S START LOOKING THERE.
OKAY.
I THINK THERE MIGHT BE SOME SECRET DOCUMENTS HIDDEN INSIDE!
IT'S THE RIGHT SIZE FOR IT.
ぞろ ZORO
THAT WOULD BE PRETTY COOL.
ぞろ ZORO (WALK)
YEAH! I CAN'T WAIT TO SEE WHAT'S INSIDE.
バタ BATA
AH!
HITOMI-SENPAI!
バタッ BATA
THERE YOU ARE!
バタ BATA

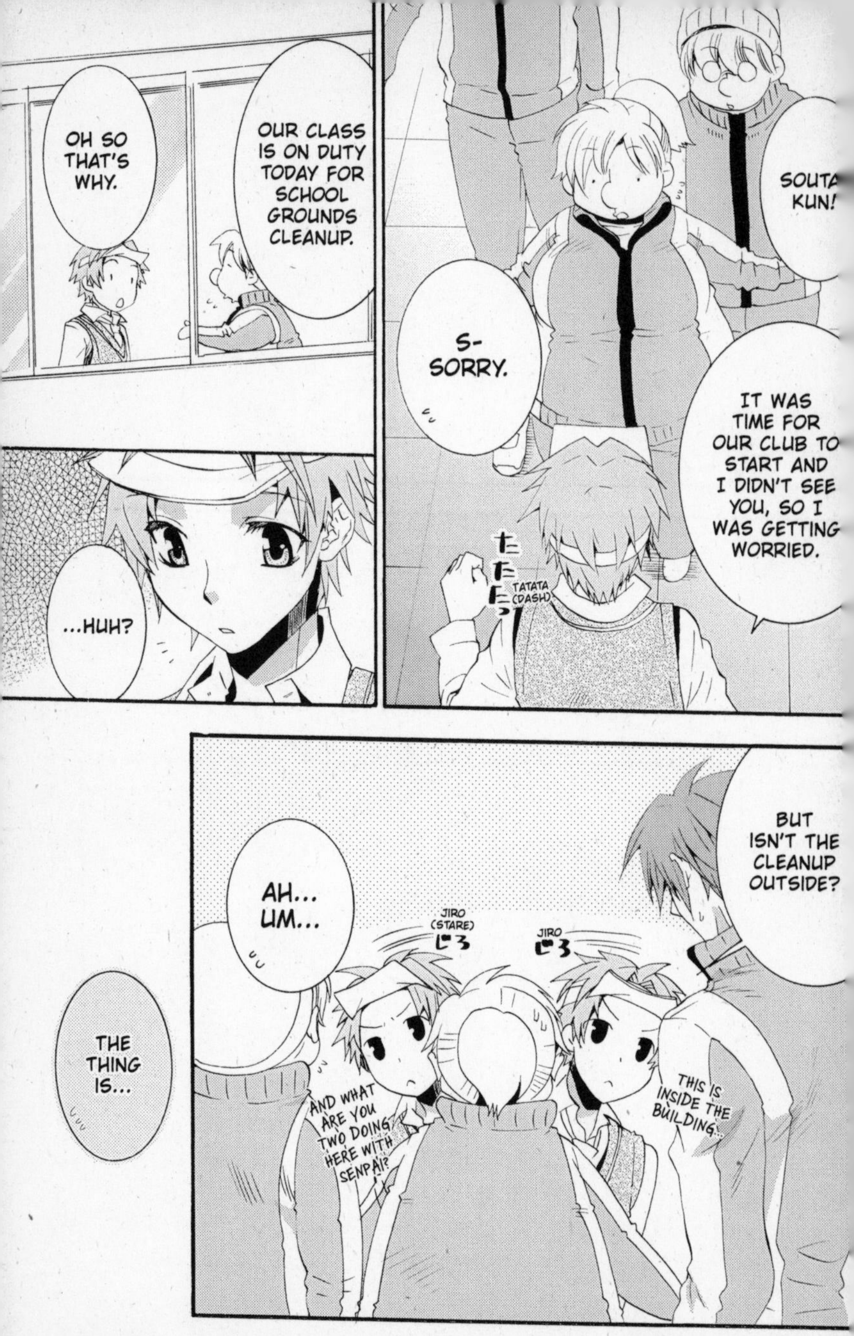
SOUTA KUN!
IT WAS TIME FOR OUR CLUB TO START AND I DIDN'T SEE YOU, SO I WAS GETTING WORRIED.
S- SORRY.
たたた
TATATA (DASH)
OUR CLASS IS ON DUTY TODAY FOR SCHOOL GROUNDS CLEANUP.
OH SO THAT'S WHY.
...HUH?
BUT ISN'T THE CLEANUP OUTSIDE?
JIRO
じろ
THIS IS INSIDE THE BUILDING..
JIRO (STARE)
じろ
AND WHAT ARE YOU TWO DOING HERE WITH SENPAI?
AH... UM...
THE THING IS...

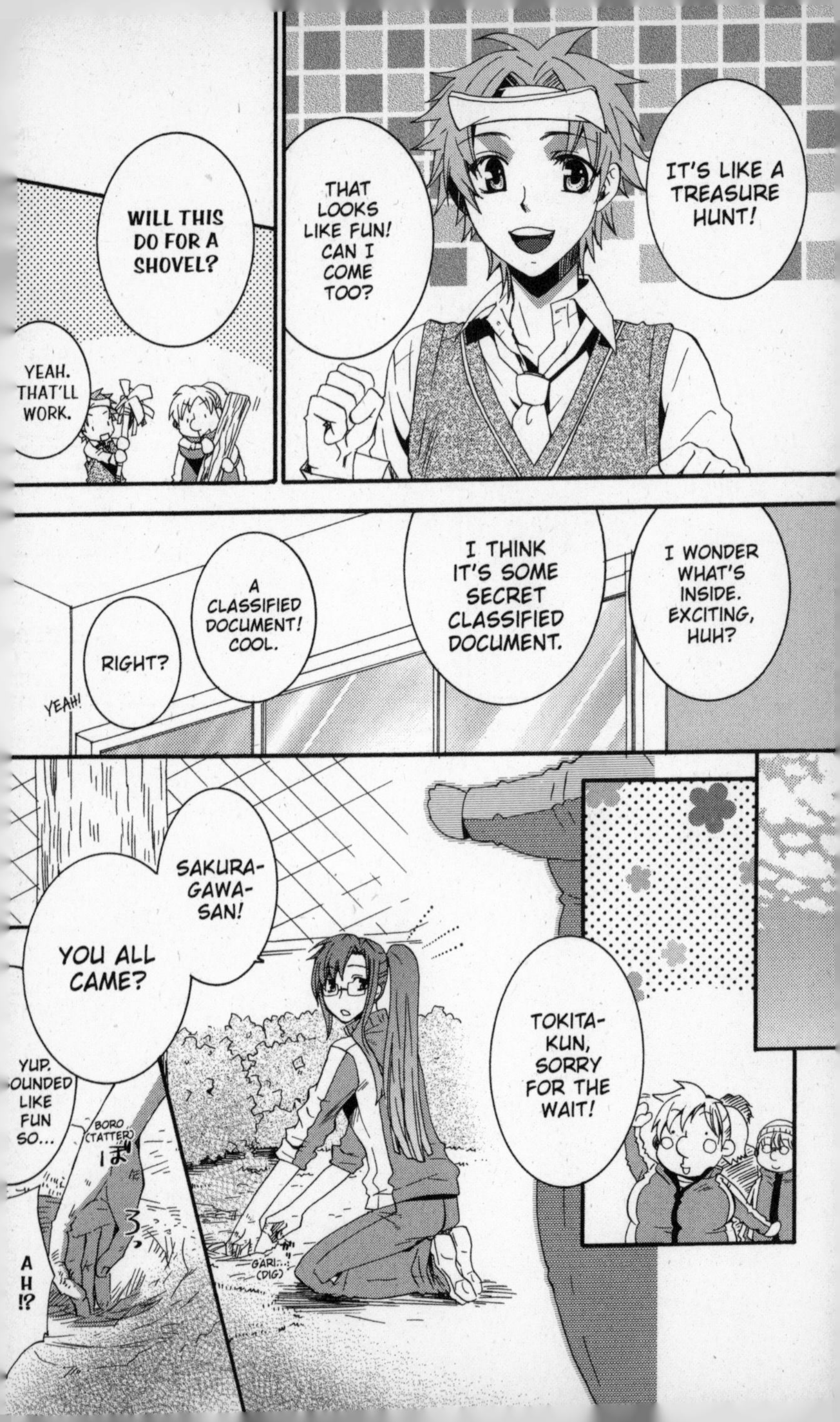
IT'S LIKE A TREASURE HUNT!
THAT LOOKS LIKE FUN! CAN I COME TOO?
WILL THIS DO FOR A SHOVEL?
YEAH. THAT'LL WORK.
I WONDER WHAT'S INSIDE. EXCITING, HUH?
I THINK IT'S SOME SECRET CLASSIFIED DOCUMENT.
A CLASSIFIED DOCUMENT! COOL.
RIGHT?
YEAH!
TOKITA-KUN, SORRY FOR THE WAIT!
SAKURA-GAWA-SAN!
YOU ALL CAME?
YUP. OUNDED LIKE FUN SO...
GARI... (DIG)
BORO (TATTER)
ぼろ
AH!?

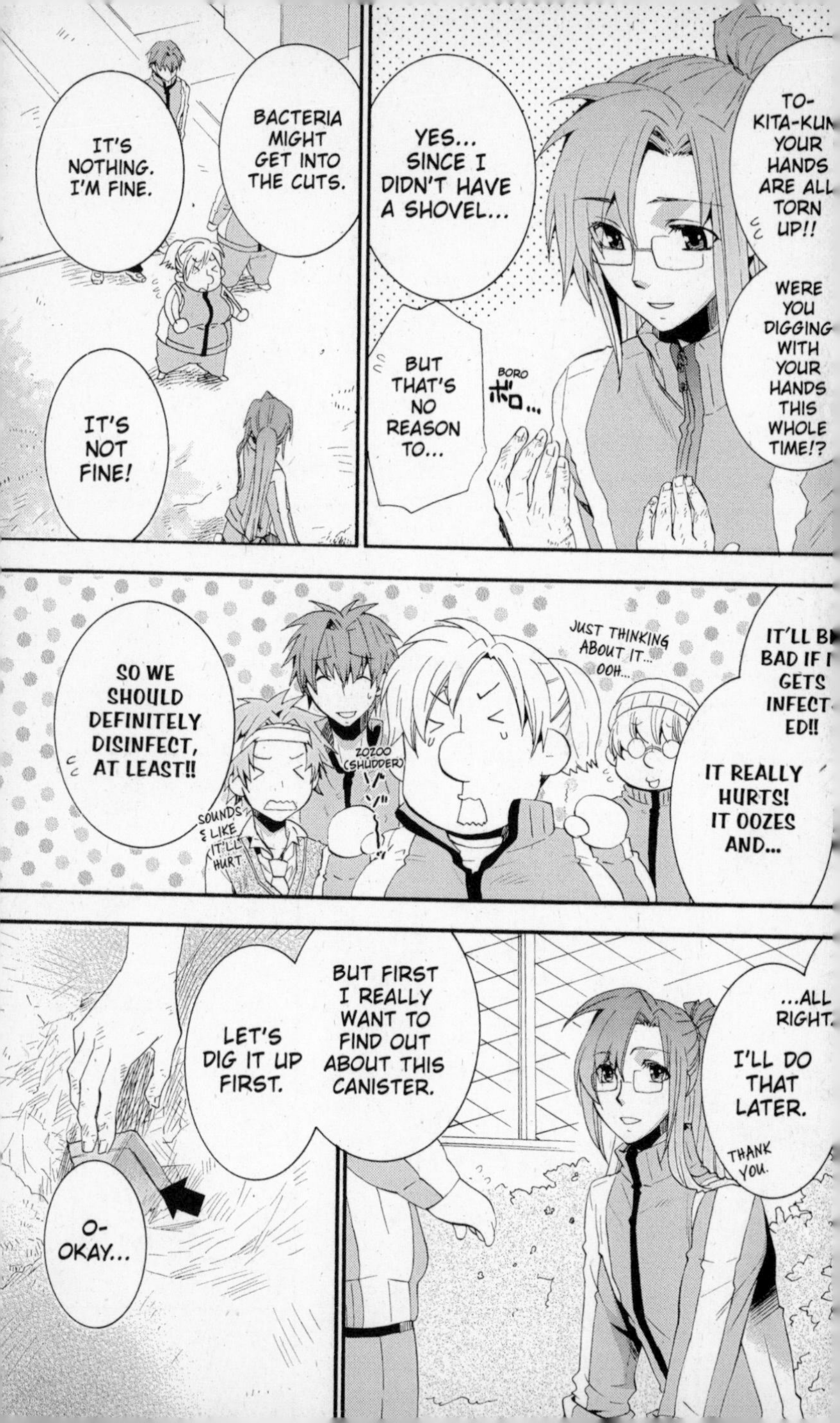
TO-KITA-KUN YOUR HANDS ARE ALL TORN UP!!
WERE YOU DIGGING WITH YOUR HANDS THIS WHOLE TIME!?
YES... SINCE I DIDN'T HAVE A SHOVEL...
BORO
ボロ...
BUT THAT'S NO REASON TO...
BACTERIA MIGHT GET INTO THE CUTS.
IT'S NOTHING. I'M FINE.
IT'S NOT FINE!
IT'LL B BAD IF I GETS INFECTED!!
IT REALLY HURTS! IT OOZES AND...
JUST THINKING ABOUT IT... OOH...
ZOZOO (SHUDDER)
SOUNDS LIKE IT'LL HURT
SO WE SHOULD DEFINITELY DISINFECT, AT LEAST!!
...ALL RIGHT.
I'LL DO THAT LATER.
THANK YOU.
BUT FIRST I REALLY WANT TO FIND OUT ABOUT THIS CANISTER.
LET'S DIG IT UP FIRST.
O-OKAY...

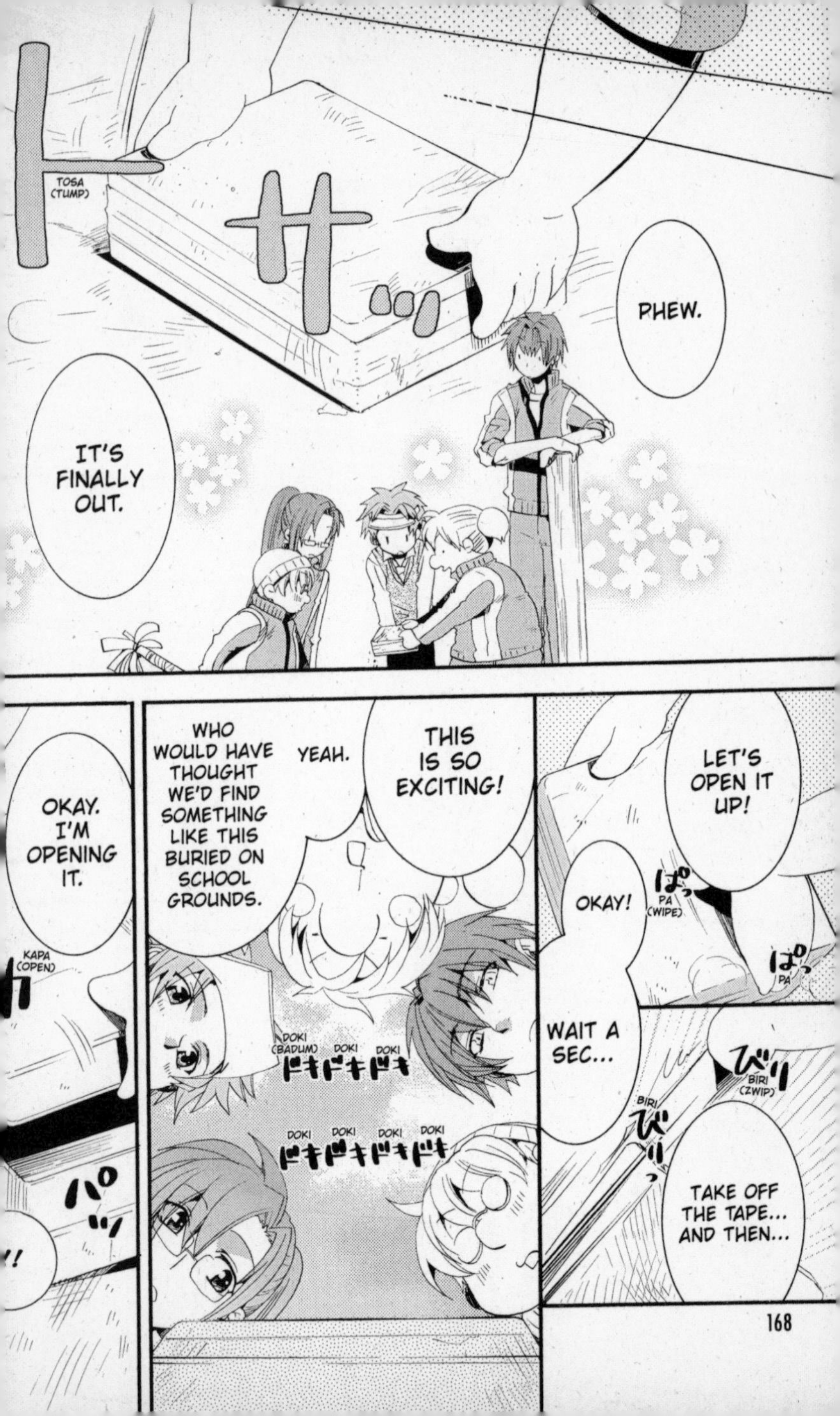
PHEW.
トサッ
TOSA (TUMP)
IT'S FINALLY OUT.
LET'S OPEN IT UP!
OKAY!
ぱっ PA (WIPE)
ぱっ PA
WAIT A SEC...
びりっ BIRI (ZWIP)
びりっ BIRI
TAKE OFF THE TAPE... AND THEN...
THIS IS SO EXCITING!
YEAH.
WHO WOULD HAVE THOUGHT WE'D FIND SOMETHING LIKE THIS BURIED ON SCHOOL GROUNDS.
ドキドキドキ DOKI (BADUM) DOKI DOKI
ドキドキドキドキ DOKI DOKI DOKI DOKI
OKAY. I'M OPENING IT.
KAPA (OPEN)
パッ

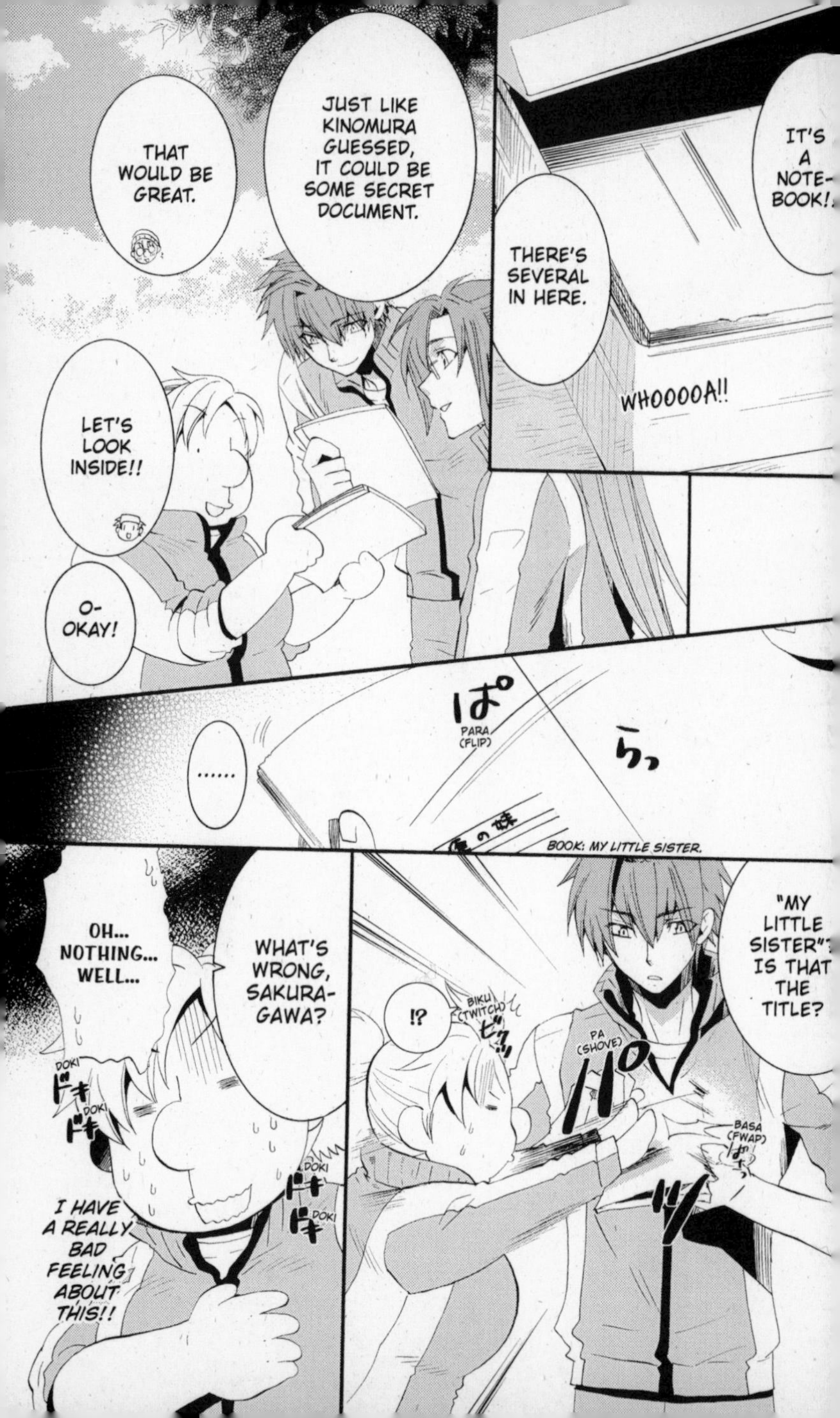
IT'S A NOTE-BOOK!.
THERE'S SEVERAL IN HERE.
WHOOOOA!!
JUST LIKE KINOMURA GUESSED, IT COULD BE SOME SECRET DOCUMENT.
THAT WOULD BE GREAT.
LET'S LOOK INSIDE!!
O-OKAY!
ぱ
PARA (FLIP)
らっ
......
BOOK: MY LITTLE SISTER.
"MY LITTLE SISTER"? IS THAT THE TITLE?
!?
BIKU (TWITCH)
PA (SHOVE)
BASA (FWAP)
WHAT'S WRONG, SAKURA-GAWA?
OH... NOTHING... WELL...
DOKI DOKI
DOKI DOKI
I HAVE A REALLY BAD FEELING ABOUT THIS!!

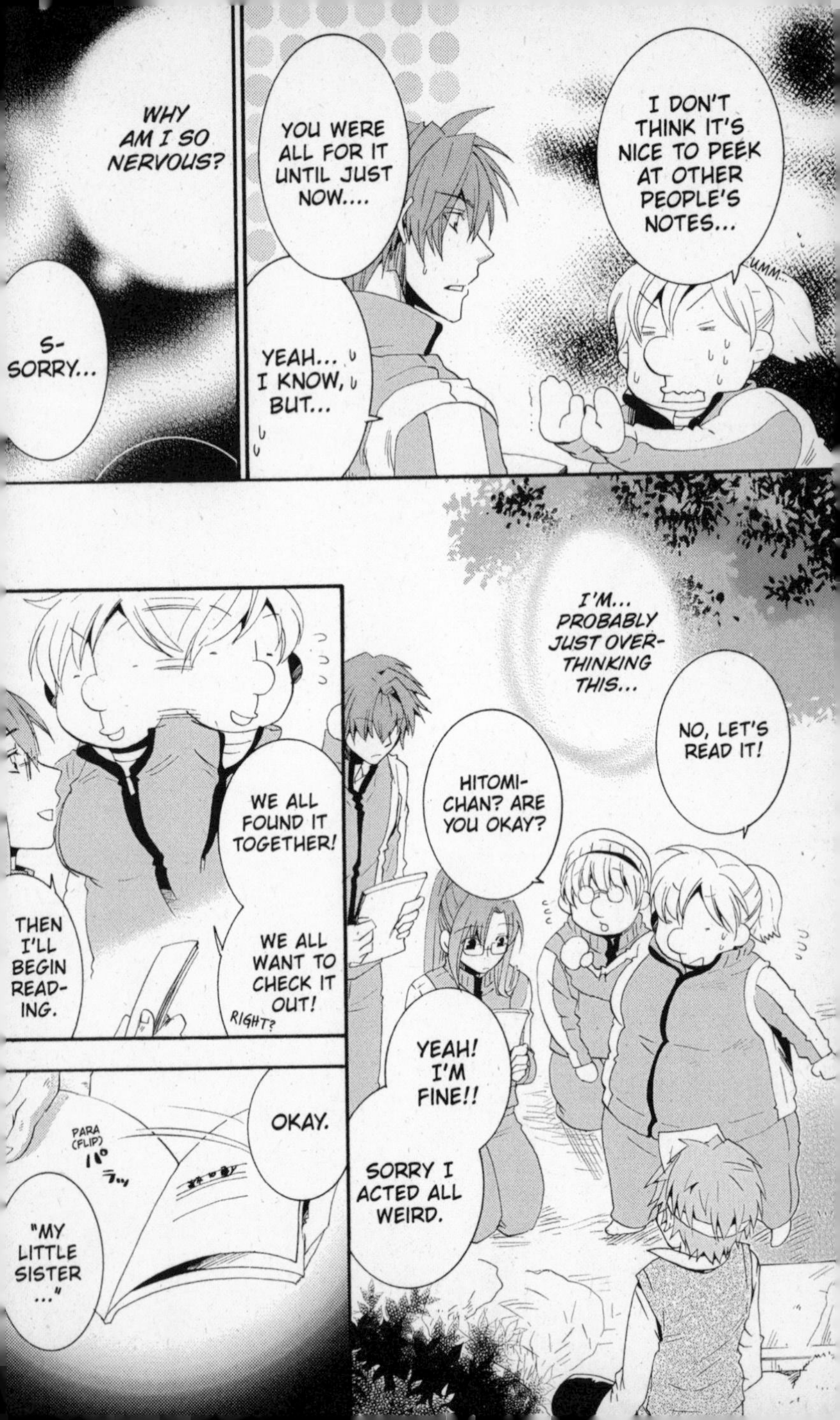
I DON'T THINK IT'S NICE TO PEEK AT OTHER PEOPLE'S NOTES...
UMM...
YOU WERE ALL FOR IT UNTIL JUST NOW....
YEAH... I KNOW, BUT...
WHY AM I SO NERVOUS?
S-SORRY...
I'M... PROBABLY JUST OVER-THINKING THIS...
NO, LET'S READ IT!
HITOMI-CHAN? ARE YOU OKAY?
YEAH! I'M FINE!!
SORRY I ACTED ALL WEIRD.
WE ALL FOUND IT TOGETHER!
WE ALL WANT TO CHECK IT OUT!
RIGHT?
THEN I'LL BEGIN READING.
OKAY.
PARA (FLIP)
"MY LITTLE SISTER ..."

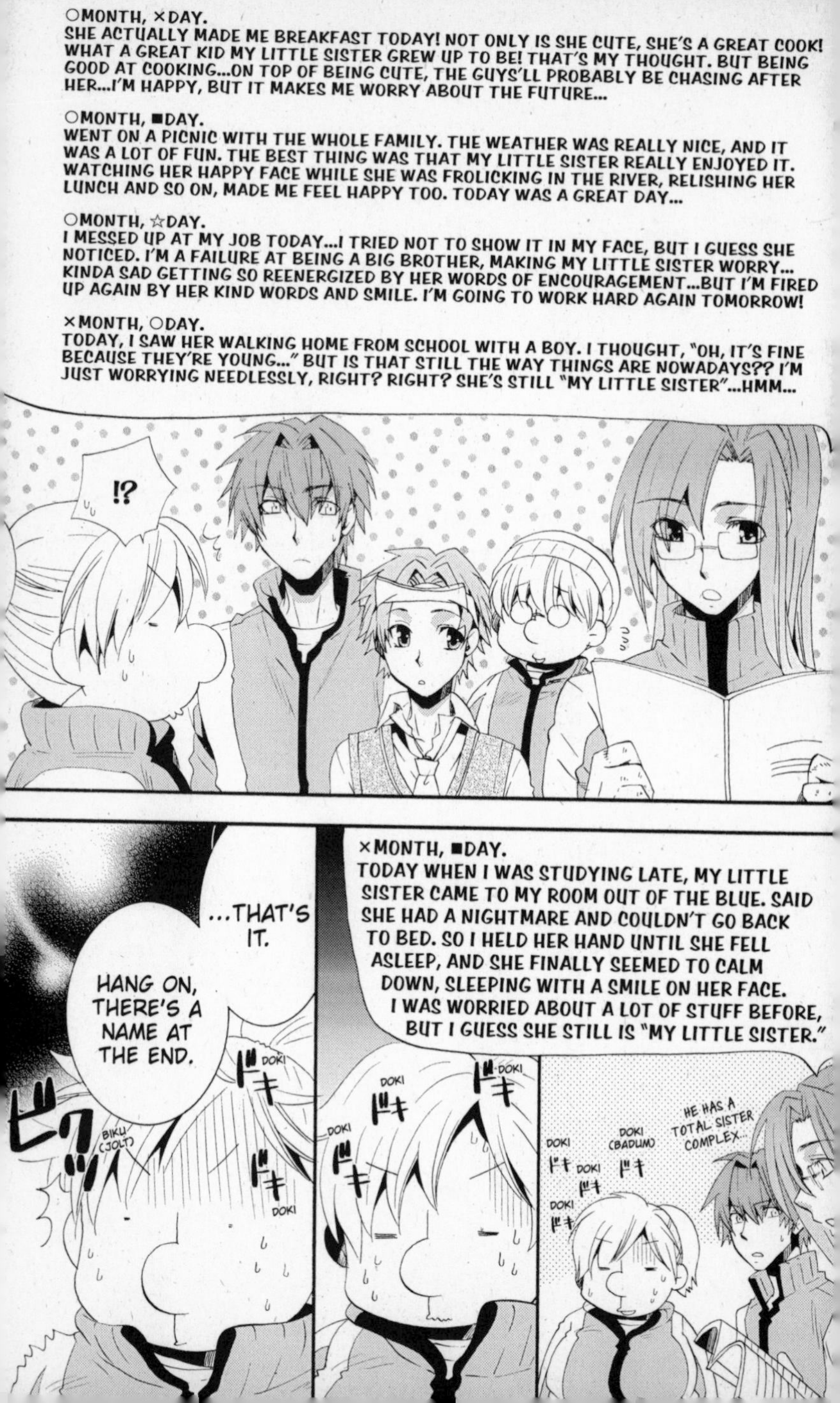
○MONTH, ×DAY.
SHE ACTUALLY MADE ME BREAKFAST TODAY! NOT ONLY IS SHE CUTE, SHE'S A GREAT COOK! WHAT A GREAT KID MY LITTLE SISTER GREW UP TO BE! THAT'S MY THOUGHT. BUT BEING GOOD AT COOKING...ON TOP OF BEING CUTE, THE GUYS'LL PROBABLY BE CHASING AFTER HER...I'M HAPPY, BUT IT MAKES ME WORRY ABOUT THE FUTURE...
○MONTH, ■DAY.
WENT ON A PICNIC WITH THE WHOLE FAMILY. THE WEATHER WAS REALLY NICE, AND IT WAS A LOT OF FUN. THE BEST THING WAS THAT MY LITTLE SISTER REALLY ENJOYED IT. WATCHING HER HAPPY FACE WHILE SHE WAS FROLICKING IN THE RIVER, RELISHING HER LUNCH AND SO ON, MADE ME FEEL HAPPY TOO. TODAY WAS A GREAT DAY...
○MONTH, ☆DAY.
I MESSED UP AT MY JOB TODAY...I TRIED NOT TO SHOW IT IN MY FACE, BUT I GUESS SHE NOTICED. I'M A FAILURE AT BEING A BIG BROTHER, MAKING MY LITTLE SISTER WORRY... KINDA SAD GETTING SO REENERGIZED BY HER WORDS OF ENCOURAGEMENT...BUT I'M FIRED UP AGAIN BY HER KIND WORDS AND SMILE. I'M GOING TO WORK HARD AGAIN TOMORROW!
×MONTH, ○DAY.
TODAY, I SAW HER WALKING HOME FROM SCHOOL WITH A BOY. I THOUGHT, "OH, IT'S FINE BECAUSE THEY'RE YOUNG..." BUT IS THAT STILL THE WAY THINGS ARE NOWADAYS?? I'M JUST WORRYING NEEDLESSLY, RIGHT? RIGHT? SHE'S STILL "MY LITTLE SISTER"...HMM...
!?
×MONTH, ■DAY.
TODAY WHEN I WAS STUDYING LATE, MY LITTLE SISTER CAME TO MY ROOM OUT OF THE BLUE. SAID SHE HAD A NIGHTMARE AND COULDN'T GO BACK TO BED. SO I HELD HER HAND UNTIL SHE FELL ASLEEP, AND SHE FINALLY SEEMED TO CALM DOWN, SLEEPING WITH A SMILE ON HER FACE. I WAS WORRIED ABOUT A LOT OF STUFF BEFORE, BUT I GUESS SHE STILL IS "MY LITTLE SISTER."
HE HAS A TOTAL SISTER COMPLEX...
DOKI (BADUM) ドキ
DOKI ドキ DOKI ドキ DOKI ドキ
DOKI ドキ DOKI ドキ DOKI ドキ
...THAT'S IT.
HANG ON, THERE'S A NAME AT THE END.
DOKI ドキ DOKI ドキ
ビクッ BIKU (JOLT)

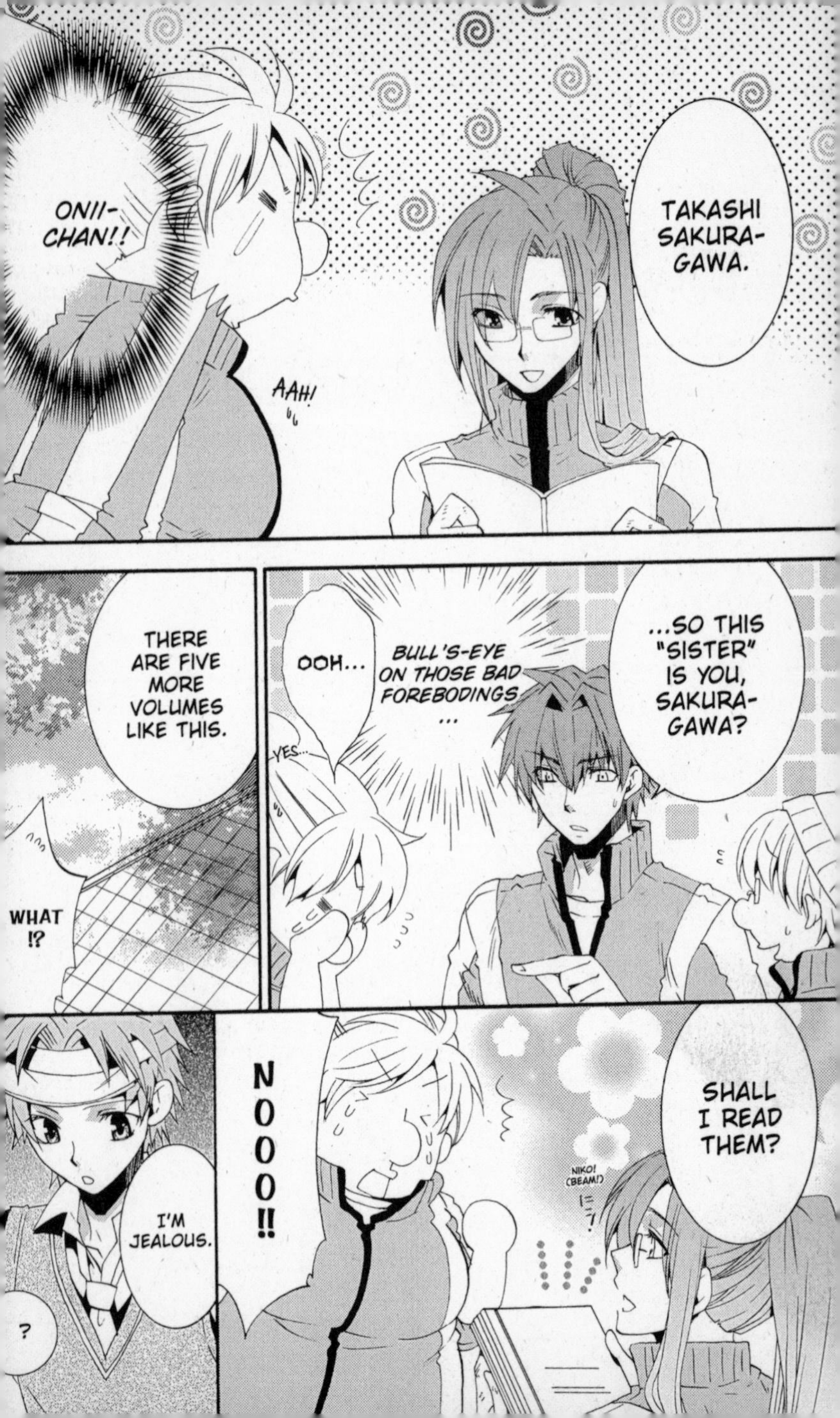
TAKASHI SAKURA-GAWA.
AAH!
ONII-CHAN!!
...SO THIS "SISTER" IS YOU, SAKURA-GAWA?
BULL'S-EYE ON THOSE BAD FOREBODINGS ...
OOH...
YES...
THERE ARE FIVE MORE VOLUMES LIKE THIS.
WHAT !?
SHALL I READ THEM?
NIKO! (BEAM!)
NOOOO!!
I'M JEALOUS.
?

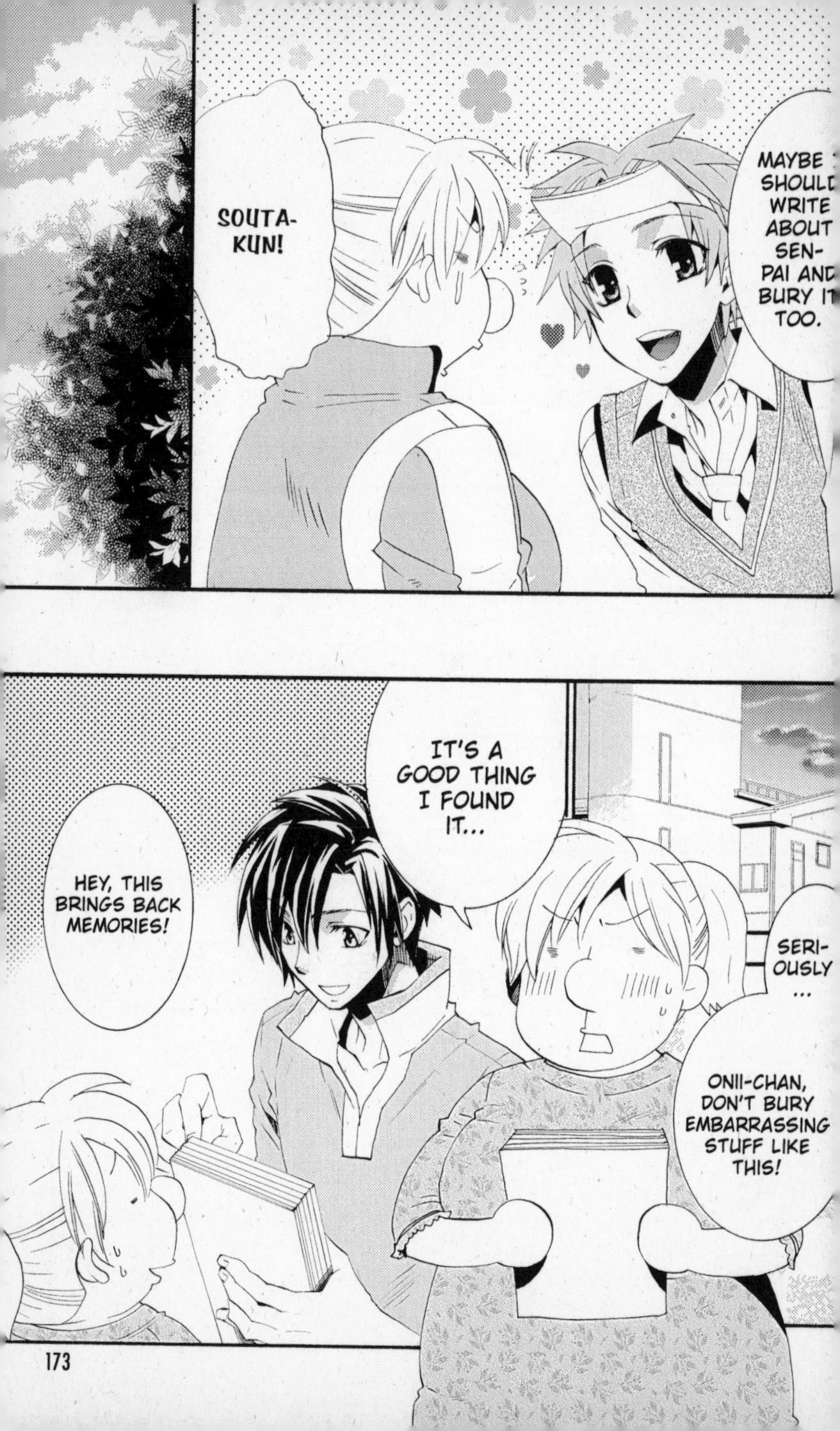
MAYBE SHOULD WRITE ABOUT SEN-PAI AND BURY IT TOO.
SOUTA-KUN!
SERI-OUSLY ...
ONII-CHAN, DON'T BURY EMBARRASSING STUFF LIKE THIS!
IT'S A GOOD THING I FOUND IT...
HEY, THIS BRINGS BACK MEMORIES!

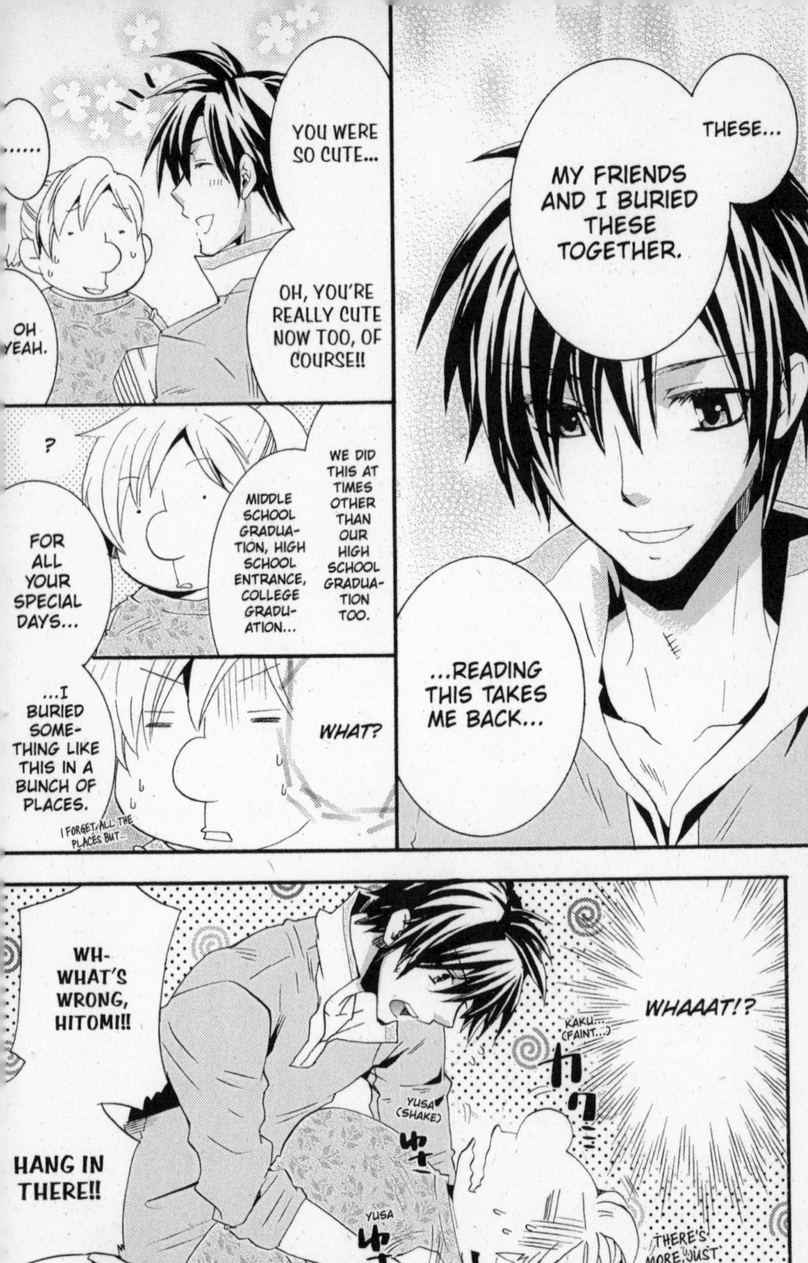
THESE...
MY FRIENDS AND I BURIED THESE TOGETHER.
...READING THIS TAKES ME BACK...
YOU WERE SO CUTE...
OH, YOU'RE REALLY CUTE NOW TOO, OF COURSE!!
......
OH YEAH.
WE DID THIS AT TIMES OTHER THAN OUR HIGH SCHOOL GRADUATION TOO.
MIDDLE SCHOOL GRADUATION, HIGH SCHOOL ENTRANCE, COLLEGE GRADUATION...
?
FOR ALL YOUR SPECIAL DAYS...
WHAT?
...I BURIED SOMETHING LIKE THIS IN A BUNCH OF PLACES.
I FORGET ALL THE PLACES BUT...
WHAAAT!?
KAKU... (FAINT...)
YUSA (SHAKE)
WH-WHAT'S WRONG, HITOMI!!
YUSA
THERE'S MORE JUST LIKE THAT...
ONII-CHAN...
HANG IN THERE!!

MASAKI

■ Hello and nice to meet you. My name is Yuuki Fujinari. Thank you for reading Volume 1 of *Ugly Duckling's Love Revolution*!! I hope you were able to enjoy the book, whether you've played the game or not.

■ It's been one year since I signed on to do the comic adaptation of *Ugly Duckling's Love Revolution*. The time really went by so quickly... It went so fast that I don't even remember writing the script (*laugh*).

■ I love gaming and was thinking of getting *Ugly Duckling's Love Revolution*, which had just been released, when I happened to get this job—boy, was I surprised! Adapting and being serialized were both firsts for me, and initially I couldn't tell my left hand from my right. But my editor and people behind the game really guided me every step of the way (still in progress). I'm finding myself being coddled and carried along. Thank you so much for everything.

■ Trying to do my own thing while at the same time keeping to the vision of the creators of *Ugly Duckling's Love Revolution* was a lot harder than I thought it would be. Now I've gotten kinda used to drawing the *Ugly Duckling* characters, but looking back at my first attempts, they look so different that it makes me wonder, "Who are they?" Especially Ren and Masaki, who looked like completely different people!

■ As for me, I've really fattened up since taking this job, with all the chaos of over-drinking and overeating (*strained laugh*). I'm planning to diet just like Hitomi-chan. Well, that's my thought as I create plots and names, but I'm not really losing weight. I guess I need to exercise too.

■ There are a lot of characters in *Ugly Duckling's Love Revolution*, and I'd like to take them one at a time. But please let me know if you'd like to see more of a certain character or another character in a certain situation, etc.!

■ A big thank you to everyone who has been helping me through this process—the game maker, my editor, the people at the publishing company, my five friends, and the designer! And most importantly, the readers. Thank you so much! For those of you who haven't played the game yet, please do try it out!

■ Sorry to ramble. Thank you so much for reading the book!

Yuuki Fujinari
Fall 2006

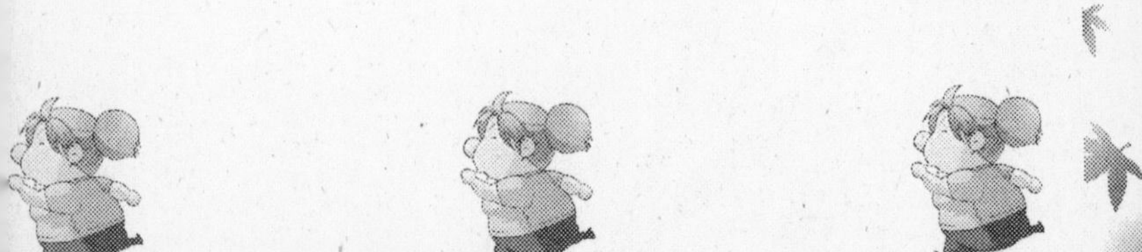

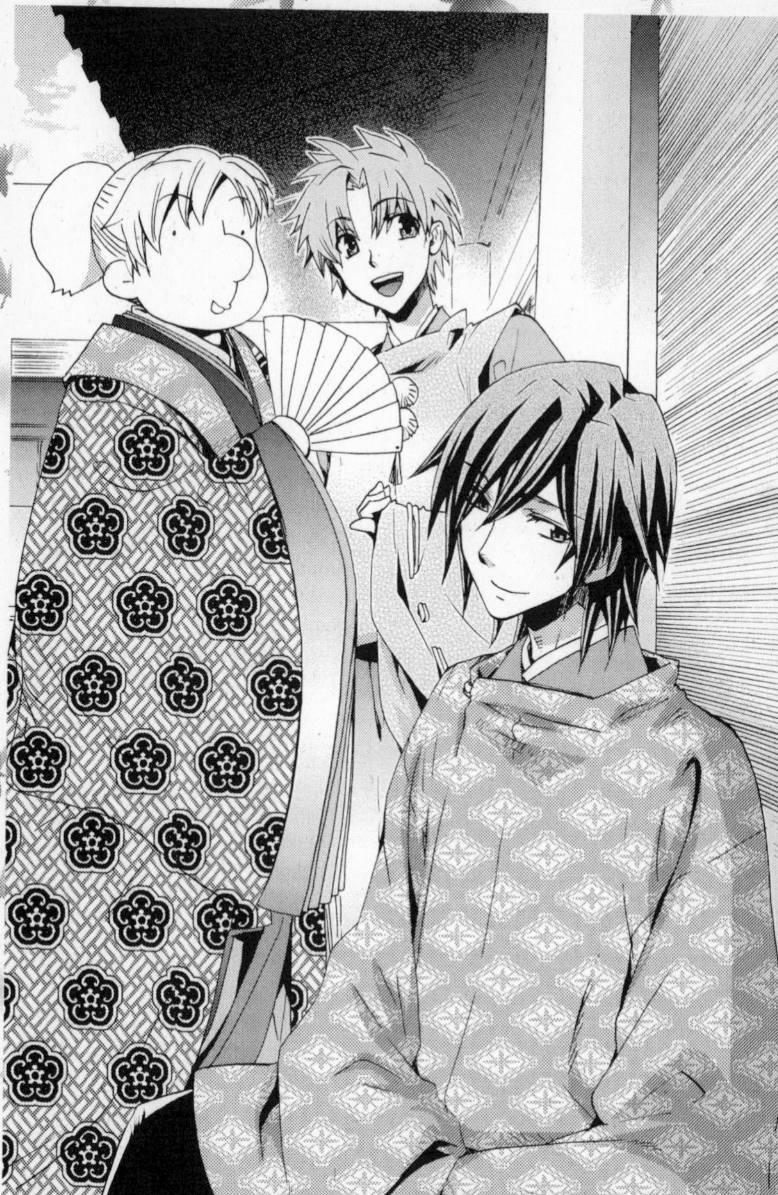

HEIAN ERA COSPLAY

UGLY DUCKLING'S LOVE REVOLUTION ❶

YUUKI FUJINARI
GUNGHO WORKS, INC.

Translation: Kaori Inoue • Lettering: Lys Blakeslee

Otometekikoikakumei★Loverevo!! Vol.1 © 2006 YUUKI FUJINARI © 2006, 2008 GUNGHO WORKS, INC./WILL. All rights reserved. First published in Japan in 2006 by ENTERBRAIN, INC., Tokyo. English translation rights arranged with ENTERBRAIN, INC. through Tuttle-Mori Agency, Inc., Tokyo.

Translation © 2010 by Hachette Book Group, Inc.

All rights reserved. Except as permitted under the U.S. Copyright Act of 1976, no part of this publication may be reproduced, distributed, or transmitted in any form or by any means, or stored in a database or retrieval system, without the prior written permission of the publisher.

The characters and events in this book are fictitious. Any similarity to real persons, living or dead, is coincidental and not intended by the author.

Yen Press
Hachette Book Group
237 Park Avenue, New York, NY 10017

www.HachetteBookGroup.com
www.YenPress.com

Yen Press is an imprint of Hachette Book Group, Inc. The Yen Press name and logo are trademarks of Hachette Book Group, Inc.

First Yen Press Edition: July 2010

ISBN: 978-0-7595-3175-8

10 9 8 7 6 5 4 3 2 1

BVG

Printed in the United States of America